Why Do You Need This New Edition?

If you're wondering why you should buy this new edition of *Poetry: A Pocket Anthology,* here are four good reasons!

1. **Compelling new selections from masters of the genre,** ranging from John Keats to e.e. cummings, Langston Hughes, and Elizabeth Bishop, offer fresh models from classic writers.

2. **Authors new to this collection,** including Amy Gerstler (named by the *Los Angeles Times* as "one of the best poets in the nation"), and award winners Rebecca Foust and Craig Arnold, provide ample evidence that poetry continues to flourish in today's world.

3. **Young writers** Ernest Hilbert and Erica Dawson bring poetry into the 21st century and provide inspiration for aspiring young poets.

4. And as always, *Poetry: A Pocket Anthology* offers a comprehensive collection at an affordable price and an appealing length.

about the author

R.S. GWYNN has edited several other books, including *Drama: A Pocket Anthology; Literature: A Pocket Anthology; Fiction: A Pocket Anthology; Inside Literature: Reading, Responding, Writing* (with Steven Zani); *The Art of the Short Story* (with Dana Gioia); and *Contempo-rary American Poetry: A Pocket Anthology* (with April Lindner). He has also authored five collections of poetry, including *No Word of Farewell: Selected Poems, 1970–2000*. He has been awarded the Michael Braude Award for verse from the American Academy of Arts and Letters. Gwynn is University Professor of English and Poet-in-Residence at Lamar University in Beaumont, Texas.

PENGUIN ACADEMICS

POETRY

A POCKET ANTHOLOGY

3⁷⁵.

PENGUIN ACADEMICS

POETRY
A POCKET ANTHOLOGY

SEVENTH EDITION

Edited by

R. S. Gwynn
Lamar University

Longman
Boston   Columbus   Indianapolis   New York   San Francisco
Upper Saddle River   Amsterdam   Cape Town   Dubai   London   Madrid
Milan   Munich   Paris   Montreal   Toronto   Delhi   Mexico City
São Paulo   Sydney   Hong Kong   Seoul   Singapore   Taipei   Tokyo

Senior Sponsoring Editor: Virginia L. Blanford
Senior Marketing Manager: Joyce Nilsen
Assistant Editor: Rebecca Gilpin
Production Project Manager: Clara Bartunek
Project Coordination, Text Design, and Electronic Page Makeup: Nitin
    Agarwal, Aptara®, Inc
Creative Art Director: Jayne Conte
Cover Designer: Bruce Kenselaar
Cover Illustration/Photo: Fotolia
Printer and Binder: Courier/Westford
Cover Printer: Lehigh Phoenix Hagerstown

For more information about the Penguin Academics series, please contact us by mail at Pearson Education, attn. Marketing Department, 51 Madison Avenue, 29th Floor, New York, NY 10010, or visit us online at www.pearsonhighered.com/english.

For permission to use copyrighted material, grateful acknowledgment is made to the copyright holders on appropriate page within text, which are hereby made part of this copyright page.

Library of Congress Cataloging-in-Publication Data
Poetry: a pocket anthology / edited by R.S. Gwynn.
    p. cm.—(Penguin academics)
    Includes indexes.
    ISBN-13: 978-0-205-10198-6 (alk. paper)
    ISBN-10: 0-205-10198-4 (alk. paper)
    1. Poetry—Collections. I. Gwynn, R. S.
PN6101.P52 2010
821.008'—dc22   2010043757

1 2 3 4 5 6 7 8 9 10—CRW—14 13 12 11
    Longman
    is an imprint of

www.pearsonhighered.com

ISBN–13: 978-0-205-10198-6
ISBN–10:   0-205-10198-4

contents

CONTENTS

xiii

preface

When the *Pocket Anthology* series first appeared, our chief aim was to offer a clear alternative to the anthologies of fiction, poetry, and drama that were available at the time. *Poetry: A Pocket Anthology*, now part of the Penguin Academic series from Pearson Longman, is here updated and revised for a seventh edition. Designed to be used in a wide range of courses, this brief anthology can be packaged with one or more of a rich selection of Penguin titles, which Pearson Longman offers at significantly reduced prices. Also, *Poetry* is published concurrently with two companion volumes, *Fiction* and *Drama*, as well as in a combined edition, *Literature: A Pocket Anthology*, which comprises most of the selections found in the three independent volumes, as well as introductions to all three genres. Your Pearson Longman representative can supply full details about these books, and about the available Penguin titles.

What's New in This Edition

As with earlier editions on *Poetry*, our goal has been to provide variety and flexibility in the selections offered. Contemporary poets new to this anthology include Rebecca Foust, Craig Arnold, Ernest Hilbert, and Erica Dawson. In addition, readers will find new selections from poets ranging from Donne, Poe, Whitman, and Hardy, to modernists including Wallace Stevens, e.e. cummings, and Richard Wilbur. More than a third of our poems are by women and minority writers, and a strong effort has been made to include poems that reflect contemporary social questions, as well as a wide range of traditional poetic forms.

The Goals of This Anthology

Poetry addresses the four wishes and concerns most commonly expressed by both instructors and students. First, of course, is the variety of selections it contains. Admittedly, a pocket anthology has to be very selective in its contents, so we are especially proud that the over three-hundred poems in this book include both a generous selection of works by poets from past centuries and a large number of contemporary poems that reflect the diversity of authorship, subject matter, and form that is essential to the study of contemporary poetry. Women and minority writers are strongly represented by such voices as Jean Toomer, Langston Hughes, Julia Alvarez, Rita Dove, and Cathy Song. We have made every effort to include poems rooted in contemporary social questions—like those of "soldier-poet" Brian Turner—and our selections profit both from the advice of experienced instructors, who have cited poems that appeal to students, and from the editor's own long experience as a poet, critic, and teacher of literature and creative writing. *Poetry* contains examples—many of them by contemporary poets—of virtually every traditional poetic form used in English-language poetry, ranging from the haiku and the cinquain to the rondeau redoublé and the sestina. These examples help to make *Poetry* invaluable for courses that emphasize analysis of poetic meter and form or composition of poems in formal patterns. Among the features in *Poetry* is a useful appendix grouping poems by form, which provides students and instructors with a quick way to locate comparable poems for discussion, analysis, and emulation.

Our second goal was flexibility. We wanted a book that could be used as both a primary and a supplemental text in a wide range of courses, from introduction to poetry to advanced classes in poetic analysis to creative writing workshops. When combined with one of its companion volumes, *Fiction* or *Drama*, or with novels, collections of short stories or poems by individual authors, or plays available from Penguin, *Poetry* may also be used in introductory literature courses. *Poetry* contains, in addition to its generous selection of poems, biographical headnotes for authors, an introduction that covers the techniques and terminology of the genre, and a concise section on writing about poetry and research procedures.

Third, we wanted an affordable book. Full-size introductory literature books—and even comprehensive anthologies of poetry—now cost well over $70. Pearson Longman is committed to keeping the price of the *Pocket Anthology* series reasonable, without compromising on design or typeface. We hope that readers will find the attractive layout of *Poetry* preferable to the cramped margins and minuscule fonts found in many literature textbooks. Because of its relatively low cost, this volume may be easily supplemented in individual courses with works of criticism, handbooks of grammar and usage, or manuals of style.

Finally, we stressed portability. Many instructors have expressed concern for students who must carry literature books comprising 2,000 or more pages in backpacks already laden with books and materials for other courses. A semester is a short time, and few courses can cover more than a fraction of the material that many full-sized collections contain. Because many instructors focus on a single genre at a time, *Poetry* and its companion volumes, *Fiction* and *Drama*, remain compact yet self-contained volumes that are reasonably easy to handle and carry.

Acknowledgments

No book is ever created in a vacuum. We would like to express our gratitude to the instructors who reviewed the current edition of this volume and offered invaluable recommendations for improvement. They are: Lucas Carpenter, Oxford College of Emory University; David Helper, College of the Redwoods; Norman W. Jones, Ohio State University, Mansfield Campus; Jo Cochran, Klamath Community College; William E. Matsen, North Hennepin Community College; Portia Weston. Point Park University.

We are also grateful to those who reviewed earlier editions, including Allan Braden, Tacoma Community College; James Hoggard, Midwestern State University; Derek Sheffield, Wenatchee Valley College; Matha Silano, Edmonds and Bellevue Community College; and Jeanne Yeasting, Western Washington University.

The editor also acknowledges the invaluable assistance of Rachel Klauss in assembling this edition.

R. S. Gwynn
Lamar University

Introduction

An Anecdote: Where Poetry Starts

The room is not particularly grand, a large lecture hall in one of the old buildings on the college campus, and the small group of first-year students whose literature class has been dismissed so that they can attend the poetry reading has taken seats near the back of the room. They have been encouraged to come for several weeks by their instructor, and when she enters she looks around the room and nods in their direction, smiling.

The seats gradually fill. The crowd is a mixed one—several men and women known by sight as senior faculty members; a scattering of other older visitors, many of them apparently from the community; a large contingent of instructors and graduate students from the English Department sitting in the front rows; and small clusters of undergraduates scattered throughout the room.

One of the students scans the crowd, wondering aloud which is the poet. On the walk to the reading, several fellow class members decided that the poet, a cadaverous gray-haired man wrapped in a black cloak, would recite his poems in a resonant baritone, preferably with a strong breeze tossing his hair. Speculating on how the wind effect might be managed inside a lecture hall made them laugh.

Now the crowd grows quiet as the students' instructor steps to the podium and adjusts the microphone. She makes a few complimentary remarks about the strong turnout and thanks several benefactors for their support of poetry at the university. Then she introduces the guest.

Her students know most of this information, for they have studied several of his poems in class that week, but they are still slightly surprised when he rises to polite applause and takes the lectern. The balding middle-age man wearing a golf shirt could be taken for a professor in any campus department, and when he adjusts his glasses and clears his throat, blinking at the audience, there is little about him that would fit anyone's romantic stereotype of a poet.

Surprisingly, he does not begin with a poem. Instead, in a relaxed voice he tells an anecdote about his younger daughter and an overdue science project. When he moves from the background story into reading the poem itself, there is little change in his volume level, and his tone remains conversational. The students find that the poem, which they had discussed in class only a couple of days before, takes on more meaning when its origins are explained by the poet himself. They find themselves listening attentively to his words, even laughing out loud several times. The hour goes by quickly, and at its end their applause, like that of the rest of the audience, is long and sincere.

At the next class meeting, the instructor asks for reactions to the reading. Although some of the class members are slightly critical, faulting the speaker for his informal manner and his failure to maintain eye contact with the room, most of the remarks are positive. The comments that surface most often have to do with how much more meaningful the poems in the textbook become when the poet explains how he came to write them. They now know that one poem is actually spoken in the voice of the poet's dead father and that another is addressed to a friend who was paralyzed in an automobile accident. Although these things could perhaps be inferred from the poems alone, the students are unanimous in their opinion that knowing the details beforehand adds a great deal to the first impression a poem makes. As one student puts it, "It's just that a poem makes a lot more sense when you know who's talking and when and where it's supposed to be taking place."

"It always helps to know where poetry starts," adds one of her classmates.

Speaker, Listener, and Context

The situation described above is hardly unique. Instructors have long been encouraging, even begging, their students to attend events like the one described, and the college poetry reading has become, for

perplex (handwritten)

many American students, the closest encounter they will have with this complex and often perplexing art form. But what students often find at such readings, sometimes to their amazement, is that poetry need not be intimidating or obscure. Poems that are *performed* provide a gentle reminder that the roots of poetry, like those of all literature, were originally part of the oral tradition. In ancient societies, stories and poems were passed down from generation to generation and recited for all members of the tribe, from the wizened elders to the youngest children. For most of its long history, poetry has been a popular art form aimed at audiences (remember that the word *audience* means "hearers"). It is only recently, in the last four or five decades, that its most visible signs of life are to be found on college campuses. Still, it is perhaps worth noting that we are exposed daily to a great deal of poetry in oral form, primarily through the medium of recorded song lyrics. The unique qualities of poetry throughout the ages, that is, its ability to tell stories or summarize complicated emotions in a few well-chosen words, are demonstrated whenever we memorize the lines of a popular song and sing them to ourselves.

Of course, poetry written primarily for the page is usually more demanding than song lyrics. Writers of popular songs aim at a wide commercial audience, and this simple fact of economics, added to the fact that the lyrics are not intended primarily for publication but for being recorded with all the resources of studio technology, tends to make many song lyrics relatively uninteresting when they appear in print. But a poem will exist primarily as a printed text, although its effect may be enhanced greatly through a skillful oral performance in which the poet can also explain the background of the poem, its setting and speaker, and the circumstances under which it was written. In general, these details, so crucial to understanding a poem yet so often only implied when the poem appears in print, are called the dramatic situation of a poem. Dramatic situation can be summed up in a question: *Who is speaking to whom under what circumstances?* If the poet fails to provide us with clues or if we are careless in picking up the information that is provided, then we may begin reading with no sense of reference and, thus, may go far astray. Even such words as "on," "upon," or "to" in titles can be crucial to our understanding of dramatic situation, telling us something about an event or object that provided the stimulus for the poem or about the identity of the "you" addressed in the poem.

An illustration may be helpful. Suppose we look at what is unquestionably the most widely known poem ever written by an American. It is a poem that virtually all Americans can recite in part and, in fact, do so by the millions every week. Yet if we were told that this poem is unusual because its best-known section is a long, unanswered question, addressed by the speaker to a nearby companion, about whether or not the object named in the title even exists, then it is likely that most of us would be confused. Before going further, let's look at the poem.

The Star-Spangled Banner

O say, can you see, by the dawn's early light,
    What so proudly we hailed at the twilight's last gleaming?
Whose broad stripes and bright stars thro' the perilous fight,
    O'er the ramparts we watched, were so gallantly streaming!
And the rockets' red glare, the bombs bursting in air,
    Gave proof through the night that our flag was still there:
O say, does that star-spangled banner yet wave
    O'er the land of the free and the home of the brave?

On the shore, dimly seen thro' the mists of the deep,
    Where the foe's haughty host in dread silence reposes,
What is that which the breeze, o'er the towering steep,
    As it fitfully blows, now conceals, now discloses?
Now it catches the gleam of the morning's first beam,
    In full glory reflected now shines on the stream:
'Tis the star-spangled banner! O long may it wave
    O'er the land of the free and the home of the brave!

And where is that band who so vauntingly swore
    That the havoc of war and the battle's confusion
A home and a country should leave us no more?
    Their blood has washed out their foul footsteps' pollution.
No refuge could save the hireling and slave
    From the terror of flight, or the gloom of the grave:
And the star-spangled banner in triumph doth wave
    O'er the land of the free and the home of the brave!

Oh! thus be it ever, when freemen shall stand
    Between their loved homes and the war's desolation!

Blest with victory and peace, may the heav'n-rescued land
Praise the Pow'r that hath made and preserved us a nation.
Then conquer we must, when our cause it is just,
And this be our motto: "In God is our trust."
And the star-spangled banner in triumph shall wave
O'er the land of the free and the home of the brave!

"Now wait a minute!" you may be complaining. "'The Star-Spangled Banner' is a *song*, not a poem. And what's this *question* business? Don't we always sing it while facing the flag? Besides, it's just a patriotic song. Nobody really worries about what it *means*."

In answer to the first comment, "The Star-Spangled Banner" *was* in fact written as a poem and was set to music only after its composition. Most of us will probably agree that the words are not particularly well-suited to the melody (which was taken, curiously, from a popular British barroom ballad) and the song remains notoriously difficult to sing, even for professional performers. In its original form, "The Star-Spangled Banner" (or "The Defense of Fort McHenry," the title under which it was first published) is an example of *occasional verse*, a poem that is written about or for an important event (or occasion), sometimes private but usually of some public significance. Although poems of this type are not often printed on the front pages of newspapers as they once were, they are still being written. Enough poems appeared after the assassination of President John F. Kennedy in 1963 to fill a book, *Of Poetry and Power*, and the *Challenger* disaster of 1986 stimulated a similar outpouring of occasional poems, one of them by Howard Nemerov, who served as poet laureate of the United States. In 1993, Maya Angelou recited "On the Pulse of Morning" at the first inauguration of President Clinton, and Miller Williams read "Of History and Hope" at the second, in 1997. The events of September 11, 2001, stimulated thousands of poems including "The Names" by then-U.S. Poet Laureate Billy Collins. The author of "The Star-Spangled Banner," Francis Scott Key (1779–1843), wrote poetry as an avocation. Yet like many men and women who are not professional writers, Key was so deeply moved by an event that he witnessed that occasional poetry was the only medium through which he could express his feelings.

Now let's go back to our question about dramatic situation, taking it one part at a time: Who is speaking? A technical word that is often used to designate the speaker of a poem is **persona** (plural: **personae**), a word that meant "mask" in ancient Greek. Even though the persona of "The Star-Spangled Banner" never uses the word "I" in the poem, the speaker seems to be Key himself, a fact that can be verified by biographical research. Still, it is probably safer to look at poems carefully to see if they give any evidence that the speaker is someone other than the poet. Poems like "Ulysses" by Alfred, Lord Tennyson or "Porphyria's Lover" by Robert Browning have titles that identify personae who are, respectively, a character from ancient epic poetry and an unnamed man who is confessing the murder of his lover, Porphyria. In neither case is the persona to be identified with the poet himself. Other poems may be somewhat more problematical. Edgar Allan Poe's famous "The Raven," like many of Poe's short stories, is spoken by a persona who is not to be identified directly with the author, even though he shares many of the same morbid preoccupations of Poe's other characters. Even Sylvia Plath, a poet usually associated with an extremely candid form of autobiographical poetry known as **confessional poetry**, on a radio broadcast identified the persona of her masterpiece "Daddy" as an invented character, "a girl with an Electra complex." Although it now is clear that Plath used many autobiographical details in her poem, readers who try to identify her as a victim of child abuse on its evidence should instead turn to Plath's journals and the many biographies that have been written about her. Sometimes poems have more than one persona, which is the case with Thomas Hardy's "The Ruined Maid" and Robert Frost's "Home Burial," two poems that consist almost entirely of dialogue. In other poems, for instance in many ballads, the voice may simply be a third-person **narrator** such as we might find in a short story or novel. Thus, although it is perhaps true that many poems (including the majority of those included here) are in fact spoken by the poet out of his or her most private feelings, it is not a good idea to leap too quickly to the assumption that the persona of a poem is identical to the poet and shares his or her views. Conclusions about the degree to which a poem is autobiographical can be verified only by research and familiarity with a poet's other works.

To return to our question: Who is speaking to whom? Another useful term is **auditor**, the person or persons spoken to in a poem. Some poems identify no auditor; others clearly do specify an auditor or auditors, in most cases identified by name or by the second-person pronoun "you" (or "thee/thou" in older poetry). Again, the title may give clues: Robert Herrick's "To the Virgins, to Make Much of Time" is addressed to a group of young women; William Cullen Bryant's "To the Fringed Gentian" is addressed to a common New England wildflower. (The figure of speech apostrophe—discussed later in this introduction—is used when a nonhuman, inanimate, or abstract thing is directly addressed.) Relatively few poems are addressed directly to the reader, so when we read the opening of William Shakespeare's Sonnet 18 ("Shall I compare thee to a summer's day?") we should keep in mind that he is not addressing us but another individual, in this case a young male friend who is referred to in many of the sonnets. Claude McKay's sonnet "If We Must Die" begins in this manner:

If we must die, let it not be like hogs
Hunted and penned in an inglorious spot,
While round us bark the mad and hungry dogs,
Making their mock at our accursed lot.

Later in the poem McKay identifies his auditors as "Kinsmen." Without outside help, about all we can say with certainty at first glance is that the poet seems to be addressing a group of companions who share his desperate situation; when we learn, possibly through research, that McKay was an African-American poet writing in reaction to the Harlem race riots of 1919, the symbolic nature of his exhortation becomes clearer.

Now the final part of the question: Who is speaking to whom *under what circumstances?* First, we might ask if there is a relationship, either implied or stated, between persona and auditor. Obviously many love poems take the form of verbal transactions between two parties and, because relationships have their ups and downs, these shifts of mood are reflected in the poetry. One famous example is Michael Drayton's "Idea: Sonnet 61" ("Since there's no help, come let us kiss and part . . ."), which begins with the persona threatening to end the relationship with the auditor but which ends with an apparent reconciliation. Such "courtship ritual" poems as John Donne's "The Flea" or Andrew Marvell's "To His Coy Mistress" are witty arguments in favor of the couple's setting aside their hesitations and engaging in sexual relations. An example from poetry about marital love is Matthew Arnold's "Dover Beach," which ends with the plea "Ah, love, let us be true / To one another" as the only hope for stability the persona can find in a world filled with uncertainty and fear. Even an age disparity between persona and auditor can lend meaning to a poem, which is the case with the

Herrick poem mentioned earlier and a dialogue poem like John Crowe Ransom's "Piazza Piece," a classic example of the debate between innocence and experience.

Other questions relating to circumstances of the dramatic situation might concern the poem's physical setting (if any), time (of day, year, historical era), even such matters as weather. Thomas Hardy's "Neutral Tones" provides a good example of a poem in which the setting, a gray winter day in a barren outdoor location, symbolically reinforces the persona's memory of the bitter end of a love affair. The shift in setting from the springtime idyll to the "cold hill side" in John Keats's "La Belle Dame sans Merci" cannot be overlooked in discussing the persona's disillusionment. Of course, many poems are explicitly occasional and may even contain an **epigraph** (see Gwendolyn Brooks's "We Real Cool"), a brief explanatory statement or quotation, or a **dedication**, which explains the setting. Sometimes footnotes or even outside research may be necessary. John Milton's "On the Late Massacre in Piedmont" will make little sense to readers if they do not know that the poet is reacting to the massacre of a group of Waldensian Protestants by Roman Catholic soldiers on Easter Sunday, 1655. Milton, an English Puritan, uses the occasion to attack the papacy as a "triple tyrant" and the "Babylonian woe."

To return, then, one final time to "The Star-Spangled Banner," let us apply our question to the poem. We have already determined that Key is the persona. Who is the "you" mentioned four words into the poem? It seems clear that Key is addressing an auditor standing close to him, either a single individual or a group, as he asks the auditor if he can see the flag that they both observed for the last time the previous day at sundown. Key tells us that it is now the first moment of dawn, and that even though the flag could be glimpsed periodically in the "rockets' red glare" of the bombardment throughout the night, it cannot be clearly seen now. It is a crucial question, for if the flag is no longer flying "o'er the ramparts," it will mean that the fort has fallen to the enemy. The tension mounts and moves into the second stanza, where at last, "thro' the mists of the deep," the flag can be discerned, "dimly seen" at first, then clearly as it "catches the gleam" of the full sunlight.

The full story of how Key came to write the poem is fairly well known and supports this reading. The events that the poem describes took place on September 13–14, 1814, during the War of 1812.

Key, a lawyer, came aboard a British warship anchored off Baltimore to argue for the release of a client and friend who had been taken hostage by the British. Key won his friend's release, but the British captain, fearing that he might reveal information he had learned on board, kept Key overnight, releasing him and his client in the morning. It was during that night that Key witnessed the bombardment and, with it, the failure of the British to take Baltimore. The final half of the poem celebrates the victory and offers a hopeful prayer that God will continue to smile on America "when our cause . . . is just." One might well argue that Key's phrase "conquer we must" contradicts the spirit of the earlier parts of the poem, but few people have argued that "The Star-Spangled Banner" is a consistently great poem. Still, it is an effective piece of patriotic verse that has a few moments of real drama, expressed in a vivid manner that lets its readers become eyewitnesses to an incident from American history.

Lyric, Narrative, Dramatic

The starting point for all literary criticism in Western civilization is Aristotle's *Poetics*, a work dating from the fourth century BC. Although Aristotle's remarks on drama, tragedy in particular, are more complete than his analysis of other types of literature, he does mention three main types of poetry: lyric, epic, and dithyrambic. In doing so, Aristotle outlines for the first time a theory of literature based on **genres**, or separate categories delineated by distinct style, form, and content. This threefold division remains useful today, although in two cases different terminology is employed. The first genre, **lyric poetry**, originally comprised brief poems that were meant to be sung or chanted to the accompaniment of a lyre. Today we still use the word "lyrics" in a specialized sense when referring to the words of a song, but lyric poetry has become such a large category that it includes virtually all poems that are primarily *about* a subject and contain little narrative content. The subject of a lyric poem may be the poet's emotions, an abstract idea, a satirical insight, or a description of a person or place. The persona in a lyric is usually closely identified with the poet himself or herself, and because we tend to identify the essence of poetry with personal, subjective expression of feelings or ideas, lyric poetry remains the largest genre, with a number of subtypes. Among them are the

epigram, a short, satirical lyric usually aimed at a specific person; the **elegy**, a lyric on the occasion of a death; and the **ode**, a long lyric in elevated language on a serious theme.

Aristotle's second genre, the epic, has been expanded to include all types of **narrative poetry**, that is, poetry whose main function is to tell a story. Like prose fiction, narrative poems have plots, characters, setting, and point-of-view, and may be discussed in roughly the same terms as, say, a short story. The **epic** is a long narrative poem about the exploits of a hero. **Folk epics** like *The Iliad* or *Beowulf* were originally intended for public recitation and existed in oral form for a long period of time before they were transcribed. Little or nothing is known about the authors of folk epics; even Homer, the purported author of the *Iliad* and the *Odyssey*, is primarily a legendary character. **Literary epics**, like Dante's *Inferno* or Henry Wadsworth Longfellow's *The Song of Hiawatha*, differ in that they are the products of known authors who *wrote* their poems for publication. **Ballads** generally are shorter narratives with song-like qualities which often include rhyme and repeated refrains. **Folk ballads**, like folk epics, come from the oral tradition and are anonymously authored; "Bonny Barbara Allan" and "Sir Patrick Spens" are typical examples. **Art** or **literary ballads** are conscious imitations of the ballad style by later poets and are generally somewhat more sophisticated than folk ballads in their techniques. Examples of this popular genre include Keats's "La Belle Dame sans Merci," Robert Burns's "John Barleycorn," and more recently, Marilyn Nelson's "The Ballad of Aunt Geneva." **Realistic narratives** of medium length (under 1000 lines) like Robert Frost's "Home Burial" have been popular since the early nineteenth century and are sometimes discussed as "poetic novels" or "short stories in verse."

There is no exact contemporary analogue for Aristotle's third category, **dithyrambic poetry**. This type of poem, composed to be chanted at religious rituals by a chorus, was the forerunner of tragedy. Today this third type is usually called **dramatic poetry**, because it has perhaps as much in common with the separate genre of drama as with lyric and narrative poetry. In general, the persona in a dramatic poem is an invented character not to be identified with the poet. The poem is presented as a speech or dialogue that might be acted out like a soliloquy or scene from a play. The **dramatic monologue** is a speech for a single character, usually delivered to a silent auditor. Notable examples are Tennyson's "Ulysses" and Browning's "My Last Duchess." A dramatic monologue sometimes implies, in the words of its persona, a distinct setting and interplay between persona and auditor. At the close of "Ulysses" the aged hero urges his "mariners" to listen closely and to observe the ship in the harbor waiting to take them off on a final voyage. Dramatic poetry can also take the form of **dialogue poetry**, in which two personae speak alternately. Examples are Christina Rossetti's "Up-Hill" and Hardy's "The Ruined Maid." A popular type of dialogue poem that originated in the Middle Ages was the **débat**, or mock-debate, in which two characters, usually personified abstractions like the Soul and the Body, argued their respective merits.

Although it is easy enough to find examples of "pure" lyrics, narratives, and dramatic monologues, sometimes the distinction between the three major types may become blurred, even in the same poem. "The Star-Spangled Banner," for example, contains elements of all three genres. The opening stanza, with its vivid re-creation of a question asked at dawn, is closest to dramatic poetry. The second and third stanzas, which tell of the outcome of the battle, are primarily narrative. The final stanza, with its patriotic effusion and religious sentiment, is lyrical. Still, the threefold division is useful in discussing a single author's various ways of dealing with subjects or in comparing examples of one type by separate authors. To cite three poems by the same poet in this collection, we might look at William Blake's "The Tyger," "A Poison Tree," and "The Chimney Sweeper." The first of these is a descriptive lyric, dwelling primarily on the symbolic meaning of the tiger's appearance; the second is a narrative that relates, in the first person and the allegorical manner of a parable, the events leading up to a murder; and the third is a short dramatic monologue spoken by the persona identified in the title.

The Language of Poetry

One of the most persistent myths about poetry is that its language is artificial, "flowery," and essentially different from the language that people speak every day. Although these beliefs may be true of some poetry, one can easily find numerous examples that demonstrate poetic diction of an entirely different sort. It is impossible to characterize poetic language narrowly, for poetry, which is after all the art of language, covers the widest possible range of linguistic possibilities. For example, here are several passages from different poets, all describing birds:

Hail to thee, blithe Spirit!
  Bird thou never wert—
That from Heaven, or near it,
  Pourest thy full heart
In profuse strains of unpremeditated art.

Higher still and higher
  From the earth thou springest
Like a cloud of fire;
  The blue deep thou wingest,
And singing still dost soar, and soaring ever singest.

Percy Bysshe Shelley, "To a Skylark"

I caught this morning morning's minion, king-
  dom of daylight's dauphin, dapple-dawn-drawn Falcon, in
    his riding
  Of the rolling level underneath him steady air, and striding
High there, how he rung upon the rein of a wimpling wing
In his ecstacy!

Gerard Manley Hopkins, "The Windhover"

When the lilac-scent was in the air and Fifth-month grass was
    growing,
Up this seashore in some briers,
Two feather'd guests from Alabama, two together,
And their nest, and four light-green eggs spotted with brown,
And every day the he-bird to and fro near at hand,
And every day the she-bird crouch'd on her nest, silent, with
    bright eyes,
And every day I, a curious boy, never too close, never disturbing
    them,
Cautiously peering, absorbing, translating.

Walt Whitman, "Out of the Cradle Endlessly Rocking"

At once a voice arose among
  The bleak twigs overhead
In a full-hearted evensong
  Of joy illimited;
An aged thrush, frail, gaunt, and small,
  In blast-beruffled plume,

Had chosen thus to fling his soul
Upon the growing gloom.

Thomas Hardy, "The Darkling Thrush"

There is a singer everyone has heard,
Loud, a mid-summer and a mid-wood bird,
Who makes the solid tree trunks sound again.
He says that leaves are old and that for flowers
Mid-summer is to spring as one to ten.

Robert Frost, "The Oven Bird"

The blue booby lives
on the bare rocks
of Galápagos
and fears nothing.
It is a simple life:
they live on fish,
and there are few predators.

James Tate, "The Blue Booby"

Of these quotes, only Shelley's, from the early nineteenth century, possesses the stereotypical characteristics of what we mean when we use the term "poetic" in a negative sense. Poetry, like any other art form, follows fashions that change over the years; by Shelley's day, the use of "thee" and "thou" and their related verb forms ("wert" and "wingest") had come full circle from their original use as a familiar form of the second person employed to address intimates and servants to an artificially heightened grammatical form reserved for prayers and poetry. Hopkins's language, from a poem of the 1870s, is artificial in an entirely different way; here the poet's **idiom**, the personal use of words that marks his poetry, is highly individual; indeed, it would be hard to mistake a poem by Hopkins, with its muscular monosyllables and rich texture of sound patterns, with one by any other poet. Whitman's diction should present few difficulties; the only oddity here is the use of "Fifth-month" instead of "May," a linguistic inheritance, perhaps, from the poet's Quaker mother. Of course, one might argue that Whitman's "naturalness" results from his use of free verse, but both Hardy and Frost, who write rhymed, metrical verse, are hardly less natural. When we move to the contemporary period, we can find little difference between the language of many poems and conversational speech, as Tate's lines indicate.

Still, in reading a poem, particularly one from the past, we should be aware of certain problems that may impede our understanding. **Diction** refers to the individual words in a poem and may be classified in several ways. A poem's **level of diction** can range from slang at one extreme to formal usage at the other, although in an age in which most poems use a level of diction that stays in the middle of the scale, ranging from conversational and standard levels, these distinctions are useful only when a poet is being self-consciously formal (perhaps for ironic effect) or going to the opposite extreme to imitate the language of the streets. In past eras the term **poetic diction** was used to indicate a level of speech somehow refined above ordinary usage and, thus, somehow superior to it. Today the same term would most likely be used as a way of criticizing a poet's language. We should keep in mind that the slang of one era may become the standard usage of another, as is the case with "O.K." which has become a universal expression. In other cases, a poet may even "invent" an idiom for a poem, the case with Lewis Carroll's famous "Jabberwocky" and Stevie Smith's "Our Bog Is Dood."

A good dictionary is useful in many ways, particularly in dealing with **archaisms** (words that are no longer in common use) and other words that may not be familiar to the reader. Take, for example, the opening lines of Edgar Allan Poe's "To Helen":

> Helen, thy beauty is to me
> > Like those Nicean barks of yore,
> That gently, o'er a perfumed sea,
> > The weary, way-worn wanderer bore
> > To his own native shore.

Several words here may give trouble to the average contemporary reader. First, "o'er," like "ne'er" or similar words like "falt'ring" and "glimm'ring," is simply a contraction; this dropping of a letter, called **syncope**, is done for the sake of maintaining the poem's meter; in the fourth stanza of "The Star-Spangled Banner," the words "Pow'r" and "heav'n" are contracted for the same reason. "Barks of yore" will probably send most of us to the dictionary, for our sense of "bark" as either the outer surface of a tree or the noise that a dog makes does not fit here; likewise, "yore" is unfamiliar, possibly archaic. Looking up the literal sense of a word in a dictionary discloses its **denotation**, or literal meaning. Thus, we find that "barks" are small sailing ships and that "yore" refers to the distant past. Of course, Poe could have said "ships of the past" or a similar phrase, but his word choice was perhaps dictated by **connotation**, the implied meaning or feel that some words have acquired; it may be that even in Poe's day "barks of yore" had a remote quality that somehow evoked ancient Greece in a way that, say, "ancient ships" would not. But what are we to make of "Nicean," a proper adjective that sounds geographical but does not appear in either the dictionary or gazetteer? In this case we have encountered an example of a **coinage**, or **neologism**, a word made up by the poet. Speculation on the source of "Nicean" has ranged from Nice, in the south of France, to Phoenician, but it is likely that Poe simply coined the word for its exotic sound. Similarly, we might note that the phrase "weary, way-worn wanderer" contains words that seem to have been chosen primarily for their alliterated sounds.

When we put a poem into our own words, we **paraphrase** it, a practice that is often useful when passages are hard to understand. Other than diction, **syntax**, the order of words in a sentence, may also give readers problems. Syntax in poetry, particularly in poems that use rhyme, is likely to be different from that of both speech and prose; if a poet decides to rhyme in a certain pattern, then word order must be modified to fit the formal design, and this may present difficulties to readers in understanding the grammar of a passage. Here is the opening of a familiar piece of American patriotic verse: "My country, 'tis of thee, / Sweet land of liberty, / Of thee I sing." What is the subject of this sentence? Would you be surprised to learn that the grammatical subject is "it" (contained in the contraction "'tis"—"It is of thee, my country, sweet land of liberty, of thee [that] I sing")? The passage from Poe's poem presents few difficulties of this order but does contain one example of **inversion**, words that fall out of their expected order (a related syntactical problem lies in **ellipsis**, words that are consciously omitted by the poet). If we do not allow for this, we are likely to be confused by "the weary, way-worn wanderer bore / To his own native shore." The wanderer bore *what*? A quick mental sentence diagram shows that "wanderer" is the direct object of "bore," not its subject. A good paraphrase should simplify both diction and syntax: "Helen, to me your beauty is like those Nicean (?) ships of the ancient past that carried the weary, travel-worn wanderer gently over a perfumed sea to his own native land." In paraphrasing, only the potentially troublesome words and phrases should be substituted, leaving the original language as intact as possible. Paraphrasing is a useful first step toward unfolding a poem's literal sense, but it obviously takes few of a poet's specific nuances of language into account; words like "cool," "cold," "chilly," and "frigid" may denote the same thing, but each has its own connotation. "Poetry," Robert Frost famously remarked, "is what is lost in translation." He might have extended the complaint to include paraphrase as well.

Several other matters relevant to poetic language are worth mentioning. **Etymology**, the study of the sources of words, is a particularly rewarding topic in English because our language has such an unusually rich history—just compare an unabridged French dictionary to its English counterpart. Old English (or Anglo-Saxon), the ancient language of the British Isles, was part of the Germanic family of languages. When the Norman French successfully invaded Britain in 1066 they brought with them their own language, part of the Romance language family (all originally derived from Latin). By the time of Chaucer's death in 1400 these two linguistic traditions had merged into a single language, Middle English, that can be read today, despite its differences in spelling, pronunciation, and vocabulary. We can still, however, distinguish the words that show their Germanic heritage from those of Latinate origin. English is rich in synonyms, and Germanic and Latinate words that "mean" the same thing often have different connotations. "Smart" (from the Old English *smeart*) is not quite the same as "intelligent" (from the Latin *intellegent*). A "mapmaker" is subtly different from a "cartographer"—ask yourself which would have ink on his fingers. Although a poet's preference for words of a certain origin is not always immediately clear, we can readily distinguish the wide gulf that separates a statement like "I live in a house with my folks" from "I occupy a residence with my parents."

A final tension exists in poems between their use of **concrete diction** and **abstract diction**. Concrete words denote that which can be perceived by the senses, and the vividness of a poem's language resides primarily in the way it uses **imagery**, sensory details denoting specific physical experiences. Because sight is the most important of the five senses, **visual imagery** ("a dim light"; "an ink-stained rag"; "a golden daffodil") predominates in poems, but we should also be alert for striking examples of the other types of imagery: **auditory** ("a pounding surf"), **tactile** ("a scratchy beard"), **olfactory** ("the scent of apple blossoms"), and **gustatory** ("the bitter tang of gin"). The use of specific imagery has always been crucial for poetry. Consider, for example, the way Chaucer uses brilliantly chosen concrete details—a nun's coral jewelry, a monk's hood lined with fur, a festering sore on a cook's shin—to bring his pilgrims to life in the prologue to *The Canterbury Tales*. In the early twentieth century, a group of poets led by Americans Ezra Pound and H. D. (Hilda Doolittle) pioneered a poetic movement called **imagism**, in which concrete details predominate in short descriptive poems (see H. D.'s "Sea Rose"). "Go in fear of abstractions," commanded Pound, and his friend William Carlos Williams modified the remark to become a poetic credo: "No ideas but in things."

Still, for most poets abstract words remain important because they carry the burden of a poem's overall meaning or theme. William Butler Yeats's "Leda and the Swan" provides a good example of how concrete and abstract diction coexists in a poem. In reading this account of the myth in which Zeus, in the form of a swan, rapes and impregnates a human woman and thus sets in action the chain of events that leads to the Trojan War (Leda was the mother of Helen of Troy), we will probably be struck at first by the way that tactile imagery ("a sudden blow," fingers attempting to "push / The feathered glory" away, "A shudder in the loins") is used to describe an act of sexual violation. Even though some abstract words ("terrified," "vague," "glory," "strange") appear in the first eight lines of the poem they are all linked closely to concrete words like "fingers," "feathered," and "heart." In the last two lines of the poem, Yeats uses three large abstractions—"knowledge," "power," and "indifferent"—to state his theme (or at least ask the crucial rhetorical question about the meaning of the myth). More often than not, one can expect to encounter the largest number of abstract words near the conclusion of poems. Probably the most famous abstract statement in English poetry—John Keats's "'Beauty is truth, truth beauty,' that is all / Ye know on earth, and all ye need to know"—appears in the last two lines of a fifty-line poem that is otherwise filled with lush, sensory details of description.

Two other devices sometimes govern a poet's choice of words. **Onomatopoeia** refers to individual words like "splash" or "thud" whose meanings are closely related to their sounds. Auditory imagery in a poem can often be enhanced by the use of onomatopoeic words. In some cases, however, a whole line can be called onomatopoeic, even if it contains no single word that illustrates the device. Thomas Hardy uses this line to describe the pounding of distant surf: "Where hill-hid tides throb, throe on throe." Here the repetition of similar sounds helps to imitate the sound of the ocean. A second device is the **pun**, the use of one word to imply the additional meaning of a similar-sounding word (the formal term is **paranomasia**). Thus, when Anne Bradstreet, in "The Author to Her Book," compares her first book to an illegitimate child, she addresses the book in this manner: "If for thy Father asked, say thou had'st none; / And for thy Mother, she alas is poor, / Which caused her thus to send thee out of door." The closeness of the interjection "alas" to the article and noun "a lass" is hardly coincidental. Poets in Bradstreet's day considered the pun a staple of their repertoire, even in serious poetry, but contemporary poets are more likely to use it primarily for comic effect:

> They have a dozen children; it's their diet,
> For they have bread too often. Please don't try it (Anonymous)

More often than not, puns like these will elicit a groan from the audience, a response that may be exactly what the poet desires.

Figurative Language

We use figurative language in everyday speech without thinking of the poetic functions of the same devices. We can always relate experience in a purely literal fashion: "His table manners were deplorable. Mother scolded him severely, and Dad said some angry words to him. He left the table embarrassed and with his feelings hurt." But a more vivid way of saying the same thing might employ language used not in the literal but in the figurative sense. Thus, another version might run, "He made an absolute pig of himself. Mother jumped on his back about it, and Dad scorched his ears. You should have seen him slink off like a scolded puppy." At least four comparisons are made here in an attempt to describe one character's table manners, his mother's scolding, his father's words, and the manner in which the character retreated from the table. In every case, the thing being described, what is called the **tenor** of the figure of speech, is linked with a concrete image or **vehicle**. All of the types of figurative language, what are called **figures of speech**, or **tropes**, involve some kind of comparison, either explicit or implied. Thus, two of the figures in the above example specifically compare aspects of the character's behavior to animal behavior. The other two imply parental words that were delivered with strong physical force or extreme anger. Some of the most common figures of speech are:

Metaphor: a direct comparison between two unlike things. Metaphors may take several forms.

> His words were sharp knives.
> The sharp knife of his words cut through the silence.
> He spoke sharp, cutting words with his knife-edged voice.
> His words knifed through the still air.

> *I will speak daggers to her but use none.* (Shakespeare, *Hamlet*)

Implied metaphor: a metaphor in which either the tenor or vehicle is implied, not stated.

> The running back gathered steam and chugged toward the end
> zone.

Here the player is compared to a steam locomotive without naming it explicitly.

> *While smoke on its chin, that slithering gun*
> *Coiled back from its windowsill* (X. J. Kennedy)

In this passage from a poem about the assassination of President John F. Kennedy, Lee Harvey Oswald's rifle is indirectly compared ("coiled back" and "slithering") to a snake that has struck its victim.

Simile: a comparison using "like," "as," or "than" as a connective device.

> *My love is like a red, red rose* (Robert Burns)

> My love smells as sweet as a rose.
> My love looks fresher than a newly budded rose.

Conceit: an extended or far-fetched metaphor, in most cases comparing things that apparently have almost nothing in common.

> *Make me, O Lord, thy spinning wheel complete.* . . . (Edward Taylor)

The poem, "Huswifery," draws an analogy between the process of salvation and the manufacture of cloth, ending with the persona attired in "holy robes for glory."

Petrarchan conceit: named after the first great master of the sonnet, is a clichéd comparison usually relating to a woman's beauty (see Thomas

Campion's "There Is a Garden in Her Face"; Shakespeare's Sonnet 130 parodies this type of trope). The **metaphysical conceit** refers to the extended comparisons favored by such so-called metaphysical poets as John Donne, George Herbert, and Edward Taylor. The conceit in the final three stanzas of Donne's "A Valediction: Forbidding Mourning" compares the poet and his wife with a pair of drafting compasses, hardly an image that most people would choose to celebrate marital fidelity.

Hyperbole: an overstatement, a comparison using conscious exaggeration.

He threw the ball so fast it caught the catcher's mitt on fire.

And I will love thee still, my dear,
Till a' the seas gang dry. (Robert Burns)

Understatement: the opposite of hyperbole.

"I don't think we're in Kansas anymore, Toto." (says Dorothy in
   The Wizard of Oz)

The space between, is but an hour,
The frail duration of a flower. (Philip Freneau)

Freneau is understating a wild honeysuckle's lifespan by saying it is "but an hour." Because, by implication, he is also talking about human life, the understatement is even more pronounced.

I watched him; and the sight was not so fair
As one or two that I have seen elsewhere. (Edwin Arlington
   Robinson)

In "How Annandale Went Out," the persona is a physician who is about to perform euthanasia on a friend dying in agony. Understatement is often used in conjunction with verbal irony (see below).

Allusion: a metaphor making a direct comparison to a historical or literary event or character, a myth, a biblical reference, and so forth.

He is a Samson of strength but a Judas of duplicity.

He dreamed of Thebes and Camelot,
And Priam's neighbors. (Edwin Arlington Robinson)

Metonymy: use of a related object to stand for the thing actually being talked about.

It's the only white-collar street in this blue-collar town.

And O ye high-flown quills that soar the skies,
And ever with your prey still catch your praise. (Anne Bradstreet)

Here, Bradstreet speaks of critics who may be hostile to her work. She identifies them as "quills," referring to their quill pens.

He stood among a crowd at Dromahair;
His heart hung all upon a silken dress. (William Butler Yeats)

The title character of "The Man Who Dreamed of Faeryland" was interested in the woman *in* the dress, not the dress itself.

Synecdoche: use of a part for the whole, or vice versa (very similar to metonymy).

The crowned heads of Europe were in attendance.
Before the indifferent beak could let her drop. (William Butler Yeats)

Personification: giving human characteristics to nonhuman things or to abstractions.

Justice weighs the evidence in her golden scales.
The ocean cursed and spat at us.

Of all her train, the hands of Spring
First plant thee in the watery mould. (William Cullen Bryant)

Bryant personifies spring by giving it hands with which to plant a yellow violet, which is one of the first wildflowers to appear in the season.

Apostrophe: a variety of personification in which a nonhuman thing, abstraction, or person not physically present is directly addressed as if it could respond.

Milton! Thou shouldst be living at this hour. (William Wordsworth)

Is it, O man, with such discordant noises,
   With such accursed instruments as these,
Thou drownest Nature's sweet and kindly voices,
   And jarrest the celestial harmonies? (Henry Wadsworth Longfellow)

Longfellow is addressing the human race in general.

Paradox: an apparent contradiction or illogical statement.

I'll never forget old what's-his-name.

His hand hath made this noble work which Stands,
His Glorious Handiwork not made by hands. (Edward Taylor)

Taylor is describing God's creation of the universe, which He willed into being out of nothingness.

Oxymoron: a short paradox, usually consisting of an adjective and noun with conflicting meanings.

The touch of her lips was sweet agony.

Progress is a comfortable disease (e. e. cummings)

A terrible beauty is born. (William Butler Yeats)

Synesthesia: a conscious mixing of two different types of sensory experience.

A raw, red wind rushed from the north.

Leaves cast in casual potpourris
Whisper their scents from pits and cellar-holes (Richard Wilbur)

Transferred epithet: not, strictly speaking, a trope, it occurs when an adjective is "transferred" from the word it actually modifies to a nearby word.

The plowman homeward plods his weary way. (Thomas Gray)

In this example, the plowman is weary, not the path ("way") he walks upon.

Allegory and Symbol

Related to the figurative devices are the various types of symbolism that may occur in poems. In many cases, a poem may seem so simple on the surface that we feel impelled to read deeper meanings into it. Robert Frost's famous lyric "Stopping by Woods on a Snowy Evening" is a classic case in point. There is nothing wrong with searching for larger significance in a poem, but the reader should perhaps be wary of leaping to conclusions about symbolic meanings before fully exhausting the literal sense of a poem. Whatever the case, both allegory and symbolism share the demand that the reader supply abstract or general meanings to the specific concrete details of the poem.

The simplest form that this substitution takes occurs in **allegory**. An allegory is usually a narrative that exists on at least two levels simultaneously, a concrete literal level and a second level of abstract meaning; throughout an allegory a consistent sequence of parallels exists between the literal and the abstract. Sometimes allegories may imply third or fourth levels of meaning as well, especially in long allegorical poems like Dante's *The Divine Comedy*, which has been interpreted on personal, political, ethical, and Christian levels. The characters and actions in an allegory explicitly signify the abstract level of meaning, and generally this second level of meaning is what the poet primarily intends to convey. For example, Robert Southwell's "The Burning Babe" is filled with fantastic incidents and paradoxical speech that are made clear in the poem's last line: "And straight I callèd unto mind that it was Christmas day." The literal burning babe of the title is the Christ child, who predicts his own future to the amazed watcher. Thus, in interpreting the poem, the reader must substitute theological terms like "redemption" or "original sin" for the literal details it contains.

Two types of prose allegories, the fable and parable, have been universally popular. A fable is a short, nonrealistic narrative that is told to illustrate a universal moral concept. A parable is similar but generally contains realistic characters and events. Thus, Aesop's fable of the tortoise and the hare, instead of telling us something about animal behavior, illustrates the virtue of persistence against seemingly unbeatable competition. Jesus's parable of the Good Samaritan tells the story of a man who is robbed and beaten and eventually rescued by a stranger of another race in order to define the concept of "neighbor" for a questioning lawyer. Poetic allegories like George Herbert's "Redemption" or Christina Rossetti's "Up-Hill" can be read in Christian terms as symbolic accounts of the process of salvation. Robert Burns's witty ballad "John Barleycorn" tells on the literal surface the story of a violent murder, but the astute reader quickly discovers that the underlying meaning involves the poet's native Scotland's legendary talent for distilling and consuming strong drink.

Many poems contain symbolic elements that are somewhat more elusive in meaning than the simple one-for-one equivalences presented by allegory. A **symbol**, then, is any concrete thing or any action in a poem that implies a meaning beyond its literal sense. Many of these things or actions are called **traditional symbols**, that is, symbols that hold roughly the same meanings for members of a given society.

Certain flowers, colors, natural objects, and religious emblems possess meanings that we can generally agree on. A white lily and a red rose suggest, respectively, mourning and passion. Few Western cultures would associate a black dress with a festive occasion or a red one with purity and innocence. Dawn and rainbows are traditional natural symbols of hope and new beginnings. It would be unlikely for a poet to mention a cross without expecting readers to think of its Christian symbolism. Other types of symbols can be identified in poems that are otherwise not allegorical. A **private symbol** is one that has acquired certain meanings from a single poet's repeated use of it. William Butler Yeats's use of "gyres" in several poems like "The Second Coming" is explained in some of his prose writings as a symbol for the turning of historical cycles, and his use of the word in his poems obviously goes beyond the literal level. Some visionary poets like Yeats and William Blake devised complicated private symbolic systems, a sort of alternative mythology, and understanding the full import of these symbols becomes primarily the task of critics who have specialized in these poets. Other poets may employ **incidental symbols**, things that are not usually considered symbolic but may be in a particular poem, or symbolic acts, a situation or response that seems of greater than literal import. As noted earlier, one of the most famous poems using these two devices is Robert Frost's "Stopping by Woods on a Snowy Evening." In this poem some readers see the "lovely, dark and deep" woods as both inviting and threatening and want to view the persona's rejection of their allure ("But I have promises to keep / And miles to go before I sleep") as some sort of life-affirming act. Frost himself was not particularly helpful in guiding his readers, often scoffing at those who had read too much metaphysical portent into such a simple lyric, although in other poems he presents objects such as a fork in the road or an abandoned woodpile in a manner that leads the reader to feel that these obviously possess some larger significance. Many modern poems remain so enigmatic that readers have consistently returned to them seeking new interpretations. Poems like these were to a degree influenced by the Symbolists, a group of French poets of the late nineteenth century, who deliberately wrote poems filled with vague nuances subject to multiple interpretations. Such American attempts at symbolist experiments as Wallace Stevens's "Anecdote of the Jar" or "The Emperor of Ice-Cream" continue to perplex and fascinate readers, particularly those who are versed in recent schools of interpretation that focus on the indeterminacy of a poetic text.

Tone of Voice

Even the simplest statement is subject to multiple interpretations if it is delivered in several different tones of voice. Consider the shift in emphasis between saying "*I* gave you the money," "I *gave* you the money," and "I gave *you* the money." Even a seemingly innocent compliment like "You look lovely this morning" takes on a different meaning if it is delivered by a woman on New Year's Day to her hungover husband. Still, these variations in **tone**, the speaker's implied attitude toward the words he or she says, depend primarily on vocal inflection. Because a poet only rarely gets the opportunity to elucidate his tones in a public performance, it is possible that readers may have difficulties in grasping the tone of a poem printed on the page. Still, many poems establish their tone quite clearly from the outset. The opening of Milton's sonnet "On the Late Massacre in Piedmont" ("Avenge, O Lord, thy slaughtered saints . . .") establishes a tone of righteous anger that is consistent throughout the poem. Thus, in many cases we can relate the tone of voice in poems to the emotions we employ in our own speech, and we would have to violate quite a few rules of common sense to argue that Milton is being flippant.

    Irony is the element of tone by which a poet may imply an attitude that is in fact contrary to what his words appear to say. Of course, the simplest form of irony is **sarcasm**, the wounding tone of voice we use to imply exactly the opposite of what we say: "That's really a *great* excuse!" or "What a *wonderful* performance!" For obvious reasons, sarcasm is appropriate primarily to spoken language. It has become almost universal to follow a bit of gentle sarcasm in an e-mail message with a symbolic :) to indicate that the remark is not to be taken "straight." **Verbal irony** is the conscious manipulation of tone by which the poet's actual attitude is the opposite of what he says. In a poem like Thomas Hardy's "The Ruined Maid," it is obvious that one speaker considers the meaning of "ruined" to be somewhat less severe than the other, and the whole poem hinges on this ironic counterpoint of definitions and the different moral and social attitudes they imply. Consider the opening lines of Oliver Wendell Holmes's "Old Ironsides," a piece of propaganda verse that succeeded in raising enough money to save the U.S.S. *Constitution* from the scrapyard: "Ay, tear her tattered ensign down! / Long has it waved on high, / And many an eye has danced to see / That banner in the sky. . . ." Because Holmes's poetic mission is to *save* the ship, it is obvious that he is speaking ironically in the opening line; he emphatically *does not* want the ship's flag stripped from her, an attitude that is made clear in the third and fourth lines. Verbal irony is also a conspicuous feature of **verse satire**, poetry that exists primarily to mock or ridicule, although often with serious intent. One famous example, in the form of a short satirical piece, or **epigram**, is Sarah N. Cleghorn's "The Golf Links," a poem written before the advent of child labor laws:

> The golf links lie so near the mill
>> That almost every day
> The laboring children can look out
>> And see the men at play.

Here the weight of the verbal irony falls on two words, "laboring" and "play," and the way each is incongruously applied to the wrong group of people.

"The Golf Links," taken as a whole, also represents a second form of irony, **situational irony**, in which the setting of the poem (laboring children watching playing adults) contains a built-in incongruity. One master of ironic situation is Thomas Hardy, who used the title "Satires of Circumstance" in a series of short poems illustrating this sort of irony. Hardy's "Ah, Are You Digging on My Grave?" hinges on this kind of irony, with a ghostly persona asking questions of living speakers who end up offering little comfort to the dead woman. **Dramatic irony**, the third type of irony, occurs when the persona of a poem is less aware of the full import of his or her words than is the reader. William Blake's "The Chimney Sweeper" (from *Songs of Innocence*) is spoken by a child who does not seem to fully realize how badly he is being exploited by his employer, who has apparently been using the promises of religion as a way of keeping his underage workers in line. A similar statement could be made of the persona of Walter Savage Landor's short dramatic monologue "Mother, I Cannot":

> Mother, I cannot mind my wheel;
>> My fingers ache, my lips are dry:
> Oh! if you felt the pain I feel!
>> But oh, who ever felt as I?
>
> No longer could I doubt him true;
>> All other men may use deceit:
> He always said my eyes were blue,
>> And often swore my lips were sweet.

The young woman who speaks here apparently has not realized (or is deliberately unwilling to admit) that she has been sexually deceived and deserted by a scoundrel; "All other men may use deceit" gives the measure of her tragic naïvete. Dramatic irony, as the term implies, is most often found in dramatic monologues, where the gap between the speaker's perception of the situation and the reader's may be wide indeed.

Repetition: Sounds and Schemes

Because poetry uses language at its most intense level, we are aware of the weight of individual words and phrases to a degree that is usually lacking when we read prose. Poets have long known that the meanings that they attempt to convey often depend as much on the sound of the words as their meaning. We have already mentioned one sound device, onomatopoeia. Consider how much richer the experience of "the murmuring of innumerable bees" is than a synonymous phrase, "the faint sound of a lot of bees." It has often been said that all art aspires to the condition of music in the way that it affects an audience on some unconscious, visceral level. By carefully exploiting the repetition of sound devices, a poet may attempt to produce some of the same effects that the musical composer does.

Of course, much of this sonic level of poetry is subjective; what strikes one listener as pleasant may overwhelm the ear of another. Still, it is useful to distinguish between a poet's use of **euphony**, a series of pleasant sounds, and **cacophony**, sounds that are deliberately unpleasant. Note the following passages from Alexander Pope's "An Essay on Criticism," a didactic poem which attempts to illustrate many of the devices poets use:

> Soft is the strain when Zephyr gently blows,
> And the smooth stream in smoother numbers flows . . .

The repetition of the initial consonant sounds is called **alliteration**, and here Pope concentrates on the s sound. The vowel sounds are generally long: strain, blows, smooth, and flows. Here the description of the gentle west wind is assisted by the generally pleasing sense of euphony. But Pope, to illustrate the opposite quality, follows this couplet with a second:

But when loud surges lash the sounding shore,
The hoarse, rough verse should like the torrent roar.

Now the wind is anything but gentle, and the repetition of the *r* sounds in *surges, shore, hoarse, rough, verse, torrent,* and *roar* force the reader to speak from the back of the throat, making sounds that are anything but euphonious.

Repetition of sounds has no inherent meaning values (although some linguists may argue that certain sounds do stimulate particular emotions), but this repetition does call attention to itself and can be particularly effective when a poet wishes to emphasize a certain passage. We have already mentioned alliteration. Other sound patterns are **assonance**, the repetition of similar vowel sounds (*st*ee*p, *e*ven, rec*ei*ve, v*ea*l*), and **consonance,** the repetition of similar consonant sounds (*du*ck*, tor*que*, stri*ke*, tri*ck*le*). It should go without saying that spelling has little to do with any sound pattern; an initial *f* will alliterate with an initial *ph*.

Rhyme is the most important sound device, and our pleasure in deftly executed rhymes (consider the possibilities of rhyming "neighbor" with "sabre," as Richard Wilbur does in one of his translations) goes beyond mere sound to include the pleasure we take when an unexpected word is magically made to fit with another. There are several types of rhyme. **Masculine rhyme** occurs between single stressed syllables: *fleece, release, surcease, niece,* and so on. **Feminine rhyme,** also called **double rhyme,** matches two syllables, the first stressed and the second usually unstressed: *stinging, upbringing, flinging.* **Triple rhyme** goes further: *slithering, withering.* **Slant rhyme** (also called **near rhyme** and **off rhyme**) contains hints of sound repetition (sometimes related to assonance and consonance): *chill, dull,* and *sale* are possibilities, although contemporary poets often grant themselves considerable leeway in counting as rhyming words pairs that often have only the slightest similarity. When rhymes fall in a pattern in a poem and are **end rhymes**, occurring at the ends of lines, it is then convenient to assign letters to the sounds and speak of a **rhyme scheme.** Thus, a stanza of four lines ending with *heaven, hell, bell, eleven* would be said to have a rhyme scheme of *abba.* Rhymes may also occasionally be found in the interior of lines, which is called **internal rhyme.** Note how both end and internal rhymes work in the complex stanza which Poe uses in "The Raven."

More complicated patterns of repetition involve more than mere sounds but whole phrases and grammatical units. Ancient rhetoricians, teaching the art of public speaking, identified several of these, and they are also found in poetry. **Parallel structure** is simply the repetition of grammatically similar phrases or clauses: Tennyson's "To strive, to seek, to find, and not to yield." **Anaphora** and **epistrophe** are repeated words or phrases at, respectively, the beginning and end of lines. Walt Whitman uses these schemes extensively, often in the same lines. This passage from "Song of Myself" illustrates both anaphora and epistrophe:

> If they are not yours as much as mine they are nothing, or next
>   to nothing,
> If they are not the riddle and the untying of the riddle they are
>   nothing,
> If they are not just as close as they are distant they are nothing.

Antithesis is the matching of parallel units that contain contrasting meanings, such as Whitman's "I am of old and young, of the foolish as much as the wise, / Regardless of others, ever regardful of others, / Maternal as well as paternal, a child as well as a man. . . ." Although the rhetorical schemes are perhaps more native to the orator, the poet can still make occasional effective use of them. Whitman's poetry was influenced by many sources but by none perhaps so powerfully as the heavily schematic language of the King James Bible.

Meter and Rhythm

The subject of poetic meter and rhythm can be a difficult one, to say the least, and it is doubtless true that such phrases as *trochaic octameter* or *spondaic substitution* have an intimidating quality. Still, discussions of meter need not be limited to experts, and even beginning readers should be able to apply a few of the metrical principles that are commonly found in poetry written in English.

First, let us distinguish between two terms that are often used synonymously: **poetry** and **verse**. Poetry refers to a whole genre of literature and thus stands with fiction and drama as one of the three major types of writing, whereas verse refers to a mode of writing in lines of a certain length; thus, many poets still retain the old practice of capitalizing the first word of each line to indicate its integrity as a unit of composition. Virtually any piece of writing can be versified (and sometimes rhymed as well). Especially useful are bits of **mnemonic verse**, in which information like the number of days in the months (thirty days hath September . . .) or simple spelling rules ("I before E / Except after

C . . .") is cast in a form that is easy to remember. Although it is not strictly accurate to do so, many writers use verse to denote metrical writing that somehow does not quite measure up to the level of true poetry; phrases like **light verse** or **occasional verse** (lines written for a specific occasion, like a birthday or anniversary) are often used in this manner.

If a writer is unconcerned about the length of individual lines and is governed only by the width of the paper being used, then he or she is not writing verse but **prose**. All verse is metrical writing; prose is not. Surprisingly enough, there is a body of writing called **prose poetry**, which uses language in a poetic manner but avoids any type of meter; Carolyn Forché's "The Colonel" is one example. Perhaps the simplest way to think of **meter** in verse is to think of its synonym **measure** (think of the use of meter in words like odometer or kilometer). Thus, meter refers to the method by which a poet determines line length.

When we talk about meter in poetry we ordinarily mean that the poet is employing some kind of consistent **prosody** or system of measurement. There are many possible prosodies, depending on what the poet decides to count as the unit of measurement in the line, but only three of these systems are common in English poetry. Perhaps the simplest is **syllabic verse**. In verse of this type, the length of the line is determined by counting the total number of syllables the line contains (Sylvia Plath's "Metaphors," for one example, uses lines of nine syllables, a witty metaphor for the poem's subject, pregnancy). Much French poetry of the past was written in twelve-syllable lines, or **Alexandrines**, and in English a word like **octosyllabic** denotes a line of eight syllables. Because English is a language of strong stresses, most of our poets have favored other prosodic systems, but syllabic poetry has been attempted by many poets, among them Marianne Moore, Richard Wilbur, and Dylan Thomas. Moore, in particular, often wrote in **quantitative syllabics**, that is, stanzas containing the same number of lines with identical numbers of syllables in the corresponding lines of different stanzas. Moore's "The Fish" uses stanzas made of lines of one, three, eight, one, six, and eight syllables, respectively.

More natural to the English language is **accentual** verse, a prosodic system in which only accented or strongly stressed syllables are counted in a line, which can also contain a varying number of unaccented syllables. Much folk poetry, perhaps intended to be recited to the beat of a percussion instrument, retains this stress-based pattern, and the oldest verse in the British tradition, Anglo-Saxon poetry like *Beowulf*, is composed in four-stress lines which were recited to musical accompaniment. Many of the verses we re-call from nursery rhymes, children's chanting games ("Red rover, red rover, / Send [any name from one to four syllables can be substituted here—*Bill, Susan, Latisha, Elizabeth*] right over"), and sports cheers ("Two bits, four bits, six bits, a dollar! / All for the [*Owls, Cowboys, Cardinals, Thundering Herd*] stand up and holler!") retain the strong sense of rhythmical pulse that characterizes much accentual verse, a fact we recognize when we clap our hands and move rhythmically to the sound of the words. Indeed, the lyrics to much current rap music are actually composed to a four-stress accentual line, and the stresses or "beats" can be heard plainly when we listen or dance. Gerard Manley Hopkins, attempting to recapture some of the flavor of Anglo-Saxon verse, pioneered a type of accentual prosody that he called **sprung rhythm**, in which he counted only the strong stresses in his lines. Accentual meters still supply possibilities for contempo-rary poets; indeed, what often appears to be free verse is revealed, on closer inspection, to be a poem written in accentual meter. Richard Wilbur's "The Writer," for example, is written in a stanza containing lines of three, five, and three strong stresses, respectively, but the stresses do not overwhelm the reader's ear.

    Accentual-syllabic verse is the most important prosodic system in English, dominating our poetry for the five centuries from Chaucer's time down to the early years of the twentieth century. Even though in the last seventy years or so free verse has become the prevailing style in which poetry is written, accentual-syllabic verse still has many able practitioners. An accentual-syllabic prosody is somewhat more compli-cated than the two systems we have mentioned because it requires that the poet count both the strongly stressed syllables and the total num-ber of syllables in the line. Because stressed and unstressed syllables al-ternate fairly regularly in this system, four **metrical feet**, representing the most common patterns, designate the subdivisions of rhythm that make up the line (think of a yardstick divided into three feet). These feet are the **iamb** (or **iambic foot**), one unstressed and one stressed syl-lable; the **trochee** (or **trochaic foot**), one stressed and one unstressed syllable; the **anapest** (or **anapestic foot**), two unstressed syllables and one stressed syllable; and the **dactyl** (or **dactylic foot**), one stressed and two unstressed syllables. The first two of these, iambic and trochaic, are called **double meters**; the second two, **triple meters**. Iambic and anapestic meters are sometimes called **rising meters** because they "rise" toward the stressed syllable; trochaic and dactylic meters are called **falling meters** for the opposite reason. Simple repetition of words or phrases can give us the sense of how these lines sound in a purely schematic sense. The **breve** (˘) and **ictus** (´) are used to denote unstressed and stressed syllables, respectively.

Iambic:

    rĕleáse / rĕleáse / rĕleáse
    tŏ fáll / iňtó /dĕspáir
    Maríe / dĭscoý /eřs cándy

Trochaic:

    méltiňg / méltiňg / méltiňg / méltiňg
    Ṕetĕr / disă /gréed eň / tírelў
    clevĕr / wŕitiňg / filled the /páge

Anapestic:

    uňcoňtrólled / uň coňtrólled
    ă rĕtríev / ĕr ăppéared
    aňd ă tér / řible thúndĕr

Dactylic:

    shĭveriňg / shĭveriňg / shĭveriňg / shĭveriňg /shĭveriňg
    térřiblॅy / ill wĭth the / sýmptoṁs ŏf / virăl pňeu / móňiă
    nóte hŏw the / míniॅstĕr / whíspeřed ăt / Émĭlॅy's / gráve

Because each of these lines contains a certain number of feet, a second specialized term is used to denote how many times a pattern is repeated in a line:

one foot	**monometer**
two feet	**dimeter**
three feet	**trimeter**
four feet	**tetrameter**
five feet	**pentameter**
six feet	**hexameter**
seven feet	**heptameter**
eight feet	**octameter**

Thus, in the examples above, the first set of lines is iambic trimeter; the second, trochaic tetrameter; the third, anapestic dimeter; and the fourth, dactylic pentameter. The third lines in the iambic and anapestic examples are **hypermetrical**; that is, they contain an extra unstressed syllable or **feminine ending**. Conversely, the third lines in the trochaic and dactylic examples are missing one and two unstressed final syllables, respectively, a common practice called **catalexis**. Although over thirty combinations of foot type and number per line theoretically are possible, relatively few are ordinarily encountered in poetry. The iambic foot is most common in English, followed by the anapest and the trochee; the dactylic foot is relatively rare. Line lengths tend to be from three to five feet, with anything shorter or longer used only sparingly. Still, there are famous exceptions like Poe's "The Raven," which is composed in trochaic octameters and tetrameters, or Southwell's "The Burning Babe," written in iambic heptameter. Long trochaic and iambic lines sometimes exhibit a kind of rhythmical counterpoint. In the opening line of John Whitworth's "The Examiners," for example, the line of trochaic octameter really has only four strong stresses: "Where the HOUSE is cold and EMPty and the GARden's over-GROWN." Verse like this is called **dipodic** ("double-footed") because two feet (/u|/u) are combined into a single unit (uu/u).

Meter denotes regularity, the "blueprint" for a line from which the poet works. Because iambic pentameter is the most common meter used in English poetry, our subsequent discussion will focus on poems written in it. Most poets quickly learn that a metronomic regularity, five iambic feet marching in lockstep line after line, is not a virtue and quickly becomes predictable. Thus, there are several ways by which poets can add variety to their lines so that the actual **rhythm** of the line, what is actually heard, plays a subtle counterpoint against the regularity of the meter. One way is to vary the placement of the **caesura** (||) or pause within a line (usually indicated by a mark of punctuation). Another is by mixing **end-stopped lines**, which clearly pause at their conclusion, with **enjambed** lines, which run on into the next line with no pause. The following lines from Tennyson's "Ulysses" illustrate these techniques:

> This is my son, mine own Telemachus,
> To whom I leave the scepter and the isle,
> Well-loved of me, discerning to fulfill
> This labor, by slow prudence to make mild
> A rugged people, and through soft degrees
> Subdue them to the useful and the good.

Lines two and six have no caesurae; the others do, after either the third, fourth, or fifth syllable. Lines one, two, and six are end-stopped; the others are enjambed (or use **enjambment**).

Another technique of varying regularity is **metrical substitution**, where feet of a different type are substituted for what the meter calls for. In iambic meter, trochaic feet are often encountered at the beginnings of lines, or after a caesura. Two other feet, the **pyrrhic** (˘˘) consisting of two unstressed syllables, and the **spondee** (´´), consisting of two stressed syllables, are also commonly substituted. Here are Tennyson's lines with their scansion marked.

> Thís iš / m̆y són, || / miňe óẃn / T̆elém / ăchús,
> T̆o whóm / Ĭ leáve / the scép / těr ařd / the ísle,
> Wéll-lóved / ŏf me, / || / discérn / iňg tŏ / fúlfíll
> Thís lá / bŏr, || by / slow prú / děnce t̆o / máke míld
> Ă rúg / gĕd peó / ple, || ařd / through sóft / degrées
> S̆ŭbdúe / thĕm tŏ / the uśe / fŭl ařd / the góod.

Even though these are fairly regular iambic pentameter lines, it should be observed that no single line is without some substitution. Still, the dominant pattern of five iambic feet per line should be apparent (out of thirty total feet, about twenty are iambs); there is even a strong tendency on the reader's part to "promote" the middle syllable of three unstressed syllables ("Subdue / them *to* / the use / ful *and* / the good") to keep the sense of the iambic rhythm.

How far can a poet depart from the pattern without losing contact with the original meter? That is a question that is impossible to answer in general terms. The following scansion will probably strike us at first as a far departure from regular iambic pentameter:

> ´ || ´/ ˘ || ´ / ˜˜ || / ´ ˘ / ˘ ´

Yet it is actually the opening line of one of Shakespeare's most often quoted passages, Mark Antony's funeral oration from *Julius Caesar*:

> Fríends, || Ró / măns, || cóun, || tr̆ymeň, || / lénd m̆e / yŏur eárs

Poets who have learned to use the full resources of meter do not consider it a restraint; instead, they are able to stretch the pattern to its limits without breaking it. A good analogy might be made between poetry and dance. Beginning dancers watch their feet and count the steps while making them; after considerable practice, the movements become second nature, and a skillful pair of partners can add dips and passes without losing the basic step of the music.

Free Verse, Open Form, and Closed Form

Nothing has been so exhaustively debated in English-language poetry as the exact nature of **free verse**. The simplest definition may be the best: free verse is verse with no consistent metrical pattern. In free verse, line length is a subjective decision made by the poet, and length may be determined by grammatical phrases, the poet's own sense of individual "breath-units," or even by the visual arrangement of lines on the page. Clearly, it is easier to speak of what free verse is not than to explain what it is. Even its practitioners do not seem very happy with the term free verse, which is derived from the French *vers libre*. The extensive use of free verse is a fairly recent phenomenon in the history of poetry. Even though there are many examples of free verse from the past (the Psalms, Ecclesiastes, and the Song of Solomon from the King James Bible), the modern history of free verse begins in 1855 with the publication of Walt Whitman's *Leaves of Grass*. Whitman, influenced by Ralph Waldo Emerson's statement that "it is not meters but meter-making argument that makes a poem," created a unique variety of long-line free verse based on grammatical units—phrases and clauses. Whitman's free verse is so distinctive that he has had few direct imitators, and subsequent poets who have used free verse have written lines that vary widely in syllable count. Good free verse, as T. S. Eliot remarked, still contains some kind of "ghost of meter," and its rhythms can be as terse and clipped as those of Philip Levine or as lushly sensuous as those of Pattiann Rogers. The poet who claims that free verse is somehow easier to write than metrical verse would find many arguments to the contrary. As Eliot said, "No verse is free for the poet who wants to do a good job."

All poems have form, the arrangement of the poem on the page that differentiates it from prose. Sometimes this arrangement indicates that the poet is following a preconceived plan—a metrical pattern, a rhyme scheme, a purely visual design like that of **concrete** or **spatial poetry**, or a scheme like that of **acrostic verse**, in which the first letters of the lines spell a message. An analysis of poetic form notes how the lines are arranged, how long they are, and how they are grouped into blocks or **stanzas**. Further analysis might reveal the existence of types of repetition, rhyme, or the use of a **refrain**, or a repeated line or groups of lines. A large number of the poems composed in the twentieth and twenty-first centuries have been written in **open form**, which simply means that there is no strict pattern of regularity in the elements mentioned above; that is, there is no consistent meter and no rhyme scheme. Still, even a famous poem in open form like William Carlos Williams's "The Red Wheelbarrow" can be described in formal terms:

so much depends
upon

a red wheel
barrow

glazed with rain
water

beside the white
chickens.

Here we observe that the eight-line poem is divided into **uniform stanzas** of two lines each (or couplets). Line length varies between four and two syllables per line. The odd-numbered lines each contain three words; the even, one. Although there is no apparent use of rhyme or repetition here, many poems in open form contain some rhyme and metrical regularity at their conclusions. Alan Dugan's "Love Song: I and Thou" falls into regular iambic tetrameter in its final lines, and a typical contemporary example of an open form poem, Naomi Shihab Nye's "The Traveling Onion," concludes with a closing rhyme on "career" and "disappear."

Closed form, unlike open form, denotes the existence of some kind of regular pattern of meter, stanza, rhyme, or repetition. **Stanza forms** are consistent patterns in the individual units of the poem (stanza means "room" in Italian); **fixed forms** are patterns that encompass a complete poem, for example, a sonnet or a villanelle. **Traditional forms** are patterns that have been used for long periods of time and thus may be associated with certain subjects, themes, or types of poems; the sonnet is one example, for it has been used primarily (but by no means exclusively) for lyric poetry. **Nonce forms** are patterns that originate in an individual poem and have not been widely used by other poets. Of course, it goes without saying that every traditional form was at first a nonce form; the Italian poet (now lost to memory) who first wrote a lyric consisting of fourteen rhymed eleven-syllable lines could not have foreseen that in subsequent centuries poets the world over would produce literally millions of sonnets that are all variations on the original model. Some of the most common stanza and fixed forms are briefly discussed herein.

Stanza Forms

Blank verse is not, strictly speaking, a stanza form because it consists of individual lines of iambic pentameter that do not rhyme. However, long poems in blank verse may be arranged into **verse paragraphs** or stanzas with a varying number of lines. Blank verse originally appeared in English with the Earl of Surrey's translation of the *Aeneid* in the fifteenth century; it has been used extensively for narrative and dramatic purposes since then, particularly in epics like Milton's *Paradise Lost* and in Shakespeare's plays. Also written in stanzas of varying lengths is the **irregular ode**, a poem which employs lines of varying lengths (although usually of a regular rhythm that is iambic or matches one of the other feet) and an irregular rhyme scheme.

Paired rhyming lines *(aabbcc . . .)* are called **couplets**, although they are only rarely printed as separate stanzas. **Short couplets** have a meter of iambic tetrameter (and are sometimes called **octosyllabic couplets**). If their rhymes are predominantly feminine and seem chosen for comic effect, they may be called **Hudibrastic couplets** after Samuel Butler's satirical poem *Hudibras* of the late 1600s. **Heroic couplets** have a meter of iambic pentameter and have often been used effectively in satirical poems like Alexander Pope's "mock heroic" poem *The Dunciad* and even in dramatic monologues like Robert Browning's "My Last Duchess," where the rhymes are so effectively buried by enjambment that the poem approximates speech. Two other couplet forms, both rare, are poulter's *measure*, rhyming pairs of alternating lines of iambic hexameter and iambic heptameter, and *fourteeners*, pairs of iambic heptameter (fourteen-syllable) lines which, because a natural caesura usually falls after the fourth foot, closely resemble common meter (see below).

A three-line stanza is called a **tercet**. If it rhymes in an *aaa bbb . . .* pattern, it is a **triplet**; sometimes triplets appear in poems written in heroic couplets, especially at the end of sections or where special emphasis is desired. Iambic pentameter tercets rhyming *aba bcb cdc . . .* form **terza rima**, a pattern invented by Dante for *The Divine Comedy*.

A four-line stanza is known as a **quatrain**. Alternating lines of tetrameter and trimeter in any foot, rhyming *abcb* or *abab*, make up a **ballad stanza**; if the feet are strictly iambic, then the quatrain is called **common meter**, the form of many popular hymns like "Amazing Grace." **Long meter**, also widely used in hymns, consists of iambic tetrameter lines rhyming *abcb* or *abab*; **short meter** has a similar rhyme scheme but contains first, second, and fourth lines of iambic trimeter and a third line of iambic tetrameter. The **In Memoriam stanza,** named after Tennyson's long poetic sequence, is iambic tetrameter rhyming *abba*. The ***Rubaiyat* stanza,** used by Frost in "Stopping by Woods on a Snowy Evening," is an import from Persia; and it consists of lines of either iambic tetrameter or pentameter, rhyming *aaba bbcb*. Lines of iambic pentameter rhyming *abab* are known as an **English quatrain;** lines of the same meter rhyming *abba* make up an **Italian quatrain.** One other unusual quatrain stanza is an import from ancient Greece, the **Sapphic stanza,** named after the poet Sappho. The Sapphic stanza consists of three **hendecasyllabic** (eleven-syllable) lines of this pattern:

$$\acute{}\,\breve{}\ /\ \acute{}\,\breve{}\ /\ \acute{}\,\breve{}\,\breve{}\ /\ \acute{}\,\breve{}\ /\ \acute{}\,\breve{}$$

and a fourth line called an **Adonic,** which is five syllables long and consists of one dactylic foot and one trochaic foot. The Sapphic stanza is usually unrhymed. The quatrain stanza is also used in another import, the **pantoum,** a poem in which the second and fourth lines of the first stanza become the first and third of the second, and the second and fourth of the second become the first and third of the fourth, and so on. Pantoums may be written in any meter and may or may not employ rhyme.

A five-line stanza is known as a **quintet** and is relatively rare in English poetry. The **sestet,** or six-line stanza, can be found with a number of different meters and rhyme schemes. A seven-line stanza is called a **septet;** one septet stanza form is **rime royal,** seven lines of iambic pentameter rhyming *ababbcc*. An eight-line stanza is called an **octave;** one widely used stanza of this length is **ottava rima,** iambic pentameter lines rhyming *abababcc*. Another octave form is the **Monk's Tale stanza,** named after one of Chaucer's tales. It is iambic pentameter and rhymes *ababbcbc*. The addition of a ninth line, rhyming *c* and having a meter of iambic hexameter, makes a **Spenserian stanza,** named after Edmund Spenser, the poet who invented it for *The Faerie Queene*, a long metrical romance.

Fixed Forms

Fixed forms are combinations of meter, rhyme scheme, and repetition that comprise complete poems. One familiar three-line fixed form is the **haiku**, a Japanese import consisting of lines of five, seven, and five syllables, respectively.

The **clerihew**, named after its inventor, Edward Clerihew Bentley, is a humorous form in which the first line is a person's name; the clerihew has a rhyme scheme of *aa bb*.

Two five-line fixed forms are the **limerick** and the **cinquain**. The common and comic limerick consists of anapestic trimeter in lines one, two, and five, and anapestic dimeter in lines three and four. The rhymes, *aabba*, are usually double rhymes used for comic effect. Robert Conquest, the great historian of the purges of the Soviet Union, is also a celebrated poet and an accomplished author of limericks. Conquest memorably summed up his political conclusions in five lines:

> There was a great Marxist called Lenin,
> Who did two or three million men in.
> That's a lot to have done in,
> But where he did one in,
> That grand Marxist Stalin did ten in.

A cinquain, the invention of American poet Adelaide Crapsey (1878–1914), consists of five unrhymed lines of two, four, six, eight, and two syllables, respectively.

Two other short fixed forms, the triolet and the double-dactyl, have also proven popular. The eight-line triolet, a French form, uses two repeating lines in the pattern *ABaAabAB* with all lines having the same meter. The double-dactyl, which also is an eight-line form, was invented by the poets Anthony Hecht and John Hollander. The meter is dactylic dimeter with a rhyme scheme of *abcd efgd*. The other "rules" for the double-dactyl include a nonsense phrase in the first line, a person's name in the second, and a single word in the sixth. Here is an example, Leon Stokesbury's "Room with a View":

> Higgledy-piggledy
> Emily Dickinson
> Looked out her front window
> Struggling for breath—
>
> Suffering slightly from
> Agoraphobia:
> "Think I'll just—stay in and—
> Write about—Death—"

The most important of the fixed forms is the **sonnet**, which consists of fourteen lines of rhymed iambic pentameter. The original form of the sonnet is called the **Italian sonnet** or the **Petrarchan sonnet** after the fourteenth-century poet who popularized it. An Italian sonnet is usually cast in two stanzas, an octave rhyming *abbaabba* and a sestet with a variable rhyme scheme; *cdcdcd, cdecde,* and *cddcee* are some of the possible patterns. A **volta** or "turn," usually a conjunction or conjunctive adverb like "but" or "then," may appear at the beginning of the sestet, signifying a slight change of direction in thought. Many Italian sonnets have a strong logical connection between octave and sestet problem/solution, cause/effect, question/answer and the volta helps to clarify the transition. The **English sonnet**, also known as the **Shakespearean sonnet** after its prime exemplar, was developed in the sixteenth century after the sonnet was imported to England and employs a different rhyme scheme that takes into consideration the relative scarcity of rhymes in English (compared with Italian). The English sonnet has a rhyme scheme of *ababcdcdefefgg* and is usually printed as a single stanza. The pattern of three English quatrains plus a heroic couplet often forces a slightly different organizational scheme on the poet, although many of Shakespeare's sonnets still employ a strong volta at the beginning of the ninth line. Other English sonnets may withhold the turn until the beginning of the closing couplet. A third sonnet type, relatively rare, is the **Spenserian sonnet,** named after Edmund Spenser, author of *Amoretti,* one of the earliest sonnet sequences in English. The Spenserian sonnet rhymes *ababbcbccdcdee.* Many other sonnets have been written over the years that have other rhyme schemes, often hybrids of the Italian and English types. These are usually termed **nonce sonnets.** Shelley's "Ozymandias," with its unusual rhyme scheme of *ababacdcedefef,* is one notable example. In "Ode to the West Wind," Shelley employs a fourteen-line stanza rhyming *aba bcb cdc ded ee,* which has been called a **terza rima sonnet.**

Several other fixed forms, all French imports, have appeared frequently in English poetry. The eight-line **triolet,** usually written in iambic tetrameter, uses two refrains: *ABaAabAB.* The **rondeau** has fifteen lines of iambic tetrameter or pentameter arranged in three stanzas: *aabba aabR aabbaR;* the R here stands for the unrhymed refrain, which repeats the first few words of the poem's first line. A maddeningly complex variation is the twenty-five line **rondeau redoublé,** through which Wendy Cope wittily maneuvers in her poem of the same name. The **villanelle** is a nineteen-line poem, usually written in iambic pentameter, employing two refrain lines, A_1 and A_2, in a pattern of five tercets and a final quatrain: A_1bA_2 abA_1 abA_2 abA_1 abA_2 abA_1A_2. A related form, also nineteen lines long, is the **terzanelle**, which uses several more repeating lines (capitalized here): A_1BA_2 bCB cDC dED efE f A_1FA_2. The **ballade** is twenty-eight lines of iambic tetrameter employing a refrain that appears at the end of its three octaves and final quatrain, or **envoy**: *ababbcbC ababbcbC ababbcbC bcbC*. Obviously the rhyming demands of the villanelle, the terzanelle, and the ballade pose serious challenges to English-language poets. A final fixed form is the thirty-nine-line **sestina**, which may be either metrical or in free verse and uses a complicated sequence repeating, in different order, the six words that end the lines of the initial stanza. The sequence for the first six sestets is *123456 615243 364125 532614 451362 246531*. A final tercet uses three words in the interior of the lines and three at the ends in the pattern *(2)5(4)3(6)1*. Many sestinas hinge on the poet's choice of six end words that have multiple meanings and can serve as more than one part of speech.

Two contemporary poets, Billy Collins and Kim Addonizio, have recently created nonce forms. Collins's tongue-in-cheek description of the **paradelle** was taken seriously by many readers, and a whole anthology of poems in the form has been assembled. Addonizio's personalized variation on the sonnet, the **sonnenizio**, has also been imitated by other poets. There are many other less familiar types of stanza forms and fixed forms. Lewis Turco's *The Book of Forms* and Miller Williams's *Patterns of Poetry* are two reference sources that are useful in identifying them.

Literary History and Poetic Conventions

What a poet attempts to do in any given poem is always governed by the tension that exists between originality and convention, or between the poet's desire, in Ezra Pound's famous phrase, to "make it new," and the various stylistic devices that other poets and readers are familiar with through their understanding of the poetic tradition. If we look at some of the most obscure passages of Pound's *Cantos* (a single page may contain passages in several foreign languages), we may think that the poet has departed about as far from conventional modes of expression as possible, leaving his audience far behind him. Yet it is important to keep two facts in mind. First, this style was not arrived at overnight; Pound's early poetry is relatively traditional and should present little difficulty to most readers. He arrived at the style of the *Cantos* after a twenty-year apprenticeship to the styles of writers as different as Li-Po, Robert Browning, and William Butler Yeats. Second, by the time Pound was writing his mature poetry the modernist movement was in full flower, forcing the public not only to read poems but also to look at paintings and sculpture and to listen to music in ways that would have been unimaginable only a decade or two earlier. When we talk about the stylistic conventions of any given literary period, we should keep in mind that poets are rarely willing to go much beyond what they have educated their audiences to understand. This mutual sense of agreement is the essence of poetic convention.

One should be wary of making sweeping generalizations about "schools" of poetry or the shared conventions of literary periods. In any era, there is always a significant amount of diversity among individual poets. Further, an anthology of this limited scope, which by its very nature must exclude most long poems, is likely to contribute to a misleading view of literary history and the development of poetry in English. When we read Shakespeare's or Milton's sonnets, we should not forget that their major reputations rest on poetry of a very different sort. The neoclassical era in English poetry, stretching from the late seventeenth century until almost the end of the eighteenth, is poorly represented in this anthology because the satires of John Dryden and Alexander Pope and long philosophical poems like Pope's *An Essay on Man* do not readily lend themselves to being excerpted (an exception is the section on meter from Pope's *An Essay on Criticism*). Edgar Allan Poe once claimed that a long poem is "simply a contradiction in terms," but the continued high reputations of *The Faerie Queene, Paradise Lost, Don Juan*, and even a modern verse-novella like Robinson Jeffers's "The Roan Stallion" demonstrate that Poe's was far from the last word on the subject.

The earliest poems in this volume, all anonymous, represent poetry's links to the oral folk tradition. The American folk songs that children learn to sing in elementary school represent our own inheritance of this rich legacy. The poets of the Tudor (1485–1558) and Elizabethan (1558–1603) eras excelled at lyric poetry; Sir Thomas Wyatt and Henry Howard, Earl of Surrey, had imported the sonnet form from Italy, and the form was perfected during this period. Much of the love poetry of the age is characterized by conventional imagery, so-called Petrarchan conceits, which even a later poet like Thomas Campion employs in "There Is a Garden in Her Face" and which Shakespeare satirizes brilliantly in his Sonnet 130 ("My mistress' eyes are nothing like the sun").

The poetry of the first half of the seventeenth century has several major schools: A smooth lyricism influenced by Ben Jonson that can be traced through the work of Robert Herrick, Edmund Waller, and Richard Lovelace; a serious body of devotional poetry by John Donne, George Herbert, and John Milton; and the metaphysical style, which uses complex extended metaphors or metaphysical conceits—Donne and Herbert are its chief exemplars, followed by the early American poets Anne Bradstreet and Edward Taylor. Shortly after the English Restoration in 1660, a profound period of conservatism began in the arts, and the neoclassical era, lasting through most of the eighteenth century, drew heavily on Greek and Roman models. Poetry written during this period—the age of Jonathan Swift, Alexander Pope, and Thomas Gray—was dominated by one form, the heroic couplet; the genres of epic and satire; and an emphasis on human reason as the poet's chief guide. Never has the private voice been so subordinated to the public as in this period when, as Pope put it, a poet's highest aspiration should be to utter "What oft was thought, but ne'er so well expressed."

The first inklings of the romantic era coincide with the American and French revolutions, and poets of the latter half of the eighteenth century like Robert Burns and William Blake exhibit some of its characteristics. But it was not until the publication of *Lyrical Ballads*, a 1798 book containing the best early work of William Wordsworth and Samuel Taylor Coleridge, that the romantic era can be said to have truly flowered. Wordsworth's famous formulation of a poem as "the spontaneous overflow of powerful feeling recollected in tranquillity" remains one of romanticism's key definitions, with its emphasis on emotion and immediacy and reflection; Wordsworth's own poetry, with its focus on the natural world, was tremendously influential. Most of the English and American poets of the first half of the nineteenth century have ties to romanticism in its various guises, and even a poet as late as Walt Whitman (b. 1819) inherits many of its liberal, democratic attitudes. Poets of the Victorian era (1837–1901), such as Alfred, Lord Tennyson and Robert Browning, continued to explore many of the same themes and genres as their romantic forebears, but certainly much of the optimism of the early years of the century had dissipated by the time poets like Thomas Hardy, A. E. Housman, and William Butler Yeats, with their omnipresent irony and pessimism, arrived on the scene in the century's last decades.

The twentieth century and the beginning of the twenty-first have been ruled by the upheavals that modernism caused in every art form. If anything characterized the first half of the twentieth century, it was its tireless experimentation with the forms of poetry. There is a continuum in English-language poetry from Chaucer through Robert Frost and Edwin Arlington Robinson, but Ezra Pound, T. S. Eliot, William Carlos Williams, and Marianne Moore, to mention only four chief modernists, published poetry that would have totally mystified readers of their grandparents' day, just as Picasso and Matisse produced paintings that represented radical breaks with the visual forms of the past. Although many of the experiments of movements like imagism and surrealism seem not much more than historical curiosities today, they parallel the unusual directions that most of the other arts took during the same period.

For the sake of convenience more than anything else, it has been useful to refer to the era following the end of World War II as the postmodern era. Certainly many of the hard-won modernist gains—open form and increased candor in language and subject matter—have been taken for granted by poets writing in the contemporary period. The confessional poem, a frankly autobiographical narrative that reveals what poets in earlier ages might have striven desperately to conceal, surfaced in the late 1950s in the works of Robert Lowell, W. D. Snodgrass, Sylvia Plath, and Anne Sexton, and remains one of the chief postmodern genres. Still, as the selections here will attest, there is considerable variety to be found in the contemporary scene, and it will perhaps be many years before critics have the necessary historical distance to assess the unique characteristics of the present period.

Writing About Poetry

WRITING ASSIGNMENTS VARY WIDELY, AND YOUR TEACHER'S instructions may range from general ("Discuss any two poems in your text which contain an effective use of imagery") to very specific ("Write an explication, in not less than 1000 words, of one of Edwin Arlington Robinson's sonnets, focusing on his use of form and his psychological insights into character"). Such processes as choosing, limiting, and developing a topic; "brainstorming" by taking notes on random ideas and refining those ideas further through group discussion or conferences with your instructor; using the library and the Internet to locate supporting secondary sources; and revising a first draft in light of critical remarks are undoubtedly techniques you have practiced in other composition classes. Basic types of organizational schemes learned in "theme-writing" courses can also be applied to writing about poetry. Formal assignments of these types should avoid contractions and jargon, and should be written in a clear, straightforward style. Most literary essays are not of the personal experience type, and you should follow common sense in avoiding the first person and slang. It goes without saying that you should carefully proofread your rough and final drafts to eliminate errors in spelling, punctuation, usage, and grammar.

Writing assignments on poetry usually fall into two categories: explication (or close reading) of single poems and analysis of poetic techniques in one or more poems. Because explication involves the careful "unfolding" of individual poems on a line-by-line basis, an assignment of this type will usually focus on a single short poem or a passage from a longer one. Some poems yield most of their meaning on a single reading; others, however, may contain complexities and nuances that deserve close inspection of how the poet utilizes the elements discussed in this introduction. A typical explication might examine both form and content. Because assignments in analysis usually involve many of the same techniques as explication, we will look at explication more closely. The following is a checklist of questions that you might ask yourself before explicating a poem; the sample passages of analysis apply to a poem from this book, Edwin Arlington Robinson's "Firelight."

Form

1. How many lines does the poem contain? How are they arranged into stanzas? Is either the whole poem or the stanza an example of a traditional poetic form?

> "Firelight" is an Italian sonnet. It is divided into two stanzas, an octave and sestet, and there is a tonal shift, or what is known in sonnets as a "turn" or *volta*, at the beginning of line nine, though here there is no single word that signals the shift.

2. Is there anything striking in the visual arrangement of the poem—indentation, spacing, etc.? Are capitalization and punctuation unusual?

> Capitalization and punctuation are standard in the poem, and Robinson follows the traditional practice of capitalizing the first word of each line.

3. In what meter, if any, is the poem written? Does the poet use any notable examples of substitution in the meter? Are the lines primarily end-stopped or enjambed?

> The meter is fairly regular iambic pentameter ("Hĕr thóughts / ă mío / meñt síñce / ŏf one / whŏ shínes") with occasional substitution of trochees ("Wíseř / fŏr sí / leňce") and spondees ("thĕir jóy / rĕcálls / Nó snáke, ‖ / nó swórd").
>
> Enjambment occurs at the ends of lines two, five, six, seven, nine, ten, twelve, and thirteen; this has the effect of masking the regular meter and rhymes and enforcing a conversational tone, an effect that is assisted by the caesurae in lines six, seven, nine, and

(most importantly) fourteen. The caesura in this last line calls attention to "Apart," which ironically contrasts with the poem's opening phrase: "Ten years together."

4. What is the rhyme scheme, if any, of the poem? What types of rhyme are used?

The rhyme scheme of this poem is *abbaabba cdecde*. Robinson uses exact masculine rime; the only possible exception is "intervals," where the meter and rhyme scheme force a secondary stress on the third syllable.

5. Are significant sound patterns evident? Is there any repetition of whole lines, phrases, or words?

Alliteration is present in "*f*irelight" and "*f*our" in line three and "*w*an" and "*o*ne" in line eleven, and there are several instances of assonance ("W*i*ser for s*i*lence"; "end*o*wed / And b*o*wered") and consonance ("Se*ren*ely and pe*ren*nially e*n*dowed"; "the *w*an face of *one* somewhere a*lone*"). However, these sound patterns do not call excessive attention to themselves and depart from the poem's relaxed, conversational sound. "Firelight" contains no prominent use of repetition, with the possible exception of the pronoun "they" and its variant forms "their" and "them" and the related use of the third-person singular pronouns "he" and "she" in the last five lines of the poem. This pronoun usage, confusing at first glance, indirectly carries the poem's theme of the separateness of the lovers' thoughts. The only notable instance of parallel phrasing occurs in line seven with "No snake, no sword."

Content

1. To what genre (lyric, narrative, dramatic) does the poem belong? Does it contain elements of more than one genre?

"Firelight" is a narrative poem. Even though it has little plot in the conventional sense, it contains two characters in a specific setting who perform actions that give the reader insight into the true nature of their relationship. The sonnet form has traditionally been used for lyric poetry.

2. Who is the persona of the poem? Is there an auditor? If so, who? What is the relationship between persona and auditor? Does the poem

have a specific setting? If so, where and when is it taking place? Is there any action that has taken place before the poem opens? What actions take place during the poem?

The persona here is a third-person omniscient narrator such as might be encountered in a short story; the narrator has the ability to read "Her thoughts a moment since" and directly comments that the couple is "Wiser for silence." The unnamed characters in the poem are a man and woman who have been married for ten years. The poem is set in their home, apparently in a comfortable room with a fireplace where they are spending a quiet evening together. Neither character speaks during the poem; the only action is their looking at "each other's eyes at intervals / Of gratefulness." Much of the poem's ironic meaning hinges on the couple's silence, "what neither says aloud."

3. Does the poem contain any difficulties with grammar or syntax? What individual words or phrases are striking because of their denotation or connotation?

The syntax of "Firelight" is straightforward and contains no inversions or ellipses. The poem's sentence structure is deceptively simple. The first four lines make up a single sentence with one main clause; the second four lines also make up a single sentence, this time with two main clauses; the final six lines also make up a single sentence, broken into two equal parts by the semicolon, and consisting of both main and dependent clauses. The poem's vocabulary is not unusual, though "obliteration" (literally an *erasure*) seems at first a curious choice to describe the effects of love. One should note the allusion implied by "bowered," "snake," and "sword" in the octave and the rather complicated use of the subjunctive "were" in lines nine, ten, and twelve. Again, this slight alteration in grammar bears indirectly on the theme of the poem. "Yet" in the first line provides an interesting touch since it injects a slight negative note into the picture of marital bliss.

4. Does the poem use any figures of speech? If so, how do they add to the overall meaning? Is the action of the poem to be taken literally, symbolically, or both ways?

"Firelight" uses several figures of speech. "Cloud" is a commonly employed metaphor for "foreboding." "Firelight" and "four walls" are a metonymy and synecdoche, respectively, for the couple's comfortable home. The allusion to the "snake" and "sword" direct the reader to the Garden of Eden story. "Wiser for silence" is a slight paradox. "The graven tale of lines / On the wan face" is an implied metaphor which compares the lines on a person's face to the written ("graven") story of her life. To say that a person "shines" instead of "excels" is another familiar metaphor. "Firelight" is to be understood primarily on the literal level. The characters are symbolic only in that the man and woman are perhaps representative of many married couples, who outwardly express happiness yet inwardly carry regrets and fantasies from past relationships.

5. Is the title of the poem appropriate? What are its subject, tone of voice, and theme? Is the theme stated or implied?

"Firelight" is a good title since it carries both the connotation of domestic tranquility and a hint of danger. "To bring to the light" means to reveal the truth, and the narrator in this poem does this. Robinson's attitude toward the couple is ironic. On the surface they seem to be the picture of ideal happiness, but he reveals that this happiness has been purchased, in the man's case, at the expense of an earlier lover and, in the woman's, by settling for someone who has achieved less than another man for whom she apparently had unrequited love. Robinson's ironic view of marital stability is summed up in the phrase "Wiser for silence." Several themes are implied: the difference between surface appearance and deeper insight; the cynical idea that in love ignorance of what one's partner is thinking may be the key to bliss; the sense that individual happiness is not without its costs. All of these are possible ways to state Robinson's bittersweet theme.

Your instructor may ask you to employ specific strategies in your explication and may require a certain type of organization for the paper. In writing the body of the explication, you will probably proceed through the poem from beginning to end, summarizing and paraphrasing some lines and quoting others fully when you feel an explanation is required. It should be stressed that there are many ways, in theory, to approach a poem and that no two explications of the same poem will agree in every detail. Some instructors may favor an explication that links the poem to events in the author's life, to the sociohistorical context in which it was written, or to some other critical approach.

An assignment in analysis, which looks closely at the way a single element—dramatic situation, meter, form, imagery, one or more figures of speech, theme—functions in poetry, would probably require that you write on two or more poems; in such cases a comparison-contrast or definition-illustration paper may be called for. An assignment of this type might examine two related poems by the same poet, or it might inspect the way that several poets have used a poetic device or theme. Comparison-contrast essays look for both similarities and differences in two poems. Definition-illustration papers usually begin with a general discussion of the topic, say, a popular theme like the *carpe diem* motif, and then go on to illustrate how this motif may be found in several different poems. Assignments in analysis often lead to longer papers, which may require the use of secondary sources.

You may be required to use secondary sources from the library or Internet in writing your paper. A subject search through your library's books is a good starting place, especially for material on older poets who have attracted extensive critical attention. Reference books (many of them now in the form of online electronic databases) like *Twentieth Century Authors, Contemporary Authors, Critical Survey of Poetry*, and the *Dictionary of Literary Biography* provide compact overviews of poets' careers. *Contemporary Literary Criticism* and *Poetry Criticism* contain excerpts from critical pieces on poets' works, and the *MLA International Bibliography* will direct you to articles on poets and poems in scholarly journals. There are several popular indexes of book reviews; one of these, the annual *Book Review Digest*, reprints brief passages from the most representative reviews. A useful index to poetry explications published in periodicals and books is *Poetry Explication: A Checklist of Interpretations Since 1925 of British and American Poems Past and Present;* many of the articles listed there first appeared in *The Explicator*, a periodical whose indexes are also worth inspecting. In recent years, the Internet has facilitated the chores of research, and many online databases, reference works, and periodicals may be quickly located using search engines like Google (http://www.google.com). The Internet also holds a wealth of information in the form of individual websites devoted to authors. Most of these websites are run by universities and organizations. Students should be aware, however, that websites vary widely in quality. Some are legitimate academic sources displaying sound scholarship; others are little more than "fan pages" that may contain erroneous or misleading information.

Careful documentation of your sources is essential; if you use any material other than what is termed "common knowledge," you must cite it in your paper. Common knowledge includes biographical information, an author's publications, prizes and awards received, and other information that can be found in more than one reference book. Anything else—direct quotes or material you have put in your own words by paraphrasing—requires both a parenthetical citation in the body of your paper and an entry on your works cited pages. Doing less than this is to commit an act of plagiarism, for which the penalties are usually severe. Internet materials, which are so easily cut and pasted into a manuscript, provide an easy temptation but are immediately noticeable. Nothing is easier to spot in a paper than an uncited "lift" from a source; in most cases, the vocabulary and sentence structure will be radically different from the rest of the paper.

The seventh edition of the *MLA Handbook for Writers of Research Papers*, which can be found in the reference section of almost any library and which, if you plan to write papers for other English courses, is a good addition to your personal library, contains formats for bibliographies and manuscripts that most instructors consider standard; indeed, most of the handbooks of grammar and usage commonly used in college courses follow MLA style and may be sufficient for your needs. If you have doubts, ask your instructor about what format is preferred. The type of parenthetical citation used today to indicate the source of quotations is simple to learn and dispenses with such time-consuming and repetitive chores as footnotes and endnotes. In using parenthetical citations remember that your goal is to direct your reader from the quoted passage in the paper to its source in your bibliography, and from there, if necessary, to the book or periodical from which the quote is taken. A good parenthetical citation gives only the *minimal* information needed to accomplish this. Following are a few examples from student papers on Edwin Arlington Robinson's poetry.

> Robinson's insights into character are never sharper than in "Miniver Cheevy," a portrait of a town drunk who loves "the days of old / When swords were bright and steeds were prancing" (5, 6) and dreams incongruously "of Thebes and Camelot, / And Priam's neighbors" (11–12).

Here you should note a couple of conventions about writing about poetry. One is that the present tense is used in discussing the poem; in general, use the present tense throughout your critical writing except when you are giving biographical or historical information. Second, note how only parts of lines are quoted here to support the sentence and how the parts fit smoothly into the author's sentence structure. In general, brackets and ellipses [. . .] are not necessary at the beginning or end of these quotes because it is clear that they are quoted fragmentarily; they should, however, be used if something is omitted from the middle of a quote ("the days of old / When [. . .] steeds were prancing"). The virgule or slash (/) is used to indicate line breaks; a double slash (//) indicates stanza breaks. Quotes of up to three lines should be treated in this manner. If a quote is longer than three lines, it should be indented ten spaces (with no quotation marks) and printed as it appears in the original poem:

> Robinson opens one of his most effective and pitiless character sketches with an unsparing portrait:
>> Miniver Cheevy, child of scorn,
>> Grew lean while he assailed the seasons;
>> He wept that he was ever born,
>> And he had reasons. (1–4)

The parenthetical citation here lists only line numbers because only one poem by Robinson appears in the bibliography (note that the *MLA Handbook* suggests that you give line numbers). If several works by the poet had been listed among the works cited, the parenthetical citation would clarify which one was being referred to by adding a shortened form of the poem's title: ("Miniver," 1–4). The reader finds the following entry among the sources:

> Robinson, Edwin Arlington. "Miniver Cheevy." *Collected Poems*. New York: MacMillan, 1934. 347. Print.

Similarly, quotes and paraphrases from secondary critical sources should follow the same rules of common sense.

> Louis O. Coxe observes that Robinson, even in using the most demanding forms, manages to avoid the artificial-sounding poetic diction of most sonneteers: "The best of Robinson's sonnets take an anti-rhetorical line though they often ride to eloquence as they progress" (50–51).

In this case, the author of the quote is identified, so only the page numbers are included in the parenthetical citation. The reader knows where to look among the sources:

Coxe, Louis O. *Edwin Arlington Robinson: The Life of Poetry*. New York: Pegasus, 1969. Print.

To simplify the whole matter of parenthetical citation, it is recommended that quotes from secondary sources be introduced, wherever possible, in a manner that identifies the author so that only the page number of the quote is needed inside of the parentheses.

Of course, different types of sources—reference book entries, poems in anthologies, articles in periodicals, and book reviews—require different bibliographical information, so be sure to check the *MLA Handbook* if you have questions. Here are a few more examples of the most commonly used bibliographical formats:

Poetry

Robinson, Edwin Arlington. "Miniver Cheevy." *Collected Poems*. New York: MacMillan, 1934. 347. Print.

Donaldson, Scott. *Edwin Arlington Robinson: A Poet's Life*. New York: Columbia UP, 2007. Print.

A Book with an Author and Editor

Robinson, Edwin Arlington. *Edwin Arlington Robinson's Letters to Edith Brower*. Ed. Richard City. Cambridge: Harvard UP, 1968. Print.

A Casebook or Collection of Critical Essays

Barnard, Ellsworth, ed. *Edwin Arlington Robinson: Centenary Essays*. Athens: U of Georgia P, 1969. Print.

A Poem Reprinted in an Anthology or Textbook

Robinson, Edwin Arlington. "Richard Cory." *Literature: An Introduction to Poetry, Fiction, and Drama*. 11th ed. Ed. X.J. Kennedy and Dana Gioia. New York: Longman, 2010. 754. Print.

An Article in a Reference Book

Seymour-Smith, Martin. "Robinson, Edwin Arlington." *Who's Who in Twentieth Century Literature*. New York: McGraw, 1976. Print.

Online Article in a Scholarly Journal

Read, Arthur M., II. "Robinson's 'The Man Against the Sky.'"
Explicator 26.6 (1968): 49. Web. 2 Feb. 2011.

Online: A Reference Work

"Robinson, Edwin Arlington." *Encyclopaedia Britannica Online.*
Encyclopedia Britannica, 2009. Web. 21 Jan. 2011.

Online: A Web Site

"A Page for Edwin." 5 Feb. 1998. Web. 12 Jan. 2011.

Online: A Book Review

Hutchinson, Percy. "Robinson's Satire and Symbolism." Rev. of *King
Jasper*, by Edwin Arlington Robinson. *New York Times Book
Review* 10 Nov. 1935. Web. 18 Jan. 2011.

POETRY

Some of the popular ballads and lyrics of England and Scotland, composed for the most part between 1300 and 1500, were first collected in their current forms by Thomas Percy, whose Reliques of Ancient English Poetry *(1765) helped to revive interest in folk poetry. Francis James Child (1825–1896), an American, gathered over a thousand variant versions of the three hundred-odd core of poems. The Romantic poets of the early nineteenth century showed their debt to the folk tradition by writing imitative "art ballads" (see Keats's "La Belle Dame sans Merci" or Burns's "John Barleycorn"), which incorporate many of their stylistic devices.*

Western Wind

Western wind, when will thou blow,
    The small rain down can rain?
Christ, if my love were in my arms
    And I in my bed again!

                   —1450?

Bonny Barbara Allan

It was in and about the Martinmas° time,
    When the green leaves were a falling,
That Sir John Græme, in the West Country,
    Fell in love with Barbara Allan.

He sent his men down through the town,   5
    To the place where she was dwelling.
"O haste and come to my master dear,
    Gin° ye be Barbara Allan."

O hooly,° hooly rose she up,
    To the place where he was lying,   10
And when she drew the curtain by:
    "Young man, I think you're dying."

"O it's I'm sick, and very, very sick,
    And 'tis a'° for Barbara Allan."

1 **Martinmas** November 11   8 **Gin** if   9 **hooly** slowly   14 **a'** all

"O the better for me ye s'° never be,   15
    Though your heart's blood were a-spilling."

"O dinna° ye mind, young man," said she,
    "When ye was in the tavern a drinking,
That ye made the healths gae° round and round,
    And slighted Barbara Allan?"   20

He turned his face unto the wall,
    And death was with him dealing:
"Adieu, adieu, my dear friends all,
    And be kind to Barbara Allan."

And slowly, slowly raise she up,   25
    And slowly, slowly left him,
And sighing said she could not stay,
    Since death of life had reft him.

She had not gane° a mile but twa,°
    When she heard the dead-bell ringing,   30
And every jow° that the dead-bell geid,°
    It cried, "Woe to Barbara Allan!"

"O mother, mother, make my bed!
    O make it saft° and narrow!
Since my love died for me to-day,   35
    I'll die for him to-morrow."

—1500?

Sir Patrick Spens

The king sits in Dumferling town,
    Drinking the blude-reid° wine:
"O whar will I get guid sailor,
    To sail this ship of mine?"

Up and spak an eldern knicht,°   5
    Sat at the king's richt° knee:
"Sir Patrick Spens is the best sailor
    That sails upon the sea."

15 s' shall   17 dinna do not   19 gae go   29 gane gone   9 twa two   31 jow stroke   11 geid gave
34 saft soft
2 blude-reid blood-red   5 eldern knicht elderly knight   6 richt right

The king has written a braid° letter,
    And signed it wi' his hand,   10
And sent it to Sir Patrick Spens,
    Was walking on the sand.

The first line that Sir Patrick read,
    A loud lauch° lauched he;
The next line that Sir Patrick read,   15
    The tear blinded his ee.°

"O wha is this has done this deed,
    This ill deed done to me,
To send me out this time o' the year,
    To sail upon the sea?   20

"Mak haste, mak haste, my mirry men all,
    Our guid ship sails the morn."
"O say na sae,° my master dear,
    For I fear a deadly storm.

"Late, late yestre'en° I saw the new moon,   25
    Wi' the auld moon in hir arm,
And I fear, I fear, my dear master,
    That we will come to harm."

O our Scots nobles wer richt laith°
    To weet° their cork-heeled shoon,°   30
But lang or a'° the play were played,
    Their hats they swam aboon.°

O lang, lang may their ladies sit,
    Wi' their fans into their hand,
Or ere they see Sir Patrick Spens   35
    Come sailing to the land.

O lang, lang may the ladies stand,
    Wi' their gold kems° in their hair,
Waiting for their ain dear lords,
    For they'll see them na mair.   40

---

9 braid long   **14 lauch** laugh   **16 ee** eye   **23 na sae** not so   **25 yestre'en** last evening   **29 laith** loath   **30 weet** wet   **23 shoon** shoes   **31 lang or a'** long before   **32 Their hats they swam aboon** their hats swam above them   **38 kems** combs

Half o'er, half o'er to Aberdour
   It's fifty fadom deep,
And there lies guid Sir Patrick Spens
   Wi' the Scots lords at his feet.

—1500?

SIR THOMAS WYATT ■ (1503?–1542)

Sir Thomas Wyatt served Henry VIII as a diplomat in Italy. Wyatt read the love poetry of Petrarch (1304–1374) and is generally credited with having imported both the fashions of these lyrics—hyperbolic "conceits" or metaphorical descriptions of the woman's beauty and the lover's suffering—and their form, the sonnet, to England. "They Flee from Me," an example of one of his original lyrics, displays Wyatt's unique grasp of the rhythms of speech.

They Flee from Me

They flee from me, that sometime did me seek,
With naked foot stalking in my chamber.
I have seen them gentle, tame and meek,
That now are wild, and do not remember
That sometime they put themself in danger   5
To take bread at my hand; and now they range,
Busily seeking with a continual change.

Thanke'd be Fortune it hath been otherwise,
Twenty times better; but once in special,
In thin array, after a pleasant guise,°   10
When her loose gown from her shoulders did fall,
And she me caught in her arms long and small,
And therewith all sweetly did me kiss
And softly said, "Dear heart, how like you this?"

It was no dream, I lay broad waking.   15
But all is turned, thorough° my gentleness,
Into a strange fashion of forsaking;
And I have leave to go, of her goodness,
And she also to use newfangleness.

10 **guise** appearance   16 **thorough** through

But since that I so kindely° am served,   20
I fain° would know what she hath deserved.

Whoso List to Hunt

Whoso list° to hunt, I know where is an hind,°
But as for me, alas, I may no more:
The vain travail hath wearied me so sore.
I am of them that farthest cometh behind;
Yet may I by no means my wearied mind   5
Draw from the deer: but as she fleeth afore,
Fainting I follow. I leave off therefore,
Since in a net I seek to hold the wind.
Who list her to hunt, I put him out of doubt,
As well as I, may spend his time in vain: 10
And, graven with diamonds, in letters plain
There is written her fair neck round about:
Noli me tangere, for Caesar's I am,°
And wild for to hold, though I seem tame.

—1557

61

EDMUND SPENSER ■ (1552–1599)

Edmund Spenser was born in London, and spent most of his adult life in Ireland, where he held a variety of minor government posts. The Faerie Queene, a long allegorical romance about Elizabethan England, was uncompleted at his death. The eighty-odd sonnets that make up the sequence called Amoretti are generally thought to detail his courtship of his second wife, Elizabeth Boyle, whom he married in 1594.

Amoretti: Sonnet 75

One day I wrote her name upon the strand,
But came the waves and washèd it away:
Agayne I wrote it with a second hand,°

20 kindely in this manner   **21 fain** gladly
1 list desire   **32 hind** doe   **13 *Noli me tangere*** *Touch me not*; the poem is said to refer to the second wife of Henry VIII, Anne Boleyn.
3 second hand second time

But came the tyde, and made my paynes his pray.
"Vayne man," sayd she, "that doest in vaine assay,°   5
A mortall thing so to immortalize,
For I my selve shall lyke° to this decay
And eek° my name bee wypèd out lykewize."
"Not so," quod° I, "let baser things devize
To dy in dust, but you shall live by fame: 10
My verse your vertues rare shall eternize,
And in the hevens wryte your glorious name.
Where whenas death shall all the world subdew
Our love shall live, and later life renew."

—1595

SIR PHILIP SIDNEY ■ (1554–1586)

Sir Philip Sidney embodied many of the aspects of the ideal man of the Renaissance; he was a courtier, scholar, patron of the arts, and soldier who died of wounds received at the battle of Zutphen. His sonnet sequence Astrophel and Stella *appeared in 1591, several years before Spenser's* Amoretti, *and helped to precipitate the fashion for sonnets that lasted in England well into the next century.*

Astrophel and Stella: Sonnet 1

1

Loving in truth, and fain° in verse my love to show,
That she dear she might take some pleasure of my pain,
Pleasure might cause her read, reading might make her know,
Knowledge might pity win, and pity grace obtain,
I sought fit words to paint the blackest face of woe: 5
Studying inventions fine, her wits to entertain,
Oft turning others' leaves,° to see if thence would flow
Some fresh and fruitful showers upon my sunburned brain.
But words came halting forth, wanting Invention's stay;

5 **assay** attempt   7 **lyke** be similar to   8 **eek** also   9 **quod** said
1 **fain** glad   7 **leaves** pages

Invention, Nature's child, fled stepdame Study's blows;   10
And others' feet° still seemed but strangers in my way.
Thus, great with child to speak, and helpless in my throes,
Biting my truant pen, beating myself for spite:
"Fool," said my Muse to me, "look in thy heart, and write."

—1582

ROBERT SOUTHWELL ▪ (1561?–1595)

Robert Southwell was a Roman Catholic priest in Elizabeth's Protestant England, who was executed for his religious beliefs. His devotional poems, most of them on the subject of spiritual love, were largely written during his three years in prison. Southwell was declared a saint in the Roman Catholic Church in 1970.

The Burning Babe

As I in hoary winter's night stood shivering in the snow,
Surprised I was with sudden heat which made my heart to glow;
And lifting up a fearful eye to view what fire was near,
A pretty babe all burning bright did in the air appear;
Who, scorchèd with excessive heat, such floods of tears did shed   5
As though his floods should quench his flames which with his
    tears were fed.
"Alas," quoth he, "but newly born in fiery heats I fry,
Yet none approach to warm their hearts or feel my fire but I!
My faultless breast the furnace is, the fuel wounding thorns,
Love is the fire, and sighs the smoke, the ashes shame
    and scorns;   10
The fuel justice layeth on, and mercy blows the coals,
The metal in this furnace wrought are men's defilèd souls,
For which, as now on fire I am to work them to their good,
So will I melt into a bath to wash them in my blood."
With this he vanished out of sight and swiftly shrunk away,   15
And straight I callèd unto mind that it was Christmas day.

—1602

11 **feet** metrical feet in poetry

Michael Drayton, like his contemporary, Shakespeare, excelled in several literary genres. He collaborated on plays with Thomas Dekker and wrote long poems on English history, biography, and topography. Drayton labored almost three decades on the sixty-three sonnets in Idea, publishing them in their present form in 1619.

Idea: Sonnet 61

Since there's no help, come let us kiss and part;
Nay, I have done, you get no more of me,
And I am glad, yea glad with all my heart
That thus so cleanly I myself can free;
Shake hands forever, cancel all our vows,   5
And when we meet at any time again,
Be it not seen in either of our brows
That we one jot of former love retain.
Now at the last gasp of love's latest breath,
When, his pulse failing, passion speechless lies,   10
When faith is kneeling by his bed of death,
And innocence is closing up his eyes,
    Now if thou wouldst, when all have given him over,
    From death to life thou mightst him yet recover.

—1619

William Shakespeare first printed his sonnets in 1609, during the last years of his active career as a playwright, but they had circulated privately a dozen years before. Given the lack of concrete details about Shakespeare's life outside the theatre, critics have found the sonnets fertile ground for biographical speculation, and the sequence of 154 poems does contain distinct characters— a handsome youth to whom most of the first 126 sonnets are addressed, a "Dark Lady" who figures strongly in the remaining poems, and the poet himself, whose name is the source of many puns in the poems. There is probably no definitive "key" to the sonnets, but there is also little doubt that their place is secure among the monuments of English lyric verse. Shakespeare's other nondramatic poems include narratives, allegories, and songs,

WILLIAM SHAKESPEARE

of which "When Daisies Pied," the companion pieces from his early comedy
Love's Labour's Lost, are perhaps the best examples.

Sonnet 18

Shall I compare thee to a summer's day?
Thou art more lovely and more temperate:
Rough winds do shake the darling buds of May,
And summer's lease hath all too short a date:
Sometimes too hot the eye of heaven shines,   5
And often is his gold complexion dimmed;
And every fair from fair° sometimes declines,
By chance or nature's changing course untrimmed;°
But thy eternal summer shall not fade,
Nor lose possession of that fair thou ow'st;°   10
Nor shall death brag thou wander'st in his shade,
When in eternal lines to time thou grow'st:
So long as men can breathe, or eyes can see,
So long lives this, and this gives life to thee.

—*1609*

Sonnet 20

A woman's face, with nature's own hand painted,
Hast thou, the master mistress of my passion—
A woman's gentle heart, but not acquainted
With shifting change, as is false women's fashion;
An eye more bright than theirs, less false in rolling,°   5
Gilding the object whereupon it gazeth;
A man in hue all hues in his controlling,
Which steals men's eyes and women's souls amazeth.
And for a woman wert thou first created,
Till nature as she wrought thee fell a-doting,   10
And by addition me of thee defeated,
By adding one thing to my purpose nothing.
But since she pricked thee out for women's pleasure,
Mine be thy love and thy love's use their treasure.

—*1609*

7 **fair from fair** every fair thing from its fairness   8 **untrimmed** stripped   10 **ow'st** ownest
5 **rolling** wandering

Sonnet 29

When, in disgrace with fortune and men's eyes,
I all alone beweep my outcast state,
And trouble deaf heaven with my bootless° cries,
And look upon myself, and curse my fate,
Wishing me like to one more rich in hope,   5
Featured like him, like him with friends possessed,
Desiring this man's art and that man's scope,
With what I most enjoy contented least;
Yet in these thoughts myself almost despising,
Haply° I think on thee—and then my state,   10
Like to the lark at break of day arising
From sullen earth, sings hymns at heaven's gate;
For thy sweet love remembered such wealth brings
That then I scorn to change my state with kings.

—1609

Sonnet 73

That time of year thou mayst in me behold
When yellow leaves, or none, or few, do hang
Upon those boughs which shake against the cold,
Bare ruined choirs, where late the sweet birds sang.
In me thou see'st the twilight of such day   5
As after sunset fadeth in the west;
Which by and by black night doth take away,
Death's second self, that seals up all in rest.
In me thou see'st the glowing of such fire,
That on the ashes of his youth doth lie,   10
As the deathbed whereon it must expire,
Consumed with that which it was nourished by.
This thou perceiv'st, which makes thy love more strong,
To love that well which thou must leave ere long.

—1609

3 **bootless** useless   10 **Haply** fortunately

Sonnet 116

Let me not to the marriage of true minds
Admit impediments. Love is not love
Which alters when it alteration finds,
Or bends with the remover to remove:
Oh, no! it is an ever-fixèd mark,   5
That looks on tempests and is never shaken:
It is the star to every wandering bark,°
Whose worth's unknown, although his height be taken.°
Love's not Time's fool, though rosy lips and cheeks
Within his bending sickle's compass° come;   10
Love alters not with his brief hours and weeks,
But bears it out even to the edge of doom.
If this be error and upon me proved,
I never writ, nor no man ever loved.

—1609

Sonnet 129

Th' expense of spirit in a waste° of shame
Is lust in action; and, till action, lust
Is perjured, murd'rous, bloody, full of blame,
Savage, extreme, rude, cruel, not to trust;
Enjoyed no sooner but despisèd straight;   5
Past reason hunted, and no sooner had,
Past reason hated, as a swallowed bait
On purpose laid to make the taker mad;
Mad in pursuit, and in possession so;
Had, having, and in quest to have, extreme;   10
A bliss in proof—and proved, a very woe;
Before, a joy proposed; behind, a dream.
All this the world well knows; yet none knows well
To shun the heaven that leads men to this hell.

—1609

7 **bark** boat 8 **height be taken** elevation be measured 10 **compass** range
1 **waste** desert

Sonnet 130

My mistress' eyes are nothing like the sun;
Coral is far more red than her lips' red;
If snow be white, why then her breasts are dun;
If hairs be wires, black wires grow on her head.
I have seen roses damasked,° red and white,   5
But no such roses see I in her cheeks;
And in some perfumes is there more delight
Than in the breath that from my mistress reeks.
I love to hear her speak, yet well I know
That music hath a far more pleasing sound;   10
I grant I never saw a goddess go;
My mistress, when she walks, treads on the ground.
And yet, by heaven, I think my love as rare
As any she belied° with false compare.°

—1609

WILLIAM SHAKESPEARE

68

When Daisies Pied°

Spring

When daisies pied and violets blue
    And ladysmocks all silver-white
And cuckoobuds of yellow hue
    Do paint the meadows with delight,
The cuckoo then, on every tree,   5
Mocks married men;° for thus sings he,
      Cuckoo;
Cuckoo, cuckoo: Oh word of fear,
Unpleasing to a married ear!
When shepherds pipe on oaten straws,   10
    And merry larks are plowmen's clocks,
When turtles tread,° and rooks, and daws,
And maidens bleach their summer smocks,
The cuckoo then, on every tree,

5 **damasked** multi-colored   14 **belied** lied about   **compare** comparisons
Pied multi-colored   6 **Mocks married men** The pun is on the similarity between "cuckoo" and
"cuckold."   12 **turtles tread** turtledoves mate

Mocks married men; for thus sings he,   15
           Cuckoo;
Cuckoo, cuckoo: Oh word of fear,
Unpleasing to a married ear!

Winter

When icicles hang by the wall
And Dick the shepherd blows his nail°   20
And Tom bears logs into the hall,
    And milk comes frozen home in pail,
When blood is nipped and ways be foul,
Then nightly sings the staring owl,
           Tu-who;   25
Tu-whit, tu-who: a merry note,
While greasy Joan doth keel° the pot.

When all aloud the wind doth blow,
    And coughing drowns the parson's saw,°
And birds sit brooding in the snow,   30
    And Marian's nose looks red and raw,
When roasted crabs° hiss in the bowl,
Then nightly sings the staring owl,
           Tu-who;
Tu-whit, tu-who: a merry note   35
While greasy Joan doth keel the pot.

—*1598*

69

THOMAS CAMPION ■ (1567–1620)

Thoman Campion was a poet and physician who wrote music and lyrics in a manner that was "chiefly aimed to couple my words and notes lovingly together." The imagery in "There Is a Garden in Her Face" represents a late flowering of the conceits of Petrarchan love poetry, so wittily mocked by Shakespeare in "Sonnet 130."

20 nail fingernails   **27 keel** stir   **29 saw** saying   **32 crabs** crabapples

There Is a Garden in Her Face

There is a garden in her face,
Where roses and white lilies grow,
A heavenly paradise is that place,
Wherein all pleasant fruits do flow.
There cherries grow which none may buy   5
Till "Cherry-ripe!" themselves do cry.

Those cherries fairly do enclose
Of orient pearl a double row,
Which when her lovely laughter shows,
They look like rosebuds filled with snow.   10
Yet them nor peer nor prince can buy,
Till "Cherry-ripe!" themselves do cry.

Her eyes like angels watch them still;
Her brows like bended bows do stand,
Threatening with piercing frowns to kill   15
All that attempt with eye or hand
Those sacred cherries to come nigh,
Till "Cherry-ripe!" themselves do cry.

—1617

JOHN DONNE ■ (1572–1631)

John Donne was trained in the law for a career in government service, but Donne became the greatest preacher of his day, ending his life as dean of St. Paul's Cathedral in London. Only two of Donne's poems and a handful of his sermons were printed during his life, but both circulated widely in manuscript and his literary reputation among his contemporaries was considerable. His poetry falls into two distinct periods: the witty love poetry of his youth and the sober religious meditations of his maturity. In both, however, Donne shows remarkable originality in rhythm, diction, and the use of metaphor and conceit, which marks him as the chief poet of what has become commonly known as the metaphysical style.

The Flea

Mark but this flea, and mark in this,
How little that which thou deniest me is;
Me it sucked first, and now sucks thee,
And in this flea our two bloods mingled be;
Thou know'st that this cannot be said   5
A sin, or shame, or loss of maidenhead,
    Yet this enjoys before it woo,
    And pampered swells with one blood made of two,
    And this, alas, is more than we would do.

Oh stay, three lives in one flea spare,   10
Where we almost, nay more than married are.
This flea is you and I, and this
Our marriage bed and marriage temple is;
Though parents grudge, and you, we are met,
And cloistered in these living walls of jet.°   15
    Though use° make you apt to kill me
    Let not to that, self-murder added be,
    And sacrilege, three sins in killing three.

Cruel and sudden, hast thou since
Purpled thy nail° in blood of innocence?   20
Wherein could this flea guilty be,
Except in that drop which it sucked from thee?
Yet thou triumph'st, and say'st that thou
Find'st not thy self nor me the weaker now;
    'Tis true; then learn how false fears be: 25
    Just so much honor, when thou yield'st to me,
    Will waste, as this flea's death took life from thee.

—*1633*

HOLY SONNET 10

71

Holy Sonnet 10

Death, be not proud, though some have callèd thee
Mighty and dreadful, for thou art not so;
For those whom thou think'st thou dost overthrow

15 **jet** black   16 **use** familiarity, especially in the sexual sense   20 **Purpled thy nail** bloodied your fingernail

Die not, poor Death, nor yet canst thou kill me.
From rest and sleep, which but thy pictures be,   5
Much pleasure; then from thee much more must flow,
And soonest our best men with thee do go,
Rest of their bones, and soul's delivery.
Thou'art slave to fate, chance, kings, and desperate men,
And dost with poison, war, and sickness dwell,   10
And poppy° or charms can make us sleep as well
And better than thy stroke; why swell'st thou then?
One short sleep past, we wake eternally,
And death shall be no more; Death, thou shalt die.

—1633

col

JOHN DONNE

72

Holy Sonnet 14

A Batter my heart, three-personed God; for You
B As yet but knock, breathe, shine, and seek to mend;
B That I may rise, and stand, o'erthrow me, and bend
A Your force to break, blow, burn, and make me new.
A I, like an usurped town, to another due,
B Labor to admit You, but O, to no end;
B Reason, Your viceroy in me, me should defend,
A But is captived, and proves weak or untrue.
C Yet dearly I love You, and would be lovèd fain,°
D But am betrothed unto Your enemy.   10
C Divorce me, untie or break that knot again;
D Take me to You, imprison me, for I,
E Except You enthrall me, never shall be free,
E Nor ever chaste, except You ravish me.

—1633

The Sun Rising

        Busy old fool, unruly sun,
        Why dost thou thus
Through windows and through curtains call on us?
Must to the motions lovers' seasons run?

11 **poppy** opium
9 **fain** gladly

Saucy pedantic wretch, go chide 5
  Late schoolboys and sour prentices,
  Go tell court huntsmen that the King will ride,
  Call country ants to harvest offices;°
Love, all alike, no season knows nor clime,
Nor hours, days, months, which are the rags of time. 10

  Thy beams, so reverend and strong
    Why shouldst thou think?
I could eclipse and cloud them with a wink,
But that I would not lose her sight so long;
  If her eyes have not blinded thine, 15
    Look, and tomorrow late, tell me,
  Whether both th' Indias of spice and mine°
Be where thou leftst them, or lie here with me.
Ask for those kings whom thou saw'st yesterday,
And thou shalt hear, All here in one bed lay. 20

  She is all states, and all princes I,
    Nothing else is.
Princes do but play us; compared to this,
All honor's mimic, all wealth alchemy.
    Thou, sun, art half as happy as we, 25
    In that the world's contracted thus;
  Thine age asks ease, and since thy duties be
To warm the world, that's done in warming us.
Shine here to us, and thou art everywhere;
This bed thy center is, these walls thy sphere. 30

—1633

A Valediction:° Forbidding Mourning

As virtuous men pass mildly away,
  And whisper to their souls to go,
Whilst some of their sad friends do say
  The breath goes now, and some say, No;

8 offices duties   **17 Indias of spice and mine** the East and West ladies, respectively
Valediction farewell speech; Donne is addressing his wife before leaving on a diplomatic mission.

So let us melt, and make no noise,   5
    No tear-floods, nor sigh-tempests move,
'Twere profanation of our joys
    To tell the laity our love.

Moving of th' earth brings harms and fears,
    Men reckon what it did and meant;   10
But trepidation of the spheres,°
    Though greater far, is innocent.

Dull sublunary° lovers' love,
    (Whose soul is sense) cannot admit
Absence, because it doth remove   15
    Those things which elemented it.

But we by a love so much refined
    That our selves know not what it is,
Inter-assurèd of the mind,
    Care less, eyes, lips, and hands to miss.   20

Our two souls therefore, which are one,
    Though I must go, endure not yet
A breach, but an expansion,
    Like gold to airy thinness beat.

If they be two, they are two so   25
    As stiff twin compasses° are two;
Thy soul, the fixed foot, makes no show
    To move, but doth, if th' other do.

And though it in the center sit,
    Yet when the other far doth roam,   30
It leans and hearkens after it,
    And grows erect, as that comes home.

Such wilt thou be to me, who must
    Like th' other foot, obliquely run;
Thy firmness makes my circle just,°   35
    And makes me end where I begun.

—1633

JOHN DONNE

74

11 **trepidation of the spheres** natural trembling of the heavenly spheres, a concept of Ptolemaic astronomy   13 **sublunary** under the moon, hence, changeable (a Ptolemaic concept)   26 **stiff twin compasses** drafting compasses   35 **just** complete

Ben Jonson was Shakespeare's chief rival on the stage, and their contentious friendship has been the subject of much speculation. Jonson became England's first unofficial poet laureate, receiving a royal stipend from James I, and was a great influence of a group of younger poets who became known as the "Tribe of Ben." His tragedies are little regarded today, and his comedies, while still performed occasionally, have nevertheless failed to hold the stage as brilliantly as Shakespeare's. Still, he was a poet of considerable talents, particularly in short forms. His elegy on Shakespeare contains a famous assessment: "He was not of an age, but for all time!"

On My First Son

Farewell, thou child of my right hand,° and joy;
My sin was too much hope of thee, loved boy:
Seven years thou'wert lent to me, and I thee pay,
Exacted by thy fate, on the just day.°
Oh, could I lose all father now! for why   5
Will man lament the state he should envy,
To have so soon 'scaped world's and flesh's rage,
And, if no other misery, yet age?
Rest in soft peace, and asked, say, "Here doth lie
Ben Jonson his best piece of poetry."   10
For whose sake henceforth all his vows be such
As what he loves may never like too much.

—1616

Slow, Slow, Fresh Fount

From Cynthia's Revels°

Slow, slow, fresh fount, keep time with my salt tears;
Yet slower, yet, O faintly, gentle springs!
List to the heavy part the music bears,

---

1 child of my right hand Benjamin, the child's name, means this in Hebrew.   **4 the just day**
Jonson's son died on his seventh birthday.
Slow, Slow, Fresh Fount: From Cynthia's Revels spoken in this masque by the nymph Echo about
the dead Narcissus

Woe weeps out her division,° when she sings.
    Droop herbs and flowers;   5
    Fall grief in showers;
Our beauties are not ours. O, I could still,
Like melting snow upon some craggy hill,
    Drop, drop, drop, drop,
Since nature's pride is now a withered daffodil.   10

—1600

MARY WROTH ■ (1587?–1651)

Mary Wroth was the niece of Sir Philip Sidney and the cousin of Sir Walter Raleigh, both distinguished poets and courtiers. A friend of poet Ben Jonson, who dedicated The Alchemist *to her, she was prominent in the court of King James I. Her prose romance,* Urania *(1621), stirred controversy because of its similarities to actual people and events. Wroth may have fallen into disfavor at court after the publication of* Urania, *and few facts are known about her later life.*

In This Strange Labyrinth How Shall I Turn

In this strange labyrinth how shall I turn,
Ways° are on all sides, while the way I miss:
If to the right hand, there in love I burn,
Let me go forward, therein danger is.
If to the left, suspicion hinders bliss: 5
Let me turn back, shame cries I ought return:
Nor faint, though crosses° with my fortunes kiss.
Stand still is harder, although sure to mourn.
Thus let me take the right, or left hand way,
Go forward, or stand still, or back retire: 10
I must these doubts endure without allay°

---

4 division part of a song
2 Ways paths   **7 crosses** troubles   **11 allay** alleviation

Or help, but travail find for my best hire
Yet that which most my troubled sense doth move,
Is to leave all and take the thread of Love°

—1621

ROBERT HERRICK ■ (1591–1674)

*Robert Herrick was the most distinguished member of the "Tribe of Ben."
Herrick is grouped with the Cavalier poets, whose graceful lyrics are marked
by wit and gentle irony. Surprisingly, Herrick was a minister; his Royalist
sympathies during the English Civil War caused him hardship during the
Puritan era, but his position in the church was returned to him by Charles II
after the Restoration.*

To the Virgins, to Make Much of Time

Gather ye rosebuds while ye may,
    Old time is still a-flying;
And this same flower that smiles today
    Tomorrow will be dying.

The glorious lamp of heaven, the sun,   5
    The higher he's a-getting,
The sooner will his race be run,
    And nearer he's to setting.

That age is best which is the first,
    When youth and blood are warmer;   10
But being spent, the worse, and worst
    Times still succeed the former.

Then be not coy, but use your time,
    And, while ye may, go marry;
For, having lost but once your prime,   15
    You may forever tarry.

—1648

---

14 Love an allusion to the myth of Theseus, who, with the help of Ariadne, unrolled a thread behind
him as he entered the labyrinth of Crete.

George Herbert was the great master of the English devotional lyric. Herbert was born into a distinguished family which included his mother, the formidable literary patroness Lady Magdalen Herbert, and his brother, the poet and statesman Edward, Lord Herbert of Cherbury. Like John Donne, with whom he shares the metaphysical label, Herbert early aimed at a political career but turned to the clergy, spending several happy years as rector of Bemerton before his death at age 40. The Temple, which contains most of his poems, was published posthumously in 1633.

Easter Wings

Lord, who createdst man in wealth and store,°
Though foolishly he lost the same,
Decaying more and more
Till he became
Most poor: 5
With Thee
O let me rise
As larks, harmoniously,
And sing this day Thy victories:
Then shall the fall further the flight in me.   10

My tender age in sorrow did begin;
And still with sicknesses and shame
Thou didst so punish sin,
That I became
Most thin.   15
With Thee
Let me combine,
And feel this day thy victory;
For, if I imp my wing on thine,°
Affliction shall advance the flight in me.   20

—*1633*

---

1 store abundance   **19 imp my wing on thine** to graft feathers from a strong wing onto a weak one, a term from falconry

The Pulley

When God at first made man,
Having a glass of blessings standing by,
    "Let us," said he, "pour on him all we can.
Let the world's riches, which dispersèd lie,
    Contract into a span."°   5

    So strength first made a way;
Then beauty flowed, then wisdom, honor, pleasure.
    When almost all was out, God made a stay,
Perceiving that, alone of all his treasure,
    Rest in the bottom lay.   10

    "For if I should," said he,
"Bestow this jewel also on my creature,
    He would adore my gifts instead of me,
And rest in Nature, not the God of Nature;
    So both should losers be.   15

"Yet let him keep the rest,
    But keep them with repining restlessness.
Let him be rich and weary, that at least,
    If goodness lead him not, yet weariness
May toss him to my breast."   20

                                                        —*1633*

Redemption

Having been tenant long to a rich lord,
    Not thriving, I resolvèd to be bold,
    And make a suit° unto him, to afford°
A new small-rented lease, and cancel the old.
In heaven at his manor I him sought;   5
    They told me there that he was lately gone
    About some land, which he had dearly bought
Long since on earth, to take possession.

---

5 span the distance between thumb tip and the tip of the little finger
3 make a suit formally request   **afford** grant (me)

I straight returned, and knowing his great birth,
    Sought him accordingly in great resorts;   10
    In cities, theaters, gardens, parks, and courts;
At length I heard a ragged noise and mirth
    Of thieves and murderers; there I him espied,°
    Who straight, *Your suit is granted*, said, and died.

—*1633*

EDMUND WALLER ▮ (1606–1687)

Edmund Waller was another Royalist sympathizer who suffered after the English Civil War, during Oliver Cromwell's protectorate. Waller is noted for having pioneered the use of the heroic couplet as a popular verse form. He has been often praised for the smoothness of his rhythms and sound patterns.

Song

    Go, lovely rose!
Tell her that wastes her time and me
    That now she knows,
When I resemble° her to thee,
How sweet and fair she seems to be.   5

    Tell her that's young,
And shuns to have her graces spied,
    That hadst thou sprung
In deserts, where no men abide,
Thou must have uncommended died.   10

    Small is the worth
Of beauty from the light retired;
    Bid her come forth,
Suffer herself to be desired,
And not blush so to be admired.   15

13 him espied saw him
4 resemble compare

Then die! that she
The common fate of all things rare
    May read in thee;
How small a part of time they share
That are so wondrous sweet and fair!   20

—1645

JOHN MILTON ■ (1608–1674)

John Milton is best known as the author of Paradise Lost, *the greatest English epic poem. His life included service in the Puritan government of Cromwell, pamphleteering for liberal political causes, and brief imprisonment after the Restoration. Milton suffered from blindness in his later years. He excelled in the sonnet, a form to which he returned throughout his long literary life.*

How Soon Hath Time

How soon hath Time, the subtle thief of youth,
    Stol'n on his wing my three and twentieth year!
    My hasting days fly on with full career,
    But my late spring no bud or blossom shew'th.°
Perhaps my semblance might deceive the truth,   5
    That I to manhood am arrived so near,
    And inward ripeness doth much less appear,
    That some more timely-happy spirits endu'th.°
Yet be it less or more, or soon or slow,
    It shall be still in strictest measure even°   10
    To that same lot, however mean or high,
Toward which Time leads me, and the will of Heaven;
    All is, if I have grace to use it so,
    As ever in my great Taskmaster's eye.

—1645

4 **shew'th** shows   8 **endu'th** endows   10 **even** equal

On the Late Massacre in Piedmont°

Avenge, O Lord, thy slaughtered saints, whose bones
    Lie scattered on the Alpine mountains cold,
    Even them who kept thy truth so pure of old
    When all our fathers worshiped stocks and stones,°
Forget not: in thy book record their groans   5
    Who were thy sheep and in their ancient fold
    Slain by the bloody Piedmontese that rolled
    Mother with infant down the rocks. Their moans
The vales redoubled to the hills, and they
    To Heaven. Their martyred blood and ashes sow   10
    O'er all th'Italian fields where still doth sway
The triple tyrant:° that from these may grow
    A hundredfold, who having learnt thy way
    Early may fly the Babylonian woe.°

—1655

JOHN MILTON

82

When I Consider How My Light Is Spent

When I consider how my light is spent
    Ere half my days, in this dark world and wide,
    And that one talent which is death to hide°
    Lodged with me useless, though my soul more bent
To serve therewith my Maker, and present   5
    My true account, lest he returning chide;
    "Doth God exact day-labor, light denied?"
    I fondly° ask; but Patience to prevent
That murmur, soon replies, "God doth not need
    Either man's work or his own gifts; who best   10
    Bear his mild yoke, they serve him best. His state

Massacre in Piedmont 1700 Protestants from this North Italian state were massacred by Papal forces on Easter Day, 1655. **4 stocks and stones** idols   **12 triple tyrant** the Pope   **14 Babylonian woe** Early Protestants often linked ancient Babylon to modern Rome as centers of vice.
3 talent which is death to hide See the Parable of the Talents, Matthew 25:14–30.   **8 fondly** foolishly

Is kingly. Thousands at his bidding speed
And post o'er land and ocean without rest:
They also serve who only stand and wait."

—1673

ANNE BRADSTREET ▣ (1612–1672)

Anne Bradstreet was an American Puritan who was one of the first settlers of the Massachusetts Bay Colony, along with her husband Simon, later governor of the colony. The Tenth Muse Lately Sprung Up in America, published abroad by a relative without her knowledge, was the first American book of poetry published in England, and the circumstances of its appearance lie behind the witty tone of "The Author to Her Book."

The Author to Her Book

Thou ill-formed offspring of my feeble brain,
Who after birth didst by my side remain,
Till snatched from thence by friends, less wise than true,
Who thee abroad, exposed to public view,
Made thee in rags, halting to th' press° to trudge,   5
Where errors were not lessened (all may judge).
At thy return my blushing was not small,
My rambling brat (in print) should mother call,
I cast thee by as one unfit for light,
Thy visage was so irksome in my sight;   10
Yet being mine own, at length affection would
Thy blemishes amend, if so I could:
I washed thy face, but more defects I saw,
And rubbing off a spot still made a flaw.
I stretched thy joints to make thee even feet,°   15
Yet still thou run'st more hobbling than is meet;
In better dress to trim thee was my mind,
But nought save homespun cloth i' th' house I find.
In this array 'mongst vulgars° may'st thou roam.

5 press printing press; also a clothes closet or chest   **15 even feet** a pun on metrical feet
19 vulgars common people, i.e., average readers

In critic's hands beware thou dost not come,   20
And take thy way where yet thou art not known;
If for thy Father asked, say thou had'st none;
And for thy Mother, she alas is poor,
Which caused her thus to send thee out of door.

—1678

RICHARD LOVELACE ■ (1618–1658)

Richard Lovelace was another Cavalier lyricist who was a staunch supporter of Charles I, serving as a soldier in Scotland and France. He composed many of his poems in prison following the English Civil War.

To Lucasta, Going to the Wars

Tell me not, sweet, I am unkind
That from the nunnery
Of thy chaste breast and quiet mind,
To war and arms I fly.

True, a new mistress now I chase,   5
The first foe in the field;
And with a stronger faith embrace
A sword, a horse, a shield.

Yet this inconstancy is such
As you too shall adore;   10
I could not love thee, dear, so much,
Loved I not honor more.

—1649

ANDREW MARVELL ■ (1621–1678)

Andrew Marvell was widely known for the playful sexual wit of this most famous example of the carpé diem *poem in English. Marvell was a learned Latin scholar who moved in high circles of government under both the Puritans and Charles II, serving as a member of Parliament for two decades. Oddly, Marvell was almost completely forgotten as a lyric poet for almost two hundred years after his death, although today he is considered the last of the great exemplars of the metaphysical style.*

To His Coy Mistress

Had we but world enough, and time,
This coyness,° lady, were no crime.
We would sit down, and think which way
To walk, and pass our long love's day.
Thou by the Indian Ganges' side   5
Shouldst rubies find; I by the tide
Of Humber° would complain. I would
Love you ten years before the flood,
And you should, if you please, refuse
Till the conversion of the Jews.°   10
My vegetable° love should grow
Vaster than empires, and more slow;
An hundred years should go to praise
Thine eyes, and on thy forehead gaze;
Two hundred to adore each breast,   15
But thirty thousand to the rest;
An age at least to every part,
And the last age should show your heart.
For, lady, you deserve this state,°
Nor would I love at lower rate.   20
   But at my back I always hear
Time's wingèd chariot hurrying near;
And yonder all before us lie
Deserts of vast eternity.
Thy beauty shall no more be found;   25
Nor, in thy marble vault, shall sound
My echoing song; then worms shall try°
That long-preserved virginity,
And your quaint° honor turn to dust,
And into ashes all my lust: 30
The grave's a fine and private place,
But none, I think, do there embrace.

2 **coyness** here, artificial sexual reluctance   7 **Humber** an English river near Marvell's home
10 **conversion of the Jews** at the end of time   11 **vegetable** flourishing   19 **state** estate   27 **try** test
29 **quaint** too subtle

Now therefore, while the youthful hue
Sits on thy skin like morning glow,
And while thy willing soul transpires   35
At every pore with instant fires,
Now let us sport us while we may,
And now, like amorous birds of prey,
Rather at once our time devour,
Than languish in his slow-chapped° power.   40
Let us roll all our strength and all
Our sweetness up into one ball,
And tear our pleasures with rough strife
Thorough the iron gates of life:
Thus, though we cannot make our sun   45
Stand still, yet we will make him run.

—1681

JOHN DRYDEN ■ (1631–1700)

John Dryden excelled at long forms—verse dramas like All for Love, *his version
of Shakespeare's* Antony and Cleopatra, *his translation of Virgil's* Aeneid, *political allegories like* Absalom and Achitophel, *and* MacFlecknoe, *the first
great English literary satire. Dryden's balance and formal conservatism introduced the neoclassical style to English poetry, a manner that prevailed for a
century after his death. He became poet laureate of England in 1668.*

To the Memory of Mr. Oldham°

Farewell, too little, and too lately known,
Whom I began to think and call my own:
For sure our souls were near allied, and thine
Cast in the same poetic mold with mine.
One common note on either lyre did strike,   5
And knaves and fools we both abhorred alike.
To the same goal did both our studies drive;
The last set out the soonest did arrive.
Thus Nisus° fell upon the slippery place,

40 **chapped** jawed
John Oldham (1653–1683) was a poet and a satirist.   **9 Nisus** In Virgil's *Aeneid* he is defeated in a
footrace by Euryalus, his friend.

While his young friend performed and won the race.   10
O early ripe! to thy abundant store
What could advancing age have added more?
It might (what nature never gives the young)
Have taught the numbers° of thy native tongue.
But satire needs not those, and wit will shine   15
Through the harsh cadence of a rugged line:
A noble error, and but seldom made,
When poets are by too much force betrayed.
Thy generous fruits, though gathered ere their prime,
Still showed a quickness, and maturing time   20
But mellows what we write to the dull sweets of rhyme.
Once more, hail and farewell; farewell, thou young,
But ah too short, Marcellus° of our tongue;
Thy brows with ivy, and with laurels bound
But fate and gloomy night encompass thee around.   25

beautiful

—1684

A DESCRIPTION OF A CITY SHOWER

JONATHAN SWIFT ■ (1667–1745)

Jonathan Swift, the author of Gulliver's Travels, *stands unchallenged as the greatest English prose satirist, but his poetry too is remarkable in the unsparing realism of its best passages. Like many poets of the neoclassical era, Swift adds tension to his poetry by ironically emphasizing parallels between the heroic past and the familiar characters and scenes of contemporary London. A native of Dublin, Swift returned to Ireland in his maturity as dean of St. Patrick's Cathedral.*

A Description of a City Shower

Careful observers may foretell the hour
(By sure prognostics)° when to dread a shower:
While rain depends,° the pensive cat gives o'er
Her frolics, and pursues her tail no more.
Returning home at night, you'll find the sink°   5

---

14 **numbers** poetic meters   23 **Marcellus** Roman military leader who died at age twenty
2 **prognostics** forecasts   3 **depends** is imminent   5 **sink** sewer

Strike your offended sense with double stink.
If you be wise, then go not far to dine;
You'll spend in coach hire more than save in wine.
A coming shower your shooting corns presage,
Old achès throb, your hollow tooth will rage.   10
Sauntering in coffeehouse is Dulman° seen;
He damns the climate and complains of spleen.°
    Meanwhile the South, rising with dabbled wings,
A sable cloud athwart the welkin° flings,
That swilled more liquor than it could contain,   15
And, like a drunkard, gives it up again.
Brisk Susan whips her linen from the rope,
While the first drizzling shower is borne aslope:
Such is that sprinkling which some careless quean°
Flirts on you from her mop, but not so clean: 20
You fly, invoke the gods; then turning, stop
To rail; she singing, still whirls on her mop.
Not yet the dust had shunned the unequal strife,
But, aided by the wind, fought still for life,
And wafted with its foe by violent gust,   25
'Twas doubtful which was rain and which was dust.
Ah! where must needy poet seek for aid,
When dust and rain at once his coat invade?
Sole coat, where dust cemented by the rain
Erects the nap, and leaves a mingled stain.   30
    Now in contiguous drops the flood comes down,
Threatening with deluge this devoted° town.
To shops in crowds the daggled° females fly,
Pretend to cheapen° goods, but nothing buy.
The Templar° spruce, while every spout's abroach,°   35
Stays till 'tis fair, yet seems to call a coach.
The tucked-up sempstress walks with hasty strides,
While streams run down her oiled umbrella's sides.
Here various kinds, by various fortunes led,
Commence acquaintance underneath a shed.   40

11 **Dulman** i.e., dull man   12 **spleen** mental depression   14 **welkin** sky   19 **quean** ill-mannered woman   32 **devoted** doomed   33 **daggled** spattered   34 **cheapen** inspect prices of   35 **Templar** law student   **abroach** pouring

Triumphant Tories and desponding Whigs°
Forget their feuds, and join to save their wigs.
Boxed in a chair° the beau impatient sits,
While spouts run clattering o'er the roof by fits,
And ever and anon with frightful din   45
The leather sounds; he trembles from within.
So when Troy chairmen bore the wooden steed,
Pregnant with Greeks impatient to be freed
(Those bully Greeks, who, as the moderns do,
Instead of paying chairmen, run them through),   50
Laocoön° struck the outside with his spear,
And each imprisoned hero quaked for fear.
    Now from all parts the swelling kennels° flow,
And bear their trophies with them as they go:
Filth of all hues and odors seem to tell   55
What street they sailed from, by their sight and smell.
They, as each torrent drives with rapid force,
From Smithfield° or St. Pulchre's shape their course,
And in huge confluence joined at Snow Hill ridge,
Fall from the conduit prone to Holborn Bridge.   60
Sweepings from butchers' stalls, dung, guts, and blood,
Drowned puppies, stinking sprats,° all drenched in mud,
Dead cats, and turnip tops, come tumbling down the flood.

                                                          —1710

ALEXANDER POPE ■ (1688–1744)

Alexander Pope was a tiny man who was afflicted in childhood by a crip-
pling disease. Pope was the dominant poet of eighteenth-century England,
particularly excelling as a master of mock-epic satire in "The Rape of the
Lock" and "The Dunciad." His translations of the Iliad and the Odyssey
made him famous and financially independent and remained the standard
versions of Homer for almost two hundred years. "An Essay on Criticism," a
long didactic poem modeled on Horace's Ars Poetica, remains the most
complete statement of the neoclassical aesthetic.

---

41 Tories . . . Whigs rival political factions   **43 chair** sedan chair   **51 Laocoön** For his attempt to
warn the Trojans, he was crushed by sea serpents sent by Poseidon.   **53 kennels** storm drains
58 Smithfield site of London cattle exchange   **62 sprats** small fish

A DESCRIPTION OF A CITY SHOWER

89

From An Essay on Criticism

But most by numbers judge a poet's song,
And smooth or rough with them is right or wrong.
In the bright Muse though thousand charms conspire,
Her voice is all these tuneful fools admire,
Who haunt Parnassus° but to please their ear,   5
Not mend their minds; as some to church repair,
Not for the doctrine, but the music there.
These equal syllables alone require,
Though oft the ear the open vowels tire,
While expletives° their feeble aid do join,   10
And ten low words oft creep in one dull line:
While they ring round the same unvaried chimes,
With sure returns of still expected rhymes;
Where'er you find "the cooling western breeze,"
In the next line, it "whispers through the trees";   15
If crystal streams "with pleasing murmurs creep,"
The reader's threatened (not in vain) with "sleep";
Then, at the last and only couplet fraught
With some unmeaning thing they call a thought,
A needless Alexandrine° ends the song   20
That, like a wounded snake, drags its slow length along.
Leave such to tune their own dull rhymes, and know
What's roundly smooth or languishingly slow;
And praise the easy vigor of a line
Where Denham's strength and Waller's° sweetness join.   25
True ease in writing comes from art, not chance,
As those move easiest who have learned to dance.
'Tis not enough no harshness gives offense,
The sound must seem an echo to the sense.
Soft is the strain when Zephyr° gently blows,   30
And the smooth stream in smoother numbers flows;
But when loud surges lash the sounding shore,
The hoarse, rough verse should like the torrent roar.

5 **Parnassus** mountain of the Muses   10 **expletives** unnecessary filler words (like "do" in this line)
20 **Alexandrine** line of six iambic feet (as in the next line)   25 **Denham's . . . Waller's** earlier
English poets praised by Pope   30 **Zephyr** the west wind

When Ajax° strives some rock's vast weight to throw,
The line too labors, and the words move slow;   35
Not so when swift Camilla° scours the plain,
Flies o'er the unbending corn, and skims along the main.
Hear how Timotheus'° varied lays surprise,
And bid alternate passions fall and rise!
While at each change the son of Libyan Jove°   40
Now burns with glory, and then melts with love;
Now his fierce eyes with sparkling fury glow,
Now sighs steal out, and tears begin to flow:
Persians and Greeks like turns of nature found
And the world's victor stood subdued by sound!   45
The power of music all our hearts allow,
And what Timotheus was is Dryden now.
     Avoid extremes; and shun the fault of such
Who still are pleased too little or too much.
At every trifle scorn to take offense: 50
That always shows great pride, or little sense.
Those heads, as stomachs, are not sure the best,
Which nauseate all, and nothing can digest.
Yet let not each gay turn thy rapture move;
For fools admire, but men of sense approve: 55
As things seem large which we through mists descry,
Dullness is ever apt to magnify.

                                        —1711

Ode on Solitude

Happy the man whose wish and care
     A few paternal acres bound,
Content to breathe his native air,
          In his own ground.

Whose herds with milk, whose fields with bread,   5
     Whose flocks supply him with attire,
Whose trees in summer yield him shade,
          In winter fire.

---

34 Ajax legendary strong man of the *Iliad*   **36 Camilla** messenger of the goddess Diana
38 Timotheus a legendary musician   **40 son of Libyan Jove** Alexander the Great

Blest, who can unconcernedly find
    Hours, days, and years slide soft away,   10
In health of body, peace of mind,
    Quiet by day,

Sound sleep by night; study and ease,
    Together mixed; sweet recreation;
And innocence, which most does please   15
    With meditation.

Thus let me live, unseen, unknown;
    Thus unlamented let me die;
Steal from the world, and not a stone
    Tell where I lie.   20

—1736

THOMAS GRAY ■ (1716–1771)

Thomas Gray possesses a contemporary reputation that rests primarily on a single poem, but it remains one of the most often quoted in the whole English canon, and the quatrain stanza is often called "elegiac" in its honor. Gray lived almost all of his adult life at Cambridge University, where he was a professor of history and languages. He declined the poet laureateship of England in 1757.

Elegy Written in a Country Churchyard

The curfew tolls the knell of parting day,
    The lowing herd wind slowly o'er the lea,
The plowman homeward plods his weary way,
    And leaves the world to darkness and to me.

Now fades the glimmering landscape on the sight,   5
    And all the air a solemn stillness holds,
Save where the beetle wheels his droning flight,
    And drowsy tinklings lull the distant folds;

Save that from yonder ivy-mantled tower
    The moping owl does to the moon complain   10
Of such, as wandering near her secret bower,
    Molest her ancient solitary reign.

Beneath those rugged elms, that yew tree's shade,
     Where heaves the turf in many a moldering heap,
Each in his narrow cell forever laid,   15
     The rude° forefathers of the hamlet sleep.

The breezy call of incense-breathing morn,
     The swallow twittering from the straw-built shed,
The cock's shrill clarion, or the echoing horn,
     No more shall rouse them from their lowly bed.   20

For them no more the blazing hearth shall burn,
     Or busy housewife ply her evening care;
No children run to lisp their sire's return,
     Or climb his knees the envied kiss to share.

Oft did the harvest to their sickle yield,   25
     Their furrow oft the stubborn glebe° has broke;
How jocund did they drive their team afield!
     How bowed the woods beneath their sturdy stroke!

Let not Ambition mock their useful toil,
     Their homely joys, and destiny obscure;   30
Nor Grandeur hear with a disdainful smile
     The short and simple annals of the poor.

The boast of heraldry, the pomp of power,
     And all that beauty, all that wealth e'er gave,
Awaits alike the inevitable hour.   35
     The paths of glory lead but to the grave.

Nor you, ye proud, impute to these the fault,
     If Memory o'er their tomb no trophies raise,
Where through the long-drawn aisle and fretted° vault
     The pealing anthem swells the note of praise.   40

Can storied urn or animated° bust
     Back to its mansion call the fleeting breath?
Can Honor's voice provoke the silent dust,
     Or Flattery soothe the dull cold ear of Death?

16 rude unlearned   **26 glebe** plot of farmland   **39 fretted** carved   **41 animated** lifelike

Perhaps in this neglected spot is laid   45
    Some heart once pregnant with celestial fire;
Hands that the rod of empire might have swayed,
    Or waked to ecstasy the living lyre.

But Knowledge to their eyes her ample page
    Rich with the spoils of time did ne'er unroll;   50
Chill Penury repressed their noble rage,
    And froze the genial current of the soul.

Full many a gem of purest ray serene,
    The dark unfathomed caves of ocean bear:
Full many a flower is born to blush unseen,   55
    And waste its sweetness on the desert air.

Some village Hampden,° that with dauntless breast
    The little tyrant of his field withstood;
Some mute inglorious Milton here may rest,
    Some Cromwell° guiltless of his country's blood.   60

The applause of listening senates to command,
    The threats of pain and ruin to despise,
To scatter plenty o'er a smiling land,
    And read their history in a nation's eyes,

Their lot forbade: nor circumscribed alone   65
    Their growing virtues, but their crimes confined;
Forbade to wade through slaughter to a throne,
    And shut the gates of mercy on mankind,

The struggling pangs of conscious truth to hide,
    To quench the blushes of ingenuous shame,   70
Or heap the shrine of Luxury and Pride
    With incense kindled at the Muse's flame.

Far from the madding° crowd's ignoble strife,
    Their sober wishes never learned to stray;
Along the cool sequestered vale of life   75
    They kept the noiseless tenor of their way.

Yet even these bones from insult to protect
    Some frail memorial still erected nigh,

THOMAS GRAY

94

57 **Hampden** hero of the English Civil War   60 **Cromwell** Lord Protector of England from 1653 to 1658   73 **madding** frenzied

With uncouth rhymes and shapeless sculpture decked,
  Implores the passing tribute of a sigh.   80

Their name, their years, spelt by the unlettered Muse,
  The place of fame and elegy supply:
And many a holy text around she strews,
  That teach the rustic moralist to die.

For who to dumb Forgetfulness a prey,   85
  This pleasing anxious being e'er resigned,
Left the warm precincts of the cheerful day,
  Nor cast one longing lingering look behind?

On some fond breast the parting soul relies,
  Some pious drops the closing eye requires;   90
Even from the tomb the voice of Nature cries,
  Even in our ashes live their wonted fires.

For thee, who mindful of the unhonored dead
  Dost in these lines their artless tale relate;
If chance, by lonely contemplation led,   95
  Some kindred spirit shall inquire thy fate,

Haply some hoary°-headed swain° may say,
  "Oft have we seen him at the peep of dawn
Brushing with hasty steps the dews away
  To meet the sun upon the upland lawn.   100

"There at the foot of yonder nodding beech
  That wreathes its old fantastic roots so high,
His listless length at noontide would he stretch,
  And pore upon the brook that babbles by.

"Hard by yon wood, now smiling as in scorn,   105
  Muttering his wayward fancies he would rove,
Now drooping, woeful wan, like one forlorn,
  Or crazed with care, or crossed in hopeless love.

"One morn I missed him on the customed hill,
  Along the heath and near his favorite tree;   110
Another came; nor yet beside the rill,
  Nor up the lawn, nor at the wood was he;

97 hoary frosty, white   **swain** peasant

"The next with dirges due in sad array
    Slow through the churchway path we saw him borne.
Approach and read (for thou canst read) the lay,   115
    Graved on the stone beneath yon aged thorn."

The Epitaph

Here rests his head upon the lap of Earth
    A youth to Fortune and to Fame unknown.
Fair Science frowned not on his humble birth,
    And Melancholy marked him for her own.   120

Large was his bounty, and his soul sincere,
    Heaven did a recompense as largely send:
He gave to Misery all he had, a tear,
    He gained from Heaven ('twas all he wished) a friend.

No farther seek his merits to disclose,   125
    Or draw his frailties from their dread abode
(There they alike in trembling hope repose),
    The bosom of his Father and his God.

—1751

WILLIAM BLAKE ▪ (1757–1827)

William Blake was a poet, painter, engraver, and visionary. Blake does not fit easily into any single category, although his political sympathies link him to the later romantic poets. His first book, Poetical Sketches, *attracted little attention, but his mature works, starting with* Songs of Innocence *and* Songs of Experience, *combine poetry with his own remarkable illustrations and are unique in English literature. Thought mad by many in his own day, Blake anticipated many future directions of both literature and modern psychology.*

The Chimney Sweeper

When my mother died I was very young,
And my father sold me while yet my tongue
Could scarcely cry "'weep! 'weep! 'weep! 'weep!"
So your chimneys I sweep & in soot I sleep.

There's little Tom Dacre, who cried when his head   5
That curl'd like a lamb's back, was shav'd, so I said,

"Hush, Tom! never mind it, for when your head's bare,
You know that the soot cannot spoil your white hair."

And so he was quiet, & that very night,
As Tom was a-sleeping, he had such a sight!   10
That thousands of sweepers, Dick, Joe, Ned, & Jack,
Were all of them lock'd up in coffins of black;

And by came an Angel who had a bright key,
And he open'd the coffins & set them all free;
Then down a green plain, leaping, laughing, they run,   15
And wash in a river and shine in the Sun.

Then naked & white, all their bags left behind,
They rise upon clouds, and sport in the wind.
And the Angel told Tom, if he'd be a good boy,
He'd have God for his father, & never want joy.   20

And so Tom awoke; and we rose in the dark,
And got with our bags & our brushes to work.
Tho' the morning was cold, Tom was happy & warm;
So if all do their duty, they need not fear harm.

—1789   97

The Little Black° Boy

My mother bore me in the southern wild,
And I am black, but O! my soul is white;
White as an angel is the English child:
But I am black as if bereav'd of light.

My mother taught me underneath a tree,   5
And sitting down before the heat of day,
She took me on her lap and kissèd me,
And pointing to the east, began to say:

"Look on the rising sun: there God does live,
And gives his light, and gives his heat away;   10
And flowers and trees and beasts and men receive
Comfort in morning, joy in the noon day.

Black probably Indian rather than African

"And we are put on earth a little space,
That we may learn to bear the beams of love,
And these black bodies and this sun-burnt face   15
Is but a cloud, and like a shady grove.

"For when our souls have learn'd the heat to bear,
The cloud will vanish; we shall hear his voice,
Saying: 'Come out from the grove, my love & care,
And round my golden tent like lambs rejoice.'"   20

Thus did my mother say, and kissèd me;
And thus I say to little English boy:
When I from black and he from white cloud free,
And round the tent of God like lambs we joy,

I'll shade him from the heat till he can bear   25
To lean in joy upon our father's knee:
And then I'll stand and stroke his silver hair,
And be like him, and he will then love me.

—1789

A Poison Tree

I was angry with my friend:
I told my wrath, my wrath did end.
I was angry with my foe:
I told it not, my wrath did grow.

And I water'd it in fears,   5
Night & morning with my tears;
And I sunnèd it with smiles,
And with soft deceitful wiles.

And it grew both day and night,
Till it bore an apple bright;   10
And my foe beheld it shine,
And he knew that it was mine,

And into my garden stole
When the night had veil'd the pole;
In the morning glad I see   15
My foe outstretch'd beneath the tree.

—1794

The Tyger

Tyger! Tyger! burning bright
In the forests of the night,
What immortal hand or eye
Could frame thy fearful symmetry?

In what distant deeps or skies   5
Burnt the fire of thine eyes?
On what wings dare he aspire?
What the hand, dare seize the fire?

And what shoulder, & what art,
Could twist the sinews of thy heart?   10
And when thy heart began to beat,
What dread hand? & what dread feet?

What the hammer? what the chain?
In what furnace was thy brain?
What the anvil? what dread grasp   15
Dare its deadly terrors clasp?

When the stars threw down their spears,
And water'd heaven with their tears,
Did he smile his work to see?
Did he who made the Lamb make thee?   20

Tyger! Tyger! burning bright
In the forests of the night,
What immortal hand or eye,
Dare frame thy fearful symmetry?

—1794

ROBERT BURNS ■ (1759–1796)

Robert Burns was a Scot known in his day as the "Ploughman Poet" and was one of the first English poets to put dialect to serious literary purpose. Chiefly known for his realistic depictions of peasant life, he was also an important lyric poet who prefigured many of the later concerns of the romantic era.

A Red, Red Rose

O my luve's like a red, red rose,
    That's newly sprung in June;
O my luve's like the melodie
    That's sweetly played in tune.

As fair art thou, my bonnie lass,   5
    So deep in luve am I;
And I will luve thee still, my dear,
    Till a' the seas gang° dry.

Till a' the seas gang dry, my dear,
    And the rocks melt wi' the sun;   10
O I will luve thee still, my dear,
    While the sands o' life shall run.

And fare thee weel, my only luve,
    And fare thee weel awhile!
And I will come again, my luve   15
    Though it were ten thousand mile.

—1791

John Barleycorn

There were three kings into the east,
Three kings both great and high;
And they has sworn a solemn oath
John Barleycorn should die.

They took a plough and plough'd him down,   5
Put clods upon his head;
And they hae sworn a solemn oath
John Barleycorn was dead.

But the cheerful spring came kindly on,
And showers began to fall;   10
John Barleycorn got up again,
And sore surprised them all.

8 gang go

ROBERT BURNS

100

The sultry suns of summer came,
And he grew thick and strong;
His head well armed wi' point'd spears,   15
That no one should him wrong.

The sober autumn enter'd mild,
When he grew wan and pale;
His bending joints and drooping head
Show'd he began to fail.   20

His colour sicken'd more and more
He faded into age;
And then his enemies began
To show their deadly rage.

They've ta'en a weapon long and sharp,   25
And cut him by the knee;
Then tied him fast upon a cart,
Like a rogue for forgery.

They laid him down upon his back,
And cudgell'd him full sore;   30
They hung him up before the storm,
And turn'd him o'er and o'er.

They fill'd up a darksome pit
With water to the brim;
They heaved in John Barleycorn,   35
There let him sink or swim.

They laid him out upon the floor,
To work him further woe;
And still as signs of life appear'd,
They toss'd him to and fro.   40

They wasted o'er a scorching flame
The marrow of his bones;
But a miller used him worst of all
He crushed him 'tween two stones.

And they has ta'en his very heart's blood,   45
And drank it round and round,
And still the more and more they drank,
Their joy did more abound.

John Barleycorn was a hero bold,
Of noble enterprise;   50
For if you do but taste his blood,
'Twill make your courage rise.

'Twill make a man forget his woe;
'Twill heighten all his joy;
'Twill make the widow's heart to sing,   55
Though the tear were in her eye.

Then let us toast John Barleycorn,
Each man a glass in hand;
And may his great posterity
Ne'er fail in old Scotland!   60

—*1786*

WILLIAM WORDSWORTH ■ (1770–1850)

*William Wordsworth is generally considered the first of the English roman-
tics. Lyrical Ballads, the 1798 volume that introduced both his poetry and
Samuel Taylor Coleridge's to a wide readership, remains one of the most influential collections of poetry ever published. Wordsworth's preface to the revised edition of 1800 contains the famous Romantic formulation of poetry
as the "spontaneous overflow of powerful feelings," a theory exemplified in
short lyrics like "I Wandered Lonely as a Cloud" and in longer meditative
pieces like "Tintern Abbey" (the title by which "Lines" is commonly known).
Wordsworth served as poet laureate from 1843 to his death.*

I Wandered Lonely as a Cloud

I wandered lonely as a cloud
That floats on high o'er vales and hills,
When all at once I saw a crowd,
A host, of golden daffodils;
Beside the lake, beneath the trees,   5
Fluttering and dancing in the breeze.

Continuous as the stars that shine
And twinkle on the milky way,
They stretched in never-ending line
Along the margin of a bay: 10

Ten thousand saw I at a glance,
Tossing their heads in sprightly dance.

The waves beside them danced, but they
Outdid the sparkling waves in glee;
A poet could not but be gay,   15
In such a jocund company;
I gazed—and gazed—but little thought
What wealth the show to me had brought:

For oft, when on my couch I lie
In vacant or in pensive mood,   20
They flash upon that inward eye
Which is the bliss of solitude;
And then my heart with pleasure fills,
And dances with the daffodils.

—1807

It Is a Beauteous Evening

It is a beauteous evening, calm and free,
The holy time is quiet as a Nun
Breathless with adoration; the broad sun
Is sinking down in its tranquillity;
The gentleness of heaven broods o'er the Sea: 5
Listen! the mighty Being is awake,
And doth with his eternal motion make
A sound like thunder—everlastingly.
Dear Child! dear Girl!° that walkest with me here,
If thou appear untouched by solemn thought,   10
Thy nature is not therefore less divine:
Thou liest in Abraham's bosom° all the year,
And worship'st at the Temple's inner shrine,
God being with thee when we know it not.

—1807

---

9 **Dear Child! dear Girl!** the poet's daughter   12 **Abraham's bosom** where souls rest in Heaven

Nuns Fret Not at Their Convent's Narrow Room

Nuns fret not at their convent's narrow room;
And hermits are contented with their cells;
And students with their pensive citadels;
Maids at the wheel, the weaver at his loom,
Sit blithe and happy; bees that soar for bloom,   5
High as the highest Peak of Furness-fells,°
Will murmur by the hour in foxglove bells: — *flowering plant*
In truth the prison, into which we doom
Ourselves, no prison is: and hence for me,
In sundry moods, 'twas pastime to be bound   10
Within the Sonnet's scanty plot of ground;
Pleased if some Souls (for such there needs must be)
Who have felt the weight of too much liberty,
Should find brief solace there, as I have found.

—1807

104

Ode

Intimations of Immortality
from Recollections of Early Childhood

The Child is Father of the Man;
And I could wish my days to be
Bound each to each by natural piety.°

1

There was a time when meadow, grove, and stream,
The earth, and every common sight,
       To me did seem
       Appareled in celestial light,
The glory and the freshness of a dream.   5
It is not now as it hath been of yore;—
       Turn wheresoe'er I may,
       By night or day,
The things which I have seen I now can see no more.

---

6 Furness-fells mountains located in the English Lake District
The Child . . . natural piety last three lines of the poet's "My Heart Leaps Up"

2

The Rainbow comes and goes, 10
And lovely is the Rose,
The Moon doth with delight
Look round her when the heavens are bare,
Waters on a starry night
Are beautiful and fair; 15
The sunshine is a glorious birth;
But yet I know, where'er I go,
That there hath past away a glory from the earth.

3

Now, while the birds thus sing a joyous song,
And while the young lambs bound 20
As to the tabor's° sound,
To me alone there came a thought of grief:
A timely utterance gave that thought relief,
And I again am strong:
The cataracts blow their trumpets from the steep; 25
No more shall grief of mine the season wrong;
I hear the Echoes through the mountains throng,
The Winds come to me from the fields of sleep,
And all the earth is gay;
Land and sea 30
Give themselves up to jollity,
And with the heart of May
Doth every Beast keep holiday;—
Thou Child of Joy,
Shout round me, let me hear thy shouts, thou happy
Shepherd-boy! 35

4

Ye blessèd Creatures, I have heard the call
Ye to each other make; I see
The heavens laugh with you in your jubilee;
My heart is at your festival, 40
My head hath its coronal,°

21 **tabor's** small drum's   41 **coronal** floral crown

The fulness of your bliss, I feel—I feel it all.
      Oh evil day! if I were sullen
      While Earth herself is adorning,
         This sweet May-morning,   45
      And the Children are culling
         On every side,
    In a thousand valleys far and wide,
    Fresh flowers; while the sun shines warm,
And the Babe leaps up on his Mother's arm:—   50
     I hear, I hear, with joy I hear!
     —But there's a Tree, of many, one,
A single Field which I have looked upon,
Both of them speak of something that is gone:
       The Pansy at my feet   55
       Doth the same tale repeat:
Whither is fled the visionary gleam?
Where is it now, the glory and the dream?

5

Our birth is but a sleep and a forgetting:
The Soul that rises with us, our life's Star,   60
      Hath had elsewhere its setting,
         And cometh from afar:
     Not in entire forgetfulness,
     And not in utter nakedness,
But trailing clouds of glory do we come   65
      From God, who is our home:
Heaven lies about us in our infancy!
Shades of the prison-house begin to close
      Upon the growing Boy,
But he beholds the light, and whence it flows,   70
      He sees it in his joy;
The Youth, who daily farther from the east
      Must travel, still is Nature's Priest,
      And by the vision splendid
      Is on his way attended;   75
At length the Man perceives it die away,
And fade into the light of common day.

6

Earth fills her lap with pleasures of her own;
Yearnings she hath in her own natural kind,
And, even with something of a Mother's mind,   80
    And no unworthy aim,
    The homely Nurse doth all she can
To make her Foster-child, her Inmate Man,
    Forget the glories he hath known,
And that imperial palace whence he came.   85

7

Behold the Child among his new-born blisses,
A six years' Darling of a pigmy size!
See where 'mid work of his own hand he lies,
Fretted° by sallies of his mother's kisses,
With light upon him from his father's eyes!   90
See, at his feet, some little plan or chart,
Some fragment from his dream of human life,
Shaped by himself with newly-learnèd art;
    A wedding or a festival,
    A mourning or a funeral;   95
      And this hath now his heart,
    And unto this he frames his song:
    Then will he fit his tongue
To dialogues of business, love, or strife;
    But it will not be long   100
    Ere this be thrown aside,
    And with new joy and pride
The little Actor cons another part;
Filling from time to time his "humorous stage"°
With all the Persons, down to palsied Age,   105
That Life brings with her in her equipage;
    As if his whole vocation
    Were endless imitation.

ODE

107

89 **Fretted** annoyed or marked   104 **"humorous stage"** phrase from poet Samuel Daniel (1563–1619)

8

Thou whose exterior semblance doth belie
    Thy Soul's immensity;   110
Thou best Philosopher, who yet dost keep
Thy heritage, thou Eye among the blind,
That, deaf and silent, read'st the eternal deep,
Haunted for ever by the eternal mind,—
    Mighty Prophet! Seer blest!   115
    On whom those truths do rest,
Which we are toiling all our lives to find,
In darkness lost, the darkness of the grave;
Thou, over whom thy Immortality
Broods like the Day, a Master o'er a Slave,   120
A Presence which is not to be put by;
Thou little Child, yet glorious in the might
Of heaven-born freedom on thy being's height,
Why with such earnest pains dost thou provoke
The years to bring the inevitable yoke,   125
Thus blindly with thy blessedness at strife?
Full soon thy Soul shall have her earthly freight,
And custom lie upon thee with a weight,
Heavy as frost, and deep almost as life!

9

    O joy! that in our embers   130
    Is something that doth live,
    That nature yet remembers
    What was so fugitive!
The thought of our past years in me doth breed
Perpetual benediction: not indeed   135
For that which is most worthy to be blest;
Delight and liberty, the simple creed
Of Childhood, whether busy or at rest,
With new-fledged hope still fluttering in his breast:—
    Not for these I raise   140
    The song of thanks and praise;
    But for those obstinate questionings
    Of sense and outward things,

Fallings from us, vanishings;
　　Blank misgivings of a Creature   145
Moving about in worlds not realized,
High instincts before which our mortal Nature
Did tremble like a guilty Thing surprised:
　　　　But for those first affections,
　　　　Those shadowy recollections,   150
　　　Which, be they what they may,
Are yet the fountain light of all our day,
Are yet a master light of all our seeing;
　　　Uphold us, cherish, and have power to make
Our noisy years seem moments in the being   155
Of the eternal Silence: truths that wake,
　　　　To perish never;
Which neither listlessness, nor mad endeavour,
　　　　Nor Man nor Boy,
Nor all that is at enmity with joy,   160
Can utterly abolish or destroy!
　　　Hence in a season of calm weather
　　　Though inland far we be,
Our Souls have sight of that immortal sea
　　　Which brought us hither,   165
　　　Can in a moment travel thither,
And see the Children sport upon the shore,
And hear the mighty waters rolling evermore.

　　10

Then sing, ye Birds, sing, sing a joyous song!
　　　And let the young Lambs bound   170
　　　As to the tabor's sound!
We in thought will join your throng,
　　　Ye that pipe and ye that play,
　　　Ye that through your hearts to-day
　　　Feel the gladness of the May!   175
What though the radiance which was once so bright
Be now for ever taken from my sight,
　　　Though nothing can bring back the hour
Of splendour in the grass, of glory in the flower;
　　　We will grieve not, rather find   180
　　　Strength in what remains behind;

In the primal sympathy
Which having been must ever be;
In the soothing thoughts that spring
Out of human suffering;   185
In the faith that looks through death,
In years that bring the philosophic mind.

11

And O, ye Fountains, Meadows, Hills, and Groves,
Forbode not any severing of our loves!
Yet in my heart of hearts I feel your might;   190
I only have relinquished one delight
To live beneath your more habitual sway.
I love the Brooks which down their channels fret,
Even more than when I tripped lightly as they;
The innocent brightness of a new-born Day   195
       Is lovely yet;
The Clouds that gather round the setting sun
Do take a sober colouring from an eye
That hath kept watch o'er man's mortality;
Another race hath been, and other palms are won.   200
Thanks to the human heart by which we live,
Thanks to its tenderness, its joys, and fears,
To me the meanest° flower that blows can give
Thoughts that do often lie too deep for tears.

—1807

110

SAMUEL TAYLOR COLERIDGE ■ (1772–1834)

Samuel Taylor Coleridge, inspired but erratic, did his best work, like Wordsworth, during the great first decade of their friendship, the period that produced Lyrical Ballads. *Coleridge's later life is a tragic tale of financial and marital problems, unfinished projects, and a ruinous addiction to opium. A brilliant critic, Coleridge lectured on Shakespeare and other writers and wrote the* Biographia Literaria, *perhaps the greatest literary autobiography ever written.*

203 meanest least significant

Frost at Midnight

The Frost performs its secret ministry,
Unhelped by any wind. The owlet's cry
Came loud—and hark, again! loud as before.
The inmates of my cottage, all at rest,
Have left me to that solitude, which suits   5
Abstruser musings: save that at my side
My cradled infant° slumbers peacefully.
'Tis calm indeed! so calm, that it disturbs
And vexes meditation, with its strange
And extreme silentness. Sea, hill, and wood,   10
This populous village! Sea, and hill, and wood,
With all the numberless goings-on of life,
Inaudible as dreams! the thin blue flame
Lies on my low-burnt fire, and quivers not;
Only that film,° which fluttered on the grate,   15
Still flutters there, the sole unquiet thing.
Methinks its motion in this hush of nature
Gives it dim sympathies with me who live,
Making it a companionable form,
Whose puny flaps and freaks the idling Spirit   20
By its own moods interprets, everywhere
Echo or mirror seeking of itself,
And makes a toy of Thought.
                                        But O! how oft,
How oft, at school, with most believing mind,
Presageful,° have I gazed upon the bars,   25
To watch that fluttering stranger! and as oft
With unclosed lids, already had I dreamt
Of my sweet birthplace, and the old church tower,
Whose bells, the poor man's only music, rang
From morn to evening, all the hot Fair-day,   30
So sweetly, that they stirred and haunted me
With a wild pleasure, falling on mine ear
Most like articulate sounds of things to come!

---

7 My cradled infant the poet's son Hartley (1796–1849)   **15 film** a piece of ash   **25 Presageful** with
hints of the future

So gazed I, till the soothing things, I dreamt,
Lulled me to sleep, and sleep prolonged my dreams!   35
And so I brooded all the following morn,
Awed by the stern preceptor's° face, mine eye
Fixed with mock study on my swimming book:
Save if the door half opened, and I snatched
A hasty glance, and still my heart leaped up,   40
For still I hoped to see the *stranger's* face,
Townsman, or aunt, or sister more beloved,
My playmate when we both were clothed alike!

    Dear Babe, that sleepest cradled by my side,
Whose gentle breathings, heard in this deep calm,   45
Fill up the interspersèd vacancies
And momentary pauses of the thought!
My babe so beautiful! it thrills my heart
With tender gladness, thus to look at thee,
And think that thou shalt learn far other lore,   50
And in far other scenes! For I was reared
In the great city, pent 'mid cloisters dim,
And saw nought lovely but the sky and stars.
But *thou*, my babe! shalt wander like a breeze
By lakes and sandy shores, beneath the crags   55
Of ancient mountain, and beneath the clouds,
Which image in their bulk both lakes and shores
And mountain crags: so shalt thou see and hear
The lovely shapes and sounds intelligible
Of that eternal language, which thy God   60
Utters, who from eternity doth teach
Himself in all, and all things in himself.
Great universal Teacher! he shall mold
Thy spirit, and by giving make it ask.

    Therefore all seasons shall be sweet to thee,   65
Whether the summer clothe the general earth
With greenness, or the redbreast sit and sing
Betwixt the tufts of snow on the bare branch
Of mossy apple tree, while the nigh thatch

37 preceptor teacher

Smokes in the sun-thaw; whether the eave-drops fall   70
Heard only in the trances of the blast,
Or if the secret ministry of frost
Shall hang them up in silent icicles,
Quietly shining to the quiet Moon.

beautiful

serene   —1798

Kubla Khan°

OR A VISION IN A DREAM,° A FRAGMENT

In Xanadu did Kubla Khan
A stately pleasure-dome decree:
Where Alph, the sacred river, ran
Through caverns measureless to man

Down to a sunless sea.   5
So twice five miles of fertile ground
With walls and towers were girdled round:
And there were gardens bright with sinuous rills,
Where blossomed many an incense-bearing tree;
And here were forests ancient as the hills,   10
Enfolding sunny spots of greenery.

But oh! that deep romantic chasm which slanted
Down the green hill athwart a cedarn cover!
A savage place! as holy and enchanted
As e'er beneath a waning moon was haunted   15
By woman wailing for her demon lover!
And from this chasm, with ceaseless turmoil seething,
As if this earth in fast thick pants were breathing,
A mighty fountain momently was forced:
Amid whose swift half-intermitted burst   20

Kubla Khan ruler of China (1216–1294)   **vision in a dream** Coleridge's own account tells how he took opium for an illness and slept for three hours, during which time he envisioned a complete poem of some 300 lines. When he awoke, he began to write down the details of his dream. "At this moment he was unfortunately called out by a person on business from Porlock, and detained by him above an hour, and on his return to the room found, to his no small surprise and mortification, that though he still retained some vague and dim recollection of the general purport of the vision, yet, with the exception of some eight or ten scattered lines and images on the surface of a stream into which a stone has been cast . . ." [Coleridge's note].

Huge fragments vaulted like rebounding hail,
Or chaffy grain beneath the thresher's flail:
And 'mid these dancing rocks at once and ever
It flung up momently the sacred river.
Five miles meandering with a mazy motion   25
Through wood and dale the sacred river ran,
Then reached the caverns measureless to man,
And sank in tumult to a lifeless ocean:
And 'mid this tumult Kubla heard from far
Ancestral voices prophesying war!   30

    The shadow of the dome of pleasure
    Floated midway on the waves;
    Where was heard the mingled measure
    From the fountain and the caves.
It was a miracle of rare device,   35
A sunny pleasure-dome with caves of ice!

    A damsel with a dulcimer
    In a vision once I saw:
    It was an Abyssinian maid,
    And on her dulcimer she played,   40
    Singing of Mount Abora.
    Could I revive within me
    Her symphony and song,

    To such a deep delight 'twould win me,
That with music loud and long,   45
I would build that dome in air,
That sunny dome! those caves of ice!
And all who heard should see them there,
And all should cry, Beware! Beware!
His flashing eyes, his floating hair!   50
Weave a circle round him thrice,
And close your eyes with holy dread,
For he on honey-dew hath fed,
And drunk the milk of Paradise.

                 —1797–98

Work Without Hope

Lines Composed 21st February 1825

All Nature seems at work. Slugs leave their lair—
The bees are stirring—birds are on the wing—
And Winter slumbering in the open air
Wears on his smiling face a dream of Spring!
And I the while, the sole unbusy thing,   5
Nor honey make, nor pair, nor build, nor sing.

    Yet well I ken° the banks where amaranths° blow,
Have traced the fount whence streams of nectar flow.
Bloom, O ye amaranths! bloom for whom ye may,
For me ye bloom not! Glide, rich streams, away!   10
With lips unbrightened, wreathless brow, I stroll:
And would you learn the spells that drowse my soul?
Work without Hope draws° nectar in a sieve,
And Hope without an object cannot live.

—1828

GEORGE GORDON, LORD BYRON ■ (1788–1824)

George Gordon, Lord Byron attained flamboyant celebrity status, leading an unconventional lifestyle that contributed to his notoriety. Byron was the most widely read of all the English romantic poets, but his verse romances and mock-epic poems like Don Juan *have not proved as popular in our era. An English aristocrat who was committed to revolutionary ideals, Byron died while lending military assistance to the cause of Greek freedom.*

She Walks in Beauty

    She walks in beauty, like the night
        Of cloudless climes and starry skies;
    And all that's best of dark and bright
        Meet in her aspect and her eyes:
    Thus mellowed to that tender light   5
        Which heaven to gaudy day denies.

7 ken know   **amaranths** legendary flowers that never fade   **13 draws** dips

One shade the more, one ray the less,
      Had half impaired the nameless grace
Which waves in every raven tress,
      Or softly lightens o'er her face;   10
Where thoughts serenely sweet express
      How pure, how dear their dwelling-place.

And on that cheek, and o'er that brow,
      So soft, so calm, yet eloquent,
The smiles that win, the tints that glow,   15
      But tell of days in goodness spent,
A mind at peace with all below,
      A heart whose love is innocent!

                                              —1815

Stanzas

When A Man Hath No Freedom To Fight For At Home

When a man hath no freedom to fight for at home,
      Let him combat for that of his neighbors;
Let him think of the glories of Greece and of Rome,
      And get knocked on his head for his labors.

To do good to mankind is the chivalrous plan,   5
      And is always as nobly requited:
Then battle for freedom wherever you can,
      And, if not shot or hanged, you'll get knighted.

                                              —1824

When We Two Parted

When we two parted
      In silence and tears,
Half broken-hearted
      To sever for years,
Pale grew thy cheek and cold,   5
      Colder thy kiss;
Truly that hour foretold
      Sorrow to this.

The dew of the morning
      Sunk chill on my brow—   10

It felt like the warning
  Of what I feel now.
Thy vows are all broken,
  And light is thy fame;
I hear thy name spoken,   15
  And share in its shame.

They name thee before me,
  A knell to mine ear;
A shudder comes o'er me—
  Why wert thou so dear?   20
They know not I knew thee,
  Who knew thee too well:—
Long, long shall I rue thee,
  Too deeply to tell.

In secret we met—   25
  In silence I grieve
That thy heart could forget,
  Thy spirit deceive.
If I should meet thee
  After long years,   30
How should I greet thee?—
  With silence and tears.

                                   —1813

PERCY BYSSHE SHELLEY ▪ (1792–1822)

Percy Bysshe Shelley, like his friend Byron, has not found as much favor in recent eras as the other English romantics, although his political liberalism anticipates many currents of our own day. Perhaps his unbridled emotionalism is sometimes too intense for modern readers. His wife, Mary Wollstonecraft Shelley, will be remembered as the author of the classic horror novel Frankenstein.

Ode to the West Wind

1

O wild West Wind, thou breath of Autumn's being,
Thou, from whose unseen presence the leaves dead
Are driven, like ghosts from an enchanter fleeing,

Yellow, and black, and pale, and hectic red,
Pestilence-stricken multitudes: O thou,   5
Who chariotest to their dark wintry bed

The wingèd seeds, where they lie cold and low,
Each like a corpse within its grave, until
Thine azure sister of the Spring° shall blow

Her clarion o'er the dreaming earth, and fill   10
(Driving sweet buds like flocks to feed in air)
With living hues and odors plain and hill:

Wild Spirit, which art moving everywhere;
Destroyer and preserver; hear, oh, hear!

2

Thou on whose stream, mid the steep sky's commotion,   15
Loose clouds like earth's decaying leaves are shed,
Shook from the tangled boughs of Heaven and Ocean,

Angels of rain and lightning: there are spread
On the blue surface of thine aëry surge,
Like the bright hair uplifted from the head   20

Of some fierce Mænad,° even from the dim verge
Of the horizon to the zenith's height,
The locks of the approaching storm. Thou dirge

Of the dying year, to which this closing night
Will be the dome of a vast sepulcher,   25
Vaulted with all thy congregated might

Of vapors, from whose solid atmosphere
Black rain, and fire, and hail will burst: oh, hear!

3

Thou who didst waken from his summer dreams
The blue Mediterranean, where he lay,   30
Lulled by the coil of his crystàlline streams,

Beside a pumice isle in Baiae's bay,°
And saw in sleep old palaces and towers
Quivering within the wave's intenser day,

9 **azure sister of the Spring** i.e., the South Wind   21 **Mænad** female worshipper of Bacchus, god
of wine   32 **Baiae's bay** near Naples

All overgrown with azure moss and flowers   35
So sweet, the sense faints picturing them! Thou
For whose path the Atlantic's level powers

Cleave themselves into chasms, while far below
The sea-blooms and the oozy woods which wear
The sapless foliage of the ocean, know   40

Thy voice, and suddenly grow gray with fear,
And tremble and despoil themselves: oh, hear!

4

If I were a dead leaf thou mightest bear;
If I were a swift cloud to fly with thee;
A wave to pant beneath thy power, and share   45

The impulse of thy strength, only less free
Than thou, O uncontrollable! If even
I were as in my boyhood, and could be

The comrade of thy wanderings over Heaven,
As then, when to outstrip thy skyey speed   50
Scarce seemed a vision; I would ne'er have striven

As thus with thee in prayer in my sore need.
Oh, lift me as a wave, a leaf, a cloud!
I fall upon the thorns of life! I bleed!

A heavy weight of hours has chained and bowed   55
One too like thee: tameless, and swift, and proud.

5

Make me thy lyre, even as the forest is:
What if my leaves are falling like its own!
The tumult of thy mighty harmonies

Will take from both a deep, autumnal tone,   60
Sweet though in sadness. Be thou, Spirit fierce,
My spirit! Be thou me, impetuous one!

Drive my dead thoughts over the universe
Like withered leaves to quicken a new birth!
And, by the incantation of this verse,   65

Scatter, as from an unextinguished hearth
Ashes and sparks, my words among mankind!
Be through my lips to unawakened earth

The trumpet of a prophecy! O Wind,
If Winter comes, can Spring be far behind?   70

—1820

Ozymandias°

I met a traveler from an antique land
Who said: Two vast and trunkless legs of stone
Stand in the desert. . . . Near them, on the sand,
Half sunk, a shattered visage lies, whose frown,
And wrinkled lip, and sneer of cold command,   5
Tell that its sculptor well those passions read
Which yet survive, stamped on these lifeless things,
The hand that mocked them, and the heart that fed:
And on the pedestal these words appear:
"My name is Ozymandias, king of kings: 10
Look on my works, ye Mighty, and despair!"
Nothing beside remains. Round the decay
Of that colossal wreck, boundless and bare
The lone and level sands stretch far away.

—1818

JOHN KEATS

120

JOHN KEATS ■ (1795–1821)

*John Keats is now perhaps the most admired of all the major romantics.
Certainly his tragic death from tuberculosis in his twenties gives poignancy
to thoughts of the doomed young poet writing feverishly in a futile race
against time; "Here lies one whose name was writ in water" are the words
he chose for his own epitaph. Many of Keats's poems are concerned with
glimpses of the eternal, whether a translation of an ancient epic poem or a
pristine artifact of a vanished civilization.*

Ozymandias Ramses II of Egypt (c. 1250 BC)

Bright Star, Would I Were Stedfast as Thou Art°

Bright star, would I were stedfast as thou art—
    Not in lone splendor hung aloft the night,
And watching, with eternal lids apart,
    Like nature's patient, sleepless eremite°,
The moving waters at their priestlike task   5
    Of pure ablution° round earth's human shores,
Or gazing on the new soft-fallen mask
    Of snow upon the mountains and the moors;
No—yet still stedfast, still unchangeable,
    Pillow'd upon my fair love's ripening breast,   10
To feel for ever its soft swell and fall,
    Awake for ever in a sweet unrest,
Still, still to hear her tender-taken breath,
    And so live ever—or else swoon to death°.

                          —1821

La Belle Dame sans Merci°

O what can ail thee, Knight at arms,
    Alone and palely loitering?
The sedge has withered from the Lake
    And no birds sing!

O what can ail thee, Knight at arms,   5
    So haggard, and so woebegone?
The squirrel's granary is full
    And the harvest's done.

I see a lily on thy brow
    With anguish moist and fever dew,   10
And on thy cheeks a fading rose
    Fast withereth too.

LA BELLE DAME SANS MERCI

Bright star, would I were stedfast as thou art While on a tour of the Lake District in 1818, Keats had said that the austere scenes "refine one's sensual vision into a sort of north star which can never cease to be open lidded and steadfast over the wonders of the great Power." The thought developed into this sonnet, which Keats drafted in 1819, then copied into his volume of Shakespeare's poems at the end of September or the beginning of October 1820, while on his way to Italy, where he died   **4 eremite** Hermit, religious solitary   **6 ablution** warhing, as part of a religious rite   **14 death** in the earlier version: "Half passionless, and so swoon on to death" **La Belle Dame sans Merci** "the beautiful lady without pity"

"I met a Lady in the Meads,
        Full beautiful, a faery's child,
Her hair was long, her foot was light,   15
        And her eyes were wild.

"I made a Garland for her head,
        And bracelets too, and fragrant Zone;°
She looked at me as she did love
        And made sweet moan.   20

"I set her on my pacing steed
        And nothing else saw all day long,
For sidelong would she bend and sing
        A faery's song.

"She found me roots of relish sweet,   25
        And honey wild, and manna dew,
And sure in language strange she said
        'I love thee true.'

"She took me to her elfin grot°
        And there she wept and sighed full sore,   30
And there I shut her wild wild eyes
        With kisses four.

"And there she lullèd me asleep,
        And there I dreamed, Ah Woe betide!
The latest dream I ever dreamt   35
        On the cold hill side.

"I saw pale Kings, and Princes too,
        Pale warriors, death-pale were they all;
They cried, 'La belle Dame sans merci
        Hath thee in thrall!'   40

"I saw their starved lips in the gloam
        With horrid warning gapèd wide,
And I awoke, and found me here
        On the cold hill's side.

"And this is why I sojourn here   45
        Alone and palely loitering;
Though the sedge is withered from the Lake,
        And no birds sing."

—1819

18 **Zone** belt   29 **grot** cave

Ode to a Nightingale

1

My heart aches, and a drowsy numbness pains
    My sense, as though of hemlock° I had drunk,
Or emptied some dull opiate to the drains
    One minute past, and Lethe-wards° had sunk.
'Tis not through envy of thy happy lot,   5
    But being too happy in thine happiness—
        That thou, light-wingèd Dryad° of the trees,
           In some melodious plot
Of beechen green, and shadows numberless,
    Singest of summer in full-throated ease.   10

2

O, for a draught of vintage! that hath been
    Cooled a long age in the deep-delvèd earth,
Tasting of Flora° and the country green,
    Dance, and Provençal° song, and sunburnt mirth!
O for a beaker full of the warm South,   15
    Full of the true, the blushful Hippocrene,°
        With beaded bubbles winking at the brim,
           And purple-stainèd mouth;
That I might drink, and leave the world unseen,
    And with thee fade away into the forest dim: 20

3

Fade far away, dissolve, and quite forget
    What thou among the leaves hast never known,
The weariness, the fever, and the fret
    Here, where men sit and hear each other groan;
Where palsy shakes a few, sad, last gray hairs,   25
    Where youth grows pale, and specter-thin, and dies;
        Where but to think is to be full of sorrow
           And leaden-eyed despairs,
Where Beauty cannot keep her lustrous eyes,
    Or new Love pine at them beyond tomorrow.   30

2 **hemlock** a deadly poison   4 **Lethe-wards** toward the waters of forgetfulness   7 **Dryad** tree
nymph   13 **Flora** Roman goddess of spring   14 **Provençal** of Provence, in South of France
16 **Hippocrene** fountain of the Muses

4

Away! away! for I will fly to thee,
　　Not charioted by Bacchus° and his pards,°
But on the viewless wings of Poesy,°
　　Though the dull brain perplexes and retards:
Already with thee! tender is the night,　　　　　　　　　　35
　　And haply the Queen-Moon is on her throne,
　　　　Clustered around by all her starry Fays;°
　　　　　　But here there is no light,
Save what from heaven is with the breezes blown
　　　　Through verdurous glooms and winding mossy ways.　40

5

I cannot see what flowers are at my feet,
　　Nor what soft incense hangs upon the boughs,
But, in embalmèd darkness, guess each sweet
　　Wherewith the seasonable month endows
The grass, the thicket, and the fruit-tree wild;　　　　　　45
　　White hawthorn, and the pastoral eglantine;
　　　　Fast fading violets covered up in leaves;
　　　　　　And mid-May's eldest child,
The coming musk-rose, full of dewy wine,
　　　　The murmurous haunt of flies on summer eves.　　50

6

Darkling° I listen; and for many a time
　　I have been half in love with easeful Death,
Called him soft names in many a musèd rhyme,
　　To take into the air my quiet breath;
Now more than ever seems it rich to die,　　　　　　　55
　　To cease upon the midnight with no pain,
　　　　While thou art pouring forth thy soul abroad
　　　　　　In such an ecstasy!
Still wouldst thou sing, and I have ears in vain—
　　　　To thy high requiem become a sod.　　　　　60

32 **Bacchus** Roman god of wine　**pards** leopards　33 **Poesy** poetry　37 **Fays** fairies　51 **Darkling** in the dark

7

Thou wast not born for death, immortal Bird!
    No hungry generations tread thee down;
The voice I hear this passing night was heard
    In ancient days by emperor and clown;
Perhaps the selfsame song that found a path   65
      Through the sad heart of Ruth, when, sick for home,
        She stood in tears amid the alien corn;°
            The same that ofttimes hath
      Charmed magic casements, opening on the foam
      Of perilous seas, in faery lands forlorn.   70

8

Forlorn! the very word is like a bell
    To toll me back from thee to my sole self!
Adieu! the fancy cannot cheat so well
    As she is famed to do, deceiving elf.
Adieu! adieu! thy plaintive anthem fades   75
      Past the near meadows, over the still stream,
        Up the hill side; and now 'tis buried deep
            In the next valley-glades:
    Was it a vision, or a waking dream?
      Fled is that music:—Do I wake or sleep?   80

—1819

On First Looking into Chapman's Homer°

Much have I traveled in the realms of gold,
    And many goodly states and kingdoms seen;
    Round many western islands have I been
Which bards in fealty to Apollo° hold.
Oft of one wide expanse had I been told   5
    That deep-browed Homer ruled as his demesne;
    Yet did I never breathe its pure serene

66–67 **Ruth . . . alien corn** in the Old Testament she is a Moabite working in the grain fields of Boaz in Judah

Chapman's Homer translation of the *Iliad* and *Odyssey* by George Chapman (1559–1634) **4 Apollo** here, the god of poetry

Till I heard Chapman speak out loud and bold:
Then felt I like some watcher of the skies
    When a new planet swims into his ken;   10
Or like stout Cortez° when with eagle eyes
    He stared at the Pacific—and all his men
Looked at each other with a wild surmise—
    Silent, upon a peak in Darien.°

—*1816*

ELIZABETH BARRETT BROWNING ▪ (1806–1861)

Elizabeth Barrett Browning was already a famous poet when she met her husband-to-be, Robert Browning, who had been corresponding with her on literary matters. She originally published her famous sonnet sequence, written in the first years of her marriage, in the guise of a translation of Portuguese poems, perhaps to mask their personal revelations.

Sonnets from the Portuguese, 18

A I never gave a lock of hair away
B To a man, dearest, except this to thee,
B Which now upon my fingers thoughtfully,
A I ring out to the full brown length and say
A "Take it." My day of youth went yesterday;   5
B My hair no longer bounds to my foot's glee,
B Nor plant I it from rose or myrtle-tree,
A As girls do, any more: it only may
C Now shade on two pale cheeks the mark of tears,
D Taught drooping from the head that hangs aside   10
C Through sorrow's trick. I thought the funeral-shears
D Would take this first, but Love is justified,—
C Take it thou,—finding pure, from all those years,
D The kiss my mother left here when she died.

—*1845–46*

---

11 **Cortez** Balboa was actually the first European to see the Pacific   14 **Darien** in modern-day Panama

Sonnets from the Portuguese, 43

How do I love thee? Let me count the ways.
I love thee to the depth and breadth and height
My soul can reach, when feeling out of sight
For the ends of Being and ideal Grace.
I love thee to the level of everyday's   5
Most quiet need, by sun and candle-light.
I love thee freely, as men strive for Right;
I love thee purely, as they turn from Praise.
I love thee with the passion put to use
In my old griefs, and with my childhood's faith.   10
I love thee with a love I seemed to lose
With my lost saints—I love thee with the breath,
Smiles, tears, of all my life!—and, if God choose,
I shall but love thee better after death.

—1845–46

HENRY WADSWORTH LONGFELLOW ■ (1807–1882)

Henry Wadsworth Longfellow was by far the most prominent nineteenth-century American poet, and his international fame led to his bust being placed in Westminster Abbey after his death. The long epic poems like Evangeline *and* Hiawatha *that were immensely popular among contemporary readers are seldom read today, but his shorter poems reveal a level of craftsmanship that few poets have equaled.*

The Arsenal at Springfield

This is the Arsenal. From floor to ceiling,
    Like a huge organ, rise the burnished arms;
But from their silent pipes no anthem pealing
    Startles the villages with strange alarms.

Ah! what a sound will rise, how wild and dreary,   5
    When the death-angel touches those swift keys!
What loud lament and dismal Miserere°
    Will mingle with their awful symphonies!

7 **Miserere** Latin hymn from Psalm 1: "Have mercy on me, Lord."

I hear even now the infinite fierce chorus,
    The cries of agony, the endless groan,   10
Which, through the ages that have gone before us,
    In long reverberations reach our own.

On helm and harness rings the Saxon hammer,
    Through Cimbric° forest roars the Norseman's song,
And loud, amid the universal clamor,   15
    O'er distant deserts sounds the Tartar gong.

I hear the Florentine, who from his palace
    Wheels out his battle-bell with dreadful din,
And Aztec priests upon their teocallis°
    Beat the wild war-drums made of serpent's skin;   20

The tumult of each sacked and burning village;
    The shout that every prayer for mercy drowns;
The soldiers' revels in the midst of pillage;
    The wail of famine in beleaguered towns;

The bursting shell, the gateway wrenched asunder,   25
    The rattling musketry, the clashing blade;
And ever and anon, in tones of thunder
    The diapason° of the cannonade.

Is it, O man, with such discordant noises,
    With such accursed instruments as these,   30
Thou drownest Nature's sweet and kindly voices,
    And jarrest the celestial harmonies?

Were half the power, that fills the world with terror,
    Were half the wealth bestowed on camps and courts,
Given to redeem the human mind from error,   35
    There were no need of arsenals or forts:

The warrior's name would be a name abhorred!
    And every nation, that should lift again
Its hand against a brother, on its forehead
    Would wear forevermore the curse of Cain!   40

---

14 Cimbric in Denmark   **19 teocallis** temples atop pyramids   **28 diapason** full range of pipe organ

Down the dark future, through long generations,
    The echoing sounds grow fainter and then cease;
And like a bell, with solemn, sweet vibrations,
    I hear once more the voice of Christ say, "Peace!"
Peace! and no longer from its brazen portals   45
    The blast of War's great organ shakes the skies!
But beautiful as songs of the immortals,
    The holy melodies of love arise.

            —1846

The Cross of Snow

In the long, sleepless watches of the night,
    A gentle face—the face of one long dead—
    Looks at me from the wall, where round its head
    The night-lamp casts a halo of pale light.
Here in this room she died; and soul more white   5
    Never through martyrdom of fire° was led
    To its repose; nor can in books be read
    The legend of a life more benedight.°
There is a mountain in the distant West
    That, sun-defying, in its deep ravines   10
    Displays a cross of snow upon its side.
Such is the cross I wear upon my breast
    These eighteen years, through all the changing scenes
    And seasons, changeless since the day she died.

            —1886

EDGAR ALLAN POE ■ (1809–1849)

*Edgar Allan Poe has survived his own myth as a deranged, drug-crazed ge-
nius, despite the wealth of evidence to the contrary that can be gleaned from
his brilliant, though erratic, career as a poet, short-story writer, critic, and editor. Poe's brand of romanticism seems at odds with that of other American
poets of his day, and is perhaps more in keeping with the spirit of Coleridge
than that of Wordsworth. "The Raven" has been parodied perhaps more than
any other American poem, yet it still retains a powerful hold on its audience.*

6 martyrdom of fire Longfellow's second wife, Frances, died as the result of a household fire
in 1861. **8 benedight** blessed

The Haunted Palace

In the greenest of our valleys,
   By good angels tenanted,
Once a fair and stately palace—
   Radiant palace—reared its head.
In the monarch Thought's dominion—   5
   It stood there!
Never seraph spread a pinion
   Over fabric half so fair!

Banners yellow, glorious, golden,
   On its roof did float and flow,   10
(This—all this—was in the olden
   Time long ago,)
And every gentle air that dallied,
   In that sweet day,
Along the ramparts plumed and pallid,   15
   A wingéd odor went away.

Wanderers in that happy valley,
   Through two luminous windows, saw
Spirits moving musically
   To a lute's well-tunéd law,   20
Round about a throne where, sitting,
   Porphyrogene!°
In state his glory well befitting,
   The ruler of the realm was seen.

And all with pearl and ruby glowing   25
   Was the fair palace door,
Through which came flowing, flowing, flowing,
   And sparkling evermore,
A troop of Echoes, whose sweet duty
   Was but to sing,   30
In voices of surpassing beauty,
   The wit and wisdom of their king.

EDGAR ALLAN POE

130

22 **Porphyrogene** born to the purple, i.e., royal

But evil things, in robes of sorrow,
    Assailed the monarch's high estate.
(Ah, let us mourn!—for never morrow   35
    Shall dawn upon him, desolate!)
And round about his home the glory
    That blushed and bloomed,
Is but a dim-remembered story
    Of the old time entombed.   40

and travellers, now, within that valley,
    Through the red-litten windows see
Vast forms that move fantastically
    To a discordant melody,
While, like a ghastly rapid river,   45
    Through the pale door
A hideous throng rush out forever,
    And laugh—but smile no more.

—1845

The Raven

Once upon a midnight dreary, while I pondered, weak
    and weary,
Over many a quaint and curious volume of forgotten lore—
While I nodded, nearly napping, suddenly there came a tapping,
As of some one gently rapping, rapping at my chamber door.
"'Tis some visitor," I muttered, "tapping at my chamber door—   5
    Only this and nothing more."

Ah, distinctly I remember it was in the bleak December;
And each separate dying ember wrought its ghost upon
    the floor.
Eagerly I wished the morrow;—vainly I had sought to borrow
From my books surcease of sorrow—sorrow for the
    lost Lenore—   10
For the rare and radiant maiden whom the angels name
    Lenore—
                Nameless *here* for evermore.
And the silken, sad, uncertain rustling of each purple curtain
Thrilled me—filled me with fantastic terrors never felt before;

So that now, to still the beating of my heart, I stood repeating   15
"'Tis some visitor entreating entrance at my chamber door;—
Some late visitor entreating entrance at my chamber door;—
     This it is and nothing more."

Presently my soul grew stronger; hesitating then no longer,
"Sir," said I, "or Madam, truly your forgiveness I implore;   20
But the fact is I was napping, and so gently you came rapping,
And so faintly you came tapping, tapping at my chamber door,
That I scarce was sure I heard you"—here I opened wide the
  door;—
     Darkness there and nothing more.

Deep into that darkness peering, long I stood there wondering,
  fearing,   25
Doubting, dreaming dreams no mortal ever dared to dream
  before;
But the silence was unbroken, and the stillness gave no token,
And the only word there spoken was the whispered word,
  "Lenore?"
This I whispered, and an echo murmured back the word,
  "Lenore!"
     Merely this and nothing more.   30

Back into the chamber turning, all my soul within me burning,
Soon again I heard a tapping somewhat louder than before.
"Surely," said I, "surely that is something at my window lattice;
Let me see, then, what thereat is, and this mystery explore—
Let my heart be still a moment and this mystery explore;—   35
     'Tis the wind and nothing more!"

Open here I flung the shutter, when, with many a flirt and flutter,
In there stepped a stately Raven of the saintly days of yore;
Not the least obeisance made he; not a minute stopped or
  stayed he;
But, with mien of lord or lady, perched above my chamber
  door—   40
Perched upon a bust of Pallas° just above my chamber door—
    Perched, and sat, and nothing more.

41 **Pallas** Athena, goddess of wisdom

Then this ebony bird beguiling my sad fancy into smiling,
By the grave and stern decorum of the countenance it wore,
"Though thy crest be shorn and shaven, thou," I said, "art sure
    no craven,   45
Ghastly grim and ancient Raven wandering from the Nightly
    shore—
Tell me what thy lordly name is on the Night's Plutonian° shore!"
             Quoth the Raven, "Nevermore."

Much I marvelled this ungainly fowl to hear discourse so plainly,
Though its answer little meaning—little relevancy bore;   50
For we cannot help agreeing that no living human being
Ever yet was blessed with seeing bird above his chamber door—
Bird or beast upon the sculptured bust above his chamber door,
             With such name as "Nevermore."

But the Raven, sitting lonely on the placid bust, spoke only   55
That one word, as if his soul in that one word he did outpour.
Nothing farther then he uttered—not a feather then he
    fluttered—
Till I scarcely more than muttered, "Other friends have flown
    before—
On the morrow *he* will leave me, as my Hopes have flown before."
            Then the bird said, "Nevermore."   60

Startled at the stillness broken by reply so aptly spoken,
"Doubtless," said I, "what it utters is its only stock and store
Caught from some unhappy master whom unmerciful Disaster
Followed fast and followed faster till his songs one burden bore—
Till the dirges of his Hope that melancholy burden bore   65
            Of 'Never—nevermore.'"

But the Raven still beguiling all my sad fancy into smiling,
Straight I wheeled a cushioned seat in front of bird and bust
    and door;
Then, upon the velvet sinking, I betook myself to linking
Fancy unto fancy, thinking what this ominous bird of yore—   70
What this grim, ungainly, ghastly, gaunt, and ominous bird of yore
            Meant in croaking "Nevermore."

THE RAVEN

47 Plutonian after Pluto, Roman god of the underworld

This I sat engaged in guessing, but no syllable expressing
To the fowl whose fiery eyes now burned into my bosom's core;
This and more I sat divining, with my head at ease reclining   75
On the cushion's velvet lining that the lamp-light gloated o'er,
But whose velvet-violet lining with the lamp-light gloating o'er,
     She shall press, ah, nevermore!

Then, methought, the air grew denser, perfumed from an
  unseen censer
Swung by seraphim whose foot-falls tinkled on the tufted floor.   80
"Wretch," I cried, "thy God hath lent thee—by these angels he
  hath sent thee.
Respite—respite and nepenthe° from thy memories of
  Lenore;
Quaff, oh quaff this kind nepenthe and forget this lost
  Lenore!"
     Quoth the Raven, "Nevermore."

"Prophet!" said I, "thing of evil!—prophet still, if bird or
  devil!—   85
Whether Tempter sent, or whether tempest tossed thee here
  ashore,
Desolate yet all undaunted, on this desert land enchanted—
On this home by Horror haunted—tell me truly, I implore—
Is there—*is* there balm in Gilead?—tell me—tell me, I implore!"
     Quoth the Raven, "Nevermore."   90

"Prophet!" said I, "thing of evil!—prophet still, if bird or devil!
By that Heaven that bends above us—by that God we both
  adore—
Tell this soul with sorrow laden if, within the distant Aidenn,°
It shall clasp a sainted maiden whom the angels name
  Lenore—
Clasp a rare and radiant maiden whom the angels name
  Lenore."   95
     Quoth the Raven, "Nevermore."

"Be that word our sign of parting, bird or fiend!" I shrieked,
  upstarting—

"Get thee back into the tempest and the Night's Plutonian shore!
Leave no black plume as a token of that lie thy soul hath
    spoken!
Leave my loneliness unbroken!—quit the bust above my
    door!   100
Take thy beak from out my heart, and take thy form from off
    my door!"
                    Quoth the Raven, "Nevermore."

And the Raven, never flitting, still is sitting, *still* is sitting
On the pallid bust of Pallas just above my chamber door;
And his eyes have all the seeming of a demon's that is
    dreaming,   105
And the lamp-light o'er him streaming throws his shadow on
    the floor;
And my soul from out that shadow that lies floating on the floor
                    Shall be lifted—nevermore!

                                                —1845

Sonnet: To Science

Science! true daughter of Old Time thou art!
    Who alterest all things with the peering eyes.
Why preyest thou thus upon the poet's heart,
    Vulture, whose wings are dull realities?
How should he love thee? or how deem thee wise?   5
    Who wouldst not leave him in his wandering
To seek for treasure in the jeweled skies,
    Albeit he soared with an undaunted wing?
Has thou not dragged Diana° from her car?
    And driven the Hamadryad from the wood   10
To seek a shelter in some happier star?
    Hast thou not torn the Naiad from her flood,
The Elfin from the green grass, and from me
    The summer dream beneath the tamarind tree?

                                        —1829, 1845

9 **Diana** Roman goddess, whose chariot was the moon.

Alfred, Lord Tennyson became the most famous English poet with the 1850 publication of In Memoriam, *a sequence of poems on the death of his friend A. H. Hallam. In the same year he became poet laureate. Modern critical opinion has focused more favorably on Tennyson's lyrical gifts than on his talents for narrative or drama. T. S. Eliot and W. H. Auden, among other critics, praised Tennyson's rhythms and sound patterns but had reservations about his depth of intellect, especially when he took on the role of official apologist for Victorian England.*

The Eagle

FRAGMENT

> He clasps the crag with crooked hands;
> Close to the sun in lonely lands,
> Ringed with the azure world, he stands.
>
> The wrinkled sea beneath him crawls;
> He watches from his mountain walls,   5
> And like a thunderbolt he falls.

—1851

The Lady of Shalott

Part I

> On either side the river lie
> Long fields of barley and of rye,
> That clothe the wold° and meet the sky;
> And through the field the road runs by
>   To many-towered Camelot;   5
> And up and down the people go,
> Gazing where the lilies blow
> Round an island there below,
>   The island of Shalott.

3 wold plain

Willows whiten, aspens quiver,   10
Little breezes dusk and shiver
Through the wave that runs forever
By the island in the river
      Flowing down to Camelot.
Four gray walls, and four gray towers,   15
Overlook a space of flowers,
And the silent isle embowers
      The Lady of Shalott.

By the margin, willow-veiled,
Slide the heavy barges trailed   20
By slow horses; and unhailed
The shallop° flitteth silken-sailed
      Skimming down to Camelot:
But who hath seen her wave her hand?
Or at the casement seen her stand?   25
Or is she known in all the land,
      The Lady of Shalott?

Only reapers, reaping early
In among the bearded barley,
Hear a song that echoes cheerly   30
From the river winding clearly,
      Down to towered Camelot;
And by the moon the reaper weary,
Piling sheaves in uplands airy,
Listening, whispers, "'Tis the fairy   35
      Lady of Shalott."

Part II

There she weaves by night and day
A magic web with colors gay.
She has heard a whisper say,
A curse is on her if she stay   40
      To look down to Camelot.

22 **shallop** open boat

She knows not what the curse may be,
And so she weaveth steadily,
And little other care hath she,
      The Lady of Shalott.   45

And moving through a mirror clear
That hangs before her all the year,
Shadows of the world appear.
There she sees the highway near
      Winding down to Camelot;   50
There the river eddy whirls,
And there the surly village-churls,
And the red cloaks of market girls,
      Pass onward from Shalott.

Sometimes a troop of damsels glad,   55
An abbot on an ambling pad,°
Sometimes a curly shepherd-lad,
Or long-haired page in crimson clad,
      Goes by to towered Camelot;
And sometimes through the mirror blue   60
The knights come riding two and two;
She hath no loyal knight and true,
      The Lady of Shalott.

But in her web she still delights
To weave the mirror's magic sights,   65
For often through the silent nights
A funeral, with plumes and lights
      And music, went to Camelot;
Or when the moon was overhead,
Came two young lovers lately wed;   70
"I am half sick of shadows," said
      The Lady of Shalott.

56 pad horse

Part III

A bow-shot from her bower eaves,
He rode between the barley sheaves;
The sun came dazzling through the leaves,   75
And flamed upon the brazen greaves°
    Of bold Sir Lancelot.
A red-cross knight forever kneeled
To a lady in his shield.
That sparkled on the yellow field,   80
    Beside remote Shalott.

The gemmy bridle glittered free,
Like to some branch of stars we see
Hung in the golden Galaxy.
The bridle bells rang merrily   85
    As he rode down to Camelot;
And from his blazoned baldric° slung
A mighty silver bugle hung,
And as he rode his armor rung,
    Beside remote Shalott.   90

All in the blue unclouded weather
Thick-jeweled shone the saddle-leather,
The helmet and the helmet-feather
Burned like one burning flame together
    As he rode down to Camelot;   95
As often through the purple night,
Below the starry clusters bright,
Some bearded meteor, trailing light,
    Moves over still Shalott.

His broad clear brow in sunlight glowed;   100
On burnished hooves his war horse trode;
From underneath his helmet flowed
His coal-black curls as on he rode,
    As he rode down to Camelot.
From the bank and from the river   105
He flashed into the crystal mirror,
"Tirra lirra," by the river
    Sang Sir Lancelot.

76 greaves armor for legs   **87 baldric** belt to support a sword

She left the web, she left the loom,
She made three paces through the room, 110
She saw the water lily bloom,
She saw the helmet and the plume,
    She looked down to Camelot.
Out flew the web and floated wide;
The mirror cracked from side to side; 115
"The curse is come upon me," cried
    The Lady of Shalott.

Part IV

ALFRED, LORD TENNYSON

140

In the stormy east wind straining,
The pale yellow woods were waning,
The broad stream in his banks complaining. 120
Heavily the low sky raining
    Over towered Camelot;
Down she came and found a boat
Beneath a willow left afloat,
And round about the prow she wrote 125
    The Lady of Shalott.

And down the river's dim expanse
Like some bold seer in a trance,
Seeing all his own mischance—
With a glassy countenance 130
    Did she look to Camelot.
And at the closing of the day
She loosed the chain, and down she lay;
The broad stream bore her far away,
    The Lady of Shalott. 135

Lying, robed in snowy white
That loosely flew to left and right—
The leaves upon her falling light—
Through the noises of the night
    She floated down to Camelot; 140
And as the boat-head wound along
The willowy hills and fields among,
They heard her singing her last song,
    The Lady of Shalott.

Heard a carol, mournful, holy,   145
Chanted loudly, chanted lowly,
Till her blood was frozen slowly,
And her eyes were darkened wholly,
    Turned to towered Camelot.
For ere she reached upon the tide   150
The first house by the waterside,
Singing in her song she died,
    The Lady of Shalott.

Under tower and balcony,
By garden wall and gallery,   155
A gleaming shape she floated by,
Dead-pale between the houses high,
    Silent into Camelot.
Out upon the wharfs they came,
Knight and burgher, lord and dame,   160
And round the prow they read her name,
    The Lady of Shalott.

Who is this? And what is here?
And in the lighted palace near
Died the sound of royal cheer;   165
And they crossed themselves for fear,
    All the knights at Camelot.
But Lancelot mused a little space;
He said, "She has a lovely face;
God in his mercy lend her grace,   170
    The Lady of Shalott."

                                            —1842

Tears, Idle Tears

from The Princess

    Tears, idle tears, I know not what they mean,
    Tears from the depth of some divine despair
    Rise in the heart, and gather to the eyes,
    In looking on the happy autumn-fields,
    And thinking of the days that are no more.   5

Fresh as the first beam glittering on a sail,
That brings our friends up from the underworld,
Sad as the last which reddens over one
That sinks with all we love below the verge;
So sad, so fresh, the days that are no more.　　　　　10

Ah, sad and strange as in dark summer dawns
The earliest pipe of half-awakened birds
To dying ears, when unto dying eyes
The casement slowly grows a glimmering square;
So sad, so strange, the days that are no more.　　　　15

Dear as remembered kisses after death,
And sweet as those by hopeless fancy feigned
On lips that are for others; deep as love,
Deep as first love, and wild with all regret;
O Death in Life, the days that are no more!　　　　　20

　　　　　　　　　　　　　　　　　　　　　　　　—1847

ALFRED, LORD TENNYSON

142

Ulysses°

It little profits that an idle king,
By this still hearth, among these barren crags,
Matched with an aged wife, I mete and dole
Unequal laws unto a savage race,
That hoard, and sleep, and feed, and know not me.　　　5
I cannot rest from travel; I will drink
Life to the lees. All times I have enjoyed
Greatly, have suffered greatly, both with those
That loved me, and alone; on shore, and when
Through scudding drifts the rainy Hyades°　　　　　10
Vexed the dim sea. I am become a name;
For always roaming with a hungry heart
Much have I seen and known—cities of men
And manners, climates, councils, governments,
Myself not least, but honored of them all—　　　　15
And drunk delight of battle with my peers,
Far on the ringing plains of windy Troy.

Ulysses Homer's *Odyssey* ends with the return of Odysseus (Ulysses) to his island kingdom, Ithaca.
Tennyson's poem takes place some years later.　**10 Hyades** a constellation thought to predict rain

I am a part of all that I have met;
Yet all experience is an arch wherethrough
Gleams that untraveled world whose margin fades   20
For ever and for ever when I move.
How dull it is to pause, to make an end,
To rust unburnished, not to shine in use!
As though to breathe were life! Life piled on life
Were all too little, and of one to me   25
Little remains; but every hour is saved
From that eternal silence, something more,
A bringer of new things; and vile it were
For some three suns to store and hoard myself,
And this gray spirit yearning in desire   30
To follow knowledge like a sinking star,
Beyond the utmost bound of human thought.

　　This is my son, mine own Telemachus,
To whom I leave the scepter and the isle,
Well-loved of me, discerning to fulfill   35
This labor, by slow prudence to make mild
A rugged people, and through soft degrees
Subdue them to the useful and the good.
Most blameless is he, centered in the sphere
Of common duties, decent not to fail   40
In offices of tenderness, and pay
Meet adoration to my household gods,
When I am gone. He works his work, I mine.

　　There lies the port; the vessel puffs her sail;
There gloom the dark, broad seas. My mariners,   45
Souls that have toiled, and wrought, and thought with me,
That ever with a frolic welcome took
The thunder and the sunshine, and opposed
Free hearts, free foreheads—you and I are old;
Old age hath yet his honor and his toil.   50
Death closes all; but something ere the end,
Some work of noble note, may yet be done,
Not unbecoming men that strove with gods.
The lights begin to twinkle from the rocks;
The long day wanes; the low moon climbs; the deep   55
Moans round with many voices. Come, my friends,

'Tis not too late to seek a newer world.
Push off, and sitting well in order smite
The sounding furrows; for my purpose holds
To sail beyond the sunset, and the baths   60
Of all the western stars, until I die.
It may be that the gulfs will wash us down;
It may be we shall touch the Happy Isles,°
And see the great Achilles, whom we knew.
Though much is taken, much abides; and though   65
We are not now that strength which in old days
Moved earth and heaven, that which we are, we are,
One equal temper of heroic hearts,
Made weak by time and fate, but strong in will
To strive, to seek, to find, and not to yield.   70

—1833

ROBERT BROWNING ■ (1812–1889)

Robert Browning wrote many successful dramatic monologues that are his lasting legacy, for he brings the genre to a level of achievement rarely equaled. Less regarded during his lifetime than his contemporary Tennyson, he has consistently risen in the esteem of modern readers. Often overlooked in his gallery of often grotesque characters are his considerable metrical skills and ability to simulate speech while working in demanding poetic forms.

My Last Duchess

FERRARA°

That's my last duchess painted on the wall,
Looking as if she were alive. I call
That piece a wonder, now: Frà Pandolf's° hands
Worked busily a day, and there she stands.
Will't please you sit and look at her? I said   5
"Frà Pandolf" by design, for never read
Strangers like you that pictured countenance,

63 **Happy Isles** Elysium, the resting place of dead heroes
Ferrara The speaker is probably Alfonso II d'Este, Duke of Ferrara (1533–158?)   **3 Frà Pandolf** an imaginary painter

The depth and passion of its earnest glance,
But to myself they turned (since none puts by
The curtain I have drawn for you, but I)   10
And seemed as they would ask me, if they durst,
How such a glance came there; so, not the first
Are you to turn and ask thus. Sir, 'twas not
Her husband's presence only, called that spot
Of joy into the Duchess' cheek: perhaps   15
Frà Pandolf chanced to say "Her mantle laps
Over my lady's wrist too much," or "Paint
Must never hope to reproduce the faint
Half-flush that dies along her throat": such stuff
Was courtesy, she thought, and cause enough   20
For calling up that spot of joy. She had
A heart—how shall I say?—too soon made glad,
Too easily impressed; she liked whate'er
She looked on, and her looks went everywhere.
Sir, 'twas all one! My favor at her breast,   25
The dropping of the daylight in the West,
The bough of cherries some officious fool
Broke in the orchard for her, the white mule
She rode with round the terrace—all and each
Would draw from her alike the approving speech,   30
Or blush, at least. She thanked men—good! but thanked
Somehow—I know not how—as if she ranked
My gift of a nine-hundred-years-old name
With anybody's gift. Who'd stoop to blame
This sort of trifling? Even had you skill   35
In speech—which I have not—to make your will
Quite clear to such an one, and say, "Just this
Or that in you disgusts me; here you miss,
Or there exceed the mark"—and if she let
Herself be lessoned so, nor plainly set   40
Her wits to yours, forsooth, and made excuse,
—E'en then would be some stooping; and I choose
Never to stoop. Oh sir, she smiled, no doubt,
Whene'er I passed her; but who passed without
Much the same smile? This grew; I gave commands;   45
Then all smiles stopped together. There she stands

As if alive. Will't please you rise? We'll meet
The company below, then. I repeat,
The Count your master's° known munificence
Is ample warrant that no just pretense
Of mine for dowry will be disallowed;   50
Though his fair daughter's self, as I avowed
At starting, is my object. Nay, we'll go
Together down, sir. Notice Neptune, though,
Taming a sea horse, thought a rarity,   55
Which Claus of Innsbruck cast in bronze for me!

—1842

Porphyria's° Lover

ROBERT BROWNING

The rain set early in tonight,
    The sullen wind was soon awake,
It tore the elm-tops down for spite,
    And did its worst to vex the lake:
        I listened with heart fit to break.   5
When glided in Porphyria; straight
    She shut the cold out and the storm,
And kneeled and made the cheerless grate
    Blaze up, and all the cottage warm;
        Which done, she rose, and from her form   10
Withdrew the dripping cloak and shawl,
    And laid her soiled gloves by, untied
Her hat and let the damp hair fall,
    And, last, she sat down by my side
        And called me. When no voice replied,   15
She put my arm about her waist,
    And made her smooth white shoulder bare,
And all her yellow hair displaced,
    And, stooping, made my cheek lie there,
        And spread, o'er all, her yellow hair,   20
Murmuring how she loved me—she
    Too weak, for all her heart's endeavor,

---

49 Count your master's The auditor is apparently an envoy sent to arrange a marriage between the
Duke of Ferrara and a count's daughter
Porphyria name suggesting purple, the color of nobility and royalty

To set its struggling passion free
        From pride, and vainer ties dissever,
        And give herself to me forever.   25
But passion sometimes would prevail,
        Nor could tonight's gay feast restrain
A sudden thought of one so pale
        For love of her, and all in vain:
        So, she was come through wind and rain.   30
Be sure I looked up at her eyes
        Happy and proud; at last I knew
Porphyria worshipped me; surprise
        Made my heart swell, and still it grew
        While I debated what to do.   35
That moment she was mine, mine, fair,
        Perfectly pure and good: I found
A thing to do, and all her hair
        In one long yellow string I wound
        Three times her little throat around,   40
And strangled her. No pain felt she;
        I am quite sure she felt no pain.
As a shut bud that holds a bee,
        I warily oped her lids: again
        Laughed the blue eyes without a stain.   45
And I untightened next the tress
        About her neck; her cheek once more
Blushed bright beneath my burning kiss:
        I propped her head up as before,
        Only, this time my shoulder bore   50
Her head, which droops upon it still:
        The smiling rosy little head
So glad it has its utmost will,
        That all it scorned at once is fled,
        And I, its love, am gained instead!   55
Porphyria's love: she guessed not how
        Her darling one wish would be heard.
And thus we sit together now,
        And all night long we have not stirred,
        And yet God has not said a word!   60

—1842

Walt Whitman pioneered the use of free verse, which established him as one of the forebears of modern poetry, but his subject matter, often dealing with sexual topics, and his unsparing realism were equally controversial in his day. An admirer of Emerson, he adapted many of the ideas of transcendentalism in Song of Myself, his first major sequence, and also incorporated many of Emerson's calls for poets to use American subjects and patterns of speech. Leaves of Grass, which he revised from 1855 until his death, expanded to include virtually all of his poems, including the graphic poems he wrote while serving as a volunteer in Civil War army hospitals.

point of view is first person   *connection*   *subjects*

A Noiseless Patient Spider

A noiseless patient spider,   *subject*   *the soul : a shift in*
I mark'd where on a little promontory it stood isolated,
Mark'd how to explore the vacant vast surrounding,
It launch'd forth filament, filament, filament, out of itself,
Ever unreeling them, ever tirelessly speeding them.   5

And you O my soul where you stand,   *metaphor*
Surrounded, detached, in measureless oceans of space,
Ceaselessly musing, venturing, throwing, seeking the spheres to
     connect them,   *antecedent*
Till the bridge you will need be form'd, till the ductile anchor
     hold,
Till the gossamer thread you fling catch somewhere, O my soul.   10
                                                vocative
                                                          —1876

O Captain! My Captain!°

1

O Captain! my Captain! our fearful trip is done;
The ship has weather'd every rack, the prize we sought is won;
The port is near, the bells I hear, the people all exulting,

O Captain! My Captain! This atypical ballad was written after the assassination of Abraham Lincoln and ironically became Whitman's most popular poem during his lifetime.

WALT WHITMAN

While follow eyes the steady keel, the vessel grim and daring:
   But O heart! heart! heart!   5
      O the bleeding drops of red,
         Where on the deck my Captain lies,
            Fallen cold and dead.

   2

O Captain! my Captain! rise up and hear the bells;
Rise up—for you the flag is flung—for you the bugle trills;   10
For you bouquets and ribbon'd wreaths—for you the shores
    a-crowding;
For you they call, the swaying mass, their eager faces turning;
   Here Captain! dear father!
      This arm beneath your head;
        It is some dream that on the deck,   15
          You've fallen cold and dead.

   3

My Captain does not answer, his lips are pale and still;
My father does not feel my arm, he has no pulse nor will;
The ship is anchor'd safe and sound, its voyage closed and done;
From fearful trip, the victor ship, comes in with object won;   20
   Exult, O shores, and ring, O bells!
     But I, with mournful tread,
       Walk the deck my Captain lies,
         Fallen cold and dead.

                  —1865

A Sight in Camp in the Daybreak Gray and Dim

A sight in camp in the daybreak gray and dim,
As from my tent I emerge so early sleepless,
As slow I walk in the cool fresh air the path near by the hospital tent,
Three forms I see on stretchers lying, brought out there untended
    lying,
Over each the blanket spread, ample brownish woolen blanket,   5
Gray and heavy blanket, folding, covering all.

Curious I halt and silent stand,
Then with light fingers I from the face of the nearest the first
    just lift the blanket;
Who are you elderly man so gaunt and grim, with well-gray'd
    hair, and flesh all sunken about the eyes?
Who are you my dear comrade?   10

Then to the second I step—and who are you my child and
    darling?
Who are you sweet boy with cheeks yet blooming?

Then to the third—a face nor child nor old, very calm, as of
    beautiful yellow-white ivory;
Young man I think I know you—I think this face is the face
    of the Christ himself,
Dead and divine and brother of all, and here again he lies.

                                          —1865

Song of Myself,° 1

I celebrate myself, and sing myself,
And what I assume you shall assume,
For every atom belonging to me as good belongs to you.

I loafe and invite my soul,
I lean and loafe at my ease observing a spear of summer grass.   5
My tongue, every atom of my blood, form'd from this soil, this air,

Born here of parents born here from parents the same, and
    their parents the same,
I, now thirty-seven years old in perfect health begin,
Hoping to cease not till death.

Creeds and schools in abeyance,   10
Retiring back a while sufficed at what they are, but never
    forgotten,
I harbor for good or bad, I permit to speak at every hazard,
Nature without check with original energy.

                                          —1855

Song of Myself Whitman originally published "Song of Myself" in 1855 in *Leaves of Grass* and revised it throughout his life. These excerpts are taken from the "deathbed edition" of 1891.

Song of Myself, 5

I believe in you my soul, the other I am must not abase itself
    to you,
And you must not be abased to the other.

Loafe with me on the grass, loose the stop from your throat,
Not words, not music or rhyme I want, not custom or lecture, not
    even the best,
Only the lull I like, the hum of your valvèd voice.   5

I mind how once we lay such a transparent summer morning,
How you settled your head athwart my hips and gently turn'd
    over upon me,
And parted the shirt from my bosom-bone, and plunged your
    tongue to my bare-stript heart,
And reach'd till you felt my beard, and reach'd till you held my
    feet.

Swiftly arose and spread around me the peace and knowledge
    that pass all the argument of the earth,   10
And I know that the hand of God is the promise of my own,
And I know that the spirit of God is the brother of my own,
And that all the men ever born are also my brothers, and the
    women my sisters and lovers,
And that a kelson° of the creation is love,
And limitless are leaves stiff or drooping in the fields,   15
And brown ants in the little wells beneath them,
And mossy scabs of the worm fence, heap'd stones, elder, mullein
    and poke-weed.

                                                              —1855

Song of Myself, 6

A child said What is the grass? fetching it to me with full hands;
How could I answer the child? I do not know what it is any
    more than he.

I guess it must be the flag of my disposition, out of hopeful
    green stuff woven.

14 **kelson** variant of keelson, a beam fastened to the keel of a ship for additional support

Or I guess it is the handkerchief of the Lord,
A scented gift and remembrancer designedly dropped,   5
Bearing the owner's name someway in the corners, that we may
    see and remark, and say *Whose?*

Or I guess the grass is itself a child, the produced babe of
the vegetation.

Or I guess it is a uniform hieroglyphic,
And it means, Sprouting alike in broad zones and narrow zones,
Growing among black folks as among white,   10
Kanuck,° Tuckahoe,° Congressman, Cuff,° I give them the same, I
    receive them the same.

And now it seems to me the beautiful uncut hair of graves.

Tenderly will I use you curling grass,
It may be you transpire from the breasts of young men,
It may be if I had known them I would have loved them,   15
It may be you are from old people, or from offspring taken soon
    out of their mothers' laps,
And here you are the mothers' laps.

This grass is very dark to be from the white heads of old mothers.
Darker than the colorless beards of old men.
Dark to come from under the faint red roofs of mouths.   20

O I perceive after all so many uttering tongues,
And I perceive they do not come from the roofs of mouths for
    nothing.

I wish I could translate the hints about the dead young men and
    women,
And the hints about old men and mothers, and the offspring
    taken soon out of their laps.

What do you think has become of the young and old men?   25
And what do you think has become of the women and children?

They are alive and well somewhere,
The smallest sprout shows there is really no death,

11 **Kanuck** French-Canadian   **Tuckahoe** coastal Virginian   **Cuff** a black slave

And if ever there was it led forward life, and does not wait at the
    end to arrest it.
And ceased the moment life appeared.

All goes onward and outward, nothing collapses.
And to die is different from what anyone supposed, and
    luckier.

—1855

Song of Myself, 11

Twenty-eight young men bathe by the shore,
Twenty-eight young men and all so friendly;
Twenty-eight years of womanly life and all so lonesome.

She owns the fine house by the rise of the bank,
She hides handsome and richly drest aft the blinds of the
    window.   5

Which of the young men does she like the best?
Ah the homeliest of them is beautiful to her.

Where are you off to, lady? for I see you,
You splash in the water there, yet stay stock still in your
    room.

Dancing and laughing along the beach came the twenty-ninth
    bather,   10
The rest did not see her, but she saw them and loved them.

The beards of the young men glisten'd with wet, it ran from
    their long hair,
Little streams pass'd all over their bodies.

An unseen hand also pass'd over their bodies,
It descended trembling from their temples and ribs.   15

The young men float on their backs, their white bellies bulge to
    the sun, they do not ask who seizes fast to them,
They do not know who puffs and declines with pendant and
    bending arch,
They do not think whom they souse with spray.

—1855

Song of Myself, 21

I am the poet of the Body and I am the poet of the Soul,
The pleasures of heaven are with me and the pains of hell are
    with me,
The first I graft and increase upon myself, the latter I translate
    into a new tongue.

I am the poet of the woman the same as the man
And I say it is as great to be a woman as to be a man,   5
And I say there is nothing greater than the mother of men.

I chant the chant of dilation or pride,
We have had ducking and deprecating about enough,
I show that size is only development.

Have you outstript the rest? are you the President?   10
It is a trifle, they will more than arrive there every one, and still
    pass on.

I am he that walks with the tender and growing night,
I call to the earth and sea half-held by the night.

Press close bare-bosom'd night—press close magnetic nourishing
    night!
Night of south winds—night of the large few stars!   15
Still nodding night—mad naked summer night.

Smile O voluptuous cool-breath'd earth!
Earth of the slumbering and liquid trees!

Earth of departed sunset—earth of the mountains misty-topt!
Earth of the vitreous pour of the full moon just tinged with
    blue!   20

Earth of shine and dark mottling the tide of the river!
Earth of the limpid gray of clouds brighter and clearer for my
    sake!
Far-swooping elbow'd earth—rich apple-blossom'd earth!
Smile, for your lover comes.
Prodigal, you have given me love—therefore I to you give
    love!   25
O unspeakable passionate love.

—1855

Song of Myself, 32

I think I could turn and live with animals, they are so placid and
    self-contain'd,
I stand and look at them long and long.
They do not sweat and whine about their condition,
They do not lie awake in the dark and weep for their sins,
They do not make me sick discussing their duty to God,   5
Not one is dissatisfied, not one is demented with the mania of
    owning things,
Not one kneels to another, nor to his kind that lived thousands of
    years ago,
Not one is respectable or unhappy over the whole earth.
So they show their relations to me and I accept them,
They bring me tokens of myself, they evince them plainly in their
    possession.

I wonder where they get those tokens,
Did I pass that way huge times ago and negligently drop them?

Myself moving forward then and now and forever,
Gathering and showing more always and with velocity,
Infinite and omnigenous,° and the like of these among them,   15
Not too exclusive toward the reachers of my remembrancers,
Picking out here one that I love, and now go with him on
    brotherly terms.

A gigantic beauty of a stallion, fresh and responsive to my caresses,
Head high in the forehead, wide between the ears,
Limbs glossy and supple, tail dusting the ground,   20
Eyes full of sparkling wickedness, ears finely cut, flexibly moving.

His nostrils dilate as my heels embrace him,
His well-built limbs tremble with pleasure as we race around and
    return.

I but use you a minute, then I resign you, stallion,
Why do I need your paces when I myself out-gallop them?   25
Even as I stand or sit passing faster than you.

—*1855*

15 **omnigenous** consisting of all types or kinds

Song of Myself, 52

The spotted hawk swoops by and accuses me, he complains of my
  gab and my loitering.

I too am not a bit tamed, I too am untranslatable,
I sound my barbaric yawp over the roofs of the world.

The last scud of day holds back for me,
It flings my likeness after the rest and true as any on the
  shadow'd wilds,   5
It coaxes me to the vapor and the dusk.

I depart as air, I shake my white locks at the runaway sun,
I effuse my flesh in eddies, and drift it in lacy jags.

I bequeath myself to the dirt to grow from the grass I love,
If you want me again look for me under your boot-soles.   10

You will hardly know who I am or what I mean,
But I shall be good health to you nevertheless,
And filter and fibre your blood.

Failing to fetch me at first keep encouraged,
Missing me one place search another,   15
I stop somewhere waiting for you.

—1855

WALT WHITMAN

156

When I Heard the Learn'd Astronomer

When I heard the learn'd astronomer,
When the proofs, the figures, were ranged in columns before me,
When I was shown the charts and diagrams, to add, divide, and
  measure them,
When I sitting heard the astronomer where he lectured with
  much applause in the lecture-room,
How soon unaccountable I became tired and sick,   5
Till rising and gliding out I wander'd off by myself,
In the mystical moist night-air, and from time to time,
Look'd up in perfect silence at the stars.

—1865

MATTHEW ARNOLD ■ (1822–1888)

Matthew Arnold was the son of the headmaster of Rugby School and himself served as an inspector of schools during much of his adult life. An influential essayist as well as a poet, Arnold was unsparing in his criticism of middle-class "Philistinism." At least part of "Dover Beach" is thought to date from his honeymoon in 1851.

Dover Beach

The sea is calm tonight.
The tide is full, the moon lies fair
Upon the straits; on the French coast the light
Gleams and is gone; the cliffs of England stand,
Glimmering and vast, out in the tranquil bay.   5
Come to the window, sweet is the night-air!
Only, from the long line of spray
Where the sea meets the moon-blanched land,
Listen! you hear the grating roar
Of pebbles which the waves draw back, and fling,   10
At their return, up the high strand,
Begin, and cease, and then again begin,
With tremulous cadence slow, and bring
The eternal note of sadness in.

Sophocles° long ago   15
Heard it on the Aegean, and it brought
Into his mind the turbid ebb and flow
Of human misery; we
Find also in the sound a thought,
Hearing it by this distant northern sea.   20

The Sea of Faith
Was once, too, at the full, and round earth's shore
Lay like the folds of a bright girdle° furled.
But now I only hear
Its melancholy, long, withdrawing roar,   25
Retreating, to the breath
Of the night-wind, down the vast edges drear
And naked shingles° of the world.

15 Sophocles Athenian tragic poet (496–406 BC)   **23 girdle** sash   **28 shingles** beach pebbles

157

Ah, love, let us be true
To one another! for the world, which seems   30
To lie before us like a land of dreams,
So various, so beautiful, so new,
Hath really neither joy, nor love, nor light,
Nor certitude, nor peace, nor help for pain;
And we are here as on a darkling plain   35
Swept with confused alarms of struggle and flight,
Where ignorant armies clash by night.

—1867

EMILY DICKINSON ■ (1830–1886)

*Emily Dickinson has been reinvented with each generation, and readers'
views of her have ranged between two extremes—one perceiving her as the
abnormally shy "Belle of Amherst" making poetry out of her own neuroses
and another seeing her as a proto-feminist carving out a world of her own
in self-willed isolation. What remains is her brilliant poetry—unique,
original, and marked with the stamp of individual talent. Dickinson published only seven poems during her lifetime, but left behind hundreds of
poems in manuscript at her death. Published by her relatives, they were
immediately popular, but it was not until the edition of Thomas Johnson
in 1955 that they were read with Dickinson's unusual punctuation and
capitalization intact.*

After Great Pain, a Formal Feeling Comes

After great pain, a formal feeling comes—
The Nerves sit ceremonious, like Tombs—
The stiff Heart questions was it He, that bore,
And Yesterday, or Centuries before?   5

The Feet, mechanical, go round—
Of Ground, or Air, or Ought—

A Wooden way
Regardless grown,
A Quartz contentment, like a stone—

This is the Hour of Lead—
Remembered, if outlived,
As Freezing persons, recollect the Snow—
First—Chill—then Stupor—then the letting go—

Because I Could Not Stop for Death

Because I could not stop for Death—
He kindly stopped for me—
The Carriage held but just Ourselves—
And Immortality.

We slowly drove—He knew no haste   5
And I had put away
My labor and my leisure too,
For His Civility—

We passed the School, where Children strove
At Recess—in the Ring—   10
We passed the Fields of Gazing Grain—
We passed the Setting Sun—

Or rather—He passed Us—
The Dews drew quivering and chill—
For only Gossamer, my Gown—   15
My Tippet°—only Tulle°—

We paused before a House that seemed
A Swelling of the Ground—
The Roof was scarcely visible—
The Cornice—in the Ground—   20

Since then—'tis Centuries—and yet
Feels shorter than the Day
I first surmised the Horses' Heads
Were toward Eternity—

—1890

16 Tippet shawl   **Tulle** net-like fabric

The Brain Is Wider than the Sky

because [handwritten annotation]

The Brain—is wider than the Sky—
For—put them side by side—
The one the other will contain
With ease—and You—beside—

homiletic mode [handwritten annotation]
诱教模式 [handwritten annotation]

5

The Brain is deeper than the sea—
For—hold them—Blue to Blue—
The one the other will absorb—
As Sponges—Buckets—do—

subsume [handwritten annotation]
格重. 把…归义 [handwritten annotation]
把…包括再内. [handwritten annotation]

The Brain is just the weight of God—
For—Heft them—Pound for Pound—
And they will differ—if they do—
As Syllable from Sound—

10

—1896

I Felt a Funeral, in My Brain

I felt a Funeral, in my Brain,
And Mourners to and fro
Kept treading—treading—till it seemed
That Sense was breaking through—

And when they all were seated,
A Service, like a Drum—
Kept beating—beating—till I thought
My Mind was going numb—

5

And then I heard them lift a Box
And creak across my Soul
With those same Boots of Lead, again,
Then Space—began to toll,

10

As all the Heavens were a Bell,
And Being, but an Ear,
And I, and Silence, some strange Race
Wrecked, solitary, here—

15

And then a Plank in Reason, broke,
And I dropped down, and down—
And hit a World, at every plunge,
And Finished knowing—then—   20

—1896

Much Madness Is Divinest Sense

有说服力的; 有洞察力的.

相关的; 完全的,

错误的

Much Madness is divinest Sense—
To a discerning Eye—
Much Sense—the starkest Madness—
'Tis the Majority
In this, as All, prevail—   5
Assent—and you are sane—
Demur—you're straightway dangerous—
And handled with a Chain—

—1890

神经的
非理性的
疯狂

161

A Narrow Fellow in the Grass

A narrow Fellow in the Grass
Occasionally rides—
You may have met Him—did you not
His notice sudden is—

The Grass divides as with a Comb—   5
A spotted shaft is seen—
And then it closes at your feet
And opens further on—

He likes a Boggy Acre
A Floor to cool for Corn—   10
Yet when a Boy, and Barefoot—
I more than once at Noon
Have passed, I thought, a Whip lash
Unbraiding in the Sun
When stooping to secure it   15
It wrinkled, and was gone—

Several of Nature's People
I know, and they know me—
I feel for them a transport
Of cordiality—   20

But never met this Fellow
Attended, or alone
Without a tighter breathing
And Zero at the Bone—

—1866

Some Keep the Sabbath Going to Church

Some keep the Sabbath going to Church—
I keep it, staying at Home—
With a Bobolink for a Chorister—
And an Orchard, for a Dome—

Some keep the Sabbath in Surplice—   5
I just wear my Wings—
And instead of tolling the Bell, for Church,
Our little Sexton—sings.

God preaches, a noted Clergyman—
And the sermon is never long,   10
So instead of getting to Heaven, at least—
I'm going, all along.

—1864

The Soul Selects Her Own Society

The Soul selects her own Society—
Then—shuts the Door—
To her divine Majority—
Present no more—

Unmoved—she notes the Chariots—pausing—   5
At her low Gate—

Unmoved—an Emperor be kneeling
Upon her Mat—

I've known her—from an ample nation—
Choose One— ·   10
Then—close the Valves° of her attention—
Like Stone—

—1890

Tell All the Truth, But Tell It Slant

Tell all the Truth but tell it slant—
Success in Circuit lies
Too bright for our infirm Delight
The Truth's superb surprise

As Lightning to the Children eased   5
With explanation kind
The Truth must dazzle gradually
Or every man be blind—

—1868

There's a Certain Slant of Light

There's a certain Slant of light,
Winter Afternoons—
That oppresses, like the Heft
Of Cathedral Tunes—

Heavenly Hurt, it gives us—   5
We can find no scar,
But internal difference,
Where the Meanings, are—

None may teach it—Any—
'Tis the Seal Despair—   10
An imperial affliction
Sent us of the Air—

11 **Valves** sliding doors

When it comes, the Landscape listens—
Shadows—hold their breath—
When it goes, 'tis like the Distance   15
On the look of Death—

—1890

Wild Nights—
Wild Nights!

Wild Nights—Wild Nights!
Were I with thee
Wild Nights should be
Our luxury!

Futile—the Winds—   5
To a Heart in port—
Done with the Compass—
Done with the Chart!

Rowing in Eden—
Ah, the Sea!   10
Might I but moor—Tonight—
In Thee!

—1891

CHRISTINA ROSSETTI

164

CHRISTINA ROSSETTI ■ (1830–1894)

Christina Rossetti was the younger sister of Dante Gabriel and William, also distinguished writers, and was the author of numerous devotional poems and prose works. Her collected poems, edited by her brother William, appeared posthumously in 1904.

Up-Hill

Does the road wind up-hill all the way?
    Yes, to the very end.
Will the day's journey take the whole long day?
    From morn to night, my friend.

But is there for the night a resting-place?   5
    A roof for when the slow dark hours begin.
May not the darkness hide it from my face?
    You cannot miss that inn.

Shall I meet other wayfarers at night?
    Those who have gone before.   10
Then must I knock, or call when just in sight?
    They will not keep you waiting at that door.

Shall I find comfort, travel-sore and weak?
    Of labor you shall find the sum.
Will there be beds for me and all who seek?   15
    Yea, beds for all who come.

—1858

THOMAS HARDY ■ (1840–1928)

Thomas Hardy, after the disappointing response to his novel Jude the Obscure *in 1895, returned to his first love, writing poetry, for the last thirty years of his long life. The language and life of Hardy's native Wessex inform both his novels and poems. His subject matter is very much of the nineteenth century, but his ironic, disillusioned point of view marks him as one of the chief predecessors of modernism.*

Ah, Are You Digging on My Grave?

"Ah, are you digging on my grave
    My loved one?—planting rue?"°
—"No: yesterday he went to wed
One of the brightest wealth has bred.
'It cannot hurt her now,' he said,   5
    'That I should not be true.'"

"Then who is digging on my grave?
    My nearest dearest kin?"

---

2 rue yellow flower traditionally associated with sadness

—"Ah, no; they sit and think, 'What use!
What good will planting flowers produce?   10
No tendance of her mound can loose
    Her spirit from Death's gin.' "°

"But some one digs upon my grave?
    My enemy?—prodding sly?"
—"Nay: when she heard you had passed the Gate   15
That shuts on all flesh soon or late,
She thought you no more worth her hate,
    And cares not where you lie."

"Then who is digging on my grave?
    Say—since I have not guessed!"   20
—"O it is I, my mistress dear,
Your little dog, who still lives near,
And much I hope my movements here
    Have not disturbed your rest?"

"Ah, yes! *You* dig upon my grave . . .   25
    Why flashed it not on me
That one true heart was left behind!
What feeling do we ever find
To equal among human kind
    A dog's fidelity!"   30

"Mistress, I dug upon your grave
    To bury a bone, in case
I should be hungry near this spot
When passing on my daily trot.
I am sorry, but I quite forgot   35
    It was your resting-place."

                        —1914

Channel Firing

That night your great guns, unawares,
Shook all our coffins as we lay,
And broke the chancel window-squares,
We thought it was the Judgment-day

12 **gin** grip

And sat upright. While drearisome
Arose the howl of weakened hounds:
The mouse let fall the alter-crumb,
The worms drew back into the mounds,

The glebe° cow drooled. Till God called, 'No;
It's gunnery practice out at sea
Just as before you went below;
The world is as it used to be:

'All nations striving strong to make
Red war yet redder. Mad as hatters
They do no more for Christés sake
Than you who are helpless in such matters.

'That this is not the judgment-hour
For some of them's a blessed thing,
For if it were they'd have to scour
Hell's floor for so much threatening. . . .

'Ha, ha. It will be warmer when
I blow the trumpet (if indeed
I ever do; for you are men,
And rest eternal sorely need).'

So down we lay again. 'I wonder,
Will the world ever saner be,'
Said one, 'than when he sent us under
In our indifferent century!'

And many a skeleton shook his head.
'Instead of preaching forty year,'
My neighbour Parson Thirdly said,
'I wish I had stuck to pipes and beer.'

Again the guns disturbed the hour,
Roaring their readiness to avenge,
As far inland as Stourton Tower,
And Camelot, and starlit Stonehenge.°

—1914

9 **glebe** farmland belonging to a church   **35–36 Stourton . . . Stonehenge** Stourton Tower was built in the late 1700s as a memorial to the Seven Years War; Camelot was the legendary Castle of King Arthur; Stonehenge dates from prehistoric times.

Neutral Tones

We stood by a pond that winter day,
And the sun was white, as though chidden of God,
And a few leaves lay on the starving sod;
    —They had fallen from an ash, and were gray.

Your eyes on me were as eyes that rove   5
Over tedious riddles solved years ago;
And some words played between us to and fro
    On which lost the more by our love.

The smile on your mouth was the deadest thing
Alive enough to have strength to die;   10
And a grin of bitterness swept thereby
    Like an ominous bird a-wing . . .

Since then, keen lessons that love deceives,
And wrings with wrong, have shaped to me
Your face, and the God-curst sun, and a tree,   15
    And a pond edged with grayish leaves.

—1898

The Ruined Maid

"O 'Melia, my dear, this does everything crown!
Who could have supposed I should meet you in Town?
And whence such fair garments, such prosperity?"
"O didn't you know I'd been ruined?" said she.

"You left us in tatters, without shoes or socks,   5
Tired of digging potatoes, and spudding up docks;°
And now you've gay bracelets and bright feathers three!"
"Yes: that's how we dress when we're ruined," said she.

"At home in the barton° you said 'thee' and 'thou,'
And 'thik oon,' and 'theäs oon,'° and 't'other'; but now   10
Your talking quite fits 'ee for high compa-ny!"
"Some polish is gained with one's ruin," said she.

"Your hands were like paws then, your face blue and bleak
But now I'm bewitched by your delicate cheek,

6 **docks** weeds   9 **barton** barnyard   10 **thik oon and theäs oon** dialect: "that one and this one"

And your little gloves fit as on any la-dy!"   15
"We never do work when we're ruined," said she.

"You used to call home-life a hag-ridden dream,
And you'd sigh, and you'd sock; but at present you seem
To know not of megrims° or melancho-ly!"
"True. One's pretty lively when ruined," said she.   20

"I wish I had feathers, a fine sweeping gown,
And a delicate face, and could strut about Town!"
"My dear—a raw country girl, such as you be,
Cannot quite expect that. You ain't ruined," said she.

—1866

GERARD MANLEY HOPKINS ▪ (1844–1889)

Gerard Manley Hopkins was an English Jesuit priest who developed elabo-rate theories of poetic meter (what he called "sprung rhythm") and language to express his own spiritual ardor. Most of his work was posthumously printed through the efforts of his Oxford friend and later correspondent Robert Bridges, who was poet laureate.

God's Grandeur

The world is charged with the grandeur of God.
    It will flame out, like shining from shook foil;°
    It gathers to a greatness, like the ooze of oil
Crushed.° Why do men then now not reck his rod?
Generations have trod, have trod, have trod;   5
    And all is seared with trade; bleared, smeared with toil;
    And wears man's smudge and shares man's smell: the soil
Is bare now, nor can foot feel, being shod.

And for all this, nature is never spent;
    There lives the dearest freshness deep down things;   10
And though the last lights off the black West went
    Oh, morning, at the brown brink eastward, springs—
Because the Holy Ghost over the bent
    World broods with warm breast and with ah! bright wings.

—1877

19 megrims migraines
2 foil gold leaf   **4 Crushed** Hopkins is referring to olive oil

Pied Beauty

Glory be to God for dappled things—
    For skies of couple-color as a brinded° cow;
        For rose-moles all in stipple upon trout that swim;
Fresh-firecoal chestnut-falls;° finches' wings;
        Landscape plotted and pieced—fold, fallow, and plough;   5
        And all trades, their gear and tackle and trim.
All things counter, original, spare, strange;
    Whatever is fickle, freckled (who knows how?)
        With swift, slow; sweet, sour; adazzle, dim;
He fathers-forth whose beauty is past change: 10
        Praise him.

—1877

GERARD MANLEY HOPKINS

Spring and Fall

to a young child

Márgarét, are you gríeving?
Over Goldengrove unleaving?
Leáves, líke the things of man, you
With your fresh thoughts care for, can you?
Ah! ás the heart grows older   5
It will come to such sights colder
By and by, nor spare a sigh
Though worlds of wanwood leafmeal lie;
And yet you wíll weep and know why.
Now no matter, child, the name: 10
Sórrow's spríngs áre the same.
Nor mouth had, no nor mind, expressed
What heart heard of, ghost guessed:
It ís the blight man was born for,
It is Margaret you mourn for.   15

—1880

---

2 brinded streaked   **4 Fresh-firecoal chestnut-falls** According to the poet, chestnuts have a red color

EMMA LAZARUS ■ (1849–1887)

Emma Lazarus was born in New York City, one of seven children of a wealthy Jewish-American sugar refiner. Her famous sonnet "The New Colossus" was written in 1883 for an art auction raising money to build a pedestal for the Statue of Liberty, which had been given to the United States by France. During Lazarus's short life she became a powerful spokesperson for the rights of immigrants and called on Jews to claim a homeland in Palestine. Sixteen years after her death, "The New Colossus" was engraved on a plaque for the statue's base.

The New Colossus

Not like the brazen giant of Greek fame,
With conquering limbs astride from land to land;
Here at our sea-washed, sunset gates shall stand
A mighty woman with a torch, whose flame
Is the imprisoned lightning, and her name   5
Mother of Exiles. From her beacon-hand
Glows world-wide welcome; her mild eyes command
The air-bridged harbor that twin cities frame.
"Keep, ancient lands, your storied pomp!" cries she
With silent lips. "Give me your tired, your poor,   10
Your huddled masses yearning to breathe free,
The wretched refuse of your teeming shore.
Send these, the homeless, tempest-tost to me,
I lift my lamp beside the golden door!"

—1883

A. E. HOUSMAN ■ (1859–1936)

A. E. Housman was educated in the classics at Oxford and was almost forty before he began to write verse seriously. His ballad-like poems of Shropshire (an area in which he never actually lived) have proved some of the most popular lyrics in English, despite their pervasive mood of bittersweet pessimism.

Eight o'Clock

He stood, and heard the steeple
    Sprinkle the quarters° on the morning town.
One, two, three, four, to market-place and people
    It tossed them down.

Strapped, noosed, nighing his hour,   5
    He stood and counted them and cursed his luck;
And then the clock collected in the tower
    Its strength, and struck.

                    —1922

Loveliest of Trees, the Cherry Now

Loveliest of trees, the cherry now
Is hung with bloom along the bough,
And stands about the woodland ride
Wearing white for Eastertide.

Now, of my threescore years and ten,   5
Twenty will not come again,
And take from seventy springs a score,
It only leaves me fifty more.

And since to look at things in bloom
Fifty springs are little room,   10
About the woodlands I will go
To see the cherry hung with snow.

                    —1896

Stars, I Have Seen Them Fall

Stars, I have seen them fall,
    But when they drop and die
No star is lost at all
    From all the star-sown sky.

A. E. HOUSMAN

172

2 quarters quarter hours

The toil of all that be   5
    Helps not the primal fault;
It rains into the sea
    And still the sea is salt.

—1936

"Terence, This Is Stupid Stuff . . ."

"Terence, this is stupid stuff:
You eat your victuals fast enough;
There can't be much amiss, 'tis clear,
To see the rate you drink your beer.
But oh, good Lord, the verse you make,   5
It gives a chap the belly-ache.
The cow, the old cow, she is dead;
It sleeps well, the hornèd head:
We poor lads, 'tis our turn now
To hear such tunes as killed the cow.   10
Pretty friendship 'tis to rhyme
Your friends to death before their time
Moping melancholy mad:
Come, pipe a tune to dance to, lad."

    Why, if 'tis dancing you would be,   15
There's brisker pipes than poetry.
Say, for what were hop-yards meant,
Or why was Burton built on Trent?°
Oh many a peer of England brews
Livelier liquor than the Muse,   20
And malt does more than Milton can
To justify God's ways to man.
Ale, man, ale's the stuff to drink
For fellows whom it hurts to think:
Look into the pewter pot   25
To see the world as the world's not.

18 **Burton built on Trent** site of breweries

And faith, 'tis pleasant till 'tis past:
The mischief is that 'twill not last.
Oh I have been to Ludlow fair
And left my necktie God knows where,   30
And carried halfway home, or near,
Pints and quarts of Ludlow beer:
Then the world seemed none so bad,
And I myself a sterling lad;
And down in lovely muck I've lain,   35
Happy till I woke again.
Then I saw the morning sky:
Heigho, the tale was all a lie;
The world, it was the old world yet,
I was I, my things were wet,   40
And nothing now remained to do
But begin the game anew.

    Therefore, since the world has still
Much good, but much less good than ill,
And while the sun and moon endure   45
Luck's a chance, but trouble's sure,
I'd face it as a wise man would,
And train for ill and not for good.
'Tis true, the stuff I bring for sale
Is not so brisk a brew as ale: 50
Out of a stem that scored the hand
I wrung it in a weary land.
But take it: if the smack is sour,
The better for the embittered hour;
It should do good to heart and head   55
When your soul is in my soul's stead;
And I will friend you, if I may,
In the dark and cloudy day.

    There was a king reigned in the East:
There, when kings will sit to feast,   60
They get their fill before they think
With poisoned meat and poisoned drink.
He gathered all that springs to birth
From the many-venomed earth;

First a little, thence to more,   65
He sampled all her killing store;
And easy, smiling, seasoned sound,
Sate the king when healths went round.
They put arsenic in his meat
And stared aghast to watch him eat;   70
They poured strychnine in his cup
And shook to see him drink it up:
They shook, they stared as white's their shirt:
Them it was their poison hurt.
—I tell the tale that I heard told.   75
Mithridates,° he died old.

—1896

WILLIAM BUTLER YEATS ■ (1865–1939)

William Butler Yeats is considered the greatest Irish poet and provides an important link between the late romantic era and early modernism. His early poetry, focusing on Irish legend and landscape, is regional in the best sense of the term, but his later work, with its prophetic tone and symbolist texture, moves on a larger stage. Yeats lived in London for many years and was at the center of British literary life. He was awarded the Nobel Prize in 1923.

The Lake Isle of Innisfree

I will arise and go now, and go to Innisfree,
And a small cabin build there, of clay and wattles° made:
Nine bean-rows will I have there, a hive for the honey-bee,
And live alone in the bee-loud glade.

And I shall have some peace there, for peace comes dropping
    slow,   5
Dropping from the veils of the morning to where the cricket
    sings;
There midnight's all a glimmer, and noon a purple glow,
And evening full of the linnet's wings.

76 Mithridates legendary King of Pontus, he protected himself from poisons by taking small doses regularly
2 wattles woven poles and reeds

I will arise and go now, for always night and day
I hear lake water lapping with low sounds by the shore;   10
While I stand on the roadway, or on the pavements gray,
I hear it in the deep heart's core.

—1892

Leda° and the Swan

A sudden blow: the great wings beating still
Above the staggering girl, her thighs caressed
By the dark webs, her nape caught in his bill,
He holds her helpless breast upon his breast.

How can those terrified vague fingers push   5
The feathered glory from her loosening thighs?
And how can body, laid in that white rush,
But feel the strange heart beating where it lies?

A shudder in the loins engenders there
The broken wall, the burning roof and tower   10
And Agamemnon dead.°
        Being so caught up,
So mastered by the brute blood of the air,
Did she put on his knowledge with his power
Before the indifferent beak could let her drop?

—1923

Sailing to Byzantium°

1

That is no country for old men. The young
In one another's arms, birds in the trees
—Those dying generations—at their song,
The salmon-falls, the mackerel-crowded seas,

Leda mortal mother of Helen of Troy and Clytemnestra, wife and assassin of Agamemnon
10–11 The broken wall . . . Agamemnon dead events that occurred during and after the Trojan War
Byzantium Constantinople or Istanbul, capital of the Eastern Roman Empire

Fish, flesh, or fowl, commend all summer long   5
Whatever is begotten, born, and dies
Caught in that sensual music all neglect
Monuments of unaging intellect.

2

An aged man is but a paltry thing,
A tattered coat upon a stick, unless   10
Soul clap its hands and sing, and louder sing
For every tatter in its mortal dress,
Nor is there singing school but studying
Monuments of its own magnificence;
And therefore I have sailed the seas and come   15
To the holy city of Byzantium.

3

O sages standing in God's holy fire
As in the gold mosaic of a wall,
Come from the holy fire, perne in a gyre,°
And be the singing-masters of my soul.   20
Consume my heart away; sick with desire
And fastened to a dying animal
It knows not what it is; and gather me
Into the artifice of eternity.

4

Once out of nature I shall never take   25
My bodily form from any natural thing,
But such a form as Grecian goldsmiths make
Of hammered gold and gold enamelling
To keep a drowsy Emperor awake;
Or set upon a golden bough to sing   30
To lords and ladies of Byzantium
Of what is past, or passing, or to come.

—1927

19 **perne in a gyre** descend in a spiral; the gyre for Yeats was a private symbol of historical cycles

The Second Coming

Turning and turning in the widening gyre°
The falcon cannot hear the falconer;
Things fall apart; the center cannot hold;
Mere anarchy is loosed upon the world,
The blood-dimmed tide is loosed, and everywhere   5
The ceremony of innocence is drowned;
The best lack all conviction, while the worst
Are full of passionate intensity.

Surely some revelation is at hand;
Surely the Second Coming is at hand.   10
The Second Coming! Hardly are those words out
When a vast image out of *Spiritus Mundi*°
Troubles my sight: somewhere in the sands of the desert
A shape with lion body and the head of a man,
A gaze blank and pitiless as the sun,   15
Is moving its slow thighs, while all about it
Reel shadows of the indignant desert birds.
The darkness drops again; but now I know
That twenty centuries of stony sleep
Were vexed to nightmare by a rocking cradle,   20
And what rough beast, its hour come round at last,
Slouches towards Bethlehem to be born?

—1921

The Song of
Wandering Aengus°

I went out to the hazel wood,
Because a fire was in my head,
And cut and peeled a hazel wand,
And hooked a berry to a thread;
And when white moths were on the wing,   5
And moth-like stars were flickering out,

1 **gyre** see note to "Sailing to Byzantium"   12 ***Spiritus Mundi*** World-Spirit
Aengus Among the Sidhe (native Irish deities), the god of youth, love, beauty, and poetry. Yeats once also called him the "Master of Love." Here, however, he seems mortal.

I dropped the berry in a stream
And caught a little silver trout.

When I had laid it on the floor
I went to blow the fire aflame,
But something rustled on the floor,
And some one called me by my name:
It had become a glimmering girl
With apple blossom in her hair
Who called me by my name and ran
And faded through the brightening air.

Though I am old with wandering
Through hollow lands and hilly lands,
I will find out where she has gone,
And kiss her lips and take her hands;
And walk among long dappled grass,
And pluck till time and times are done
The silver apples of the moon,
The golden apples of the sun.

—1899

rhyme + repetition 10

beautiful 20

EDWIN ARLINGTON ROBINSON ■ (1869–1935)

Edwin Arlington Robinson wrote many poems set in "Tilbury," a re-creation of his hometown of Gardiner, Maine. These poems continue to present readers with a memorable cast of eccentric characters who somehow manifest universal human desires. Robinson languished in poverty and obscurity for many years before his reputation began to flourish as a result of the interest taken in his work by President Theodore Roosevelt, who obtained a government job for Robinson and wrote a favorable review of one of his books.

Firelight

Ten years together without yet a cloud,
They seek each other's eyes at intervals
Of gratefulness to firelight and four walls
For love's obliteration of the crowd.
Serenely and perennially endowed
And bowered as few may be, their joy recalls

5

No snake, no sword; and over them there falls
The blessing of what neither says aloud.
Wiser for silence, they were not so glad
Were she to read the graven° tale of lines   10
On the wan face of one somewhere alone;
Nor were they more content could he have had
Her thoughts a moment since of one who shines
Apart, and would be hers if he had known.

—1920

EDWIN ARLINGTON ROBINSON

The Mill

The miller's wife had waited long,
    The tea was cold, the fire was dead;
And there might yet be nothing wrong
    In how he went and what he said:
"There are no millers any more,"   5
    Was all that she had heard him say;
And he had lingered at the door
    So long that it seemed yesterday.

Sick with a fear that had no form
    She knew that she was there at last;   10
And in the mill there was a warm
    And mealy fragrance of the past.
What else there was would only seem
    To say again what he had meant;
And what was hanging from a beam   15
    Would not have heeded where she went.

And if she thought it followed her,
    She may have reasoned in the dark
That one way of the few there were
    Would hide her and would leave no mark: 20
Black water, smooth above the weir
    Like starry velvet in the night,
Though ruffled once, would soon appear
    The same as ever to the sight.

—1920

10 graven engraved

Richard Cory

wow

Whenever Richard Cory went down town,
We people on the pavement looked at him:
He was a gentleman from sole to crown,
Clean favored, and imperially slim.

And he was always quietly arrayed,   5
And he was always human when he talked;
But still he fluttered pulses when he said,
"Good-morning," and he glittered when he walked.

And he was rich—yes, richer than a king—
And admirably schooled in every grace: 10
In fine, we thought that he was everything
To make us wish that we were in his place.

So on we worked, and waited for the light,
And went without the meat, and cursed the bread;
And Richard Cory, one calm summer night,   15
Went home and put a bullet through his head.

this hit you —1896

STEPHEN CRANE ■ (1871–1900)

Stephen Crane was the brilliant young journalist who wrote The Red Badge
of Courage *and was also an unconventional poet whose skeptical epigrams
and fables today seem far ahead of their time. In many ways he mirrors the
cosmic pessimism of contemporaries like Hardy, Housman, and Robinson,
all of whom were influenced by the currents of determinism that ran so
strongly at the end of the nineteenth century.*

The Trees in the Garden Rained Flowers

The trees in the garden rained flowers.
Children ran there joyously.
They gathered the flowers
Each to himself.
Now there were some   5

Who gathered great heaps—
Having opportunity and skill—
Until, behold, only chance blossoms
Remained for the feeble.
Then a little spindling tutor   10
Ran importantly to the father, crying:
"Pray, come hither!
See this unjust thing in your garden!"
But when the father had surveyed,
He admonished the tutor: 15
"Not so, small sage!
This thing is just.
For, look you,
Are not they who possess the flowers
Stronger, bolder, shrewder   20
Than they who have none?
Why should the strong—
The beautiful strong—
Why should they not have the flowers?"
Upon reflection, the tutor bowed to the ground,   25
"My lord," he said,
"The stars are displaced
By this towering wisdom."

—1899

The Wayfarer

The wayfarer.
Perceiving the pathway to truth,
Was struck with astonishment.
It was thickly grown with weeds.
"Ha," he said,   5
"I see that none has passed here
In a long time."
Later he saw that each weed
Was a singular knife.
"Well," he mumbled at last,   10
"Doubtless there are other roads."

—1899

Paul Laurence Dunbar, a native of Dayton, Ohio, was one of the first black poets to make a mark in American literature. Many of his dialect poems reflect a sentimentalized view of life in the South, which he did not know directly. However, he was also capable of powerful expressions of racial protest.

We Wear the Mask

We wear the mask that grins and lies,
It hides our cheeks and shades our eyes,—
This debt we pay to human guile;
With torn and bleeding hearts we smile,
And mouth with myriad subtleties.   5

Why should the world be over-wise,
In counting all our tears and sighs?
Nay, let them only see us, while
    We wear the mask.

We smile, but, O great Christ, our cries   10
To thee from tortured souls arise.
We sing, but oh the clay is vile
Beneath our feet, and long the mile;
But let the world dream otherwise,
    We wear the mask!   15

—1896

Robert Frost, during the second half of his long life, was a public figure who attained a popularity unmatched by any American poet of the last century. His reading at the inauguration of John F. Kennedy in 1961 capped an impressive career that included four Pulitzer Prizes. Unattracted by the more exotic aspects of modernism, Frost nevertheless remains a poet who speaks eloquently to contemporary uncertainties about humanity's place in a universe that does not seem to care much for its existence. While Frost is rarely directly an autobiographical poet ("Home Burial" may reflect the death of Frost's son Elliot at age three), his work always bears the stamp of his powerful personality and identification with the New England landscape.

Acquainted with the Night

I have been one acquainted with the night.
I have walked out in rain—and back in rain.
I have outwalked the furthest city light.

I have looked down the saddest city lane.
I have passed by the watchman on his beat   5
And dropped my eyes, unwilling to explain.

I have stood still and stopped the sound of feet
When far away an interrupted cry
Came over houses from another street,

But not to call me back or say good-bye;   10
And further still at an unearthly height
One luminary clock against the sky

Proclaimed the time was neither wrong nor right.
I have been one acquainted with the night.

—1928

ROBERT FROST

After Apple-Picking

My long two-pointed ladder's sticking through a tree
Toward heaven still,
And there's a barrel that I didn't fill
Beside it, and there may be two or three
Apples I didn't pick upon some bough.   5
But I am done with apple-picking now.
Essence of winter sleep is on the night,
The scent of apples: I am drowsing off.
I cannot rub the strangeness from my sight
I got from looking through a pane of glass   10
I skimmed this morning from the drinking trough
And held against the world of hoary grass.
It melted, and I let it fall and break.
But I was well
Upon my way to sleep before it fell,   15
And I could tell
What form my dreaming was about to take.

Magnified apples appear and disappear,
Stem end and blossom end,
And every fleck of russet showing clear. 20
My instep arch not only keeps the ache,
It keeps the pressure of a ladder-round.
I feel the ladder sway as the boughs bend.
And I keep hearing from the cellar bin
The rumbling sound 25
Of load on load of apples coming in.
For I have had too much
Of apple-picking: I am overtired
Of the great harvest I myself desired.
There were ten thousand thousand fruit to touch, 30
Cherish in hand, lift down, and not let fall.
For all
That struck the earth,
No matter if not bruised or spiked with stubble,
Went surely to the cider-apple heap 35
As of no worth.
One can see what will trouble
This sleep of mine, whatever sleep it is.
Were he not gone,
The woodchuck could say whether it's like his 40
Long sleep, as I describe its coming on,
Or just some human sleep.

—1914

Design *Sonet* *traditionally*

used as wedding day *poetry*

I found a dimpled spider, fat and white, A
On a white heal-all,° holding up a moth B
Like a white piece of rigid satin cloth— B *del*
Assorted characters of death and blight A
creepy Mixed ready to begin the morning right, A 5
Like the ingredients of a witches' broth— B *simile*
A snow-drop spider, a flower like a froth, B
And dead wings carried like a paper kite. A

simile

2 **heal-all** a wildflower, usually blue

What had that flower to do with being white,
The wayside blue and innocent heal-all?   10
What brought the kindred spider to that height,
Then steered the white moth thither in the night?
What but design of darkness to appall?—
If design govern in a thing so small.

—1936

Home Burial

He saw her from the bottom of the stairs
Before she saw him. She was starting down,
Looking back over her shoulder at some fear.
She took a doubtful step and then undid it
To raise herself and look again. He spoke   5
Advancing toward her: "What is it you see
From up there always?—for I want to know."
She turned and sank upon her skirts at that,
And her face changed from terrified to dull.
He said to gain time: "What is it you see?"   10
Mounting until she cowered under him.
"I will find out now—you must tell me, dear."
She, in her place, refused him any help,
With the least stiffening of her neck and silence.
She let him look, sure that he wouldn't see,   15
Blind creature; and awhile he didn't see.
But at last he murmured, "Oh," and again, "Oh."

"What is it—what?" she said.

                    "Just that I see."

"You don't," she challenged. "Tell me what it is."

"The wonder is I didn't see at once.   20
I never noticed it from here before.
I must be wonted to it—that's the reason.
The little graveyard where my people are!
So small the window frames the whole of it.
Not so much larger than a bedroom, is it?   25
There are three stones of slate and one of marble,
Broad-shouldered little slabs there in the sunlight

On the sidehill. We haven't to mind *those*.
But I understand: it is not the stones, *Variation*
But the child's mound—"

                              "Don't, don't, don't, don't," she cried.   30

She withdrew, shrinking from beneath his arm
That rested on the banister, and slid downstairs;
And turned on him with such a daunting look,
He said twice over before he knew himself:
"Can't a man speak of his own child he's lost?"   35

"Not you!—Oh, where's my hat? Oh, I don't need it!
I must get out of here. I must get air.—
I don't know rightly whether any man can."

"Amy! Don't go to someone else this time.
Listen to me. I won't come down the stairs."   40
He sat and fixed his chin between his fists.
"There's something I should like to ask you, dear."

"You don't know how to ask it."

                              "Help me, then."

Her fingers moved the latch for all reply.

"My words are nearly always an offense.   45
I don't know how to speak of anything
So as to please you. But I might be taught,
I should suppose. I can't say I see how.
A man must partly give up being a man
With womenfolk. We could have some arrangement   50
By which I'd bind myself to keep hands off
Anything special you're a-mind to name.
Though I don't like such things 'twixt those that love.
Two that don't love can't live together without them.
But two that do can't live together with them."   55
She moved the latch a little. "Don't—don't go.
Don't carry it to someone else this time.
Tell me about it if it's something human.
Let me into your grief. I'm not so much
Unlike other folks as your standing there   60
Apart would make me out. Give me my chance.
I do think, though, you overdo it a little.

What was it brought you up to think it the thing
To take your mother-loss of a first child
So inconsolably—in the face of love.   65
You'd think his memory might be satisfied—"

"There you go sneering now!"

                              "I'm not, I'm not!
You make me angry. I'll come down to you.
God, what a woman! And it's come to this,
A man can't speak of his own child that's dead."   70

"You can't because you don't know how to speak.
If you had any feelings, you that dug
With your own hand—how could you?—his little grave;
I saw you from that very window there,
Making the gravel leap and leap in air,   75
Leap up, like that, like that, and land so lightly
And roll back down the mound beside the hole.
I thought, Who is that man? I didn't know you.
And I crept down the stairs and up the stairs
To look again, and still your spade kept lifting.   80
Then you came in. I heard your rumbling voice
Out in the kitchen, and I don't know why,
But I went near to see with my own eyes.
You could sit there with the stains on your shoes
Of the fresh earth from your own baby's grave   85
And talk about your everyday concerns.
You had stood the spade up against the wall
Outside there in the entry, for I saw it."

"I shall laugh the worst laugh I ever laughed.
I'm cursed. God, if I don't believe I'm cursed."   90

"I can repeat the very words you were saying:
'Three foggy mornings and one rainy day
Will rot the best birch fence a man can build.'
Think of it, talk like that at such a time!
What had how long it takes a birch to rot   95
To do with what was in the darkened parlor?
You *couldn't* care! The nearest friends can go
With anyone to death, comes so far short

They might as well not try to go at all.
No, from the time when one is sick to death,   100
One is alone, and he dies more alone.
Friends make pretense of following to the grave,
But before one is in it, their minds are turned
And making the best of their way back to life
And living people, and things they understand.   105

But the world's evil. I won't have grief so
If I can change it. Oh, I won't, I won't!"

"There, you have said it all and you feel better.
You won't go now. You're crying. Close the door.
The heart's gone out of it: why keep it up?   110
Amy! There's someone coming down the road!"

"*You*—oh, you think the talk is all. I must go—
Somewhere out of this house. How can I make you—"

"If—you—do!" She was opening the door wider.
"Where do you mean to go? First tell me that.   115
I'll follow and bring you back by force. I *will!*—"

—1914

like a conversation

The Need of Being Versed in Country Things

has rhythm (2nd & 4th) but doesn't seem to have a set meter (5) maybe free verse?

it would be long

anapest

"loose iambic"

The house had gone to bring again a
To the midnight sky a sunset glow. b
Now the chimney was all of the house that stood, X
Like a pistil after the petals go. b

The barn opposed across the way, a
That would have joined the house in flame a
Had it been the will of the wind, was left b
To bear forsaken the place's name. b

every line continues forward

No more it opened with all one end
For teams that came by the stony road   10
To drum on the floor with scurrying hoofs
And brush the mow with the summer load.

The birds that came to it through the air
At broken windows flew out and in,
Their murmur more like the sigh we sigh   15
From too much dwelling on what has been.

Yet for them the lilac renewed its leaf,
And the aged elm, though touched with fire;
And the dry pump flung up an awkward arm;
And the fence post carried a strand of wire.   20

For them there was really nothing sad.
But though they rejoiced in the nest they kept,
One had to be versed in country things
Not to believe the phoebes wept.

—1923

The Road Not Taken

Two roads diverged in a yellow wood,
And sorry I could not travel both
And be one traveler, long I stood
And looked down one as far as I could
To where it bent in the undergrowth;   5

Then took the other, as just as fair,
And having perhaps the better claim,
Because it was grassy and wanted wear;
Though as for that, the passing there
Had worn them really about the same,   10

And both that morning equally lay
In leaves no step had trodden black.
Oh, I kept the first for another day!
Yet knowing how way leads on to way,
I doubted if I should ever come back.   15

I shall be telling this with a sigh
Somewhere ages and ages hence:
Two roads diverged in a wood, and I,
I took the one less traveled by,
And that has made all the difference.   20

—1916

Stopping by Woods on a Snowy Evening

Whose woods these are I think I know.
His house is in the village though;
He will not see me stopping here
To watch his woods fill up with snow.

My little horse must think it queer   5
To stop without a farmhouse near
Between the woods and frozen lake
The darkest evening of the year.

He gives his harness bells a shake
To ask if there is some mistake.   10
The only other sound's the sweep
Of easy wind and downy flake.

The woods are lovely, dark and deep,
But I have promises to keep,
And miles to go before I sleep,   15
And miles to go before I sleep.

—1923

ADELAIDE CRAPSEY ■ (1878–1914)

Adelaide Crapsey was born in Brooklyn, New York, the daughter of an Episcopalian minister. After graduation from college and travel abroad, she became an instructor of poetics at Smith College, but her declining health forced her to resign after only one year of teaching, and she died three years later from tuberculosis. Chiefly remembered as the inventor of the cinquain form, Crapsey was influenced by Asian poetry and anticipated many of the practices of imagists, who were coming to prominence in her final years. Her poetry and criticism were published posthumously.

Amaze

I know
Not these my hands
And yet I think there was

A woman like me once had hands
Like these.   5

Languor After Pain

Pain ebbs,
And like cool balm,
An opiate weariness
Settles on eye-lids, on relaxed
Pale wrists.   5

—1915

Trapped

Well and
If day on day
Follows, and weary year
On year . . . and ever days and years . . .
Well?   5

—1915

WALLACE STEVENS ■ (1879–1955)

*Wallace Stevens was a lawyer specializing in surety bonds and rose to be a
vice-president of the Hartford Accident and Indemnity Company. His poetry
was collected for the first time in Harmonium when he was forty-five, and
while he published widely during his lifetime, his poetry was only slowly recognized as the work of a major modernist whose originality has not been
surpassed. Stevens's idea of poetry as a force taking the place of religion has
had a profound influence on poets and critics of this century.*

Anecdote of the Jar

I placed a jar in Tennessee,
And round it was, upon a hill.
It made the slovenly wilderness
Surround that hill.

The wilderness rose up to it,   5
And sprawled around, no longer wild.
The jar was round upon the ground
And tall and of a port in air.

It took dominion everywhere.
The jar was gray and bare.   10
It did not give of bird or bush,
Like nothing else in Tennessee.

—1923

Disillusionment of Ten o'Clock

The houses are haunted
By white night-gowns.
None are green,
Or purple with green rings,
Or green with yellow rings,   5
Or yellow with blue rings.
None of them are strange,
With socks of lace
And beaded ceintures.°
People are not going   10
To dream of baboons and periwinkles.°
Only, here and there, an old sailor,
Drunk and asleep in his boots,
Catches tigers
In red weather.   15

—1923

The Emperor of Ice-Cream

Call the roller of big cigars,
The muscular one, and bid him whip
In kitchen cups concupiscent° curds.
Let the wenches dawdle in such dress

9 ceintures sashes   **11 periwinkles** either wildflowers or small mollusks
3 concupiscent lustful

As they are used to wear, and let the boys   5
Bring flowers in last month's newspapers.
Let be be finale of seem.
The only emperor is the emperor of ice-cream.

Take from the dresser of deal,°
Lacking the three glass knobs, that sheet   10
On which she embroidered fantails° once
And spread it so as to cover her face.
If her horny feet protrude, they come
To show how cold she is, and dumb.
Let the lamp affix its beam.   15
The only emperor is the emperor of ice-cream.

—1923

The Snow Man

One must have a mind of winter
To regard the frost and the boughs
Of the pine-trees crusted with snow;

And have been cold a long time
To behold the junipers shagged with ice,   5
The spruces rough in the distant glitter

Of the January sun; and not to think
Of any misery in the sound of the wind,
In the sound of a few leaves,

Which is the sound of the land   10
Full of the same wind
That is blowing in the same bare place

For the listener, who listens in the snow,
And, nothing himself, beholds
Nothing that is not there and the nothing that is.   15

—1923

9 **deal** cheap wood   11 **fantails** pigeons

Sunday Morning

I

Complacencies of the peignoir,° and late
Coffee and oranges in a sunny chair,
And the green freedom of a cockatoo
Upon a rug mingle to dissipate
The holy hush of ancient sacrifice.   5
She dreams a little, and she feels the dark
Encroachment of that old catastrophe,
As a calm darkens among water-lights.
The pungent oranges and bright, green wings
Seem things in some procession of the dead,   10
Winding across wide water, without sound.
The day is like wide water, without sound,
Stilled for the passing of her dreaming feet
Over the seas, to silent Palestine,
Dominion of the blood and sepulchre.   15

II

Why should she give her bounty to the dead?
What is divinity if it can come
Only in silent shadows and in dreams?
Shall she not find in comforts of the sun,
In pungent fruit and bright, green wings, or else   20
In any balm or beauty of the earth,
Things to be cherished like the thought of heaven?
Divinity must live within herself:
Passions of rain, or moods in falling snow;
Grievings in loneliness, or unsubdued   25
Elations when the forest blooms; gusty
Emotions on wet roads on autumn nights;
All pleasures and all pains, remembering
The bough of summer and the winter branch.
These are the measures destined for her soul.   30

---

1 **peignoir** woman's dressing gown

III

Jove° in the clouds had his inhuman birth.
No mother suckled him, no sweet land gave
Large-mannered motions to his mythy mind.
He moved among us, as a muttering king,
Magnificent, would move among his hinds,°   35
Until our blood, commingling, virginal,
With heaven, brought such requital to desire
The very hinds discerned it, in a star.
Shall our blood fail? Or shall it come to be
The blood of paradise? And shall the earth   40
Seem all of paradise that we shall know?
The sky will be much friendlier then than now,
A part of labor and a part of pain,
And next in glory to enduring love,
Not this dividing and indifferent blue.   45

IV

She says, "I am content when wakened birds,
Before they fly, test the reality
Of misty fields, by their sweet questionings;
But when the birds are gone, and their warm fields
Return no more, where, then, is paradise?"   50
There is not any haunt of prophecy,
Nor any old chimera° of the grave,
Neither the golden underground, nor isle
Melodious, where spirits gat them home,
Nor visionary south, nor cloudy palm   55
Remote on heaven's hill, that has endured
As April's green endures; or will endure
Like her remembrance of awakened birds,
Or her desire for June and evening, tipped
By the consummation of the swallow's wings.   60

---

31 Jove Roman name of Zeus   **35 hinds** inferiors or shepherds who saw the star of the nativity
52 chimera imagined monster

V

She says, "But in contentment I still feel
The need of some imperishable bliss."
Death is the mother of beauty; hence from her,
Alone, shall come fulfilment to our dreams
And our desires. Although she strews the leaves   65
Of sure obliteration on our paths,
The path sick sorrow took, the many paths
Where triumph rang its brassy phrase, or love
Whispered a little out of tenderness,
She makes the willow shiver in the sun   70
For maidens who were wont to sit and gaze
Upon the grass, relinquished to their feet.
She causes boys to pile new plums and pears
On disregarded plate. The maidens taste
And stray impassioned in the littering leaves.   75

VI

Is there no change of death in paradise?
Does ripe fruit never fall? Or do the boughs
Hang always heavy in that perfect sky,
Unchanging, yet so like our perishing earth,
With rivers like our own that seek for seas   80
They never find, the same receding shores
That never touch with inarticulate pang?
Why set the pear upon those river-banks
Or spice the shores with odors of the plum?
Alas, that they should wear our colors there,   85
The silken weavings of our afternoons,
And pick the strings of our insipid lutes!
Death is the mother of beauty, mystical,
Within whose burning bosom we devise
Our earthly mothers waiting, sleeplessly.   90

VII

Supple and turbulent, a ring of men
Shall chant in orgy on a summer morn
Their boisterous devotion to the sun,

Not as a god, but as a god might be,
Naked among them, like a savage source.   95
Their chant shall be a chant of paradise,
Out of their blood, returning to the sky;
And in their chant shall enter, voice by voice,
The windy lake wherein their lord delights,
The trees, like serafin,° and echoing hills,   100
That choir among themselves long afterward.
They shall know well the heavenly fellowship
Of men that perish and of summer morn.
And whence they came and whither they shall go
The dew upon their feet shall manifest.   105

VIII

She hears, upon that water without sound,
A voice that cries, "The tomb in Palestine
Is not the porch of spirits lingering.
It is the grave of Jesus, where he lay."
We live in an old chaos of the sun,   110
Or old dependency of day and night,
Or island solitude, unsponsored, free,
Of that wide water, inescapable.
Deer walk upon our mountains, and the quail
Whistle about us their spontaneous cries;   115
Sweet berries ripen in the wilderness;
And, in the isolation of the sky,
At evening, casual flocks of pigeons make
Ambiguous undulations as they sink,
Downward to darkness, on extended wings.   120

—1923

The Worms at Heaven's Gate

Out of the tomb, we bring Badroulbadour,°
Within our bellies, we her chariot.
Here is an eye. And here are, one by one,
The lashes of that eye and its white lid.

100 **serafin** seraphim, a type of angel
1 **Badroulbadour** a princess in *The Arabian Nights*

Here is the cheek on which that lid declined,   5
And, finger after finger, here, the hand,
The genius of that cheek. Here are the lips,
The bundle of the body and feet.

.   .   .   .

Out of the tomb we bring Badroulbadour.   10

—*1923*

WILLIAM CARLOS WILLIAMS ■ (1883–1963)

William Carlos Williams, like his friend Wallace Stevens, followed an uncon-
ventional career for a poet, working until his death as a pediatrician in
Rutherford, New Jersey. Williams is modern poetry's greatest proponent of
the American idiom. His plainspoken poems have been more widely imitated
than those of any other American poet of the twentieth century, perhaps
because he represents a homegrown modernist alternative to the intellectu-
alized Europeanism of Eliot and Ezra Pound (a friend of his from college
days). In his later years, Williams assisted many younger poets, among them
Allen Ginsberg, for whose controversial book Howl *he wrote an introduction.*

The Last Words of My English Grandmother

There were some dirty plates
and a glass of milk
beside her on a small table
near the rank, disheveled bed—

Wrinkled and nearly blind   5
she lay and snored
rousing with anger in her tones
to cry for food,

Gimme something to eat—
They're starving me—   10
I'm all right—I won't go
to the hospital. No, no, no

Give me something to eat!
Let me take you
to the hospital, I said   15
and after you are well

you can do as you please.
She smiled, Yes
you do what you please first
then I can do what I please—   20

Oh, oh, oh! she cried
as the ambulance men lifted
her to the stretcher—
Is this what you call

making me comfortable?   25
By now her mind was clear—
Oh you think you're smart
you young people,

she said, but I'll tell you
you don't know anything.   30
Then we started.
On the way

We passed a long row
of elms. She looked at them
awhile out of   35
the ambulance window and said,

What are all those
fuzzy-looking things out there?
Trees? Well, I'm tired
of them and rolled her head away.   40

                                                      —1920

The Red Wheelbarrow

so much depends
upon

a red wheel
barrow

glazed with rain   5
water

beside the white
chickens.

—1923

Spring and All

By the road to the contagious hospital°
under the surge of the blue
mottled clouds driven from the
northeast—a cold wind. Beyond, the
waste of broad, muddy fields   5
brown with dried weeds, standing and fallen

patches of standing water
the scattering of tall trees
All along the road the reddish
purplish, forked, upstanding, twiggy   10
stuff of bushes and small trees
with dead, brown leaves under them
leafless vines—

Lifeless in appearance, sluggish
dazed spring approaches—   15

They enter the new world naked,
cold, uncertain of all
save that they enter. All about them
the cold, familiar wind—

Now the grass, tomorrow   20
the stiff curl of wildcarrot leaf
One by one objects are defined—
It quickens: clarity, outline of leaf

But now the stark dignity of
entrance—Still, the profound change   25
has come upon them: rooted, they
grip down and begin to awaken

—1923

1 **contagious hospital** a hospital for quarantined patients

Ezra Pound was the greatest international proponent of modernist poetry. Born in Idaho and reared in Philadelphia, he emigrated to England in 1909, where he befriended Yeats, promoted the early work of Frost, and discovered Eliot. Pound's early promotion of the imagist movement assisted a number of important poetic principles and reputations, including those of H. D. (Hilda Doolittle) and, later, William Carlos Williams. Pound's support of Mussolini during World War II, expressed in controversial radio broadcasts, caused him to be held for over a decade after the war as a mental patient in the United States, after which he returned to Italy for the final years of his long and controversial life.

In a Station of the Metro

The apparition of these faces in the crowd;
Petals on a wet, black bough.

—1916

EZRA POUND

202

Portrait d'une Femme°

Your mind and you are our Sargasso Sea,°
London has swept about you this score years
And bright ships left you this or that in fee:
Ideas, old gossip, oddments of all things,
Strange spars of knowledge and dimmed wares of price.   5
Great minds have sought you—lacking someone else.
You have been second always. Tragical?
No. You preferred it to the usual thing:
One dull man, dulling and uxorious,°
One average mind—with one thought less, each year   10
Oh, you are patient, I have seen you sit
Hours, where something might have floated up.
And now you pay one. Yes, you richly pay.
You are a person of some interest, one comes to you
And takes strange gain away: 15

Portrait d'une Femme Portrait of a Lady   **1 Sargasso Sea** area of seaweed in the mid-Atlantic where flotsam accumulates   **9 uxorious** doting and submissive

Trophies fished up; some curious suggestion;
Fact that leads nowhere; and a tale or two,
Pregnant with mandrakes,° or with something else
That might prove useful and yet never proves,
That never fits a corner or shows use,   20
Or finds its hour upon the loom of days:
The tarnished, gaudy, wonderful old work;
Idols and ambergris° and rare inlays,
These are your riches, your great store; and yet
For all this sea-hoard of deciduous things,   25
Strange woods half sodden, and new brighter stuff:
In the slow float of differing light and deep,
No! there is nothing! In the whole and all,
Nothing that's quite your own.
            Yet this is you

                                        —1912

The River-Merchant's Wife: A Letter°

While my hair was still cut straight across my forehead
I played about the front gate, pulling flowers.
You came by on bamboo stilts, playing horse,
You walked about my seat, playing with blue plums.
And we went on living in the village of Chokan: 5
Two small people, without dislike or suspicion.
At fourteen I married My Lord you.
I never laughed, being bashful.
Lowering my head, I looked at the wall.
Called to, a thousand times, I never looked back.   10

At fifteen I stopped scowling,
I desired my dust to be mingled with yours
Forever and forever and forever.
Why should I climb the lookout?

---

18 mandrakes plants with roots shaped like the lower half of the human body   **23 ambergris**
intestinal secretion of the sperm whale; valuable and used in making perfumes
The River-Merchant's Wife: A Letter imitation of a poem by Li-Po (AD 701–762)

At sixteen you departed, 15
You went into far Ku-to-yen, by the river of swirling eddies,
And you have been gone five months.
The monkeys make sorrowful noise overhead.

You dragged your feet when you went out.
By the gate now, the moss is grown, the different mosses, 20
Too deep to clear them away!
The leaves fall early this autumn, in wind.
The paired butterflies are already yellow with August
Over the grass in the West garden;
They hurt me. I grow older. 25
If you are coming down through the narrows of the river Kiang,
Please let me know beforehand,
And I will come out to meet you
    As far as Cho-Fu-Sa.

—*1915*

ELINOR WYLIE ■ (1885–1928)

Elinor Wylie, whose considerable lyrical skills found wide popularity during her relatively brief career, has recently come to the notice of the present generation. For many readers in the post–World War I era, Wylie, along with her slightly younger contemporary Edna St. Vincent Millay, helped to define the literary role of the New Woman of the 1920s. A poetic traditionalist whose lifestyle was thoroughly modern, Wylie now seems overdue for a serious reassessment of her place in the development of twentieth-century women's poetry.

Let No Charitable Hope

Now let no charitable hope
Confuse my mind with images
Of eagle and of antelope:
I am in nature none of these.

I was, being human, born alone; 5
I am, being woman, hard beset;
I live by squeezing from a stone
The little nourishment I get.

In masks outrageous and austere
The years go by in single file;   10
But none has merited my fear,
And none has quite escaped my smile.

—1923

Ophelia°

My locks are shorn for sorrow
Of love which may not be;
Tomorrow and tomorrow
Are plotting cruelty.

The winter wind tangles   5
These ringlets half-grown,
The sun sprays with spangles
And rays like his own.

Oh, quieter and colder
Is the stream; he will wait;   10
When my curls touch my shoulder
He will comb them straight.

—1921

H. D. (HILDA DOOLITTLE) ■ (1886–1961)

H. D. (Hilda Doolittle) was born in Bethlehem, Pennsylvania. Hilda Doolittle was a college friend of both Williams and Pound and moved to Europe permanently in 1911. With her husband Richard Aldington, H. D. was an important member of the imagist group promoted by Pound.

Pear Tree

Silver dust,
lifted from the earth,
higher than my arms reach,
you have mounted,

Ophelia character in Shakespeare's *Hamlet* who drowns herself after her father, Polonius, is killed by Hamlet

O, silver,
higher than my arms reach,
you front us with great mass;

no flower ever opened
so staunch a white leaf,
no flower ever parted silver   10
from such rare silver;

O, white pear,
your flower-tufts
thick on the branch
bring summer and ripe fruits   15
in their purple hearts.

—1916

Sea Rose

Rose, harsh rose,
marred and with stint of petals,
meager flower, thin,
sparse of leaf,

more precious   5
than a wet rose
single on a stem—
you are caught in the drift.

Stunted, with small leaf,
you are flung on the sand,   10
you are lifted
in the crisp sand
that drives in the wind.

Can the spice-rose
drip such acrid fragrance   15
hardened in a leaf?

—1916

Siegfried Sassoon was a decorated hero who publicly denounced World War I and became a friend and supporter of other British war poets, including Robert Graves and Wilfred Owen. His sardonic, anti-heroic war poems owe much to Thomas Hardy, whom he acknowledged as his chief poetic influence.

Dreamers

Soldiers are citizens of death's grey land,
    Drawing no dividend from time's tomorrows.
In the great hour of destiny they stand,
    Each with his feuds, and jealousies, and sorrows.

Soldiers are sworn to action; they must win   5
    Some flaming, fatal climax with their lives.
Soldiers are dreamers, when the guns begin
    They think of firelit homes, clean beds, and wives.

I see them in foul dug-outs, gnawed by rats,
    And in the ruined trenches, lashed with rain,   10
Dreaming of things they did with balls and bats,
    And mocked by hopeless longing to regain
Bank-holidays, and picture shows, and spats,°
    And going to the office in the train.

—1918

Robinson Jeffers lived with his wife and children for many years in Carmel, California, in a rock house that he built himself by the sea. Many of his ideas about man's small place in the larger world of nature have gained in relevance through the years since his death. Largely forgotten for many years, his poetry, particularly his book-length verse narratives, is once more regaining the attention of serious readers.

13 spats once-fashionable shoe coverings

The Purse-Seine°

Our sardine fishermen work at night in the dark of the moon;
    daylight or moonlight
They could not tell where to spread the net, unable to see the
    phosphorescence of the shoals of fish.
They work northward from Monterey, coasting Santa Cruz; off
    New Year's Point or off Pigeon Point
The look-out man will see some lakes of milk-color light on the
    sea's night-purple; he points, and the helmsman
Turns the dark prow, the motorboat circles the gleaming shoal
    and drifts out her seine-net. They close the circle   5
and purse the bottom of the net, then with great labor haul
    it in.

                                    I cannot tell you
How beautiful the scene is, and a little terrible, then, when the
    crowded fish
Know they are caught, and wildly beat from one wall to the other
    of their closing destiny the phosphorescent
Water to a pool of flame, each beautiful slender body sheeted
    with flame, like a live rocket   10
A comet's tail wake of clear yellow flame; while outside the
    narrowing
Floats and cordage of the net great sea-lions come up to
    watch, sighing in the dark; the vast walls of night
Stand erect to the stars.

                        Lately I was looking from a night mountain-top
On a wide city, the colored splendor, galaxies of light: how could
    I help but recall the seine-net   15
Gathering the luminous fish? I cannot tell you how beautiful
    the city appeared, and a little terrible.
I thought, We have geared the machines and locked all together
    into interdependence; we have built the great cities; now
There is no escape. We have gathered vast populations
    incapable of free survival, insulated

Purse-Seine large circular fishing net; the bottom is closed (or pursed) before it is hauled in

From the strong earth, each person in himself helpless, on
    all dependent. The circle is closed, and the net
Is being hauled in. They hardly feel the cords drawing, yet
    they shine already. The inevitable mass-disasters   20
Will not come in our time nor in our children's, but we and
    our children
Must watch the net draw narrower, government take all powers—
    or revolution, and the new government
Take more than all, add to kept bodies kept souls—or anarchy,
    the mass-disasters.

                           These things are Progress;
Do you marvel our verse is troubled or frowning, while it keeps
    its reason? Or it lets go, lets the mood flow   25
In the manner of the recent young men into mere hysteria,
    splintered gleams, crackled laughter. But they are quite wrong.
There is no reason for amazement: surely one always knew
    that cultures decay, and life's end is death.

                                     —1937

MARIANNE MOORE ■ (1887–1972)

*Marianne Moore called her own work poetry—unconventional and marked
with the stamp of a rare personality—because, as she put it, there was no
other category for it. For four years she was editor of the* Dial, *one of the
chief modernist periodicals. Moore's wide range of reference, which can leap
from the commonplace to the wondrous within a single poem, reflects her
unique set of personal interests—which range from exotic natural species to
baseball.*

The Fish

wade
through black jade.
    Of the crow-blue mussel-shells, one
        keeps
        adjusting the ash-heaps;   5
    opening and shutting itself like

an
injured fan.
    The barnacles which encrust the
        side10
        of the wave, cannot hide
    there for the submerged shafts of the

sun,
split like spun
    glass, move themselves with spotlight swift-15
        ness
        into the crevices—
    in and out, illuminating

the
turquoise sea20
    of bodies. The water drives a
        wedge
        of iron through the iron edge
    of the cliff; whereupon the stars,

pink25
rice-grains, ink-
    bespattered jelly-fish, crabs like
        green
        lilies, and submarine
    toadstools, slide each on the other.30

All
external
    marks of abuse are present on
        this
        defiant edifice—35
    all the physical features of

ac-
cident—lack
    of cornice, dynamite grooves, burns,
        and40
        hatchet strokes, these things stand
    out on it; the chasm-side is

dead.
Repeated
 evidence has proved that it can   45
  live
  on what can not revive
  its youth. The sea grows old in it.

—1921

Silence

My father used to say,
"Superior people never make long visits,
have to be shown Longfellow's grave
or the glass flowers at Harvard.
Self-reliant like the cat—   5
that takes its prey to privacy,
the mouse's limp tail hanging like a shoelace from its mouth—
they sometimes enjoy solitude
and can be robbed of speech
by speech which has delighted them.   10
The deepest feeling always shows itself in silence;
not in silence, but restraint."
Nor was he insincere in saying, "Make my house your inn."
Inns are not residences.

—1935

T. S. ELIOT ■ (1888–1965)

T. S. Eliot was the author of The Waste Land, *one of the most famous and difficult modernist poems, and became an international figure. Born in St. Louis and educated at Harvard, he moved to London in 1914, where he remained for the rest of his life, becoming a British subject in 1927. This chief prophet of modern despair turned to the Church of England in later life, and wrote successful dramas on religious themes. As a critic and influential editor, Eliot dominated poetic taste in England and America for over twenty-five years. He was awarded the Nobel Prize in 1948.*

Journey of the Magi°

'A cold coming we had of it,
Just the worst time of the year
For a journey, and such a long journey:
The ways deep and the weather sharp,
The very dead of winter.'°   5
And the camels galled, sore-footed, refractory,
Lying down in the melting snow.
There were times we regretted
The summer palaces on slopes, the terraces,
And the silken girls bringing sherbet.   10
Then the camel men cursing and grumbling
And running away, and wanting their liquor and women,
And the night-fires going out, and the lack of shelters,
And the cities hostile and the towns unfriendly
And the villages dirty and charging high prices: 15
A hard time we had of it.
At the end we preferred to travel all night,
Sleeping in snatches,
With the voices singing in our ears, saying
That this was all folly.   20

Then at dawn we came down to a temperate valley,
Wet, below the snow line, smelling of vegetation;
With a running stream and a water-mill beating the darkness,
And three trees on the low sky.
And an old white horse galloped away in the meadow.   25
Then we came to a tavern with vine-leaves over the lintel,
Six hands at an open door dicing for pieces of silver,
And feet kicking the empty wine-skins.
But there was no information, and so we continued
And arrived at evening, not a moment too soon   30
Finding the place; it was (you may say) satisfactory.

Magi Wise Men mentioned in Matthew 2:1–2   **1–5 'A cold . . . winter'** The quotation marks
indicated Eliot's source, a sermon by Lancelot Andrewes (1555–1626).

All this was a long time ago, I remember,
And I would do it again, but set down
This° set down
This: were we led all that way for   35
Birth or Death? There was a Birth, certainly,
We had evidence and no doubt. I had seen birth and death,
But had thought they were different; this Birth was
Hard and bitter agony for us, like Death, our death.
We returned to our places, these Kingdoms,   40
But no longer at ease here, in the old dispensation,°
With an alien people clutching their gods.
I should be glad of another death.

                                                        —1927

The Love Song of
J. Alfred Prufrock

S'io credesse che mia risposta fosse
A persona che mai tornasse al mondo,
Questa fiamma staria senza più scosse.
Ma perciocche giammai di questo fondo
Non tornò vivo alcun, s'i'odo il vero,
Senza tema d'infamia ti rispondo.°

Let us go then, you° and I,
When the evening is spread out against the sky
Like a patient etherised upon a table;
Let us go, through certain half-deserted streets,
The muttering retreats   5
Of restless nights in one-night cheap hotels
And sawdust restaurants with oyster-shells:
Streets that follow like a tedious argument
Of insidious intent

33–34 set down . . . This The Magus is dictating his memoirs to a scribe.   **41 old dispensation**
world before the birth of Christ
S'io credesse . . . rispondo From Dante's *Inferno* (Canto 27). The speaker is Guido da Montefeltro: "If I
thought I spoke to someone who would return to the world, this flame would tremble no longer. But,
if what I hear is true, since no one has ever returned alive from this place I can answer you without
fear of infamy." **1 you** Eliot said that the auditor of the poem was a male friend of Prufrock.

To lead you to an overwhelming question . . .   10
Oh, do not ask, "What is it?"
Let us go and make our visit.

In the room the women come and go
Talking of Michelangelo.°

The yellow fog that rubs its back upon the window-panes,   15
The yellow smoke that rubs its muzzle on the window-panes,
Licked its tongue into the corners of the evening,
Lingered upon the pools that stand in drains,
Let fall upon its back the soot that falls from chimneys,
Slipped by the terrace, made a sudden leap,   20
And seeing that it was a soft October night,
Curled once about the house, and fell asleep.

And indeed there will be time
For the yellow smoke that slides along the street,

Rubbing its back upon the window-panes;   25
There will be time, there will be time
To prepare a face to meet the faces that you meet;
There will be time to murder and create,
And time for all the works and days of hands
That lift and drop a question on your plate: 30
Time for you and time for me,
And time yet for a hundred indecisions,
And for a hundred visions and revisions,
Before the taking of a toast and tea.

In the room the women come and go   35
Talking of Michelangelo.

And indeed there will be time
To wonder, "Do I dare?" and, "Do I dare?"—
Time to turn back and descend the stair,
With a bald spot in the middle of my hair—   40
(They will say: "How his hair is growing thin!")
My morning coat, my collar mounting firmly to the chin,

14 **Michelangelo** Italian painter and sculptor (1475–1564)

My necktie rich and modest, but asserted by a simple pin—
(They will say: "But how his arms and legs are thin!")
Do I dare   45
Disturb the universe?
In a minute there is time
For decisions and revisions which a minute will reverse.

For I have known them all already, known them all:
Have known the evenings, mornings, afternoons,   50
I have measured out my life with coffee spoons;
I know the voices dying with a dying fall
Beneath the music from a farther room.
          So how should I presume?

And I have known the eyes already, known them all—   55
The eyes that fix you in a formulated phrase,
And when I am formulated, sprawling on a pin,
When I am pinned and wriggling on the wall,
Then how should I begin
To spit out all the butt-ends of my days and ways?   60
          And how should I presume?

And I have known the arms already, known them all—
Arms that are braceleted and white and bare
(But in the lamplight, downed with light brown hair!)
Is it perfume from a dress   65
That makes me so digress?
Arms that lie along a table, or wrap about a shawl.
          And should I then presume?
          And how should I begin?

          . . . . .

Shall I say, I have gone at dusk through narrow streets,   70
And watched the smoke that rises from the pipes
Of lonely men in shirtsleeves, leaning out of windows? . . .

I should have been a pair of ragged claws
Scuttling across the floors of silent seas.

          . . . . .

And the afternoon, the evening, sleeps so peacefully!   75
Smoothed by long fingers,

Asleep . . . tired . . . or it malingers,
Stretched on the floor, here beside you and me.
Should I, after tea and cakes and ices,
Have the strength to force the moment to its crisis?   80
But though I have wept and fasted, wept and prayed,
Though I have seen my head (grown slightly bald) brought in
      upon a platter,
I am no prophet°—and here's no great matter;
I have seen the moment of my greatness flicker,
And I have seen the eternal Footman hold my coat, and
      snicker,   85
            And in short, I was afraid.

And would it have been worth it, after all,
After the cups, the marmalade, the tea,
Among the porcelain, among some talk of you and me,
Would it have been worth while,   90
To have bitten off the matter with a smile,
To have squeezed the universe into a ball
To roll it towards some overwhelming question,
To say: "I am Lazarus,° come from the dead,
Come back to tell you all, I shall tell you all"—   95
If one, settling a pillow by her head,
      Should say: "That is not what I meant at all;
      That is not it, at all."

And would it have been worth it, after all,
Would it have been worth while,   100
After the sunsets and the dooryards and the sprinkled
      streets,
After the novels, after the teacups, after the skirts that trail
      along the floor—
And this, and so much more?—
It is impossible to say just what I mean!
But as if a magic lantern° threw the nerves in patterns on a
      screen: 105

Would it have been worth while
If one, settling a pillow or throwing off a shawl,
And turning toward the window, should say:
    "That is not it at all,
    That is not what I meant, at all."   110

        . . . . .

No! I am not Prince Hamlet, nor was meant to be;
Am an attendant lord, one that will do
To swell a progress, start a scene or two,
Advise the prince; no doubt, an easy tool,
Deferential, glad to be of use,   115
Politic, cautious, and meticulous;
Full of high sentence, but a bit obtuse;
At times, indeed, almost ridiculous—
Almost, at times, the Fool.°

I grow old . . . I grow old . . .   120
I shall wear the bottoms of my trousers rolled.

Shall I part my hair behind? Do I dare to eat a peach?
I shall wear white flannel trousers, and walk upon the beach.
I have heard the mermaids singing, each to each.

I do not think that they will sing to me.   125

I have seen them riding seaward on the waves
Combing the white hair of the waves blown back
When the wind blows the water white and black.

We have lingered in the chambers of the sea
By sea-girls wreathed with seaweed red and brown   130
Till human voices wake us, and we drown.

                                                    —1917

111–119 **not Prince Hamlet . . . the Fool** The allusion is probably to Polonius, a character in *Hamlet*.

Preludes

I

The winter evening settles down
With smell of steaks in passageways.
Six o'clock.
The burnt-out ends of smoky days.
And now a gusty shower wraps   5
The grimy scraps
Of withered leaves about your feet
And newspapers from vacant lots;
The showers beat
On broken blinds and chimney-pots,   10
And at the corner of the street
A lonely cab-horse steams and stamps.

And then the lighting of the lamps.

II

The morning comes to consciousness
Of faint stale smells of beer   15
From the sawdust-trampled street
With all its muddy feet that press
To early coffee-stands.

With the other masquerades
That time resumes,   20
One thinks of all the hands
That are raising dingy shades
In a thousand furnished rooms.

III

You tossed a blanket from the bed,
You lay upon your back, and waited;   25
You dozed, and watched the night revealing
The thousand sordid images
Of which your soul was constituted;
They flickered against the ceiling.

And when all the world came back   30
And the light crept up between the shutters
And you heard the sparrows in the gutters,
You had such a vision of the street
As the street hardly understands;
Sitting along the bed's edge, where   35
You curled the papers from your hair,
Or clasped the yellow soles of feet
In the palms of both soiled hands.

IV

His soul stretched tight across the skies
That fade behind a city block,   40
Or trampled by insistent feet
At four and five and six o'clock;
And short square fingers stuffing pipes,
And evening newspapers, and eyes
Assured of certain certainties,   45
The conscience of a blackened street
Impatient to assume the world.

I am moved by fancies that are curled
Around these images, and cling:
The notion of some infinitely gentle   50
Infinitely suffering thing.

Wipe your hand across your mouth, and laugh;
The worlds revolve like ancient women
Gathering fuel in vacant lots.

—1917

Raised in the coastal village of Camden, Maine, Edna St. Vincent Millay was extremely popular in the 1920s, when her sonnets seemed the ultimate expression of the liberated sexuality of what was then called the New Woman. Neglected for many years, her poems have recently generated renewed interest, and it seems likely that she will eventually regain her status as one of the most important female poets of the twentieth century.

If I Should Learn, in Some Quite Casual Way

If I should learn, in some quite casual way,
That you were gone, not to return again—
Read from the back-page of a paper, say,
Held by a neighbor in a subway train,
How at the corner of this avenue   5
And such a street (so are the papers filled)
A hurrying man, who happened to be you,
At noon today had happened to be killed—
I should not cry aloud—I could not cry
Aloud, or wring my hands in such a place—   10
I should but watch the station lights rush by
With a more careful interest on my face;
Or raise my eyes and read with greater care
Where to store furs and how to treat the hair.

—1917

Oh, Oh, You Will Be Sorry for That Word

Oh, oh, you will be sorry for that word!
Give back my book and take my kiss instead.
Was it my enemy or my friend I heard,
"What a big book for such a little head!"
Come, I will show you now my newest hat,   5
And you may watch me purse my mouth and prink!°

6 **prink** primp

Oh, I shall love you still, and all of that.
I never again shall tell you what I think.
I shall be sweet and crafty, soft and sly;
You will not catch me reading any more: 10
I shall be called a wife to pattern by;
And some day when you knock and push the door,
Some sane day, not too bright and not too stormy,
I shall be gone, and you may whistle for me.

—*1923*

What Lips My Lips Have Kissed, and Where, and Why

What lips my lips have kissed, and where, and why,
I have forgotten, and what arms have lain
Under my head till morning; but the rain
Is full of ghosts tonight, that tap and sigh
Upon the glass and listen for reply,   5
And in my heart there stirs a quiet pain
For unremembered lads that not again
Will turn to me at midnight with a cry.
Thus in the winter stands the lonely tree,
Nor knows what birds have vanished one by one,   10
Yet knows its boughs more silent than before:
I cannot say what loves have come and gone,
I only know that summer sang in me
A little while, that in me sings no more.

—*1923*

WILFRED OWEN ■ (1893–1918)

Wilfred Owen was killed in the trenches only a few days before the armistice that ended World War I. Owen showed more promise than any other English poet of his generation. A decorated officer whose nerves broke down after exposure to battle, he met Siegfried Sassoon at Craiglockhart military hospital. His work was posthumously collected by his friend. A novel by Pat Barker, Regeneration *(also made into a film), deals with their poetic and personal relationship.*

Dulce et Decorum Est°

Bent double, like old beggars under sacks,
Knock-kneed, coughing like hags, we cursed through sludge,
Till on the haunting flares we turned our backs
And towards our distant rest began to trudge.
Men marched asleep. Many had lost their boots   5
But limped on, blood-shod. All went lame; all blind;
Drunk with fatigue; deaf even to the hoots
Of tired, outstripped Five-Nines° that dropped behind.

Gas! Gas! Quick, boys!—An ecstasy of fumbling
Fitting the clumsy helmets just in time;   10
But someone still was yelling out and stumbling
And flound'ring like a man in fire or lime . . .
Dim, through the misty panes and thick green light,°
As under a green sea, I saw him drowning.

In all my dreams, before my helpless sight,   15
He plunges at me, guttering, choking, drowning.
If in some smothering dreams you too could pace
Behind the wagon that we flung him in,
And watch the white eyes writhing in his face,
His hanging face, like a devil's sick of sin;   20
If you could hear, at every jolt, the blood
Come gargling from the froth-corrupted lungs,
Obscene as cancer, bitter as the cud
Of vile, incurable sores on innocent tongues,—
My friend,° you would not tell with such high zest   25
To children ardent for some desperate glory,
The old Lie: Dulce et decorum est
Pro patria mori.

—1920

WILFRED OWEN

222

Dulce et Decorum Est (pro patria mori) from the Roman poet Horace: "It is sweet and proper to
die for one's country"   **8 Five-Nines** German artillery shells (59 mm)   **13 misty panes and thick
green light** i.e., through the gas mask   **25 My friend** The poem was originally addressed to Jessie
Pope, a writer of patriotic verse.

E. E. CUMMINGS ■ (1894–1962)

e. e. cummings was the son of a Harvard professor and Unitarian clergyman. Edward Estlin Cummings served as a volunteer ambulance driver in France during World War I. cummings's experimentation with the typographical aspects of poetry reveals his serious interest in cubist painting, which he studied in Paris in the 1920s. A brilliant satirist, he also excelled as a writer of lyrical poems whose unusual appearance and idiosyncratic grammar, spelling, and punctuation often overshadow their traditional themes.

pity this busy monster, manunkind

pity this busy monster, manunkind,

not. Progress is a comfortable disease:
your victim (death and life safely beyond)

plays with the bigness of his littleness
—electrons° deify one razorblade   5
into a mountainrange; lenses extend

unwish through curving wherewhen till unwish
returns on its unself.
                         A world of made
is not a world of born—pity poor flesh

and trees, poor stars and stones, but never this   10
fine specimen of hypermagical

ultraomnipotence. We doctors know

a hopeless case if—listen: there's a hell
of a good universe next door; let's go

—1944

---

5 electrons in an electron microscope

plato told

plato told

him: he couldn't
believe it (jesus

told him; he
wouldn't believe   5
it) lao

tsze
certainly told
him, and general
(yes

mam)   10
sherman;°

and even
(believe it
Or   15

not) you
told him: i told

him; we told him
(he didn't believe it, no

sir) it took   20
a nipponized° bit of
the old sixth

avenue
el; in the top of his head: to tell
him   25

1944

---

11 William Tecumseh Sherman (1820–1891), Union general in the American Civil War. cummings alludes to his famous statement "War is hell," a sentiment presumably shared by Plato, the Greek philosopher (427?–347 BC), Jesus, and Lao-tze (c. 604 BC), Chinese philosopher credited as the founder of Taoism.   **21** Scrap metal from the Sixth Avenue elevated railway in New York City, torn down in the 1930s, was sold to Japan and turned into armaments used in World War II.

r-p-o-p-h-e-s-s-a-g-r

r-p-o-p-h-e-s-s-a-g-r
                who
a)s w(e loo)k
upnowgath
          PPEGORHRASS   5
                    eringint(o-
aThe):l
     eA
       !p:
S   a   10
          (r
rIvInG   .gRrEaPsPhOs)
                    to
rea(be)rran(com)gi(e)ngly
,grasshopper;   15
                              —1932

Somewhere I have never travelled

somewhere i have never travelled, gladly beyond
any experience, your eyes have their silence:
in your most frail gesture are things which enclose me,
or which i cannot touch because they are too near

your slightest look will easily unclose me   5
though i have closed myself as fingers,
you open always petal by petal myself as Spring opens
(touching skilfully,mysteriously) her first rose

or if your wish be to close me, i and
my life will shut very beautifully ,suddenly,   10
as when the heart of this flower imagines
the snow carefully everywhere descending;

nothing which we are to perceive in this world equals
the power of your intense fragility:whose texture
compels me with the color of its countries,   15
rendering death and forever with each breathing

(i do not know what it is about you that closes
and opens;only something in me understands
the voice of your eyes is deeper than all roses)
nobody,not even the rain,has such small hands   20

—1931

JEAN TOOMER ■ (1894–1967)

*Jean Toomer was born in Washington, D.C., the grandson of a black man who
served as governor of Louisiana during Reconstruction. His book* Cane *(1923) is
a mixed collection of prose and verse based on his observations of life in rural
Georgia, where he was a schoolteacher. A complete edition of his poetry, most of
it unpublished during his life, was assembled over twenty years after his death.*

Georgia Dusk

The sky, lazily disdaining to pursue
    The setting sun, too indolent to hold
    A lengthened tournament for flashing gold,
Passively darkens for night's barbecue,

A feast of moon and men and barking hounds,   5
    An orgy for some genius of the South
    With blood-hot eyes and cane-lipped scented mouth,
Surprised in making folk-songs from soul sounds.

The sawmill blows its whistle, buzz-saws stop,
    And silence breaks the bud of knoll and hill,   10
Soft settling pollen where plowed lands fulfill
Their early promise of a bumper crop.

Smoke from the pyramidal sawdust pile
    Curls up, blue ghosts of trees, tarrying low
    Where only chips and stumps are left to show   15
The solid proof of former domicile.

Meanwhile, the men, with vestiges of pomp,
    Race memories of king and caravan,
    High-priests, an ostrich, and a juju-man,
Go singing through the footpaths of the swamp.   20

Their voices rise . . the pine trees are guitars,
    Strumming, pine-needles fall like sheets of rain . . .

Their voices rise . . the chorus of the cane
Is caroling a vesper to the stars . .

O singers, resinous and soft your songs   25
    Above the sacred whisper of the pines,
    Give virgin lips to cornfield concubines,
Bring dreams of Christ to dusky cane-lipped throngs.

—1923

LOUISE BOGAN ▪ (1897–1970)

Louise Bogan was for many years the poetry editor and resident critic of The
New Yorker, *and the opinions expressed in her many book reviews have held
up well in the years since her death. In her later years, Bogan suffered from
severe bouts of clinical depression and wrote little poetry, but her relatively
slim output reveals a unique poetic voice.*

Women

Women have no wilderness in them,
They are provident instead,
Content in the tight hot cell of their hearts
To eat dusty bread.

They do not see cattle cropping red winter grass,   5
They do not hear
Snow water going down under culverts
Shallow and clear.

They wait, when they should turn to journeys,
They stiffen, when they should bend.   10
They use against themselves that benevolence
To which no man is friend.

They cannot think of so many crops to a field
Or of clean wood cleft by an axe.
Their love is an eager meaninglessness   15
Too tense, or too lax.

They hear in every whisper that speaks to them
A shout and a cry.

As like as not, when they take life over their door-sills
They should let it go by.   20

—1923

LANGSTON HUGHES ■ (1902–1967)

*Langston Hughes was a leading figure in the Harlem Renaissance of the
1920s, and he became the most famous black writer of his day. Phrases from
his poems and other writings have become deeply ingrained in the American
consciousness. An important experimenter with poetic form, Hughes is credited with incorporating the rhythms of jazz into poetry.*

Dream Boogie

Good morning, daddy!
Ain't you heard
The boogie-woogie rumble
Of a dream deferred?
Listen closely: 5
You'll hear their feet
Beating out and beating out a—

　　*You think
　　It's a happy beat?*

Listen to it closely: 10
Ain't you heard
something underneath
like a—

　　What did I say?

Sure,   15
I'm happy!
Take it away!

　　*Hey, pop!
　　Re-bop!
　　Mop!*   20
　　　Y-e-a-h!

—1951

Harlem Sweeties

Have you dug the spill
Of Sugar Hill?
Cast your gims
On this sepia thrill:
Brown sugar lassie,   5
Caramel treat,
Honey-gold baby
Sweet enough to eat.
Peach-skinned girlie,
Coffee and cream,   10
Chocolate darling
Out of a dream.
Walnut tinted
Or cocoa brown,
Pomegranate-lipped   15
Pride of the town.
Rich cream-colored
To plum-tinted black,
Feminine sweetness
In Harlem's no lack.   20
Glow of the quince
To blush of the rose.
Persimmon bronze
To cinnamon toes.
Blackberry cordial,   25
Virginia Dare wine—
All those sweet colors
Flavor Harlem of mine!
Walnut or cocoa,
Let me repeat: 30
Caramel, brown sugar,
A chocolate treat.
Molasses taffy,
Coffee and cream,
Licorice, clove, cinnamon   35
To a honey-brown dream.
Ginger, wine-gold,

Persimmon, blackberry,
All through the spectrum
Harlem girls vary—   40
So if you want to know beauty's
Rainbow-sweet thrill,
Stroll down luscious,
Delicious, *fine* Sugar Hill.

—1940

The Weary Blues

LANGSTON HUGHES

Droning a drowsy syncopated tune,
Rocking back and forth to a mellow croon,
     I heard a Negro play.
Down on Lenox Avenue the other night
By the pale dull pallor of an old gas light   5
     He did a lazy sway. . . .
     He did a lazy sway. . . .
To the tune o' those Weary Blues.
With his ebony hands on each ivory key
He made that poor piano moan with melody.   10
     O Blues!
Swaying to and fro on his rickety stool
He played that sad raggy tune like a musical fool.
     Sweet Blues!
Coming from a black man's soul.   15
     O Blues!
In a deep song voice with a melancholy tone
I heard that Negro sing, that old piano moan—
     "Ain't got nobody in all this world,
     Ain't got nobody but ma self.   20
     I's gwine to quit ma frownin'
     And put ma troubles on the shelf."

Thump, thump, thump, went his foot on the floor.
He played a few chords then he sang some more—
     "I got the Weary Blues   25
     And I can't be satisfied.
     Got the Weary Blues
     And can't be satisfied—

I ain't happy no mo'
And I wish that I had died."   30
And far into the night he crooned that tune.
The stars went out and so did the moon.
The singer stopped playing and went to bed
While the Weary Blues echoed through his head.
He slept like a rock or a man that's dead.   35

—1926

STEVIE SMITH ■ (1902–1971)

Stevie (Florence Margaret) Smith worked for many years as a secretary to a London publisher and first attracted attention with the autobiographical Novel on Yellow Paper in 1936. Always something of a literary outsider who nevertheless found popular success with her highly original and idiosyncratic fiction, poetry, and drawings, Smith was brilliantly portrayed by Glenda Jackson in the 1978 film Stevie.

Our Bog Is Dood

Our Bog is dood, our Bog is dood,
They lisped in accents mild,
But when I asked them to explain
They grew a little wild.
How do you know your Bog is dood   5
My darling little child?

We know because we wish it so
That is enough, they cried,
And straight within each infant eye
Stood up the flame of pride,   10
And if you do not think it so
You shall be crucified.

Then tell me, darling little ones,
What's dood, suppose Bog is?
Just what we think, the answer came,   15
Just what we think it is.
They bowed their heads. Our Bog is ours
And we are wholly his.

But when they raised them up again
They had forgotten me   20
Each one upon each other glared
In pride and misery
For what was dood, and what their Bog
They never could agree.

Oh sweet it was to leave them then,   25
And sweeter not to see,
And sweetest of all to walk alone
Beside the encroaching sea,
The sea that soon should drown them all,
That never yet drowned me.   30

—1950

COUNTEE CULLEN ■ (1903–1946)

Countee Cullen, among black writers of the first half of the twentieth century, crafted poetry representing a more conservative style than that of his contemporary, Hughes. Although he wrote a number of lyrics on standard poetic themes, he is best remembered for his eloquent poems on racial subjects.

Incident

Once riding in old Baltimore,
  Heart-filled, head-filled with glee,
I saw a Baltimorean
  Keep looking straight at me.

Now I was eight and very small,   5
  And he was no whit bigger,
And so I smiled, but he poked out
  His tongue, and called me, "Nigger."

I saw the whole of Baltimore
  From May until December;   10
Of all the things that happened there
  That's all that I remember.

—1925

Yet Do I Marvel

I doubt not God is good, well-meaning, kind,
And did He stoop to quibble could tell why
The little buried mole continues blind,
Why flesh that mirrors Him must some day die,
Make plain the reason tortured Tantalus°   5
Is baited by the fickle fruit, declare
If merely brute caprice dooms Sisyphus°
To struggle up a never-ending stair.
Inscrutable His ways are, and immune
To catechism by a mind too strewn   10
With petty cares to slightly understand
What awful brain compels His awful hand.
Yet do I marvel at this curious thing:
To make a poet black and bid him sing!

—1925

W. H. AUDEN ■ (1907–1973)

W. H. Auden was already established as an important younger British poet before he moved to America in 1939 (he later became a U.S. citizen). As a transatlantic link between two literary cultures, Auden was one of the most influential literary figures and cultural spokespersons in the English-speaking world for almost forty years, giving a name to the postwar era when he dubbed it "The Age of Anxiety" in a poem. In his last years he returned briefly to Oxford, where he occupied the poetry chair.

As I Walked Out One Evening

As I walked out one evening,
    Walking down Bristol Street,
The crowds upon the pavement
    Were fields of harvest wheat.

5 **Tantalus** mythological character tortured by unreachable fruit   7 **Sisyphus** figure in myth who endlessly rolls a boulder uphill

And down by the brimming river   5
    I heard a lover sing
Under an arch of the railway:
    "Love has no ending.

"I'll love you, dear, I'll love you
    Till China and Africa meet,   10
And the river jumps over the mountain
    And the salmon sing in the street.

"I'll love you till the ocean
    Is folded and hung up to dry,
And the seven stars go squawking   15
    Like geese about the sky.

"The years shall run like rabbits,
    For in my arms I hold
The Flower of the Ages,
    And the first love of the world."   20

But all the clocks in the city
    Began to whirr and chime:
"O let not Time deceive you,
    You cannot conquer Time.

"In the burrows of the Nightmare   25
    Where Justice naked is,
Time watches from the shadow
    And coughs when you would kiss.

"In headaches and in worry
    Vaguely life leaks away,   30
And Time will have his fancy
    Tomorrow or to-day.

"Into many a green valley
    Drifts the appalling snow;
Time breaks the threaded dances   35
    And the diver's brilliant bow.

"O plunge your hands in water,
    Plunge them in up to the wrist;
Stare, stare in the basin
    And wonder what you've missed.   40

"The glacier knocks in the cupboard,
   The desert sighs in the bed,
And the crack in the tea-cup opens
   A lane to the land of the dead.

"Where the beggars raffle the banknotes   45
   And the Giant is enchanting to Jack,
And the Lily-white Boy is a Roarer,
   And Jill goes down on her back.

"O look, look in the mirror,
   O look in your distress;   50
Life remains a blessing
   Although you cannot bless.

"O stand, stand at the window
   As the tears scald and start;
You shall love your crooked neighbor   55
   With your crooked heart."

It was late, late in the evening,
   The lovers they were gone;
The clocks had ceased their chiming,
   And the deep river ran on.   60

—1940

Musée des Beaux Arts°

About suffering they were never wrong,
The Old Masters: how well they understood
Its human position; how it takes place
While someone else is eating or opening a window or just
   walking dully along;
How, when the aged are reverently, passionately waiting   5
For the miraculous birth, there always must be
Children who did not specially want it to happen, skating
On a pond at the edge of the wood:
They never forgot
That even the dreadful martyrdom must run its course   10

Musée des Beaux Arts Museum of Fine Arts

Anyhow in a corner, some untidy spot
Where the dogs go on with their doggy life and the torturer's horse
Scratches its innocent behind on a tree.

In Brueghel's *Icarus*,° for instance: how everything turns away
Quite leisurely from the disaster; the ploughman may   15
Have heard the splash, the forsaken cry,
But for him it was not an important failure; the sun shone
As it had to on the white legs disappearing into the green
Water; and the expensive delicate ship that must have seen
Something amazing, a boy falling out of the sky,   20
Had somewhere to get to and sailed calmly on.

—1938

The Unknown Citizen

W. H. AUDEN

236

To JS/07/M/378
This Marble Monument Is Erected by the State

He was found by the Bureau of Statistics to be
One against whom there was no official complaint,
And all the reports on his conduct agree
That, in the modern sense of an old-fashioned word, he was a saint,
For in everything he did he served the Greater Community.   5
Except for the War till the day he retired
He worked in a factory and never got fired,
But satisfied his employers, Fudge Motors Inc.
Yet he wasn't a scab or odd in his views,
For his Union reports that he paid his dues,   10
(Our report on his Union shows it was sound)
And our Social Psychology workers found
That he was popular with his mates and liked a drink.
The Press are convinced that he bought a paper every day
And that his reactions to advertisements were normal
    in every way.   15
Policies taken out in his name prove that he was fully insured,

---

14 Brueghel's *Icarus* In this painting (c. 1550) the famous event from Greek myth is almost
inconspicuous among the other details Auden mentions.

And his Health-card shows he was once in hospital but left
    it cured.
Both Producers Research and High-Grade Living declare
He was fully sensible to the advantages of the Installment Plan
And had everything necessary to the Modern Man,   20
A phonograph, a radio, a car and a frigidaire.
Our researchers into Public Opinion are content
That he held the proper opinions for the time of year;
When there was peace, he was for peace; when there was war,
    he went.
He was married and added five children to the population,   25
Which our Eugenist says was the right number for a parent
    of his generation,
And our teachers report that he never interfered with their
    education.
Was he free? Was he happy? The question is absurd:
Had anything been wrong, we should certainly have heard.

—1939

THEODORE ROETHKE ■ (1908–1963)

*Theodore Roethke was born in Michigan. Roethke was an influential teacher
of poetry at the University of Washington for many years. His father was the
owner of a greenhouse, and Roethke's childhood closeness to nature was an
important influence on his mature poetry. His periodic nervous breakdowns,
the result of bipolar manic-depression, presaged his early death.*

Dolor°

I have known the inexorable sadness of pencils,
Neat in their boxes, dolor of pad and paper-weight,
All of the misery of manilla folders and mucilage,
Desolation in immaculate public places,
Lonely reception room, lavatory, switchboard,   5
The unalterable pathos of basin and pitcher,
Ritual of multigraph, paper-clip, comma,

Dolor sadness

Endless duplication of lives and objects.
And I have seen dust from the walls of institutions,
Finer than flour, alive, more dangerous than silica,°   10
Sift, almost invisible, through long afternoons of tedium,
Dropping a fine film on nails and delicate eyebrows,
Glazing the pale hair, the duplicate grey standard faces.

—*1948*

My Papa's Waltz

THEODORE ROETHKE

238

A The whiskey on your breath
B Could make a small boy dizzy;
A But I hung on like death:
B Such waltzing was not easy.

C We romped until the pans   5
D Slid from the kitchen shelf;
C My mother's countenance
D Could not unfrown itself.

E The hand that held my wrist
F Was battered on one knuckle;   10
E At every step you missed
F My right ear scraped a buckle.

G You beat time on my head
H With a palm caked hard by dirt,
G Then waltzed me off to bed   15
H Still clinging to your shirt.

—*1948*

Root Cellar

Nothing would sleep in that cellar, dank as a ditch,
Bulbs broke out of boxes hunting for chinks in the dark,
Shoots dangled and drooped,
Lolling obscenely from mildewed crates,
Hung down long yellow evil necks, like tropical snakes.   5

---

10 **silica** rock dust, a cause of silicosis, an occupational disease of miners and quarry workers

And what a congress of stinks!—
Roots ripe as old bait,
Pulpy stems, rank, silo-rich,
Leaf-mold, manure, lime, piled against slippery planks.
Nothing would give up life: 10
Even the dirt kept breathing a small breath.

—1948

ELIZABETH BISHOP ■ (1911–1979)

*Elizabeth Bishop for most of her life was highly regarded as a "poet's poet,"
winning the Pulitzer Prize for* North *and* South *in 1956, but in the years
since her death she has gained a wider readership. She traveled widely and
lived in Brazil for a number of years before returning to the United States to
teach at Harvard during the last years of her life.*

The Fish

I caught a tremendous fish
and held him beside the boat
half out of water, with my hook
fast in a corner of his mouth.
He didn't fight.   5
He hadn't fought at all.
He hung a grunting weight,
battered and venerable
and homely. Here and there
his brown skin hung in strips   10
like ancient wallpaper,
and its pattern of darker brown
was like wallpaper:
shapes like full-blown roses
stained and lost through age.   15
He was speckled with barnacles,
fine rosettes of lime,
and infested
with tiny white sea-lice,
and underneath two or three   20

rags of green weed hung down.
While his gills were breathing in
the terrible oxygen
—the frightening gills,
fresh and crisp with blood,   25
that can cut so badly—
I thought of the coarse white flesh
packed in like feathers,
the big bones and the little bones,
the dramatic reds and blacks   30
of his shiny entrails,
and the pink swim-bladder
like a big peony.
I looked into his eyes
which were far larger than mine   35
but shallower, and yellowed,
the irises backed and packed
with tarnished tinfoil
seen through the lenses
of old scratched isinglass.°   40
They shifted a little, but not
to return my stare.
—It was more like the tipping
of an object toward the light.
I admired his sullen face,   45
the mechanism of his jaw,
and then I saw
that from his lower lip
—if you could call it a lip—
grim, wet, and weapon-like,   50
hung five old pieces of fish-line,
or four and a wire leader
with the swivel still attached,
with all their five big hooks
grown firmly in his mouth.   55
A green line, frayed at the end
where he broke it, two heavier lines,

40 isinglass semitransparent material made from fish bladders

and a fine black thread
still crimped from the strain and snap
when it broke and he got away.   60
Like medals with their ribbons
frayed and wavering,
a five-haired beard of wisdom
trailing from his aching jaw.
I stared and stared   65
and victory filled up
the little rented boat,
from the pool of bilge
where oil had spread a rainbow
around the rusted engine   70
to the bailer° rusted orange,
the sun-cracked thwarts,
the oarlocks on their strings,
the gunnels°—until everything
was rainbow, rainbow, rainbow!   75
And I let the fish go.

—1946

One Art

The art of losing isn't hard to master;
so many things seem filled with the intent
to be lost that their loss is no disaster.

Lose something every day. Accept the fluster
of lost door keys, the hour badly spent.   5
The art of losing isn't hard to master.

Then practice losing farther, losing faster:
places, and names, and where it was you meant
to travel. None of these will bring disaster.

I lost my mother's watch. And look! my last, or   10
next-to-last, of three loved houses went.
The art of losing isn't hard to master.

71 **bailer** bucket   74 **gunnels** gunwales

I lost two cities, lovely ones. And, vaster,
some realms I owned, two rivers, a continent.
I miss them, but it wasn't a disaster. 15

—Even losing you (the joking voice, a gesture
I love) I shan't have lied. It's evident
the art of losing's not too hard to master
though it may look like *(Write it!)* like disaster.

—1976

The Shampoo

ROBERT HAYDEN

The still explosions on the rocks,
the lichens, grow
by spreading, gray, concentric shocks.
They have arranged
to meet the rings around the moon, although 5
within our memories they have not changed.

And since the heavens will attend
as long on us,
you've been, dear friend,
precipitate and pragmatical; 10
and look what happens. For Time is
nothing if not amenable.

The shooting stars in your black hair
in bright formation
are flocking where, 15
so straight, so soon?
—Come, let me wash it in this big tin basin,
battered and shiny like the moon.

—1976

ROBERT HAYDEN ■ (1913–1980)

*Robert Hayden named Countee Cullen as one of the chief early influences on
his poetry. A native of Michigan, he taught for many years at Fisk University
in Nashville and at the University of Michigan. Although many of Hayden's
poems are on African-American subjects, he wished to be considered a poet
with strong links to the mainstream English-language tradition.*

Those Winter Sundays

Sundays too my father got up early
and put his clothes on in the blueblack cold,
then with cracked hands that ached
from labor in the weekday weather made
banked fires blaze. No one ever thanked him.   5

I'd wake and hear the cold splintering, breaking.
When the rooms were warm, he'd call,
and slowly I would rise and dress,
fearing the chronic angers of that house,

Speaking indifferently to him,   10
who had driven out the cold
and polished my good shoes as well.
What did I know, what did I know
of love's austere and lonely offices?°

—1962

DUDLEY RANDALL ■ (1914—2000)

Dudley Randall was the founder of Broadside Press, a black-owned publishing firm that eventually attracted important writers like Gwendolyn Brooks and Don L. Lee. For most of his life a resident of Detroit, Randall spent many years working in that city's library system before taking a similar position at the University of Detroit.

Ballad of Birmingham

(On the Bombing of a Church in
Birmingham, Alabama, 1963)°

"Mother dear, may I go downtown
Instead of out to play,
And march the streets of Birmingham
In a Freedom March today?"

---

14 offices daily religious ceremonies
Birmingham, Alabama, 1963 during the height of the civil rights movement

"No, baby, no, you may not go,   5
For the dogs are fierce and wild,
And clubs and hoses, guns and jail
Aren't good for a little child."

"But, mother, I won't be alone.
Other children will go with me,   10
And march the streets of Birmingham
To make our country free."

"No, baby, no, you may not go,
For I fear those guns will fire.
But you may go to church instead   15
And sing in the children's choir."

She has combed and brushed her night-dark hair,
And bathed rose petal sweet,
And drawn white gloves on her small brown hands,
And white shoes on her feet.   20

The mother smiled to know her child
Was in the sacred place,
But that smile was the last smile
To come upon her face.

For when she heard the explosion,   25
Her eyes grew wet and wild.
She raced through the streets of Birmingham
Calling for her child.

She clawed through bits of glass and brick,
Then lifted out a shoe.   30
"O, here's the shoe my baby wore,
But, baby, where are you?"

—*1969*

WILLIAM STAFFORD ■ (1914–1993)

William Stafford was one of the most prolific poets of the postwar era. Stafford published in virtually every magazine in the United States. Raised in Kansas as a member of the pacifist Church of the Brethren, Stafford served in a camp for conscientious objectors during World War II. His first book did not appear until he was in his forties, but he published over thirty collections before his death at age seventy-nine.

Traveling Through the Dark

Traveling through the dark I found a deer
dead on the edge of the Wilson River road.
It is usually best to roll them into the canyon:
that road is narrow; to swerve might make more dead.

By glow of the tail-light I stumbled back of the car   5
and stood by the heap, a doe, a recent killing;
she had stiffened already, almost cold.
I dragged her off; she was large in the belly.

My fingers touching her side brought me the reason—
her side was warm; her fawn lay there waiting,   10
alive, still, never to be born.
Beside that mountain road I hesitated.

The car aimed ahead its lowered parking lights;
under the hood purred the steady engine.
I stood in the glare of the warm exhaust turning red;   15
around our group I could hear the wilderness listen.

I thought hard for us all—my only swerving—
then pushed her over the edge into the river.

assumption that is connected.

—1960

DYLAN THOMAS ■ (1914–1953)

Dylan Thomas was a legendary performer of his and others' poetry. His popularity in the United States led to several collegiate reading tours, punctuated with outrageous behavior and self-destructive drinking that led to his early death in New York City, the victim of what the autopsy report labeled "insult to the brain." The Wales of his childhood remained a constant source of inspiration for his poetry and for radio dramas like Under Milk Wood, *which was turned into a film by fellow Welshman Richard Burton and his then-wife, Elizabeth Taylor.*

Do Not Go Gentle into That Good Night

Do not go gentle into that good night,
Old age should burn and rave at close of day;
Rage, rage against the dying of the light.

Though wise men at their end know dark is right,
Because their words had forked no lightning they   5
Do not go gentle into that good night.

Good men, the last wave by, crying how bright
Their frail deeds might have danced in a green bay,
Rage, rage against the dying of the light.

Wild men who caught and sang the sun in flight,   10
And learn, too late, they grieved it on its way,
Do not go gentle into that good night.

Grave men, near death, who see with blinding sight
Blind eyes could blaze like meteors and be gay,
Rage, rage against the dying of the light.   15

And you, my father, there on the sad height,
Curse, bless, me now with your fierce tears, I pray,
Do not go gentle into that good night.
Rage, rage against the dying of the light.

—1952

Poem in October

It was my thirtieth year to heaven
Woke to my heating from harbour and neighbour wood
    And the mussel pooled and the heron
        Priested shore
        The morning beckon   5
With water praying and call of seagull and rock
And the knock of sailing boats on the net webbed wall
    Myself to set foot
        That second
    In the still sleeping town and set forth.   10

My birthday began with the water-
Birds and the birds of the winged trees flying my name
   Above the farms and the white horses
       And I rose
     In the rainy autumn   15
And walked abroad in a shower of all my days.
High tide and the heron dived when I took the road
   Over the border
     And the gates
Of the town closed as the town awoke.   20

   A springful of larks in a rolling
Cloud and the roadside bushes brimming with whistling
   Blackbirds and the sun of October
      Summary
     On the hill's shoulder,   25
Here were fond climates and sweet singers suddenly
Come in the morning where I wandered and listened
   To the rain wringing
     Wind blow cold
In the wood faraway under me.   30

   Pale rain over the dwindling harbour
And over the sea wet church the size of a snail
   With its horns through mist and the castle
     Brown as owls
     But all the gardens   35
Of spring and summer were blooming in the tall tales
Beyond the border and under the lark full cloud.
   There could I marvel
     My birthday
Away but the weather turned around.   40

   It turned away from the blithe country
And down the other air and the blue altered sky
   Streamed again a wonder of summer
      With apples
     Pears and red currants   45
And I saw in the turning so clearly a child's
Forgotten morning when he walked with his mother
   Through the parables

Of sun light
And the legends of the green chapels 50

And the twice told fields of infancy
That his tears burned my cheeks and his heart moved in mine.
    These were the woods the river and sea
        Where a boy
        In the listening 55
Summertime of the dead whispered the truth of his joy
To tree and the stones and the fish in the tide.
        And the mystery
            Sang alive
        Still in the water and singingbirds. 60

And there could I marvel my birthday
Away but the weather turned around. And the true
    Joy of the long dead child sang burning
        In the sun.
        It was my thirtieth 65
Year to heaven stood there then in the summer noon
Though the town below lay leaved with October blood.
        O may my heart's truth
            Still be sung
        On this high hill in a year's turning. 70

—1946

WELDON KEES ■ (1914–1955)

Weldon Kees was a multitalented poet, painter, jazz musician, and film-maker who went from the University of Nebraska to New York to California. His reputation, aided by posthumous publication of his stories, criticism, letters, and novels, has grown steadily since his apparent suicide by leaping from the Golden Gate Bridge.

For My Daughter

Looking into my daughter's eyes I read
Beneath the innocence of morning flesh
Concealed, hintings of death she does not heed.

Coldest of winds have blown this hair, and mesh
Of seaweed snarled these miniatures of hands;   5
The night's slow poison, tolerant and bland,
Has moved her blood. Parched years that I have seen
That may be hers appear; foul, lingering
Death in certain war, the slim legs green.
Or, fed on hate, she relishes the sting   10
Of others' agony; perhaps the cruel
Bride of a syphilitic or a fool.
These speculations sour in the sun.
I have no daughter. I desire none.

—1943

MARGARET WALKER ▪ (1915–1998)

Margaret Walker, as a female African-American poet, was perhaps overshadowed by Gwendolyn Brooks, even though Walker's receipt of the Yale Younger Poets Award in 1942 for For My People *came some years before Brooks's own recognition. A longtime teacher at Jackson State University, she influenced several generations of young writers.*

For Malcolm X

All you violated ones with gentle hearts;
You violent dreamers whose cries shout heartbreak;
Whose voices echo clamors of our cool capers,
And whose black faces have hollowed pits for eyes.
All you gambling sons and hooked children and bowery bums   5
Hating white devils and black bourgeoisie,
Thumbing your noses at your burning red suns,
Gather round this coffin and mourn your dying swan.

Snow-white moslem head-dress around a dead black face!
Beautiful were your sand-papering words against our skins!   10
Our blood and water pour from your flowing wounds.
You have cut open our breasts and dug scalpels in our brains.
When and Where will another come to take your holy place?
Old man mumbling in his dotage, or crying child, unborn?

—1970

Gwendolyn Brooks was the first African American to win a Pulitzer Prize for poetry. Brooks reflected many changes in black culture during her long career, and she wrote about the stages of her own life candidly in In the Mecca *(1968), her literary autobiography. Brooks was the last poetry consultant of the Library of Congress before that position became poet laureate of the United States. At the end of her life, Brooks was one of the most honored and beloved of American poets.*

the ballad of chocolate Mabbie

It was Mabbie without° the grammar school gates.
And Mabbie was all of seven.
And Mabbie was cut from a chocolate bar.
And Mabbie thought life was heaven.

The grammar school gates were the pearly gates,   5
For Willie Boone went to school.
When she sat by him in history class
Was only her eyes were cool.

It was Mabbie without the grammar school gates
Waiting for Willie Boone.   10
Half hour after the closing bell!
He would surely be coming soon.

Oh, warm is the waiting for joys, my dears!
And it cannot be too long.
Oh, pity the little poor chocolate lips   15
That carry the bubble of song!

Out came the saucily bold Willie Boone.
It was woe for our Mabbie now.
He wore like a jewel a lemon-hued lynx
With sand-waves loving her brow.   20

1 **without** outside

It was Mabbie alone by the grammar school gates.
Yet chocolate companions had she:
Mabbie on Mabbie with hush in the heart.
Mabbie on Mabbie to be.

—1945

the mother

Abortions will not let you forget.
You remember the children you got that you did not get,
The damp small pulps with a little or with no hair,
The singers and workers that never handled the air.
You will never neglect or beat   5
them, or silence or buy with a sweet.
You will never wind up the sucking-thumb
Or scuttle off ghosts that come.
You will never leave them, controlling your luscious sigh,
Return for a snack of them, with gobbling mother-eye.   10

I have heard in the voices of the wind the voices of my dim
     killed children.
I have contracted. I have eased
My dim dears at the breasts they could never suck.
I have said, Sweets, if I sinned, if I seized
Your luck   15
And your lives from your unfinished reach,
If I stole your births and your names,
Your straight baby tears and your games,
Your stilted or lovely loves, your tumults, your marriages,
     aches, and your deaths,
If I poisoned the beginnings of your breaths,   20
Believe that even in my deliberateness I was not deliberate.
Though why should I whine,
Whine that the crime was other than mine?—
Since anyhow you are dead.
Or rather, or instead,   25
You were never made.
But that too, I am afraid,
Is faulty: oh, what shall I say, how is the truth to be said?

You were born, you had body, you died.
It is just that you never giggled or planned or cried.   30
Believe me, I loved you all.
Believe me, I knew you, though faintly, and I loved, I
  loved you
All.

—1945

We Real Cool

The Pool Players.
Seven at the Golden Shovel.

We real cool. We
Left school. We

Lurk late. We
Strike straight. We

Sing sin. We   5
Thin gin. We

Jazz June. We
Die soon.

—1960

LAWRENCE FERLINGHETTI ■ (b. 1919)

Lawrence Ferlinghetti, first owner of a literary landmark, San Francisco's City Lights Bookstore, has promoted and published the voice of the American avant-garde since the early 1950s. His own output has been relatively small, but Ferlinghetti's A Coney Island of the Mind *remains one of the quintessential documents of the Beat Generation.*

A Coney Island of the Mind, #15

Constantly risking absurdity
      and death
  whenever he performs
     above the heads
       of his audience   5

                the poet like an acrobat
                                climbs on rime
                                to a high wire of his own making
        and balancing on eyebeams
                                above a sea of faces   10
                paces his way
                                to the other side of day
                performing entrechats
                                and sleight-of-foot tricks
        and other high theatrics   15
                                and all without mistaking
                any thing
                                for what it may not be
        For he's the super realist
                                who must perforce perceive   20
                taut truth
                                before the taking of each stance or step
        in his supposed advance
                                toward that still higher perch
        where Beauty stands and waits   25
                                with gravity
                                to start her death-defying leap
        And he
                a little charleychaplin man
                                who may or may not catch   30
        her fair eternal form
                                spreadeagled in the empty air
        of existence

                                                —1958

MAY SWENSON ■ (1919–1989)

May Swenson displayed an inventiveness in poetry that ranges from traditional formalism to many spatial or concrete poems. A careful observer of the natural world, Swenson often attempted to mimic directly the rhythms of the physical universe in her self-labeled "iconographs."

How Everything Happens

(Based on a Study of the Wave)

```
                                                    happen.
                                                to
                                            up
                                    stacking
                                is
                        something
When nothing is happening
When it happens
                something
                        pulls
                            back
                                not
                                    to
                                        happen.
When                                has happened.
        pulling back         stacking up
                    happens
        has happened                        stacks up.
When it             something          nothing
                        pulls back while
Then nothing is happening
                                        happens.
                                    and
                            forward
                    pushes
                up
            stacks
        something
Then
```

—1967

HOWARD NEMEROV ■ (1920–1991)

Howard Nemerov served as poet laureate of the United States during 1988 and 1989. A poet of brilliant formal inventiveness, he was also a skilled satirist and observer of the American scene. His sister, Diane Arbus, was a famous photographer. His Collected Poems *won the Pulitzer Prize in 1978.*

A Primer of the Daily Round

A peels an apple, while B kneels to God,
C telephones to D, who has a hand
On E's knee, F coughs, G turns up the sod
For H's grave, I do not understand
But J is bringing one clay pigeon down   5
While K brings down a nightstick on L's head,
And M takes mustard, N drives into town,
O goes to bed with P, and Q drops dead,
R lies to S, but happens to be heard
By T, who tells U not to fire V   10
For having to give W the word
That X is now deceiving Y with Z,
Who happens just now to remember A
Peeling an apple somewhere far away.

—1958

this couplet is indented

RICHARD WILBUR ■ (b. 1921)

Richard Wilbur will be remembered by posterity as perhaps the most skillful metricist and exponent of wit that American poetry has produced. His highly polished poetry—against the grain of much contemporary writing—is a monument to his craftsmanship and intelligence. Perhaps the most honored of all living American poets, Wilbur served as poet laureate of the United States in 1987. His translations of the verse dramas of Molière and Racine are regularly performed throughout the world. Collected Poems, 1943–2004 *appeared in 2004.*

Junk

Huru Welandes
            wore ne geswices
monna a'nigum
            ᵹara ᵹe Mimming can
heardne gehealdan.

—*Waldere*°

The epigraph, taken from a fragmentary Anglo-Saxon poem, concerns the legendary smith Wayland, and may roughly be translated: "Truly, Wayland's handiwork—the sword Mimming which he made—will never fail any man who knows how to use it bravely." [Wilbur's note]

An axe angles
                    from my neighbor's ashcan;
It is hell's handiwork,
                    the wood not hickory,
The flow of the grain
                    not faithfully followed.
The shivered shaft
                    rises from a shellheap
Of plastic playthings,
                    paper plates,   5
And the sheer shards
                    of shattered tumblers
That were not annealed
                    for the time needful.
At the same curbside,
                    a cast-off cabinet
Of wavily-warped
                    unseasoned wood
Waits to be trundled
                    in the trash-man's truck.   10
Haul them off! Hide them!
                    The heart winces
For junk and gimcrack,
                    for jerrybuilt things
And the men who make them
                    for a little money,
Bartering pride
                    like the bought boxer
Who pulls his punches,
                    or the paid-off jockey   15
Who in the home stretch
                    holds in his horse.
Yet the things themselves
                    in thoughtless honor
Have kept composure,
                    like captives who would not
Talk under torture.
                    Tossed from a tailgate
Where the dump displays

its random dolmens,   20

Its black barrows

      and blazing valleys,

They shall waste in the weather

          toward what they were.

The sun shall glory

      in the glitter of glass-chips,

Foreseeing the salvage

      of the prisoned sand,

And the blistering paint

      peel off in patches,   25

That the good grain

      be discovered again.

Then burnt, bulldozed,

      they shall all be buried

To the depth of diamonds,

      in the making dark

Where halt Hephaestus

      keeps his hammer

And Wayland's work

      is worn away.   30

          —1961

For C.

After the clash of elevator gates
And the long sinking, she emerges where,
A slight thing in the morning's crosstown glare,
She looks up toward the window where he waits,
Then in a fleeting taxi joins the rest   5
Of the huge traffic bound forever west.

On such grand scale do lovers say good-bye—
Even this other pair whose high romance
Had only the duration of a dance,
And who, now taking leave with stricken eye,   10
See each in each a whole new life forgone.
For them, above the darkling clubhouse lawn,

Bright Perseids flash and crumble; while for these
Who part now on the dock, weighed down by grief
And baggage, yet with something like relief,   15
It takes three thousand miles of knitting seas
To cancel out their crossing, and unmake
The amorous rough and tumble of their wake.

We are denied, my love, their fine tristesse
And bittersweet regrets, and cannot share   20
The frequent vistas of their large despair,
Where love and all are swept to nothingness;
Still, there's a certain scope in that long love
Which constant spirits are the keepers of,

And which, though taken to be tame and staid,   25
Is a wild sostenuto of the heart,
A passion joined to courtesy and art
Which has the quality of something made,
Like a good fiddle, like the rose's scent,
Like a rose window or the firmament.   30

—2000

The Writer —

pure accentual meter *~no syllabic*

5 stress

In her room at the prow of the house
Where light breaks, and the windows are tossed with linden,
My daughter is writing a story.

I pause in the stairwell, hearing
From her shut door a commotion of typewriter-keys   5
Like a chain hauled over a gunwale. *boat*

Young as she is, the stuff
Of her life is a great cargo, and some of it heavy:
I wish her a lucky passage.

But now it is she who pauses,   10
As if to reject my thought and its easy figure.
A stillness greatens, in which

The whole house seems to be thinking,
And then she is at it again with a bunched clamor
Of strokes, and again is silent.   15

I remember the dazed starling
Which was trapped in that very room, two years ago;
How we stole in, lifted a sash

And retreated, not to affright it;
And how for a helpless hour, through the crack of the door,   20
We watched the sleek, wild, dark

And iridescent creature
Batter against the brilliance, drop like a glove
To the hard floor, or the desk-top.

And wait then, humped and bloody,   25
For the wits to try it again; and how our spirits
Rose when, suddenly sure,

It lifted off from a chair-back,
Beating a smooth course for the right window
And clearing the sill of the world.   30

It is always a matter, my darling,
Of life or death, as I had forgotten. I wish
What I wished you before, but harder.

—1976

Year's End

Now winter downs the dying of the year,
And night is all a settlement of snow;
From the soft street the rooms of houses show
A gathered light, a shapen atmosphere,
Like frozen-over lakes whose ice is thin   5
And still allows some stirring down within.

I've known the wind by water banks to shake
The late leaves down, which frozen where they fell
And held in ice as dancers in a spell
Fluttered all winter long into a lake;   10
Graved on the dark in gestures of descent,
They seemed their own most perfect monument.

There was perfection in the death of ferns
Which laid their fragile cheeks against the stone
A million years. Great mammoths overthrown   15
Composedly have made their long sojourns,
Like palaces of patience, in the gray
And changeless lands of ice. And at Pompeii°

The little dog lay curled and did not rise
But slept the deeper as the ashes rose   20
And found the people incomplete, and froze
The random hands, the loose unready eyes
Of men expecting yet another sun
To do the shapely thing they had not done.

These sudden ends of time must give us pause.   25
We fray into the future, rarely wrought
Save in the tapestries of afterthought.
More time, more time. Barrages of applause
Come muffled from a buried radio.
The New-year bells are wrangling with the snow.   30

—1950

PHILIP LARKIN ■ (1922–1985)

*Philip Larkin was perhaps the latest British poet to establish a significant
body of readers in the United States. The general pessimism of his work is
mitigated by a wry sense of irony and brilliant formal control. For many
years he was a librarian at the University of Hull, and he was also a dedicated fan and critic of jazz.*

Next, Please

Always too eager for the future, we
Pick up bad habits of expectancy.
Something is always approaching; every day
Till then we say,

---

18 **Pompeii** Roman city destroyed by volcanic eruption in AD 79.

Watching from a bluff the tiny, clear,   5
Sparkling armada of promises draw near.
How slow they are! And how much time they waste,
Refusing to make haste!

Yet still they leave us holding wretched stalks
Of disappointment, for, though nothing balks   10
Each big approach, leaning with brasswork prinked,
Each rope distinct,

Flagged, and the figurehead with golden tits
Arching our way, it never anchors; it's
No sooner present than it turns to past.   15
Right to the last

We think each one will heave to and unload
All good into our lives, all we are owed
For waiting so devoutly and so long.
But we are wrong: 20

Only one ship is seeking us, a black-
Sailed unfamiliar, towing at her back
A huge and birdless silence. In her wake
No waters breed or break.

—1951

This Be the Verse

They fuck you up, your mum and dad.
    They may not mean to, but they do.
They fill you with the faults they had
    And add some extra, just for you.

But they were fucked up in their turn   5
    By fools in old-style hats and coats,
Who half the time were soppy-stern
    And half at one another's throats.

Man hands on misery to man.
    It deepens like a coastal shelf.   10
Get out as early as you can,
    And don't have any kids yourself.

—1971

The Whitsun° Weddings

That Whitsun, I was late getting away:
    Not till about
One-twenty on the sunlit Saturday
Did my three-quarters-empty train pull out,
All windows down, all cushions hot, all sense   5
Of being in a hurry gone. We ran
Behind the backs of houses, crossed a street
Of blinding windscreens, smelt the fish-dock; thence
The river's level drifting breadth began,
Where sky and Lincolnshire and water meet.   10

All afternoon, through the tall heat that slept
    For miles inland,
A slow and stopping curve southwards we kept.
Wide farms went by, short-shadowed cattle, and
Canals with floatings of industrial froth;   15
A hothouse flashed uniquely: hedges dipped
And rose: and now and then a smell of grass
Displaced the reek of buttoned carriage-cloth
Until the next town, new and nondescript,
Approached with acres of dismantled cars.   20

At first, I didn't notice what a noise
    The weddings made
Each station that we stopped at: sun destroys
The interest of what's happening in the shade,
And down the long cool platforms whoops and skirls   25
I took for porters larking with the mails,
And went on reading. Once we started, though,
We passed them, grinning and pomaded, girls
In parodies of fashion, heels and veils,
All posed irresolutely, watching us go,   30

As if out on the end of an event
    Waving goodbye
To something that survived it. Struck, I leant
More promptly out next time, more curiously,

Whitsun the seventh Sunday after Easter

And saw it all again in different terms: 35
The fathers with broad belts under their suits
And seamy foreheads; mothers loud and fat;
An uncle shouting smut; and then the perms,
The nylon gloves and jewellery-substitutes,
The lemons, mauves, and olive-ochres that   40

Marked off the girls unreally from the rest.
     Yes, from cafés
And banquet-halls up yards, and bunting-dressed
Coach-party annexes, the wedding-days
Were coming to an end. All down the line
Fresh couples climbed aboard: the rest stood round;   45
The last confetti and advice were thrown,
And, as we moved, each face seemed to define
Just what it saw departing: children frowned
At something dull; fathers had never known   50

Success so huge and wholly farcical;
     The women shared
The secret like a happy funeral;
While girls, gripping their handbags tighter, stared
At a religious wounding. Free at last,   55
And loaded with the sum of all they saw,
We hurried towards London, shuffling gouts of steam.
Now fields were building-plots, and poplars cast
Long shadows over major roads, and for
Some fifty minutes, that in time would seem   60

Just long enough to settle hats and say
     I nearly died,
A dozen marriages got under way.
They watched the landscape, setting side by side
—An Odeon° went past, a cooling tower,   65
And someone running up to bowl°—and none
Thought of the others they would never meet
Or how their lives would all contain this hour.
I thought of London spread out in the sun,
Its postal districts packed like squares of wheat: 70

65 Odeon a movie theatre   **66 bowl** to throw a cricket ball

There we were aimed. And as we raced across
    Bright knots of rail
Past standing Pullmans, walls of blackened moss
Came close, and it was nearly done, this frail
Traveling coincidence; and what it held   75
Stood ready to be loosed with all the power
That being changed can give. We slowed again,
And as the tightened brakes took hold, there swelled
A sense of falling, like an arrow-shower
Sent out of sight, somewhere becoming rain.   80

                                                    —1964

JAMES DICKEY ■ (1923–1997)

James Dickey became a national celebrity with the success of his novel Delive-
rance *(1970) and the celebrated film version. There was a long background to
Dickey's success, with years spent in the advertising business before he devoted
himself fully to writing. Born in Atlanta and educated at Clemson, Vanderbilt,
and Rice Universities, Dickey rarely strayed long from the South and taught at
the University of South Carolina for over two decades.*

The Heaven of Animals

Here they are. The soft eyes open
If they have lived in a wood
It is a wood.
If they have lived on plains
It is grass rolling
Under their feet forever.   5

Having no souls, they have come,
Anyway, beyond their knowing.
Their instincts wholly bloom
And they rise.
The soft eyes open.   10

To match them, the landscape flowers,
Outdoing, desperately
Outdoing what is required:
The richest wood,
The deepest field.   15

For some of these,
It could not be the place
It is, without blood.
These hunt, as they have done,
But with claws and teeth grown perfect,

More deadly than they can believe.
They stalk more silently,
And crouch on the limbs of trees,
And their descent
Upon the bright backs of their prey   25

May take years
In a sovereign floating of joy.
And those that are hunted
Know this as their life,
Their reward: to walk   30

Under such trees in full knowledge
Of what is in glory above them,
And to feel no fear,
But acceptance, compliance.
Fulfilling themselves without pain   35

At the cycle's center,
They tremble, they walk
Under the tree,
They fall, they are torn,
They rise, they walk again.   40

—1962

ALAN DUGAN ■ (1923–2003)

*Alan Dugan received the 1961 Yale Younger Poets Award, leading to the
publication of his first collection as he neared forty. His plainspoken poetic
voice, often with sardonic overtones, is appropriate for the anti-romantic
stance of his most characteristic poems. For many years Dugan was associated with the Fine Arts Work Center in Provincetown, Massachusetts, on
Cape Cod.*

ʟove Song: I and Thou

Nothing is plumb, level or square:
    the studs are bowed, the joists
are shaky by nature, no piece fits
    any other piece without a gap
or pinch, and bent nails   5
    dance all over the surfacing
like maggots. By Christ
    I am no carpenter. I built
the roof for myself, the walls
    for myself, the floors   10
for myself, and got
    hung up in it myself. I
danced with a purple thumb
    at this house-warming, drunk
with my prime whiskey: rage.   15
    Oh I spat rage's nails
into the frame-up of my work:
    it held. It settled plumb,
level, solid, square and true
    for that great moment. Then   20
it screamed and went on through,
    skewing as wrong the other way.
God damned it. This is hell,
    but I planned it, I sawed it,
I nailed it, and I   25
    will live in it until it kills me.
I can nail my left palm
    to the left-hand cross-piece but
I can't do everything myself.
    I need a hand to nail the right,   30
a help, a love, a you, a wife.

—1961

ANTHONY HECHT
266

ANTHONY HECHT ■ (1923–2004)

Anthony Hecht is most often linked with Richard Wilbur as one of the American poets of the postwar era who has most effectively utilized traditional poetic forms. The brilliance of Hecht's technique, however, must be set beside the powerful moral intelligence that informs his poetry. The Hard Hours, his second collection, won the Pulitzer Prize in 1968.

The Dover Bitch: *A Criticism of Life*

for Andrews Wanning

So there stood Matthew Arnold° and this girl
With the cliffs of England crumbling away behind them,
And he said to her, "Try to be true to me,
And I'll do the same for you, for things are bad
All over, etc., etc."   5
Well now, I knew this girl. It's true she had read
Sophocles° in a fairly good translation
And caught that bitter allusion to the sea,
But all the time he was talking she had in mind
The notion of what his whiskers would feel like   10
On the back of her neck. She told me later on
That after a while she got to look out
At the lights across the channel, and really felt sad,
Thinking of all the wine and enormous beds
And blandishments in French and the perfumes.   15
And then she got really angry. To have been brought
All the way down from London, and then be addressed
As a sort of mournful cosmic last resort
Is really tough on a girl, and she was pretty.
Anyway, she watched him pace the room   20
And finger his watch-chain and seem to sweat a bit,
And then she said one or two unprintable things.
But you mustn't judge her by that. What I mean to say is,
She's really all right. I still see her once in a while
And she always treats me right. We have a drink   25
And I give her a good time, and perhaps it's a year
Before I see her again, but there she is,
Running to fat, but dependable as they come.
And sometimes I bring her a bottle of *Nuit d'Amour*.

—1967

1 **Matthew Arnold** Victorian poet, author of "Dover Beach"   7 **Sophocles** Ancient Greek playwright

Third Avenue in Sunlight

Third Avenue in sunlight. Nature's error.
Already the bars are filled and John is there.
Beneath a plentiful lady over the mirror°
He tilts his glass in the mild mahogany air.

I think of him when he first got out of college,   5
Serious, thin, unlikely to succeed;
For several months he hung around the Village,
Boldly T-shirted, unfettered but unfreed.

Now he confides to a stranger, "I was first scout,
And kept my glimmers peeled till after dark.   10
Our outfit had as its sign a bloody knout,
We met behind the museum in Central Park.

Of course, we were kids." But still those savages,
War-painted, a flap of leather at the loins,
File silently against him. Hostages   15
Are never taken. One summer, in Des Moines,

They entered his hotel room, tomahawks
Flashing like barracuda. He tried to pray.
Three years of treatment. Occasionally he talks
About how he almost didn't get away.   20

Daily the prowling sunlight whets its knife
Along the sidewalk. We almost never meet.
In the Rembrandt dark he lifts his amber life.
My bar is somewhat further down the street.

—1967

DANIEL HOFFMAN ■ (b. 1923)

Daniel Hoffman has published ten books of poetry, including Beyond Silence: Selected Shorter Poems 1948–2003 *(2003). He also has published a memoir and seven volumes of criticism. W. H. Auden chose Hoffman's first poetry collection,* An Armada of Thirty Whales *(1954), for the Yale*

3 **lady over the mirror** a painting

Series of Younger Poets. *Hoffman served as Consultant in Poetry to the Library of Congress from 1973 to 1974. He is the Felix E. Schelling Professor of English Emeritus at the University of Pennsylvania, and lives in Swarthmore, Pennsylvania, and Harborside, Maine. Recently, Hoffman edited* Over the Summer Water, *a collection of poems by his late wife, Elizabeth McFarland, who served for many years as poetry editor for* Ladies' Home Journal.

As I Was Going to Saint-Ives

As I was going to Saint-Ives
In stormy, windy, sunny weather
I met a man with seven wives
(The herons stand in the swift water).

One drinks her beer out of his can   5
In stormy, windy, and bright weather,
And who laughs more, she or her man?
(The herons stand still on the water.)

One knows the room his candle lit
In stormy, lightning, cloudburst weather,   10
That glows again at the thought of it
(Two herons still the swift water).

His jealous, wild-tongued, Wednesday's wife—
In dreepy, wintry, wind-lashed weather
—What's better than that ranting strife?   15
(Two herons still the roaring water.)

There's one whose mind's so like his mind
In streaming wind or balmy weather
All joy, all wisdom seem one kind
(The herons stand in the swift water).   20

And one whose secret mazes he
In moon-swept, in torrential weather
Ransacks, and cannot find the key
(Two herons stand in the white water).

8 leviathan great sea-creature mentioned in the book of Job

He'll think of none save one's slim thighs   25
In heat and sleet and windy weather
Till death has plucked his dreaming eyes
(Two herons guard the streaming water).

And the one whose love moves all he's done,
In windy, warm, and wintry weather,   30
—What can he leave but speaks thereon?
(Two herons still the swift water.)

—1963

LOUIS SIMPSON ■ (b. 1923)

Louis Simpson was born in Jamaica to a colonial lawyer father and an American mother. Simpson came to the United States in his teens and served in the U.S. Army in World War II. He won the Pulitzer Prize in 1964 for At the End of the Open Road, *a volume that attempts to reexamine Walt Whitman's nineteenth-century definitions of the American experience. Subsequent collections have continued to demonstrate Simpson's unsentimental view of American suburban life.*

American Classic

It's a classic American scene—
a car stopped off the road
and a man trying to repair it.

The woman who stays in the car
in the classic American scene   5
stares back at the freeway traffic.

They look surprised, and ashamed
to be so helpless . . .
let down in the middle of the road!

To think that their car would do this!   10
They look like mountain people
whose son has gone against the law.

But every night they set out food
and the robber goes skulking back to the trees.
That's how it is with the car . . .   15

it's theirs, they're stuck with it.
Now they know what it's like to sit
and see the world go whizzing by.

In the fume of carbon monoxide and dust
they are not such good Americans   20
as they thought they were.

The feeling of being left out
through no fault of your own, is common.
That's why I say, an American classic.

—1980

My Father in the Night Commanding No

My father in the night commanding No
Has work to do. Smoke issues from his lips;
  He reads in silence.
The frogs are croaking and the street lamps glow.

And then my mother winds the gramophone: 5
The Bride of Lammermoor° begins to shriek—
  Or reads a story
About a prince, a castle, and a dragon.

The moon is glittering above the hill.
I stand before the gateposts of the King—   10
  So runs the story—
Of Thule, at midnight when the mice are still.

And I have been in Thule! It has come true—
The journey and the danger of the world,
  All that there is   15
To bear and to enjoy, endure and do.

---

6 Bride of Lammermoor *Lucia di Lammermoor,* opera by Donizetti

Landscapes, seascapes . . . Where have I been led?
The names of cities—Paris, Venice, Rome—
    Held out their arms.
A feathered god, seductive, went ahead.   20

Here is my house. Under a red rose tree
A child is swinging; another gravely plays.
    They are not surprised
That I am here; they were expecting me.

And yet my father sits and reads in silence,   25
My mother sheds a tear, the moon is still,
    And the dark wind
Is murmuring that nothing ever happens.

Beyond his jurisdiction as I move,
Do I not prove him wrong? And yet, it's true   30
    They will not change
There, on the stage of terror and of love.

The actors in that playhouse always sit
In fixed positions—father, mother, child
    With painted eyes.   35
How sad it is to be a little puppet!

Their heads are wooden. And you once pretended
To understand them! Shake them as you will,
    They cannot speak.
Do what you will, the comedy is ended.   40

Father, why did you work? Why did you weep,
Mother? Was the story so important?
    "*Listen!*" the wind
Said to the children, and they fell asleep.

                                —1963

VASSAR MILLER ▪ (1924–1997)

*Vassar Miller was a lifelong resident of Houston, born with cerebral palsy.
Miller published both traditional devotional verse and a large body of autobiographical poetry in open forms. If I Had Wheels or Love, her collected
poems, appeared in 1990.*

VASSAR MILLER

Subterfuge

I remember my father, slight,
staggering in with his Underwood,°
bearing it in his arms like an awkward bouquet

for his spastic child who sits down
on the floor, one knee on the frame   5
of the typewriter, and holding her left wrist

with her right hand, in that precision known
to the crippled, pecks at the keys
with a sparrow's preoccupation.

Falling by chance on rhyme, novel and curious bubble   10
blown with a magic pipe, she tries them over and over,
spellbound by life's clashing in accord or against itself,

pretending pretense and playing at playing,
she does her childhood backward as children do,
her fun a delaying action against what she knows.   15

My father must lose her, his runaway on her treadmill,
will lose the terrible favor that life has done him
as she toils at tomorrow, tensed at her makeshift toy.

—1981

DONALD JUSTICE ■ (1925–2004)

*Donald Justice published more selectively than most of his contemporaries.
His Pulitzer Prize–winning volume of selected poems displays considerable
literary sophistication and reveals the poet's familiarity with the traditions
of contemporary European and Latin American poetry. As an editor, he was
responsible for rescuing the important work of Weldon Kees from obscurity.*

Counting the Mad

This one was put in a jacket,
This one was sent home,
This one was given bread and meat
But would eat none,
And this one cried No No No No   5
All day long.

2 **Underwood** popular brand of manual typewriter

This one looked at the window
As though it were a wall,
This one saw things that were not there,
This one things that were,   10
And this one cried No No No No
All day long.

This one thought himself a bird,
This one a dog,
And this one thought himself a man,   15
An ordinary man,
And this one cried No No No No
All day long.

—1960

CAROLYN KIZER ■ (b. 1925)

*Carolyn Kizer has had a fascinating career that included a year's study in Tai-
wan and another year in Pakistan, where she worked for the U.S. State
Department. Her first collection,* The Ungrateful Garden *(1961), demonstrates
an equal facility with formal and free verse, but her subsequent books (including the Pulitzer Prize–winning* Yin *of 1985) have tended more toward
the latter. A committed feminist, Kizer anticipated many of today's women's
issues as early as the mid-1950s, just as the poem "The Ungrateful Garden"
was published a decade before "ecology" became a household word.*

The Ungrateful Garden

Midas watched the golden crust
That formed over his streaming sores,
Hugged his agues, loved his lust,
But damned to hell the out-of-doors

Where blazing motes of sun impaled   5
The serried° roses, metal-bright.
"Those famous flowers," Midas wailed,
"Have scorched my retina with light."

---

6 serried crowded in rows

This gift, he'd thought, would gild his joys,
Silt up the waters of his grief;   10
His lawns a wilderness of noise,
The heavy clang of leaf on leaf.

Within, the golden cup is good
To heft, to sip the yellow mead.
Outside, in summer's rage, the rude   15
Gold thorn has made his fingers bleed.

"I strolled my halls in golden shift,
As ruddy as a lion's meat.
Then I rushed out to share my gift,
And golden stubble cut my feet."   20

Dazzled with wounds, he limped away
To climb into his golden bed.
Roses, roses can betray.
"Nature is evil," Midas said.

It's all nonmetrfanto

—1961

Pro Femina: Part Three

I will speak about women of letters, for I'm in the racket.
Our biggest successes to date? Old maids to a woman.
And our saddest conspicuous failures? The married spinsters
On loan to the husbands they treated like surrogate fathers.
Think of that crew of self-pitiers, not-very-distant,   5
Who carried the torch for themselves and got first-degree burns.
Or the sad sonneteers, toast-and-teasdales we loved at thirteen;
Middle-aged virgins seducing the puerile anthologists
Through lust-of-the-mind; barbiturate-drenched Camilles
With continuous periods, murmuring softly on sofas   10
When poetry wasn't a craft but a sickly effluvium.
The air thick with incense, musk, and emotional blackmail.

I suppose they reacted from an earlier womanly modesty
When too many girls were scabs to their stricken sisterhood.
Impugning our sex to stay in good with the men,   15
Commencing their insecure bluster. How they must have
    swaggered

When women themselves endorsed their own inferiority!
Vestals, vassals, and vessels, rolled into several,
They took notes in rolling syllabics, in careful journals,
Aiming to please a posterity that despises them.   20
But we'll always have traitors who swear that a woman
      surrenders
Her Supreme Function, by equating Art with aggression
And failure with Femininity. Still, it's just as unfair
To equate Art with Femininity, like a prettily packaged
      commodity
When we are the custodians of the world's best-kept secret: 25
Merely the private lives of one-half of humanity.

But even with masculine dominance, we mares and mistresses
Produced some sleek saboteuses, making their cracks
Which the porridge-brained males of the day were too thick
      to perceive,
Mistaking young hornets for perfectly harmless bumblebees.   30
Being thought innocuous rouses some women to frenzy;
They try to be ugly by aping the ways of men
And succeed. Swearing, sucking cigars and scorching the
      bedspread,

Slopping straight shots, eyes blotted, vanity-blown
In the expectation of glory: *she writes like a man!*   35
This drives other women mad in a mist of chiffon.
(One poetess draped her gauze over red flannels, a practical
      feminist.)

But we're emerging from all that, more or less,
Except for some ladylike laggards and Quarterly priestesses
Who flog men for fun, and kick women to maim competition.   40
Now, if we struggle abnormally, we may almost seem normal;
If we submerge our self-pity in disciplined industry;
If we stand up and be hated, and swear not to sleep with
      editors;
If we regard ourselves formally, respecting our true limitations
Without making an unseemly show of trying to unfreeze our
      assets;   45
Keeping our heads and our pride while remaining unmarried;
And if wedded, kill guilt in its tracks when we stack up the dishes

And defect to the typewriter. And if mothers, believe in the luck
  of our children,
Whom we forbid to devour us, whom we shall not devour,
And the luck of our husbands and lovers, who keep free
  women.   50

—1984

MAXINE KUMIN ■ (b. 1925)

Maxine Kumin was born in Philadelphia and educated at Radcliffe. Kumin was an early literary ally and friend of Anne Sexton, with whom she co-authored several children's books. The winner of the 1973 Pulitzer Prize, Kumin has preferred a rural life raising horses for some years. Her increased interest in the natural world has paralleled the environmental awareness of many of her readers. Her most recent poetry collection is Still to Mow.

Noted in the *New York Times*

Lake Buena Vista, Florida, June 16, 1987

Death claimed the last pure dusky seaside sparrow
today, whose coastal range was narrow,
as narrow as its two-part buzzy song.
From hummocks lost to Cape Canaveral
this mouselike skulker in the matted grass,   5
a six-inch bird, plain brown, once thousands strong,
sang *toodle-raeee azhee*, ending on a trill
before the air gave way to rocket blasts.

It laid its dull white eggs (brown specked) in small
neat cups of grass on plots of pickleweed,   10
bulrushes, or salt hay. It dined
on caterpillars, beetles, ticks, the seeds
of sedges. Unremarkable
the life it led with others of its kind.
Tomorrow we can put it on a stamp,   15
a first-day cover with Key Largo rat,
Schaus swallowtail, Florida swamp
crocodile, and fading cotton mouse.

How simply symbols replace habitat!
The tower frames of Aerospace   20
quiver in the flush of another shot
where, once indigenous, the dusky sparrow
soared trilling twenty feet above its burrow.

                                                        —1989

ALLEN GINSBERG ■ (1926–1997)

*Allen Ginsberg became the chief poetic spokesman of the Beat Generation.
He was a force—as poet and celebrity—who continued to outrage and delight four decades after the appearance of* Howl, *the monumental poem describing how Ginsberg saw "the best minds of my generation destroyed by
madness." Ginsberg's poems are cultural documents that provide a key to
understanding the radical changes in American life, particularly among
youth, that began in the mid-1950s.*

A Supermarket in California

What thoughts I have of you tonight, Walt Whitman, for I
walked down the sidestreets under the trees with a headache self-
conscious looking at the full moon.

In my hungry fatigue, and shopping for images, I went into
the neon fruit supermarket, dreaming of your enumerations!

What peaches and what penumbras?° Whole families
shopping at night! Aisles full of husbands! Wives in the avocados,
babies in the tomatoes!—and you, García Lorca,° what were you
doing down by the watermelons?

I saw you, Walt Whitman, childless, lonely old grubber, poking
among the meats in the refrigerator and eyeing the grocery boys.

I heard you asking questions of each: Who killed the pork
chops? What price bananas? Are you my Angel?   5

I wandered in and out of the brilliant stacks of cans following
you, and followed in my imagination by the store detective.

We strode down the open corridors together in our solitary
fancy tasting artichokes, possessing every frozen delicacy, and
never passing the cashier.

3 penumbras shadows   **García Lorca** Federico García Lorca, Spanish poet (1899–1936)

Where are we going, Walt Whitman? The doors close in an
hour. Which way does your beard point tonight?
(I touch your book and dream of our odyssey in the supermarket and feel absurd.)
Will we walk all night through solitary streets? The trees add
shade to shade, lights out in the houses, we'll both be lonely.   10
Will we stroll dreaming of the lost America of love past blue
automobiles in driveways, home to our silent cottage?
Ah, dear father, graybeard, lonely old courage-teacher, what
America did you have when Charon° quit poling his ferry and you
got out on a smoking bank and stood watching the boat disappear
on the black waters of Lethe?°

—1956

JAMES MERRILL ■ (1926–1995)

*James Merrill wrote "The Changing Light at Sandover," a long poem that
resulted from many years of sessions with a Ouija board. The book became
his major work and, among many other things, a remarkable memoir of a
long-term gay relationship. Merrill's shorter poems, collected in 2001, reveal
meticulous craftsmanship and a play of wit unequaled among contemporary
American poets.*

Casual Wear

Your average tourist: Fifty. 2.3
Times married. Dressed, this year, in Ferdi Plinthbower°
Originals. Odds 1 to 9^{10}
Against her strolling past the Embassy

Today at noon. Your average terrorist: 5
Twenty-five. Celibate. No use for trends,
At least in clothing. Mark, though, where it ends.
People have come forth made of colored mist

---

12 **Charon** ferryman of Hades   **Lethe** river in Hades, means forgetfulness
2 **Ferdi Plinthbower** a fictional designer

Unsmiling on one hundred million screens
To tell of his prompt phone call to the station,   10
"Claiming responsibility"—devastation
Signed with a flourish, like the dead wife's jeans.

—1984

FRANK O'HARA ▪ (1926–1966)

Frank O'Hara suffered an untimely death in a dune buggy accident on Fire Island that robbed American poetry of one its most refreshing talents. An authority on modern art, O'Hara incorporated many of the spontaneous techniques of abstract painting in his own poetry, which was often written as an immediate reaction to the events of his daily life.

The Day Lady° Died

It is 12:20 in New York a Friday
three days after Bastille day,° yes
it is 1959 and I go get a shoeshine
because I will get off the 4:19 in Easthampton
at 7:15 and then go straight to dinner   5
and I don't know the people who will feed me

I walk up the muggy street beginning to sun
and have a hamburger and a malted and buy
an ugly NEW WORLD WRITING to see what the poets
in Ghana are doing these days   10
                              I go on to the bank
and Miss Stillwagon (first name Linda I once heard)
doesn't even look up my balance for once in her life
and in the GOLDEN GRIFFIN I get a little Verlaine
for Patsy with drawings by Bonnard although I do   15
think of Hesiod, trans. Richard Lattimore or
Brendan Behan's new play or *Le Balcon* or *Les Nègres*
of Genet, but I don't, I stick with Verlaine
after practically going to sleep with quandariness

Lady Billie Holiday (1915–1959), blues singer   **2 Bastille day** July 14

and for Mike I just stroll into the PARK LANE   20
Liquor Store and ask for a bottle of Strega and
then I go back where I came from to 6th Avenue
and the tobacconist in the Ziegfeld Theatre and
casually ask for a carton of Gauloises and a carton
of Picayunes, and a NEW YORK POST with her face on it   25
and I am sweating a lot by now and thinking of
leaning on the john door in the 5 SPOT
while she whispered a song along the keyboard
to Mal Waldron° and everyone and I stopped breathing.

—1964

W. D. SNODGRASS ■ (b. 1926–2009)

W. D. Snodgrass won the Pulitzer Prize for his first collection, Heart's Needle *(1959), and is generally considered one of the first important confessional poets. However, in his later career he has turned away from autobiographical subjects, writing, among other poems, a long sequence of
dramatic monologues spoken by leading Nazis during the final days of the
Hitler regime.*

MEMENTOS, I

281

Mementos, I

Sorting out letters and piles of my old
    Canceled checks, old clippings, and yellow note cards
That meant something once, I happened to find
    Your picture. *That* picture. I stopped there cold,
Like a man raking piles of dead leaves in his yard   5
    Who has turned up a severed hand.

Still, that first second, I was glad: you stand
    Just as you stood—shy, delicate, slender,
In that long gown of green lace netting and daisies
    That you wore to our first dance. The sight of you stunned   10
Us all. Well, our needs were different, then,
    And our ideals came easy.

29 **Mal Waldron** Holiday's accompanist.

Then through the war and those two long years
    Overseas, the Japanese dead in their shacks
Among dishes, dolls, and lost shoes; I carried   15
    This glimpse of you, there, to choke down my fear,
Prove it had been, that it might come back.
       That was before we got married.

—Before we drained out one another's force
    With lies, self-denial, unspoken regret   20
And the sick eyes that blame; before the divorce
    And the treachery. Say it: before we met. Still,
I put back your picture. Someday, in due course,
    I will find that it's still there.

              —1968

JOHN ASHBERY ■ (b. 1927)

John Ashbery was born in upstate New York and educated at Harvard University. His first full-length book, Some Trees, *was chosen by W. H. Auden as winner of the Yale Younger Poets Award in 1956. His enigmatic poems have intrigued readers for so long that much contemporary literary theory seems to have been created expressly for explicating his poems. Impossible to dismiss, Ashbery is now seen as the chief inheritor of the symbolist tradition brought to American locales by Wallace Stevens.* Notes from the Air: Selected Later Poems *appeared in 2007.*

Farm Implements and Rutabagas in a Landscape

The first of the undecoded messages read: "Popeye sits in
    thunder,
Unthought of. From that shoebox of an apartment,
From livid curtain's hue, a tangram emerges: a country."
Meanwhile the Sea Hag was relaxing on a green couch: "How
    pleasant
To spend one's vacation *en la casa de Popeye*," she scratched   5
Her cleft chin's solitary hair. She remembered spinach

JOHN ASHBERY

And was going to ask Wimpy if he had bought any spinach.
"M'love," he intercepted, "the plains are decked out in thunder
Today, and it shall be as you wish." He scratched
The part of his head under his hat. The apartment   10
Seemed to grow smaller. "But what if no pleasant
Inspiration plunge us now to the stars? *For this is my country.*"
Suddenly they remembered how it was cheaper in the country.
Wimpy was thoughtfully cutting open a number 2 can of spinach
When the door opened and Swee'pea crept in. "How pleasant!"   15
But Swee'pea looked morose. A note was pinned to his bib.
    "Thunder
And tears are unavailing," it read. "Henceforth shall Popeye's
    apartment
Be but remembered space, toxic or salubrious, whole or scratched."
Olive came hurtling through the window; its geraniums scratched
Her long thigh. "I have news!" she gasped. "Popeye, forced as
    you know to flee the country   20
One musty gusty evening, by the schemes of his wizened,
    duplicate father, jealous of the apartment
And all that it contains, myself and spinach
In particular, heaves bolts of loving thunder
At his own astonished becoming, rupturing the pleasant

Arpeggio of our years. No more shall pleasant   25
Rays of the sun refresh your sense of growing old, nor the
    scratched
Tree-trunks and mossy foliage, only immaculate darkness
    and thunder."
She grabbed Swee'pea. "I'm taking the brat to the country."
"But you can't do that—he hasn't even finished his spinach,"
Urged the Sea Hag, looking fearfully around at the apartment.   30

But Olive was already out of earshot. Now the apartment
Succumbed to a strange new hush. "Actually it's quite pleasant
Here," thought the Sea Hag. "If this is all we need fear from
    spinach
Then I don't mind so much. Perhaps we could invite Alice the
    Goon over"—she scratched
One dug pensively—"but Wimpy is such a country   35
Bumpkin, always burping like that." Minute at first, the thunder

ion filled the apartment. It was domestic thunder,
ie color of spinach. Popeye chuckled and scratched
is balls: it sure was pleasant to spend a day in the country.

—1966

Paradoxes and Oxymorons

The poem is concerned with language on a very plain level.
Look at it talking to you. You look out a window
Or pretend to fidget. You have it but you don't have it.
You miss it, it misses you. You miss each other.

The poem is sad because it wants to be yours, and cannot.   5
What's a plain level? It is that and other things,
Bringing a system of them into play. Play?
Well, actually, yes, but I consider play to be

A deeper outside thing, a dreamed role-pattern,
As in the division of grace these long August days   10
Without proof. Open-ended. And before you know
It gets lost in the steam and chatter of typewriters.

It has been played once more. I think you exist only
To tease me into doing it, on your level, and then you aren't there
Or have adopted a different attitude. And the poem   15
Has set me softly down beside you. The poem is you.

—1981

W. S. MERWIN ■ (b. 1927)

W. S. Merwin often displays environmental concerns that have motivated much poetry in recent years. Even in earlier work, his fears of the results of uncontrolled destruction of the environment are presented allegorically. Born in New York City, he currently resides in Hawaii. He was appointed U. S. Poet Laureate in 2010..

For the Anniversary of My Death

Every year without knowing it I have passed the day
When the last fires will wave to me
And the silence will set out
Tireless traveller
Like the beam of a lightless star   5

Then I will no longer
Find myself in life as in a strange garment
Surprised at the earth
And the love of one woman
And the shamelessness of men   10
As today writing after three days of rain
Hearing the wren sing and the falling cease
And bowing not knowing to what

                                                    —1969

The Last One

Well they'd made up their minds to be everywhere because
        why not.
Everywhere was theirs because they thought so.
They with two leaves they whom the birds despise.
In the middle of stones they made up their minds.
They started to cut.   5

Well they cut everything because why not.
Everything was theirs because they thought so.
It fell into its shadows and they took both away.
Some to have some for burning.

Well cutting everything they came to the water.   10
They came to the end of the day there was one left standing.
They would cut it tomorrow they went away.
The night gathered in the last branches.
The shadow of the night gathered in the shadow on the water.
The night and the shadow put on the same head.   15
And it said Now.

Well in the morning they cut the last one.
Like the others the last one fell into its shadow.
It fell into its shadow on the water.
They took it away its shadow stayed on the water.   20

Well they shrugged they started trying to get the shadow
        away.
They cut right to the ground the shadow stayed whole.
They laid boards on it the shadow came out on top.
They shone lights on it the shadow got blacker and clearer.

They exploded the water the shadow rocked.   25
They built a huge fire on the roots.
They sent up black smoke between the shadow and the sun.
The new shadow flowed without changing the old one.
They shrugged they went away to get stones.

They came back the shadow was growing.   30
They started setting up stones it was growing.
They looked the other way it went on growing.
They decided they would make a stone out of it.
They took stones to the water they poured them into the shadow.
They poured them in they poured them in the stones vanished.   35
The shadow was not filled it went on growing.
That was one day.

The next day was just the same it went on growing.
They did all the same things it was just the same.
They decided to take its water from under it.   40
They took away water they took it away the water went down.
The shadow stayed where it was before.
It went on growing it grew onto the land.
They started to scrape the shadow with machines.
When it touched the machines it stayed on them.   45
They started to beat the shadow with sticks.
Where it touched the sticks it stayed on them.
They started to beat the shadow with hands.
Where it touched the hands it stayed on them.
That was another day.   50

Well the next day started about the same it went on growing.
They pushed lights into the shadow.
Where the shadow got onto them they went out.
They began to stomp on the edge it got their feet.
And when it got their feet they fell down.   55
It got into eyes the eyes went blind.
The ones that fell down it grew over and they vanished.
The ones that went blind and walked into it vanished.
The ones that could see and stood still
It swallowed their shadows.   60
Then it swallowed them too and they vanished.
Well the others ran.

The ones that were left went away to live if it would let them.
They went as far as they could.
The lucky ones with their shadows.   65

                                                                —*1969*

JAMES WRIGHT ■ (1927–1980)

*James Wright showed compassion for losers and underdogs of all types, an
attitude evident everywhere in his poetry. A native of Martins Ferry, Ohio, he
often described lives of quiet desperation in the blue-collar towns of his
youth. Like many poets of his generation, Wright wrote formal verse in his
early career and shifted to open forms during the 1960s.*

Autumn Begins in Martins Ferry, Ohio

In the Shreve High football stadium,
I think of Polacks nursing long beers in Tiltonsville,
And gray faces of Negroes in the blast furnace at Benwood,
And the ruptured night watchman of Wheeling Steel,
Dreaming of heroes.   5

All the proud fathers are ashamed to go home.
Their women cluck like starved pullets,
Dying for love.

Therefore,
Their sons grow suicidally beautiful   10
At the beginning of October
And gallop terribly against each other's bodies.

                                                                —*1963*

Saint Judas

When I went out to kill myself, I caught
A pack of hoodlums beating up a man.
Running to spare his suffering, I forgot
My name, my number, how my day began,

How soldiers milled around the garden stone   5
And sang amusing songs; how all that day
Their javelins measured crowds; how I alone
Bargained the proper coins, and slipped away.

Banished from heaven, I found this victim beaten,
Stripped, kneed, and left to cry. Dropping my rope   10
Aside, I ran, ignored the uniforms:
Then I remembered bread my flesh had eaten,
The kiss that ate my flesh. Flayed without hope,
I held the man for nothing in my arms.

—1959

PHILIP LEVINE ■ (b. 1928)

*Philip Levine was born in Detroit, Michigan. He is one of many contempo-
rary poets to hold a degree from the University of Iowa Writers' Workshop.
The gritty urban landscapes and characters trapped in dead-end industrial
jobs that provide Levine subjects for many poems match exactly with his
unadorned, informal idiom. As teacher and mentor, Levine has influenced
many younger poets.*

You Can Have It

My brother comes home from work
and climbs the stairs to our room.
I can hear the bed groan and his shoes drop
one by one. You can have it, he says.

The moonlight streams in the window   5
and his unshaven face is whitened
like the face of the moon. He will sleep
long after noon and waken to find me gone.

Thirty years will pass before I remember
that moment when suddenly I knew each man   10
has one brother who dies when he sleeps
and sleeps when he rises to face this life,

and that together they are only one man
sharing a heart that always labors, hands
yellowed and cracked, a mouth that gasps   15
for breath and asks, Am I gonna make it?

All night at the ice plant he had fed
the chute its silvery blocks, and then I
stacked cases of orange soda for the children
of Kentucky, one gray box-car at a time   20

with always two more waiting. We were twenty
for such a short time and always in
the wrong clothes, crusted with dirt
and sweat. I think now we were never twenty.

In 1948 in the city of Detroit, founded   25
by de la Mothe Cadillac for the distant purposes
of Henry Ford, no one wakened or died,
no one walked the streets or stoked a furnace,

for there was no such year, and now
that year has fallen off all the old newspapers,   30
calendars, doctors' appointments, bonds,
wedding certificates, drivers licenses.

The city slept. The snow turned to ice.
The ice to standing pools or rivers
racing in the gutters. Then bright grass rose   35
between the thousands of cracked squares,

and that grass died. I give you back 1948.
I give you all the years from then
to the coming one. Give me back the moon
with its frail light falling across a face.   40

Give me back my young brother, hard
and furious, with wide shoulders and a curse
for God and burning eyes that look upon
all creation and say, You can have it.

—1979

Anne Sexton lived a tortured life of mental illness and family troubles, becoming the model of the confessional poet. A housewife with two small daughters, she began writing poetry as the result of a program on public television, later taking a workshop from Robert Lowell in which Sylvia Plath was a fellow student. For fifteen years until her suicide, she was a vibrant, exciting presence in American poetry. A controversial biography of Sexton by Diane Wood Middlebrook appeared in 1991.

Cinderella

You always read about it:
the plumber with twelve children
who wins the Irish Sweepstakes.
From toilets to riches.
That story.   5

Or the nursemaid,
some luscious sweet from Denmark
who captures the oldest son's heart.
From diapers to Dior.
That story.   10

Or a milkman who serves the wealthy,
eggs, cream, butter, yogurt, milk,
the white truck like an ambulance
who goes into real estate
and makes a pile.   15
From homogenized to martinis at lunch.

Or the charwoman
who is on the bus when it cracks up
and collects enough from the insurance.
From mops to Bonwit Teller.°
That story.   20

---

20 **Bonwit Teller** an upscale department store

Once
the wife of a rich man was on her deathbed
and she said to her daughter Cinderella:
Be devout. Be good. Then I will smile   25
down from heaven in the seam of a cloud.
The man took another wife who had
two daughters, pretty enough
but with hearts like blackjacks.
Cinderella was their maid.   30
She slept on the sooty hearth each night
and walked around looking like Al Jolson.°
Her father brought presents home from town,
jewels and gowns for the other women
but the twig of a tree for Cinderella.   35
She planted that twig on her mother's grave
and it grew to a tree where a white dove sat.
Whenever she wished for anything the dove
would drop it like an egg upon the ground.
The bird is important, my dears, so heed him.   40

Next came the ball, as you all know.
It was a marriage market.
The prince was looking for a wife.
All but Cinderella were preparing
and gussying up for the big event.   45
Cinderella begged to go too.
Her stepmother threw a dish of lentils
into the cinders and said: Pick them
up in an hour and you shall go.
The white dove brought all his friends;   50
all the warm wings of the fatherland came,
and picked up the lentils in a jiffy.
No, Cinderella, said the stepmother,
you have no clothes and cannot dance.
That's the way with stepmothers.   55

32 Al Jolson (1885–1950) American singer and entertainer who often performed in blackface

Cinderella went to the tree at the grave
and cried forth like a gospel singer:
Mama! Mama! My turtledove,
send me to the prince's ball!
The bird dropped down a golden dress   60
and delicate little gold slippers.
Rather a large package for a simple bird.
So she went. Which is no surprise.
Her stepmother and sisters didn't
recognize her without her cinder face   65
and the prince took her hand on the spot
and danced with no other the whole day.

As nightfall came she thought she'd
better get home. The prince walked her home
and she disappeared into the pigeon house   70
and although the prince took an axe and broke
it open she was gone. Back to her cinders.
These events repeated themselves for three days.
However on the third day the prince
covered the palace steps with cobbler's wax   75
And Cinderella's gold shoe stuck upon it.
Now he would find whom the shoe fit
and find his strange dancing girl for keeps.
He went to their house and the two sisters
were delighted because they had lovely feet.   80
The eldest went into a room to try the slipper on
but her big toe got in the way so she simply
sliced it off and put on the slipper.

The prince rode away with her until the white dove
told him to look at the blood pouring forth.   85
That is the way with amputations.
They don't just heal up like a wish.
The other sister cut off her heel
but the blood told as blood will.
The prince was getting tired.   90
He began to feel like a shoe salesman.
But he gave it one last try.
This time Cinderella fit into the shoe
like a love letter into its envelope.

At the wedding ceremony
the two sisters came to curry favor
and the white dove pecked their eyes out.
Two hollow spots were left
like soup spoons.

Cinderella and the prince
lived, they say, happily ever after,
like two dolls in a museum case
never bothered by diapers or dust,
never arguing over the timing of an egg,
never telling the same story twice,
never getting a middle-aged spread,
their darling smiles pasted on for eternity
Regular Bobbsey Twins.°
That story.

—1970

THOM GUNN ■ (1929–2004)

*Thom Gunn was a British expatriate who lived in San Francisco for over
four decades. Gunn managed to retain his ties to the traditions of British
literature while writing about motorcycle gangs, surfers, gay bars, and drug
experiences. The Man with Night Sweats, his 1992 collection, contains a
number of forthright poems on AIDS, of which "Terminal" is one.*

From the Wave

It mounts at sea, a concave wall
    Down-ribbed with shine,
And pushes forward, building tall
    Its steep incline.

Then from their hiding rise to sight
    Black shapes on boards
Bearing before the fringe of white
    It mottles towards.

---

108 **Bobbsey Twins** characters in a series of popular juvenile novels by Laura Lee Hope

Their pale feet curl, they poise their weight
    With a learn'd skill.   10
It is the wave they imitate
    Keeps them so still.

The marbling bodies have become
    Half wave, half men,
Grafted it seems by feet of foam   15
    Some seconds, then,

Late as they can, they slice the face
    In timed procession:
Balance is triumph in this place,
    Triumph possession.   20

The mindless heave of which they rode
    A fluid shelf
Breaks as they leave it, falls and, slowed,
    Loses itself.

Clear, the sheathed bodies slick as seals   25
    Loosen and tingle;
And by the board the bare foot feels
    The suck of shingle.

They paddle in the shallows still;
    Two splash each other;   30
Then all swim out to wait until
    The right waves gather.

                                          —1971

Terminal

The eight years difference in age seems now
Disparity so wide between the two
That when I see the man who armoured stood
Resistant to all help however good
Now helped through day itself, eased into chairs,   5
Or else led step by step down the long stairs
With firm and gentle guidance by his friend,

Who loves him, through each effort to descend,
Each wavering, each attempt made to complete
An arc of movement and bring down the feet   10
As if with that spare strength he used to enjoy,
I think of Oedipus, old, led by a boy.

—1992

X. J. KENNEDY ▪ (b. 1929)

X. J. Kennedy is one the few contemporary American poets who has not been attracted to free verse, preferring to remain what he calls a "dinosaur," one of those poets who continue to write in meter. He is also rare among his contemporaries in his commitment to writing poems with strong ties to song. Kennedy is also the author of Literature: An Introduction to Fiction, Poetry, and Drama, *perhaps the most widely used college literature text ever written.*

In a Prominent Bar in Secaucus One Day

*To the tune of "The Old Orange Flute" or the tune of
"Sweet Betsy from Pike"*

In a prominent bar in Secaucus one day
Rose a lady in skunk with a topheavy sway,
Raised a knobby red finger—all turned from their beer—
While with eyes bright as snowcrust she sang high and clear:

"Now who of you'd think from an eyeload of me   5
That I once was a lady as proud as could be?
Oh I'd never sit down by a tumbledown drunk
If it wasn't, my dears, for the high cost of junk.

"All the gents used to swear that the white of my calf
Beat the down of the swan by a length and a half.   10
In the kerchief of linen I caught to my nose
Ah, there never fell snot, but a little gold rose.

"I had seven gold teeth and a toothpick of gold,
My Virginia cheroot° was a leaf of it rolled
And I'd light it each time with a thousand in cash—   15
Why the bums used to fight if I flicked them an ash.

"Once the toast of the Biltmore, the belle of the Taft,
I would drink bottle beer at the Drake,° never draft,
And dine at the Astor on Salisbury steak
With a clean tablecloth for each bite I did take.   20

"In a car like the Roxy I'd roll to the track,
A steel-guitar trio, a bar in the back,
And the wheels made no noise, they turned over so fast,
Still it took you ten minutes to see me go past.

"When the horses bowed down to me that I might choose,   25
I bet on them all, for I hated to lose.
Now I'm saddled each night for my butter and eggs
And the broken threads race down the backs of my legs.

"Let you hold in mind, girls, that your beauty must pass
Like a lovely white clover that rusts with its grass.   30
Keep your bottoms off barstools and marry you young
Or be left—an old barrel with many a bung.

"For when time takes you out for a spin in his car
You'll be hard-pressed to stop him from going too far
And be left by the roadside, for all your good deeds,   35
Two toadstools for tits and a face full of weeds."

All the house raised a cheer, but the man at the bar
Made a phonecall and up pulled a red patrol car
And she blew us a kiss as they copped her away
From that prominent bar in Secaucus, N.J.   40

—1961

Little Elegy

for a child who skipped rope

Here lies resting, out of breath,
Out of turns, Elizabeth
Whose quicksilver toes not quite
Cleared the whirring edge of night.

Earth whose circles round us skim   5
Till they catch the lightest limb,
Shelter now Elizabeth
And for her sake trip up Death.

—1961

ADRIENNE RICH ■ (b. 1929)

Adrienne Rich's most recent books of poetry are Telephone Ringing in the
Labyrinth: Poems 2004-2006 *and* The School Among the Ruins: 2000-2004.
She edited Muriel Rukeyser's Selected Poems *for the Library of America.* A
Human Eye: Essays on Art in Society, *appeared in April 2009.* Tonight No
Poetry Will Serve: Poems 2007-2010, *will appear in 2011 from Norton. She
is a recipient of the National Book Foundation's 2006 Medal for Distin-
guished Contribution to American Letters among other honors. She lives in
California.*

Aunt Jennifer's Tigers

Aunt Jennifer's tigers prance across a screen,
Bright topaz denizens of a world of green.
They do not fear the men beneath the tree;
They pace in sleek chivalric certainty.

Aunt Jennifer's fingers fluttering through her wool   5
Find even the ivory needle hard to pull.
The massive weight of Uncle's wedding band
Sits heavily upon Aunt Jennifer's hand.

When Aunt is dead, her terrified hands will lie
Still ringed with ordeals she was mastered by.   10
The tigers in the panel that she made
Will go on prancing, proud and unafraid.

—1950

Diving into the Wreck

First having read the book of myths,
and loaded the camera,
and checked the edge of the knife-blade,
I put on
the body-armor of black rubber   5
the absurd flippers
the grave and awkward mask.
I am having to do this
not like Cousteau° with his
assiduous team   10
aboard the sun-flooded schooner
but here alone.

There is a ladder.
The ladder is always there
hanging innocently   15
close to the side of the schooner.
We know what it is for,
we who have used it.
Otherwise
it is a piece of maritime floss   20
some sundry equipment.

I go down.
Rung after rung and still
the oxygen immerses me
the blue light   25
the clear atoms
of our human air.
I go down.
My flippers cripple me,
I crawl like an insect down the ladder   30
and there is no one
to tell me when the ocean
will begin.

ADRIENNE RICH

---

9 Cousteau Jacques-Yves Cousteau (1910–1997), underwater explorer and inventor of the scuba tank

First the air is blue and then
it is bluer and then green and then   35
black I am blacking out and yet
my mask is powerful
it pumps my blood with power
the sea is another story
the sea is not a question of power   40
I have to learn alone
to turn my body without force
in the deep element.

And now: it is easy to forget
what I came for   45
among so many who have always
lived here
swaying their crenellated fans
between the reefs
and besides   50
you breathe differently down here.

I came to explore the wreck.
The words are purposes.
The words are maps.
I came to see the damage that was done   55
and the treasures that prevail.
I stroke the beam of my lamp
slowly along the flank
of something more permanent
than fish or weed   60

the thing I came for:
the wreck and not the story of the wreck
the thing itself and not the myth
the drowned face always staring
toward the sun   65
the evidence of damage
worn by salt and sway into this threadbare beauty
the ribs of the disaster
curving their assertion
among the tentative haunters.   70

This is the place.
And I am here, the mermaid whose dark hair
streams black, the merman in his armored body.
We circle silently
about the wreck   75
we dive into the hold.
I am she: I am he

whose drowned face sleeps with open eyes
whose breasts still bear the stress
whose silver, copper, vermeil cargo lies   80
obscurely inside barrels
half-wedged and left to rot
we are the half-destroyed instruments
that once held to a course
the water-eaten log°   85
the fouled compass

We are, I am, you are
by cowardice or courage
the one who find our way
back to this scene   90
carrying a knife, a camera
a book of myths
in which
our names do not appear.

—1972

Rape

There is a cop who is both prowler and father:
he comes from your block, grew up with your brothers,
had certain ideals.
You hardly know him in his boots and silver badge,
on horseback, one hand touching his gun.   5

You hardly know him but you have to get to know him:
he has access to machinery that could kill you.
He and his stallion clop like warlords among the trash,
his ideals stand in the air, a frozen cloud
from between his unsmiling lips.   10

85 log log book

And so, when the time comes, you have to turn to him,
the maniac's sperm still greasing your thighs,
your mind whirling like crazy. You have to confess
to him, you are guilty of the crime
of having been forced.   15

And you see his blue eyes, the blue eyes of all the family
whom you used to know, grow narrow and glisten,
his hand types out the details
and he wants them all
but the hysteria in your voice pleases him best.   20

You hardly know him but now he thinks he knows you:
he has taken down your worst moment
on a machine and filed it in a file.
He knows, or thinks he knows, how much you imagined;
he knows, or thinks he knows, what you secretly wanted.   25

He has access to machinery that could get you put away;
and if, in the sickening light of the precinct,
and if, in the sickening light of the precinct,
your details sound like a portrait of your confessor,
will you swallow, will you deny them, will you lie your way 30
    home?

—1972

TED HUGHES ■ (1930–1998)

*Ted Hughes was a native of Yorkshire, England. Hughes never ventured far
from the natural world of his childhood for his subject matter. Hughes was
married to Sylvia Plath until her death in 1963. At the time of his death,
Hughes was the British poet laureate and had recently published* Birthday
Letters, *a collection of poems about Plath's and his marriage.*

Pike

Pike, three inches long, perfect
Pike in all parts, green tigering the gold.
Killers from the egg: the malevolent aged grin.
They dance on the surface among the flies.

Or move, stunned by their own grandeur,   5
Over a bed of emerald, silhouette
Of submarine delicacy and horror.
A hundred feet long in their world.

In ponds, under the heat-struck lily pads—
Gloom of their stillness: 10
Logged on last year's black leaves, watching upwards.
Or hung in an amber cavern of weeds

The jaw's hooked clamp and fangs
Not to be changed at this date;
A life subdued to its instrument;   15
The gills kneading quietly, and the pectorals.

Three we kept behind glass,
Jungled in weed: three inches, four,
And four and a half: fed fry to them—
Suddenly there were two. Finally one   20

With a sag belly and the grin it was born with.
And indeed they spare nobody.
Two, six pounds each, over two feet long,
High and dry and dead in the willow-herb—

One jammed past its gills down the other's gullet: 25
The outside eye stared: as a vice locks—
The same iron in this eye
Though its film shrank in death.

A pond I fished, fifty yards across,
Whose lilies and muscular tench°   30
Had outlasted every visible stone
Of the monastery that planted them—

Stilled legendary depth:
It was as deep as England. It held
Pike too immense to stir, so immense and old   35
That past nightfall I dared not cast

30 **tench** European freshwater fish

But silently cast and fished
With the hair frozen on my head
For what might move, for what eye might move.
The still splashes on the dark pond,   40

Owls hushing the floating woods
Frail on my ear against the dream
Darkness beneath night's darkness had freed,
That rose slowly towards me, watching.

—1960

GARY SNYDER ■ (b. 1930)

Gary Snyder was deeply involved in poetic activity in his hometown, San Francisco, when that city became the locus of the Beat Generation in the mid-1950s. Yet Snyder, whose studies in Zen Buddhism and Oriental cultures preceded his acquaintance with Allen Ginsberg and Jack Kerouac, has always exhibited a seriousness of purpose that sets him apart from his peers. His long familiarity with the mountains of the Pacific Northwest dates from his jobs with logging crews during his college days.

A Walk

Sunday the only day we don't work:
Mules farting around the meadow,
        Murphy fishing,
The tent flaps in the warm
Early sun: I've eaten breakfast and I'll   5
        take a walk
To Benson Lake. Packed a lunch,
Goodbye. Hopping on creekbed boulders
Up the rock throat three miles
        Piute Creek—   10
In steep gorge glacier-slick rattlesnake country
Jump, land by a pool, trout skitter,
The clear sky. Deer tracks.
Bad place by a falls, boulders big as houses,
Lunch tied to belt,   15
I stemmed up a crack and almost fell

But rolled out safe on a ledge
    and ambled on.
Quail chicks freeze underfoot, color of stone
Then run cheep! away, hen quail fussing.   20
Craggy west end of Benson Lake—after edging
Past dark creek pools on a long white slope—
Lookt down in the ice-black lake
    lined with cliff
From far above: deep shimmering trout.   25
A lone duck in a gunsightpass
    steep side hill
Through slide-aspen and talus, to the east end
Down to grass, wading a wide smooth stream
Into camp. At last.   30
    By the rusty three-year-
Ago left-behind cookstove
Of the old trail crew,
Stoppt and swam and ate my lunch.

                                        —1968

MILLER WILLIAMS ■ (b. 1930)

Miller Williams won the Poets' Prize in 1990 for Living on the Surface, *a volume of selected poems. A skillful translator of both Giuseppe Belli, a Roman poet of the early nineteenth century, and of Nicanor Parra, a contemporary Chilean, Williams has written many poems about his travels throughout the world yet has retained the relaxed idiom of his native Arkansas. He read a poem at the 1997 presidential inauguration.*

The Book

I held it in my hands while he told the story.

He had found it in a fallen bunker,
a book for notes with all the pages blank.
He took it to keep for a sketchbook and diary.

He learned years later, when he showed the book   5
to an old bookbinder, who paled, and stepped back
a long step and told him what he held,
what he had laid the days of his life in.
It's bound, the binder said, in human skin.

I stood turning it over in my hands,   10
turning it in my head. Human skin.

What child did this skin fit? What man, what woman?
Dragged still full of its flesh from what dream?

Who took it off the meat? Some other one
who stayed alive by knowing how to do this?   15

I stared at the changing book and a horror grew,
I stared and a horror grew, which was, which is,
how beautiful it was until I knew.

—1989

LINDA PASTAN ■ (b. 1932)

*Linda Pastan served as poet laureate of Maryland, where she has lived and
taught for many years. Her first book,* A Perfect Circle of Sun, *appeared in
1971, and a dozen more collections have been published since.*

Ethics

In ethics class so many years ago
our teacher asked this question every fall:
if there were a fire in a museum
which would you save, a Rembrandt painting
or an old woman who hadn't many   5
years left anyhow? Restless on hard chairs
caring little for pictures or old age
we'd opt one year for life, the next for art
and always half-heartedly. Sometimes
the woman borrowed my grandmother's face   10
leaving her usual kitchen to wander
some drafty, half-imagined museum.
One year, feeling clever, I replied
why not let the woman decide herself?
Linda, the teacher would report, eschews   15
the burdens of responsibility.
This fall in a real museum I stand
Before a real Rembrandt, old woman,
or nearly so, myself. The colors

within this frame are darker than autumn,   20
darker even than winter—the browns of earth,
though earth's most radiant elements burn
through the canvas. I know now that woman
and painting and season are almost one   25
and all beyond saving by children.

—*1998*

SYLVIA PLATH ■ (1932–1963)

Sylvia Plath, whose personal life is often difficult to separate from her poetry, is almost always read as an autobiographical and confessional poet. Brilliant and precocious, she served a long apprenticeship to the tradition of modern poetry before attaining her mature style in the final two years of her life. Only one collection, The Colossus *(1960), appeared in her lifetime, and her fame has mainly rested on her posthumous books of poetry and the success of her lone novel,* The Bell Jar *(1963). She committed suicide in 1963. Plath has been the subject of a half-dozen biographical studies and a feature film,* Sylvia *(2003), reflecting the intense interest that readers have in her life and work.*

Daddy

You do not do, you do not do
Any more, black shoe
In which I have lived like a foot
For thirty years, poor and white,
Barely daring to breathe or Achoo.   5

Daddy, I have had to kill you.
You died before I had time—
Marble-heavy, a bag full of God,
Ghastly statue with one gray toe
Big as a Frisco seal   10

And a head in the freakish Atlantic
Where it pours bean green over blue
In the waters off beautiful Nauset.
I used to pray to recover you.
Ach, du.°   15

15 **Ach, du** "Oh, you"

In the German tongue, in the Polish town
Scraped flat by the roller
Of wars, wars, wars.
But the name of the town is common.
My Polack friend   20

Says there are a dozen or two.
So I never could tell where you
Put your foot, your root,
I never could talk to you.
The tongue stuck in my jaw.   25

It stuck in a barb wire snare.
Ich, ich, ich, ich,°
I could hardly speak.
I thought every German was you.
And the language obscene   30

An engine, an engine
Chuffing me off like a Jew.
A Jew to Dachau, Auschwitz, Belsen.°
I began to talk like a Jew.
I think I may well be a Jew.   35

The snows of the Tyrol, the clear beer of Vienna
Are not very pure or true.
With my gypsy ancestress and my weird luck
And my Taroc pack and my Taroc pack
I may be a bit of a Jew.   40

I have always been scared of *you*,
With your Luftwaffe,° your gobbledygoo.
And your neat mustache
And your Aryan eye, bright blue.
Panzer-man, panzer-man, O You—   45

Not God but a swastika
So black no sky could squeak through.
Every woman adores a Fascist,
The boot in the face, the brute
Brute heart of a brute like you.   50

27 Ich, ich, ich, ich "I, I, I, I"   **33 Dachau, Auschwitz, Belsen** German concentration camps
42 Luftwaffe German Air Force

You stand at the blackboard, daddy,
In the picture I have of you,
A cleft in your chin instead of your foot
But no less a devil for that, no not
Any less the black man who   55

Bit my pretty red heart in two.
I was ten when they buried you.
At twenty I tried to die
And get back, back, back to you.
I thought even the bones would do.   60

But they pulled me out of the sack,
And they stuck me together with glue.
And then I knew what to do.
I made a model of you,
A man in black with a Meinkampf° look   65

And a love of the rack and the screw.
And I said I do, I do.
So daddy, I'm finally through.
The black telephone's off at the root,
The voices just can't worm through.   70

If I've killed one man, I've killed two—
The vampire who said he was you
And drank my blood for a year,
Seven years, if you want to know.
Daddy, you can lie back now.   75

There's a stake in your fat black heart
And the villagers never liked you.
They are dancing and stamping on you.
They always *knew* it was you.
Daddy, daddy, you bastard, I'm through.   80

—*1966*

---

65 Meinkampf title of Hitler's autobiography ("My Struggle")

Edge

The woman is perfected.
Her dead

Body wears the smile of accomplishment,
The illusion of a Greek necessity

Flows in the scrolls of her toga,   5
Her bare

Feet seem to be saying:
We have come so far, it is over.

Each dead child coiled, a white serpent,
One at each little   10

Pitcher of milk, now empty.
She has folded

Them back into her body as petals
Of a rose close when the garden

Stiffens and odors bleed   15
From the sweet, deep throats of the night flower.

The moon has nothing to be sad about,
Staring from her hood of bone.

She is used to this sort of thing.
Her blacks crackle and drag.   20

—1965

Metaphors

I'm a riddle in nine syllables,
An elephant, a ponderous house,
A melon strolling on two tendrils.
O red fruit, ivory, fine timbers!
This loaf's big with its yeasty rising.   5
Money's new-minted in this fat purse.
I'm a means, a stage, a cow in calf.
I've eaten a bag of green apples,
Boarded the train there's no getting off.

—1960

Gerald Barrax served as the editor of Obsidian II: Black Literature in Review, *one of the most influential journals of African-American writing. The author of five collections of poetry, he taught at North Carolina State University.*

Strangers Like Us: Pittsburgh, Raleigh, 1945–1985

The sounds our parents heard echoing over
housetops while listening to evening radios
were the uninterrupted cries running and cycling
we sent through the streets and yards, where spring summer
fall we were entrusted to the night, boys   5
and girls together, to send us home for bath
and bed after the dark had drifted down and eased
contests between pitcher and batter, hider and seeker.

Our own children live imprisoned in light.
They are cycloned into our yards and hearts,   10
whose gates flutter shut on unfamiliar smiles.
At the rumor of a moon, we call them in
before the monsters who hunt, who hurt, who haunt
us, rise up from our own dim streets.

—1992

Mark Strand displays a simplicity in his best poems that reveals the influence of Spanish-language poets like Nicanor Parra, the father of "anti-poetry," and Rafael Alberti, whom Strand has translated. Strand was named U.S. poet laureate in 1990.

The Tunnel

A man has been standing
in front of my house
for days. I peek at him
from the living room

MARK STRAND

310

window and at night,
unable to sleep,
I shine my flashlight
down on the lawn.
He is always there.

After a while
I open the front door
just a crack and order
him out of my yard.
He narrows his eyes
and moans. I slam
the door and dash back
to the kitchen, then up
to the bedroom, then down.

I weep like a schoolgirl
and make obscene gestures
through the window. I
write large suicide notes
and place them so he
can read them easily.
I destroy the living
room furniture to prove
I own nothing of value.

When he seems unmoved
I decide to dig a tunnel
to a neighboring yard.
I seal the basement off
from the upstairs with
a brick wall. I dig hard
and in no time the tunnel
is done. Leaving my pick
and shovel below,

I come out in front of a house
and stand there too tired to
move or even speak, hoping
someone will help me.
I feel I'm being watched

and sometimes I hear
a man's voice,
but nothing is done
and I have been waiting for days.   45

—1968

LEWIS TURCO ■ (b. 1934)

Lewis Turco (who also writes under the anagrammatic pseudonym Wesli Court) is best known as the author of The Book of Forms, *a widely used poetry reference book. Retired from teaching at SUNY–Oswego, Turco is presently a bookseller in Dresden, Maine.* The Collected Lyrics of Lewis Turco/Wesli Court *appeared in 2004. Turco invented the terzanelle form, of which "The Premonition" is an example.*

The Premonition

The first two planes had crashed. He'd known they would
as he watched AirOps from the Gunner's Bridge,
and he'd seen everything from where he stood.

The wings folded along the fuselage
on this new day relieved him. He was glad,   5
as he watched AirOps from the Gunner's Bridge,

that this third time there would be nothing bad
about to happen. His instincts had been wrong
on this new day. He was deeply glad

this pilot would be safe. He looked along   10
the deck as the plane was parked, then looked away
before it happened—his gut had not been wrong!

The jet had not cut out! He saw it sway,
then disappear over the *Hornet's* side
near where it had been parked. He looked away—   15

at least the first two pilots hadn't died!
Those first two planes had crashed. He'd known they would,
but this one fell along the *Hornet's* side,
and he'd seen everything from where he stood.

—2004

Russell Edson is the son of a cartoonist, and his surrealistic poems (often illustrated by himself) perhaps owe as much to the whimsical drawings and essays of New Yorker *writer James Thurber than to the direct influence of any modern poet. Edson has been called "the godfather of the prose poem in America," and the sheer originality of his imagination and his defiance of poetic "rules" set him apart from other poets and ally him with such contemporary masters of cartooning as R. Crumb and Harvey Pekar.*

Ape

You haven't finished your ape, said mother to father, who had monkey hair and blood on his whiskers.

I've had enough monkey, cried father.

You didn't eat the hands, and I went to all the trouble to make onion rings for its fingers, said mother.   5

I'll just nibble on its forehead, and then I've had enough, said father.

I stuffed its nose with garlic, just like you like it, said mother.

Why don't you have the butcher cut these apes up? You lay the whole thing on the table every night; the same fractured skull, the same singed fur; like someone who died horribly. These aren't dinners,   10
these are postmortem dissections.

Try a piece of its gum, I've stuffed its mouth with bread, said mother.

Ugh, it looks like a mouth full of vomit. How can I bite into its cheek with bread spilling out of its mouth? cried father.

Break one of the ears off, they're so crispy, said mother.   15

I wish to hell you'd put underpants on these apes; even a jockstrap, screamed father.

Father, how dare you insinuate that I see the ape as anything more than simple meat, screamed mother.

Well, what's with this ribbon tied in a bow on its privates? screamed father.   20

Are you saying that I am in love with this vicious creature? That I
would submit my female opening to this brute? That after we had
love on the kitchen floor I would put him in the oven, after breaking
his head with a frying pan; and then serve him to my husband, that
my husband might eat the evidence of my infidelity . . . ?   25

I'm just saying that I'm damn sick of ape every night, cried father.

—1994

MARY OLIVER ■ (b. 1935)

Mary Oliver was born in Cleveland, Ohio, and educated at Ohio State University and Vassar College. She has served as a visiting professor at a number of universities and at the Fine Arts Work Center in Provincetown, Massachusetts. She has won both the Pulitzer Prize and the National Book Award for her work. Red Bird, *a new collection of poems, appeared in 2008.*

The Black Walnut Tree

My mother and I debate:
we could sell
the black walnut tree
to the lumberman,
and pay off the mortgage.   5
Likely some storm anyway
will churn down its dark boughs,
smashing the house. We talk
slowly, two women trying
in a difficult time to be wise.   10
Roots in the cellar drains,
I say, and she replies
that the leaves are getting heavier
every year, and the fruit
harder to gather away.   15
But something brighter than money
moves in our blood—an edge
sharp and quick as a trowel
that wants us to dig and sow.

So we talk, but we don't do
anything. That night I dream
of my fathers out of Bohemia
filling the blue fields
of fresh and generous Ohio
with leaves and vines and orchards.
What my mother and I both know
is that we'd crawl with shame
in the emptiness we'd made
in our own and our fathers' backyard.
So the black walnut tree
swings through another year
of sun and leaping winds,
of leaves and bounding fruit,
and, month after month, the whip-
crack of the mortgage.

—1979

Honey at the Table

It fills you with the soft
essence of vanished flowers, it becomes
a trickle sharp as a hair that you follow
from the honey pot over the table

and out the door and over the ground,
and all the while it thickens,

grows deeper and wilder, edged
with pine boughs and wet boulders,
pawprints of bobcat and bear, until

deep in the forest you
shuffle up some tree, you rip the bark,

you float into and swallow the dripping combs,
bits of the tree, crushed bees—a taste
composed of everything lost, in which everything
lost is found.

—1978

Fred Chappell wrote the epic-length poem Midquest *(1981), and his achievement was recognized when he was awarded the Bollingen Prize in 1985. A four-part poem written over a decade,* Midquest *uses the occasion of the poet's thirty-fifth birthday as a departure for a complex sequence of autobiographical poems that are heavily indebted to Dante for their formal structure. A versatile writer of both poetry and prose, Chappell displays his classical learning brilliantly and in unusual contexts.*

Narcissus and Echo°

Shall the water not remember *Ember*
my hand's slow gesture, tracing above *of*
its mirror my half-imaginary *airy*
portrait? My only belonging *longing*
is my beauty, which I take *ache*   5
away and then return as love *of*
teasing playfully the one being *unbeing.*

whose gratitude I treasure *Is your*
moves me. I live apart *heart*
from myself, yet cannot *not*   10
live apart. In the water's tone, *stone?*
that brilliant silence, a flower *Hour,*
whispers my name with such slight *light,*
moment, it seems filament of air, *fare*
the world become cloudswell. *well.*   15

—*1985*

Narcissus and Echo In the myth, the vain Narcissus drowned attempting to embrace his own reflection in the water. Echo, a nymph who loved him, pined away until only her voice remained.

FRED CHAPPELL

Lucille Clifton, a native of Depew, New York, was educated at SUNY–Fredonia and Howard University, and has taught at several colleges, including American University in Washington, D.C. About her own work, she has commented succinctly, "I am a Black woman poet, and I sound like one." Clifton won a National Book Award in 2000.

homage to my hips

these hips are big hips
they need space to
move around in.
they don't fit into little
petty places. these hips   5
are free hips.
they don't like to be held back.
these hips have never been enslaved,
they go where they want to go
they do what they want to do.   10
these hips are mighty hips.
these hips are magic hips.
i have known them
to put a spell on a man and
spin him like a top!   15

—1980

wishes for sons

i wish them cramps.
i wish them a strange town
and the last tampon.
I wish them no 7-11.

i wish them one week early   5
and wearing a white skirt.
i wish them one week late.

later i wish them hot flashes
and clots like you
wouldn't believe. let the   10

flashes come when they
meet someone special.
let the clots come
when they want to.

let them think they have accepted   15
arrogance in the universe,
then bring them to gynecologists
not unlike themselves.

—1991

MARGE PIERCY ■ (b. 1936)

Marge Piercy was a political radical during her student days at the University of Michigan. Piercy has continued to be outspoken on political, cultural, and sexual issues. Her phrase "to be of use" has become a key measure by which feminist writers and critics have gauged the meaning of their own life experiences.

What's That Smell in the Kitchen?

All over America women are burning dinners.
It's lambchops in Peoria; it's haddock
in Providence; it's steak in Chicago;
tofu delight in Big Sur; red
rice and beans in Dallas.   5
All over America women are burning
food they're supposed to bring with calico
smile on platters glittering like wax.
Anger sputters in her brainpan, confined
but spewing out missiles of hot fat.   10
Carbonized despair presses like a clinker
from a barbecue against the back of her eyes.
If she wants to grill anything, it's
her husband spitted over a slow fire.
If she wants to serve him anything   15

it's a dead rat with a bomb in its belly
ticking like the heart of an insomniac.
Her life is cooked and digested,
nothing but leftovers in Tupperware.
Look, she says, once I was roast duck   20
on your platter with parsley but now I am Spam.
Burning dinner is not incompetence but war.

—1982

BETTY ADCOCK ■ (b. 1938)

Betty Adcock was born in San Augustine, Texas. Adcock has lived for many years in Raleigh, North Carolina, where she is poet-in-residence at Meredith College. Her volume of selected poems, Intervale, *appeared in 2001.*

Voyages

We were five girls prowling alleyways behind the houses,
having skipped math class for any and no reason.
Equipped with too many camelhair coats, too many cashmeres,
we were privileged and sure and dumb, isolated
without knowing it, smug in our small crime, playing   5
hooky from Miss Hockaday's Boarding School for young ladies.
Looking for anything that wouldn't be boring
as we defined that, we'd gone off exploring the going-downhill
neighborhoods around our tight Victorian schoolgrounds.
The houses were fronted with concrete porches,   10
venetian blinds drawn tight against the sun.
Somebody had told us an eccentric lived where one
back fence got strangely high and something stuck over
the top. We didn't care what it was, but we went anyway,
giggling with hope for the freakish: bodies stashed and
        decaying,   15
a madwoman pulling her hair, maybe a maniac in a cage.
Anything sufficiently awful would have done.

But when we came close enough to look through
the inch of space between two badly placed fenceboards,
we saw only the ordinary, grown grotesque and huge: 20

somebody was building a sailboat bigger than most city
    backyards,
bigger almost than the house it belonged to,
mast towering high in a brass-and-blue afternoon.
This was in the middle of Dallas, Texas—
the middle of the 1950s, which had us   25
(though we didn't yet know this) by the throat.
Here was a backyard entirely full of boat,
out of scale, out of the Bible, maybe out of a movie,
all rescue and ornament. It looked to be something between
a galleon and a Viking ship, larger than we could imagine   30
in such a space, with sails and riggings and a face on the prow
(about which we made much but which neither smiled nor
    frowned).
Gasping, overplaying the scene, we guessed at the kind
of old fool who would give a lifetime to building this thing.
Then one of us asked for a light for a cigarette   35
and we all knew how easy it would be to swipe
a newspaper, light it, and toss it onto the deck
of that great wooden landlocked ark, watch it go up.

But of course we didn't do it and nobody of course came out
of that house and we of course went back   40
in time for English and to sneak out of P.E. later
for hamburgers at Mitch's where the blue-collar boys
leaned in their ducktails against the bar.

But before we did that, we stood for a while clumped
and smoking, pushed into silence by palpable obsession   45
where it sat as if it belonged on parched Dallas grass,
a stunned, unfinished restlessness.

And didn't the ground just then, under our penny-
loafers, give the tiniest heave? Didn't we feel how thin
the grass was, like a coat of light paint, like green ice   50
over something unmanageable? How thin the sun
became for a minute, the rest of our future dimming
and wavy and vast, even tomorrow's pop quiz and softball
    practice—

as if all around us were depths we really could drown in.

—1995

Robert Phillips labored for over thirty years as a New York advertising executive, a remarkable fact when one considers his many books of poetry, fiction, and criticism and the numerous books he has edited. He currently lives in Houston, where he teaches in the creative writing program at the University of Houston.

The Stone Crab: A Love Poem

> Joe's serves approximately 1,000 pounds of crab
> claws each day.
> > —*Florida Gold Coast Leisure Guide*

Delicacy of warm Florida waters,
his body is undesirable. One giant claw
is his claim to fame, and we claim it,

more than once. Meat sweeter than lobster,
less dear than his life, when grown that claw   5
is lifted, broken off at the joint.

Mutilated, the crustacean is thrown back
into the water, back upon his own resources.
One of nature's rarities, he replaces

an entire appendage as you or I   10
grow a nail. (No one asks how he survives
that crabby sea with just one claw;

two-fisted menaces real as night-
mares, ten-tentacled nights cold
as fright.) In time he grows another,   15

large, meaty, magnificent as the first.
And one astonished day, *snap!* it too
is twigged off, the cripple dropped

back into treachery. Unlike a twig,
it sprouts again. How many losses   20
can he endure? Well,

his shell is hard, the sea is wide.
Something vital broken off, he doesn't
nurse the wound; develops something new.

—1994

DABNEY STUART ■ (b. 1938)

Dabney Stuart has written many poems populated by the supporting cast of the American family romance—parents, wives and ex-wives, and children. A Virginian who taught for many years at Washington and Lee University, Stuart published Light Years, *a volume of selected poems, in 1995.*

Discovering My Daughter

Most of your life we have kept our separate places:
After I left your mother you knew an island,
Rented rooms, a slow coastal slide northward
To Boston, and, in summer, another island
Hung at the country's tip. Would you have kept going   5
All the way off the map, an absolute alien?

Sometimes I shiver, being almost forgetful enough
To have let that happen. We've come the longer way
Under such pressure, from one person to
Another. Our trip proves again the world is   10
Round, a singular island where people may come
Together, as we have, making a singular place.

—1987

MARGARET ATWOOD ■ (b. 1939)

Margaret Atwood is the leading woman writer of Canada, and she excels at both poetry and prose fiction. Among her many novels, The Handmaid's Tale *is perhaps the best known, becoming a bestseller in the United States and the subject of a motion picture. Atwood's* Selected Poems *appeared in 1976.*

Siren° Song

This is the one song everyone
would like to learn: the song
that is irresistible:

Siren in Greek myth, one of the women whose irresistible song lured sailors onto the rocks

the song that forces men
to leap overboard in squadrons   5
even though they see the beached skulls

the song nobody knows
because anyone who has heard it
is dead, and the others can't remember.

Shall I tell you the secret   10
and if I do, will you get me
out of this bird suit?

I don't enjoy it here
squatting on this island
looking picturesque and mythical   15

with these two feathery maniacs,
I don't enjoy singing
this trio, fatal and valuable.

I will tell the secret to you,
to you, only to you.   20
Come closer. This song

is a cry for help: Help me!
Only you, only you can,
you are unique

at last. Alas   25
it is a boring song
but it works every time.

—1974

STEPHEN DUNN ■ (b. 1939)

Stephen Dunn is a graduate of the creative writing program at Syracuse University. Dunn teaches at The Richard Stockton College of New Jersey in Pomona, New Jersey. His attempt to blend ordinary experience with larger significance is illustrated in the duality of his book titles like Full of Lust and Good Usage, Work and Love, *and* Between Angels. *Dunn was awarded the Pulitzer Prize in 2001.*

The Sacred

After the teacher asked if anyone had
    a sacred place
and the students fidgeted and shrank

in their chairs, the most serious of them all
    said it was his car,   5
being in it alone, his tape deck playing

things he'd chosen, and others knew the truth
    had been spoken
and began speaking about their rooms,

their hiding places, but the car kept coming up,   10
    the car in motion,
music filling it, and sometimes one other person

who understood the bright altar of the dashboard
    and how far away
a car could take him from the need   15

to speak, or to answer, the key
    in having a key
and putting it in, and going.

—1989

SEAMUS HEANEY ■ (b. 1939)

Seamus Heaney was born in the troubled country of Northern Ireland. Heaney has largely avoided the type of political divisions that have divided his homeland. Instead, he has chosen to focus on the landscape of the rural Ireland he knew while growing up as a farmer's son. Since 1982, Heaney has taught part of the year at Harvard University. He was awarded the Nobel Prize for Literature in 1995.

Digging

Between my finger and my thumb
The squat pen rests; snug as a gun.

Under my window, a clean rasping sound
When the spade sinks into gravelly ground:
My father, digging. I look down   5

Till his straining rump among the flowerbeds
Bends low, comes up twenty years away
Stooping in rhythm through potato drills°
Where he was digging.

The coarse boot nestled on the lug, the shaft   10
Against the inside knee was levered firmly.
He rooted out tall tops, buried the bright edge deep
To scatter new potatoes that we picked
Loving their cool hardness in our hands.

By God, the old man could handle a spade.   15
Just like his old man.

My grandfather cut more turf in a day
Than any other man on Toner's bog.
Once I carried him milk in a bottle
Corked sloppily with paper. He straightened up   20
To drink it, then fell to right away

Nicking and slicing neatly, heaving sods
Over his shoulder, going down and down
For the good turf. Digging.

The cold smell of potato mould, the squelch and slap   25
Of soggy peat, the curt cuts of an edge
Through living roots awaken in my head.
But I've no spade to follow men like them.

Between my finger and my thumb
The squat pen rests.   30
I'll dig with it.

—1980

8 **drills** furrows

Punishment

I can feel the tug
of the halter at the nape
of her neck, the wind
on her naked front.

It blows her nipples   5
to amber beads,
it shakes the frail rigging
of her ribs.

I can see her drowned
body in the bog,   10
the weighing stone,
the floating rods and boughs.

Under which at first
she was a barked sapling
that is dug up   15
oak-bone, brain-firkin:°

her shaved head
like a stubble of black corn,
her blindfold a soiled bandage,
her noose a ring   20

to store
the memories of love.
Little adulteress,
before they punished you

you were flaxen-haired,   25
undernourished, and your
tar-black face was beautiful.
My poor scapegoat,

I almost love you
but would have cast, I know,   30
the stones of silence.
I am the artful voyeur

16 **firkin** a small barrel

of your brain's exposed
and darkened combs,
your muscles' webbing   35
and all your numbered bones:

I who have stood dumb
when your betraying sisters,
cauled in tar,
wept by the railings,   40

who would connive
in civilized outrage
yet understand the exact
and tribal, intimate revenge.

—1975

TED KOOSER ■ (b. 1939)

Ted Kooser, who lives in Nebraska, writes plainspoken poems about life in America's heartland. Born in Iowa, Kooser studied at Iowa State University and the University of Nebraska. His poetry collections include Winter Morning Walks: One Hundred Postcards to Jim Harrison, *which was written during Kooser's recovery from cancer surgery and radiation treatment. It received the 2001 Nebraska Book Award for poetry. Kooser is editor and publisher of* Windflower Press, *a small press specializing in contemporary poetry. A retired vice president of Lincoln Benefit Life, an insurance company, Kooser teaches at the University of Nebraska, Lincoln. In 2004, Kooser was appointed U.S. Poet Laureate.*

Abandoned Farmhouse

He was a big man, says the size of his shoes
on a pile of broken dishes by the house;
a tall man too, says the length of the bed
in an upstairs room; and a good, God-fearing man,
says the Bible with a broken back   5
on the floor below the window, dusty with sun;
but not a man for farming, say the fields
cluttered with boulders and the leaky barn.

A woman lived with him, says the bedroom wall
papered with lilacs and the kitchen shelves   10
covered with oilcloth, and they had a child,
says the sandbox made from a tractor tire.
Money was scarce, say the jars of plum preserves
and canned tomatoes sealed in the cellar hole.
And the winters cold, say the rags in the window frames.   15
It was lonely here, says the narrow country road.

Something went wrong, says the empty house
in the weed-choked yard. Stones in the fields
say he was not a farmer; the still-sealed jars
in the cellar say she left in a nervous haste.   20
And the child? Its toys are strewn in the yard
like branches after a storm—a rubber cow,
a rusty tractor with a broken plow,
a doll in overalls. Something went wrong, they say.

—1980

TOM DISCH ■ (b 1940–2008)

Tom Disch was a science-fiction writer, author of interactive computer fiction, resident critic for magazines as diverse as Playboy *and* The Nation, *and poet. Disch was possibly the most brilliant satirist in contemporary American poetry.* Yes, Let's, *a collection of his selected poems, appeared in 1989.*

Ballade of the New God

I have decided I'm divine.
Caligula and Nero knew
A godliness akin to mine,
But they are strictly hitherto.
They're dead, and what can dead gods do?   5
I'm here and now. I'm dynamite.
I'd worship me if I were you.
A new religion starts tonight!

No booze, no pot, no sex, no swine:
I have decreed them all taboo.   10
My words will be your only wine,
The thought of me your honeydew.
All other thoughts you will eschew
And call yourself a Thomasite
And hymn my praise with loud yahoo.   15
A new religion starts tonight.

But (you might think) that's asinine!
I'm just as much a god as you.
You may have built yourself a shrine
But I won't bend my knee. Who   20
Asked you to be my god? I do,
Who am, as god, divinely right.
Now you must join my retinue:
A new religion starts tonight.

All that I have said is true.   25
I'm god and you're my acolyte.
Surrender's bliss: I envy you.
A new religion starts tonight.

—1995

FLORENCE CASSEN MAYERS ■ (b. 1940)

Florence Cassen Mayers is a widely published poet and children's author. Her "ABC" books include children's guides to baseball and to the National Basketball Association.

All-American Sestina

One nation, indivisible
two-car garage
three strikes you're out
four-minute mile
five-cent cigar   5
six-string guitar

six-pack Bud
one-day sale
five-year warranty
two-way street   10
fourscore and seven years ago
three cheers

three-star restaurant
sixty-
four-dollar question   15
one-night stand
two-pound lobster
five-star general

five-course meal
three sheets to the wind   20
two bits
six-shooter
one-armed bandit
four-poster

four-wheel drive   25
five-and-dime
hole in one
three-alarm fire
sweet sixteen
two-wheeler   30

two-tone Chevy
four rms, hi flr, w/vu
six-footer
high five
three-ring circus   35
one-room schoolhouse

two thumbs up, five-karat diamond
Fourth of July, three-piece suit
six feet under, one-horse town

—1996

Pattiann Rogers is the foremost naturalist among contemporary American poets. Her poems resound with the rich names of unfamiliar species of plants and animals, most of which she seems to know on intimate terms. Song of the World Becoming: New and Collected Poems 1981–2001 was published in 2001. A new collection, Wayfare, *appeared in 2008.*

Foreplay

When it first begins, as you might expect,
the lips and thin folds are closed, the pouting
layers pressed, lapped lightly,
almost languidly, against one another
in a sealed bud.   5

However, with certain prolonged
and random strokings of care
along each binding line, with soft
intrusions traced beneath each pursed
gathering and edge, with inquiring   10
intensities of gesture—as the sun
swinging slowly from winter back

to spring, touches briefly,
between moments of moon and masking
clouds, certain stunning points   15
and inner nubs of earth—so
with such ministrations, a slight
swelling, a quiver of reaching,
a tendency toward space,
might be noticed to commence.   20

Then with dampness from the dark,
with moisture from the falling
night of morning, from hidden places
within the hills, each seal begins
to loosen, each recalcitrant clasp   25

sinks away into itself, and every tucked
grasp, every silk tack willingly relents,
releases, gives way, proclaims a turning,
declares a revolution, assumes,
in plain sight, a surging position   30
that offers, an audacious offering
that beseeches, every petal parted wide.

Remember the spiraling, blue
valerian, remember the violet, sucking
larkspur, the laurel and rosebay   35
and pea cockle flung backwards, remember
the fragrant, funnelling lily, the lifted
honeysuckle, the sweet, open pucker
of the ground ivy blossom?

Now even the darkest crease possessed,   40
the most guarded, pulsing, least drop
of pearl bead, moon grain trembling
deep within is fully revealed, fully exposed
to any penetrating wind or shaking fur
or mad hunger or searing, plunging surprise   45
the wild descending sky in delirium
has to offer.

—1994

BILLY COLLINS ■ (b. 1941)

Billy Collins was born in New York City and continues to teach there. One of the few contemporary poets to reach a wide popular audience, Collins has been an enthusiastic performer, commentator on National Public Radio, and advocate for poetry. Beginning in 2001, he served two years as U.S. poet laureate, establishing the online anthology "Poetry 180," a website that presents a poem for every day in the school year. Sailing Alone Around the Room: New and Selected Poems *was published in 2001. A new book,* The Trouble with Poetry, *was published in 2007.*

Litany

You are the bread and the knife,
The crystal goblet and the wine.
—*Jacques Crickillon*

You are the bread and the knife,
the crystal goblet and the wine.
You are the dew on the morning grass,
and the burning wheel of the sun.
You are the white apron of the baker   5
and the marsh birds suddenly in flight.

However, you are not the wind in the orchard,
the plums on the counter,
or the house of cards.
And you are certainly not the pine-scented air.   10
There is no way you are the pine-scented air.

It is possible that you are the fish under the bridge,
maybe even the pigeon on the general's head,
but you are not even close
to being the field of cornflowers at dusk.   15

And a quick look in the mirror will show
that you are neither the boots in the corner
nor the boat asleep in its boathouse.

It might interest you to know,
speaking of the plentiful imagery of the world,   20
that I am the sound of rain on the roof.

I also happen to be the shooting star,
the evening paper blowing down an alley,
and the basket of chestnuts on the kitchen table.

I am also the moon in the trees   25
and the blind woman's teacup.
But don't worry, I am not the bread and the knife.
You are still the bread and the knife.
You will always be the bread and the knife,
not to mention the crystal goblet and—somehow—the wine.   30

—2002

Paradelle° for Susan

I remember the quick, nervous bird of your love.
I remember the quick, nervous bird of your love.
Always perched on the thinnest, highest branch.
Always perched on the thinnest, highest branch.
Thinnest love, remember the quick branch.   5
Always nervous, I perched on your highest bird the.

It is time for me to cross the mountain.
It is time for me to cross the mountain.
And find another shore to darken with my pain.
And find another shore to darken with my pain.   10
Another pain for me to darken the mountain.
And find the time, cross my shore, to with it is to.

The weather warm, the handwriting familiar.
The weather warm, the handwriting familiar.
Your letter flies from my hand into the waters below.   15
Your letter flies from my hand into the waters below.
The familiar waters below my warm hand.
Into handwriting your weather flies you letter the from the.

I always cross the highest letter, the thinnest bird.
Below the waters of my warm familiar pain,   20
Another hand to remember your handwriting.
The weather perched for me on the shore.
Quick, your nervous branch flew from love.
Darken the mountain, time and find was my into it was with to to.

—1998

The paradelle is one of the more demanding French fixed forms, first appearing in the *langue d'oc* love poetry of the eleventh century. It is a poem of four six-line stanzas in which the first and second lines, as well as the third and fourth lines of the first three stanzas, must be identical. The fifth and sixth lines, which traditionally resolve these stanzas, must use *all* the words from the preceding lines and *only* those words. Similarly, the final stanza must use *every* word from *all* the preceding stanzas and *only* those words.
[Collins's note]

Robert Hass was born and reared in San Francisco, and teaches at U. C. Berkeley. His first book, Field Guide, *was chosen for the Yale Series of Younger Poets in 1973. Recently he has collaborated with Nobel Prize–winner Czeslaw Milosz on English translations of the latter's poetry. He was appointed U.S. poet laureate in 1995.*

Meditation at Lagunitas°

All the new thinking is about loss.
In this it resembles all the old thinking.
The idea, for example, that each particular erases
the luminous clarity of a general idea. That the clown-
faced woodpecker probing the dead sculpted trunk   5
of that black birch is, by his presence,
some tragic falling off from a first world
of undivided light. Or the other notion that,
because there is in this world no one thing
to which the bramble of *blackberry* corresponds,   10
a word is elegy to what it signifies.
We talked about it late last night and in the voice
of my friend, there was a thin wire of grief, a tone
almost querulous. After a while I understood that,
talking this way, everything dissolves: *justice,*   15
pine, hair, woman, you and *I.* There was a woman
I made love to and I remembered how, holding
her small shoulders in my hands sometimes,
I felt a violent wonder at her presence
like a thirst for salt, for my childhood river   20
with its island willows, silly music from the pleasure boat,
muddy places where we caught the little orange-silver fish
called *pumpkinseed.* It hardly had to do with her.
Longing, we say, because desire is full
of endless distances. I must have been the same to her   25
But I remember so much, the way her hands dismantled bread,
the thing her father said that hurt her, what

Lagunitas in California

she dreamed. There are moments when the body is as numinous
as words, days that are the good flesh continuing.
Such tenderness, those afternoons and evenings,   30
saying *blackberry, blackberry, blackberry.*

—*1979*

SIMON J. ORTIZ ▪ (b. 1941)

*Simon J. Ortiz was born in the Pueblo of Acoma, near Albuquerque, New
Mexico. Ortiz has explained why he writes: "Because Indians always tell a
story. The only way to continue is to tell a story." The author of collections of
poetry and prose and of several children's books, Ortiz has taught creative
writing and Native American literature at many universities.*

The Serenity in Stones

I am holding this turquoise
in my hands.
My hands hold the sky
wrought in this little stone.
There is a cloud   5
at the furthest boundary.
The world is somewhere underneath.

I turn the stone, and there is more sky.
This is the serenity possible in stones,
the place of a feeling to which one belongs.   10
I am happy as I hold this sky
in my hands, in my eyes, and in myself.

—*1975*

GIBBONS RUARK ▪ (b. 1941)

*Gibbons Ruark is a native of North Carolina. Ruark is the author of five col-
lections of poetry.* Passing Through Customs, *a volume of new and selected
poems, appeared in 1999. He recently retired from teaching at the University
of Delaware.*

The Visitor

Holding the arm of his helper, the blind
Piano tuner comes to our piano.
He hesitates at first, but once he finds
The keyboard, his hands glide over the slow
Keys, ringing changes finer than the eye   5
Can see. The dusty wires he touches, row
On row, quiver like bowstrings as he
Twists them one notch tighter. He runs his
Finger along a wire, touches the dry
Rust to his tongue, breaks into a pure bliss   10
And tells us, "One year more of damp weather
Would have done you in, but I've saved it this
Time. Would one of you play now, please? I hear
It better at a distance." My wife plays
Stardust. The blind man stands and smiles in her   15
Direction, then disappears into the blaze
Of new October. Now the afternoon,
The long afternoon that blurs in a haze
Of music . . . Chopin nocturnes, *Clair de Lune*,
All the old familiar, unfamiliar   20
Music-lesson pieces, *Papa Haydn's*
Dead and gone, gently down the stream . . . Hours later,
After the latest car has doused its beams,
Has cooled down and stopped its ticking, I hear
Our cat, with the grace of animals free   25
To move in darkness, strike one key only,
And a single lucid drop of water stars my dream.

—1971

Gladys Cardiff is a member of the Cherokee nation. "Combing" is taken from her first collection, To Frighten a Storm, *which was originally published in 1976.*

Combing

Bending, I bow my head
And lay my hand upon
Her hair, combing, and think
How women do this for
Each other. My daughter's hair   5
Curls against the comb,
Wet and fragrant—orange
Parings. Her face, downcast,
Is quiet for one so young.

I take her place. Beneath   10
My mother's hands I feel
The braids drawn up tight
As a piano wire and singing,
Vinegar-rinsed. Sitting
Before the oven I hear   15
The orange coils tick
The early hour before school.

She combed her grandmother
Mathilda's hair using
A comb made out of bone.   20
Mathilda rocked her oak wood
Chair, her face downcast,
Intent on tearing rags
In strips to braid a cotton
Rug from bits of orange   25
and brown. A simple act,

Preparing hair. Something
Women do for each other,
Plaiting the generations.

—1976

B. H. Fairchild grew up in Liberal, Kansas, and his father's machine shop provides the title and the setting for his prize-winning collection, The Art of the Lathe. *Fairchild teaches at the California State University, San Bernardino. His most recent collection,* Early Occult Memory Systems of the Lower Midwest *(2002), won the National Book Critics Circle Award.*

Body and Soul

Half-numb, guzzling bourbon and Coke from coffee mugs,
our fathers fall in love with their own stories, nuzzling
the facts but mauling the truth, and my friend's father begins
to lay out with the slow ease of a blues ballad a story
about sandlot baseball in Commerce, Oklahoma decades ago.   5
These were men's teams, grown men, some in their thirties
and forties who worked together in zinc mines or on oil rigs,
sweat and khaki and long beers after work, steel guitar music
whanging in their ears, little white rent houses to return to
where their wives complained about money and broken
    Kenmores°   10
and then said the hell with it and sang *Body and Soul*
in the bathtub and later that evening with the kids asleep
lay in bed stroking their husband's wrist tattoo and smoking
Chesterfields from a fresh pack until everything was O.K.
Well, you get the idea. Life goes on, the next day is Sunday,   15
another ball game, and the other team shows up one man short.

They say, we're one man short, but can we use this boy,
he's only fifteen years old, and at least he'll make a game.
They take a look at the kid, muscular and kind of knowing
the way he holds his glove, with the shoulders loose,   20
the thick neck, but then with that boy's face under
a clump of angelic blonde hair, and say, oh, hell, sure,
let's play ball. So it all begins, the men loosening up,
joking about the fat catcher's sex life, it's so bad
last night he had to hump his wife, that sort of thing,   25
pairing off into little games of catch that heat up into

10 **Kenmores** a brand of appliance

throwing matches, the smack of the fungo bat, lazy jogging
into right field, big smiles and arcs of tobacco juice,
and the talk that gives a cool, easy feeling to the air,
talk among men normally silent, normally brittle and a little   30
angry with the empty promise of their lives. But they chatter
and say rock and fire, babe, easy out, and go right ahead
and pitch to the boy, but nothing fancy, just hard fastballs
right around the belt, and the kid takes the first two
but on the third pops the bat around so quick and sure   35
that they pause a moment before turning around to watch
the ball still rising and finally dropping far beyond
the abandoned tractor that marks left field. Holy shit.
They're pretty quiet watching him round the bases,
but then, what the hell, the kid knows how to hit a ball,   40
so what, let's play some goddamned baseball here.
And so it goes. The next time up, the boy gets a look
at a very nifty low curve, then a slider, and the next one
is the curve again, and he sends it over the Allis Chalmers,°
high and big and sweet. The left fielder just stands there, frozen.   45
As if this isn't enough, the next time up he bats left-handed.
They can't believe it, and the pitcher, a tall, mean-faced
man from Okarche who just doesn't give a shit anyway
because his wife ran off two years ago leaving him with
three little ones and a rusted-out Dodge with a cracked block,   50
leans in hard, looking at the fat catcher like he was the
        sonofabitch
who ran off with his wife, leans in and throws something
out of the dark, green hell of forbidden fastballs, something
that comes in at the knees and then leaps viciously towards
the kid's elbow. He swings exactly the way he did right-handed,   55
and they all turn like a chorus line toward deep right field
where the ball loses itself in sagebrush and the sad burnt
dust of dustbowl Oklahoma. It is something to see.
But why make a long story long: runs pile up on both sides,
the boy comes around five times, and five times the pitcher   60
is cursing both God and His mother as his chew of tobacco sours
into something resembling horse piss, and a ragged and bruised

44 **Allis Chalmers** manufacturer of tractors and agricultural equipment

Spalding baseball disappears into the far horizon. Goodnight,
Irene. They have lost the game and some painful side bets
and they have been suckered. And it means nothing to them   65
though it should to you when they are told the boy's name is
Mickey Mantle.° And that's the story and those are the facts.
But the facts are not the truth. I think, though, as I scan
the faces of these old men now lost in the innings of their youth,
I think I know what the truth of this story is, and I imagine   70
it lying there in the weeds behind that Allis Chalmers
just waiting for the obvious question to be asked: why, oh
why in hell didn't they just throw around the kid, walk him,
after he hit the third homer? Anybody would have,
especially nine men with disappointed wives and dirty socks   75
and diminishing expectations for whom winning at anything
meant everything. Men who know how to play the game,
who had talent when the other team had nothing except
    this ringer
who without a pitch to hit was meaningless, and they could
    go home
with their little two-dollar side bets and stride into the house   80
singing *If You've Got the Money, Honey, I've Got the Time*
with a bottle of Southern Comfort under their arms and grab
Dixie or May Ella up and dance across the gray linoleum
as if it were V-Day° all over again. But they did not.
And they did not because they were men, and this was a boy.   85
And they did not because sometimes after making love,
after smoking their Chesterfields in the cool silence and
listening to the big bands on the radio that sounded so
    glamorous,
so distant, they glanced over at their wives and noticed the lines
growing heavier around the eyes and mouth, felt what
    their wives   90
felt: that Les Brown and Glenn Miller and all those dancing
    couples
and in fact all possibility of human gaiety and light-heartedness

67 Mickey Mantle (1931–1995) Oklahoma-born baseball star **84 V-Day** V-E Day (May 8, 1945) marked
the end of World War II in Europe; V-J Day (August 15, 1945) marked the end of the war in the Pacific

were as far away and unreachable as Times Square or the
    Avalon
ballroom. They did not because of the gray linoleum lying
    there
in the half-dark, the free calendar from the local mortuary   95
that said one day was pretty much like another, the work
    gloves
looped over the doorknob like dead squirrels. And they did not
because they had gone through a depression and a war that
    had left
them with the idea that being a man in the eyes of their
    fathers
and everyone else had cost them just too goddamned much to
    lay it   100
at the feet of a fifteen year-old boy. And so they did not walk
    him,
and lost, but at least had some ragged remnant of themselves
to take back home. But there is one thing more, though it
    is not
a fact. When I see my friend's father staring hard into the
    bottomless
well of home plate as Mantle's fifth homer heads toward
    Arkansas,   105
I know that this man with the half-orphaned children and
worthless Dodge has also encountered for his first and
    possibly
only time that vast gap between talent and genius, has seen
as few have in the harsh light of an Oklahoma Sunday,
    the blonde
and blue-eyed bringer of truth, who will not easily be forgiven. 110

—1998

CHARLES MARTIN ■ (b. 1942)

Charles Martin is a lifelong resident of New York City. Martin has taught for many years at Queensborough College. "E.S.L." appeared as a prefatory poem to Martin's sequence "Passages from Friday," an ironic retelling of the Robinson Crusoe story from his servant's point of view. A respected classicist, Martin has translated Ovid and Catullus.

E.S.L.°

My frowning students carve
Me monsters out of prose:
This one—a gargoyle—thumbs its contemptuous nose
At how, in English, subject must agree
With verb—for any such agreement shows 5
    Too great a willingness to serve,
        A docility

    Which wiry Miss Choi
    Finds un-American.
She steals a hard look at me. I wink. Her grin 10
Is my reward. *In his will, our peace, our Pass:*
Gargoyle erased, subject and verb now in
    Agreement, reach object, enjoy
        Temporary truce.

    Tonight my students must 15
    Agree or disagree:
America is still a land of opportunity.
The answer is always, uniformly, *Yes*—even though
"It has no doubt that here were to much free,"
    As Miss Torrico will insist. 20
        She and I both know

    That Language binds us fast,
    And those of us without
Are bound and gagged by those within. Each fledgling
Polyglot must shake old habits: tapping her sneakered feet, 25
Miss Choi exorcises incensed ancestors, flout-
    ing the ghosts of her Chinese past.
        Writhing in the seat

    Next to Miss Choi, Mister
    Fedakis, in anguish 30
Labors to express himself in a tongue which
Proves *Linear B* to me, when I attempt to read it
Later. They're here for English as a Second Language,
    Which I'm teaching this semester.
        God knows they need it, 35

E.S.L. English as a Second Language

And so, thank God, do they.
    The night's made easier
By our agreement: I am here to help deliver
Them into the good life they write me papers about.
English is pre-requisite for that endeavor,   40
    Explored in their nightly essays
        Boldly setting out

    To reconnoiter the fair
    New World they would enter:
Suburban Paradise, the endless shopping center   45
Where one may browse for hours before one chooses
Some new necessity—gold-flecked magenta
    Wallpaper to re-do the spare
        Bath no one uses,

    Or a machine which can,   50
    In seven seconds, crush
A newborn calf into such seamless mush
As a *mousse* might be made of—or our true sublime:
The gleaming counters where frosted cosmeticians brush
    Decades from the allotted span,   55
        Abrogating Time

    As the spring tide brushes
    A single sinister
Footprint from the otherwise unwrinkled shore
Of America the Blank. In absolute confusion   60
Poor Mister Fedakis rumbles with despair
    And puts the finishing smutches
        To his conclusion

    While Miss Choi erases:
    One more gargoyle routed.   65
Their pure, erroneous lines yield an illuminated
Map of the new found land. We will never arrive there,
Since it exists only in what we say about it,
    As all the rest of my class is
        Bound to discover.   70

—1987

SHARON OLDS ■ (b. 1942)

Sharon Olds displays a candor in dealing with the intimacies of family romance covering three generations that has made her one of the chief contemporary heirs to the confessional tradition. A powerful and dramatic reader, she is much in demand on the lecture circuit. Born in San Francisco, she currently resides in New York City.

The One Girl at the Boys Party

When I take my girl to the swimming party
I set her down among the boys. They tower and
bristle, she stands there smooth and sleek,
her math scores unfolding in the air around her.
They will strip to their suits, her body hard and   5
indivisible as a prime number,
they'll plunge into the deep end, she'll subtract
her height from ten feet, divide it into
hundreds of gallons of water, the numbers
bouncing in her mind like molecules of chlorine   10
in the bright blue pool. When they climb out,
her ponytail will hang its pencil lead
down her back, her narrow silk suit
with hamburgers and french fries printed on it
will glisten in the brilliant air, and they will   15
see her sweet face, solemn and
sealed, a factor of one, and she will
see their eyes, two each,
their legs, two each, and the curves of their sexes,
one each, and in her head she'll be doing her   20
wild multiplying, as the drops
sparkle and fall to the power of a thousand from her body.

—1983

HENRY TAYLOR ■ (b. 1942)

Henry Taylor is best known for The Flying Change, *which won the Pulitzer Prize in 1985, and* Understanding Fiction: Poems 1986–1996. *A noted horseman as well as poet, Taylor retired from teaching at American University in*

2003. Brief Candles, *the 2001 book from which the following three selections are taken, is a collection of clerihews, a light-verse form.*

from Brief Candles

Alexander Graham Bell
has shuffled off this mobile cell.
He's not talking any more,
but he has a lot to answer for.

*

Friedrich Nietzsche
strove vainly to reach a
steadfast decision
between Apollonian and Dionysian.°

*

Judas Iscariot
missed the sweet chariot
but swung pretty low
in his wasteland of woe

—2001

DIANE LOCKWARD ▪ (b. 1943)

Diane Lockward is a former high school English teacher who now works as a poet-in-the-schools for both the New Jersey State Council on the Arts and the Geraldine R. Dodge Foundation. She has received numerous awards for her poetry, which has appeared in many literary journals, but her first full-length collection, Eve's Red Dress, *did not appear until 2003. "My Husband Discovers Poetry" has been read by Garrison Keillor several times on National Public Radio's* The Writer's Almanac. *Lockward has commented that "My Husband Discovers Poetry" is, in fact, her husband's favorite poem.*

Nietzsche argued that the two ancient Gods defined stages of civilization.

My Husband Discovers Poetry

Because my husband would not read my poems,
I wrote one about how I did not love him.
In lines of strict iambic pentameter,
I detailed his coldness, his lack of humor.
It felt good to do this.   5

Stanza by stanza, I grew bolder and bolder.
Towards the end, struck by inspiration,
I wrote about my old boyfriend,
a boy I had not loved enough to marry
but who could make me laugh and laugh.   10
I wrote about a night years after we parted
when my husband's coldness drove me from the house
and back to my old boyfriend.
I even included the name of a seedy motel
well-known for hosting quickies.   15
I have a talent for verisimilitude.

In sensuous images, I described
how my boyfriend and I stripped off our clothes,
got into bed, and kissed and kissed,
then spent half the night telling jokes,   20
many of them about my husband.
I left the ending deliberately ambiguous,
then hid the poem away
in an old trunk in the basement.

You know how this story ends,   25
how my husband one day loses something,
goes into the basement,
and rummages through the old trunk,
how he uncovers the hidden poem
and sits down to read it.   30

But do you hear the strange sounds
that floated up the stairs that day,
the sounds of an animal, its paw caught
in one of those traps with teeth of steel?
Do you see the wounded creature   35

at the bottom of the stairs,
his shoulders hunched over and shaking,
fist in his mouth and choking back sobs?
It was my husband paying tribute to my art.

—2003

ELLEN BRYANT VOIGT ■ (b. 1943)

Ellen Bryant Voigt is a native of Virginia. Voigt was trained as a concert pi-anist before earning her creative writing degree from the University of Iowa. She has taught poetry at a number of colleges in New England and the South.

Daughter

There is one grief worse than any other.

When your small feverish throat clogged, and quit,
I knelt beside the chair on the green rug
and shook you and shook you,
but the only sound was mine shouting you back,   5
the delicate curls at your temples,
the blue wool blanket,
your face blue,
your jaw clamped against remedy—

how could I put a knife to that white neck?   10
With you in my lap,
my hands fluttering like flags,
I bend instead over your dead weight
to administer a kiss so urgent, so ruthless,
pumping breath into your stilled body,   15
counting out the rhythm for how long until
the second birth, the second cry
oh Jesus that sudden noisy musical inhalation
that leaves me stunned
by your survival.   20

—1983

Robert Morgan is a native of the mountains of North Carolina, and has retained a large measure of regional ties in his poetry. One of his collections, Sigodlin, *takes its title from an Appalachian word for things that are built slightly out of square.* Gap Creek: The Story of a Marriage, *a novel of turn-of-the-century mountain life, was a bestseller in 2000.*

Mountain Bride

They say Revis found a flatrock
on the ridge just
perfect for a natural hearth,
and built his cabin with a stick

and clay chimney right over it.   5
On their wedding night he lit
the fireplace to dry away the mountain
chill of late spring, and flung on

applewood to dye
the room with molten color while   10
he and Martha that was a Parrish
warmed the sheets between the tick

stuffed with leaves and its feather
cover. Under that wide hearth
a nest of rattlers,   15
they'll knot a hundred together,

had wintered and were coming awake.
The warming rock
flushed them out early.
It was she   20

who wakened to their singing near
the embers and roused him to go look.
Before he reached the fire
more than a dozen struck

and he died yelling her to stay   25
on the big four-poster.
Her uncle coming up the hollow
with a gift bearham two days later

found her shivering there
marooned above a pool   30
of hungry snakes,
and the body beginning to swell.

—1979

CRAIG RAINE ■ (b. 1944)

Craig Raine early in his career displayed a comic surrealism that was responsible for so many imitations that critic James Fenton dubbed him the founder of the "Martian School" of contemporary poetry. Born in Bishop Auckland, England, and educated at Oxford, Raine is publisher of the literary magazine Arete.

A Martian Sends a Postcard Home

Caxtons° are mechanical birds with many wings
and some are treasured for their markings—

they cause the eyes to melt
or the body to shriek without pain.

I have never seen one fly, but   5
sometimes they perch on the hand.

Mist is when the sky is tired of flight
and rests its soft machine on ground:

then the world is dim and bookish
like engravings under tissue paper.   10

Rain is when the earth is television.
It has the property of making colours darker.

Model T is a room with the lock inside—
a key is turned to free the world

for movement, so quick there is a film   15
to watch for anything missed.

But time is tied to the wrist
or kept in a box, ticking with impatience.

---

1 **Caxtons** i.e., books after William Caxton (1422–1491), first English printer

In homes, a haunted apparatus sleeps,
that snores when you pick it up.

If the ghost cries, they carry it
to their lips and soothe it to sleep

with sounds. And yet, they wake it up
deliberately, by tickling with a finger.

Only the young are allowed to suffer
openly. Adults go to a punishment room

with water but nothing to eat.
They lock the door and suffer the noises

alone. No one is exempt
and everyone's pain has a different smell.

At night, when all the colours die,
they hide in pairs

and read about themselves—
in colour, with their eyelids shut.

—1978

ENID SHOMER ■ (b. 1944)

Enid Shomer grew up in Washington, D.C., and lived for a number of years in Florida. Her first collection, Stalking the Florida Panther *(1987), explored both the Jewish traditions of her childhood and her adult attachment to her adopted state. In recent years she has published* Imaginary Men, *a collection of short stories, and* Black Drum, *a collection of poetry.*

Women Bathing at Bergen-Belsen°

April 24, 1945

Twelve hours after the Allies arrive
there is hot water, soap. Two women bathe
in a makeshift, open-air shower while nearby
fifteen thousand are flung naked into mass graves
by captured SS guards. Clearly legs and arms   5

Bergen-Belsen German concentration camp in WWII

are the natural handles of a corpse. The bathers,
taken late in the war, still have flesh
on their bones, still have breasts. Though nudity was
a death sentence here, they have undressed,
oblivious to the soldiers and the cameras.   10
The corpses push through the limed earth like upended
headstones. The bathers scrub their feet, bending
in beautiful curves, mapping the contours
of the body, that kingdom to which they've returned.

—1987

WENDY COPE ■ (b. 1945)

Wendy Cope says, "I hardly ever tire of love or rhyme. / That's why I'm poor and have a rotten time." Her first collection, Making Cocoa for Kingsley Amis (1986), *was a bestseller in England. Whether reducing T. S. Eliot's modernist classic "The Waste Land" to a set of five limericks or chronicling the life and loves of Jason Strugnell, her feckless poetic alter-ego, Cope remains one of the wisest and wittiest poets writing today. "I dislike the term 'light verse' because it is used as a way of dismissing poets who allow humor into their work. I believe that a humorous poem can also be 'serious'; deeply felt and saying something that matters." She lives in Winchester, England.*

Rondeau Redoublé

There are so many kinds of awful men—
One can't avoid them all. She often said
She'd never make the same mistake again:
She always made a new mistake instead.

The chinless type who made her feel ill-bred;   5
The practised charmer, less than charming when
He talked about the wife and kids and fled—
There are so many kinds of awful men.

The half-crazed hippy, deeply into Zen,
Whose cryptic homilies she came to dread;   10
The fervent youth who worshipped Tony Benn°—
'One can't avoid them all,' she often said.

---

11 Tony Benn British politician of the 1960s

The ageing banker, rich and overfed,
who held forth on the dollar and the yen—
Though there were many more mistakes ahead,   15
She'd never make the same mistake again.

The budding poet, scribbling in his den
Odes not to her but to his pussy, Fred;
The drunk who fell asleep at nine or ten—
She always made a new mistake instead.   20

And so the gambler was at least unwed
And didn't preach or sneer or wield a pen
Or hoard his wealth or take the Scotch to bed.
She'd lived and learned and lived and learned but then
There are so many kinds.   25

—1986

DICK DAVIS ■ (b. 1945)

*Dick Davis was born in Portsmouth, England, and, following graduation
from Cambridge and the University of Manchester, taught for many years in
England and in Iran. A scholar and translator as well as a poet, he came to
the United States in the 1980s and is currently a professor of Persian at Ohio
State University.*

A Monorhyme for the Shower

Lifting her arms to soap her hair
Her pretty breasts respond—and there
The movement of that buoyant pair
Is like a spell to make me swear
Twenty-odd years have turned to air;   5
Now she's the girl I didn't dare
Approach, ask out, much less declare
My love to, mired in young despair.

Childbearing, rows, domestic care—
All the prosaic wear and tear   10
That constitute the life we share—

Slip from her beautiful and bare
Bright body as, made half aware
Of my quick surreptitious stare,
She wrings the water from her hair   15
And turning smiles to see me there.

—2002

KAY RYAN ■ (b. 1945)

Kay Ryan has taught for many years in California. She published her first
collection at the age of thirty-eight in 1983, and her poems have appeared in
four subsequent books and numerous appearances in Poetry *and* The New
Yorker. *Ryan has often been compared to Emily Dickinson and Marianne*
Moore for her attention to details from the natural world and for her gentle,
often witty moralizing. She is a former U. S. Poet Laureate.

Bestiary

A bestiary catalogs
bests. The mediocres
both higher and lower
are suppressed in favor
of the singularly savage   5
or clever, the spectacularly
pincered, the archest
of the arch deceivers
who press their advantage
without quarter even after   10
they've won as of course they would.
Best is not to be confused with *good*—
a different creature altogether,
and treated of in the goodiary—
a text alas lost now for centuries.   15

—1996

LEON STOKESBURY ■ (b. 1945)

Leon Stokesbury, as an undergraduate at Lamar State College of Technology (now Lamar University), published a poem in The New Yorker. The author of three collections of poetry, including Autumn Rhythm: New and Selected Poems, Stokesbury has also edited anthologies of contemporary Southern poetry and the poetry of World War II.

The Day Kennedy Died

Suppose that on the day Kennedy died
you had a vision. But this was no inner movie
with a discernible plot or anything like it.
Not even very visual when you get down
to admitting what actually occurred.   5
About two-thirds of the way through 4th period
Senior Civics, fifteen minutes before
the longed-for lunchtime, suppose you stood up
for no good reason—no reason at all really—
and announced, as you never had before,   10
to the class in general and to yourself
as well, "Something. Something is happening.
I see. Something coming. I can see. I . . ."

And that was all. You stood there: blank.
The class roared. Even Phyllis Hoffpaur, girl   15
most worshipped by you from afar that year,
turned a vaguely pastel shade of red
and smiled, and Richard Head, your best friend,
Dick Head to the chosen few, pulled you down
to your desk whispering, "Jesus, man! Jesus   20
Christ!" Then you went numb. You did not know
for sure what had occurred. But less than one hour
later, when Stella (despised) Vandenburg, teacher
of twelfth grade English, came sashaying
into the auditorium, informing, left and right,   25
as many digesting members of the student body
as she could of what she had just heard,

several students began to glance at you,
remembering what you'd said. A few pointed,
whispering to their confederates, and on that   30
disturbing day they slinked away in the halls.
Even Dick Head did not know what to say.

In 5th period Advanced Math, Principal
Crawford played the radio over the intercom
and the school dropped deeper into history.   35
For the rest of that day, everyone slinked away—
except for the one moment Phyllis Hoffpaur
stared hard, the look on her face asking,
assuming you would know, "Will it be ok?"

And you did not know. No one knew.   40
Everyone staggered back to their houses
that evening aimless and lost, not knowing,
certainly sensing something had been
changed forever. *Silsbee High forever!*
That is our claim! Never, no never!   45
Will we lose our fame! you often sang.
But this was to be the class of 1964,
afraid of the future at last, who would select,
as the class song, Terry Stafford's *Suspicion.*
And this was November—even in Texas   50
the month of failings, month of sorrows—
from which there was no turning.
It would be a slow two-months slide until
the manic beginnings of the British Invasion,
three months before Clay's ascension to the throne,   55
but all you saw walking home that afternoon
were the gangs of gray leaves clotting the curbs
and culverts, the odors of winter forever
in the air: cold, damp, bleak, dead, dull:
dragging you toward the solstice like a tide.   60

—2004

John Whitworth was born in Nasik, India, the son of a civil servant, and grew up in Edinburgh. After graduating from Merton College, Oxford, he taught English as a foreign language for some years before becoming a full-time writer. The author of numerous collections of verse, including the children's book The Complete Poetical Works of Phoebe Flood, *he lives in Canterbury. "The Examiners" was a finalist in a readers' poll run by the* Times Literary Supplement.

The Examiners

Where the house is cold and empty and the garden's overgrown,
　　They are there.
Where the letters lie unopened by a disconnected phone,
　　They are there.
Where your footsteps echo strangely on each moonlit cobblestone, 5
Where a shadow streams behind you but the shadow's not
　　　　your own,
You may think the world's your oyster but it's bone, bone, bone:
　　They are there, they are there, they are there.

They can parse a Latin sentence; they're as learned as Plotinus,°
　　They are there. 10
They're as sharp as Ockham's razor,° they're as subtle as Aquinas,°
　　They are there.
They define us and refine us with their beta-query-minus,°
They're the wall-constructing Emperors of undiscovered Chinas,
They confine us, then malign us, in the end they undermine us, 15
　　They are there, they are there, they are there.

They assume it as an impost or they take it as a toll,
　　They are there.
The contractors grant them all that they incontinently stole,
　　They are there. 20
They will shrivel your ambition with their quality control,

---

9 Plotinus neo-Platonic philosopher (204–270)　　**11 Ockham 's razor** a philosophical proposition by William of Ockham (1288–1347) that the simplest solution to a problem is always the best choice
Aquinas (1225–1274) Italian Catholic philosopher and theologian　　**13 beta-query-minus** in British universities a mediocre grade (B-)

They will dessicate your passion, then eviscerate your soul,
Wring your life out like a sponge and stuff your body down a hole,
    They are there, they are there, they are there.

In the desert of your dreaming they are humped behind the
    dunes,   25
    They are there.
On the undiscovered planet with its seven circling moons,
    They are there.
They are ticking all the boxes, making sure you eat your prunes,
They are sending secret messages by helium balloons,   30
They are humming Bach cantatas, they are playing looney tunes
    They are there, they are there, they are there.

They are there, they are there like a whisper on the air,
    They are there.
They are slippery and soapy with our hope and our despair,   35
    They are there.
So it's idle if we bridle or pretend we never care,
If the questions are superfluous and the marking isn't fair,
For we know they're going to get us, we just don't know when or
    where,
    They are there, they are there, they are there.   40

—2007

MARILYN NELSON ■ (b. 1946)

Marilyn Nelson is the author of The Homeplace, *a sequence of poems on family history.* The Homeplace *is remarkable for its sensitive exploration of the mixed white and black bloodlines in the poet's family history.* Carver: A Life in Poems, *a poetic biography of George Washington Carver, appeared in 2001 and won a National Book Award.* A Wreath for Emmett Till, *a sonnet sequence about a famous hate crime in 1995 Mississippi, appeared in 2005. Both of these books are for young readers.*

The Ballad of Aunt Geneva

Geneva was the wild one.
Geneva was a tart.
Geneva met a blue-eyed boy
and gave away her heart.

Geneva ran a roadhouse.
Geneva wasn't sent
to college like the others:
Pomp's pride her punishment.

She cooked out on the river,
watching the shore slide by,   10
her lips pursed into hardness,
her deep-set brown eyes dry.

They say she killed a woman
over a good black man
by braining the jealous heifer   15
with an iron frying pan.

They say, when she was eighty,
she got up late at night
and sneaked her old, white lover in
to make love, and to fight.   20

First, they heard the tell-tale
singing of the springs,
then Geneva's voice rang out:
I need to buy some things,

So next time, bring more money.   25
And bring more moxie, too.
I ain't got no time to waste
on limp white mens like you.

Oh yeah? Well, Mister White Man,
it sure might be stone-white,   30
but my thing's white as it is.
And you know damn well I'm right.

Now listen: take your heart pills
and pay the doctor mind.
If you up and die on me,   35
I'll whip your white behind.

They tiptoed through the parlor
on heavy, time-slowed feet.
She watched him, from her front door,
walk down the dawnlit street.   40

Geneva was the wild one.
Geneva was a tart.
Geneva met a blue-eyed boy
and gave away her heart.

—1990

A I ■ (b. 1947–2010)

*Ai wrote a number of realistic dramatic monologues that often reveal the
agonies of characters trapped in unfulfilling or even dangerous lives. With
her gallery of social misfits, she was the contemporary heir to the tradition
begun by Robert Browning.*

Child Beater

Outside, the rain, pinafore of gray water, dresses the town
and I stroke the leather belt,
as she sits in the rocking chair,
holding a crushed paper cup to her lips.
I yell at her, but she keeps rocking;   5
back, her eyes open, forward, they close.
Her body, somehow fat, though I feed her only once a day,
reminds me of my own just after she was born.
It's been seven years, but I still can't forget how I felt.
How heavy it feels to look at her.   10

I lay the belt on a chair
and get her dinner bowl.
I hit the spoon against it, set it down
and watch her crawl to it,
pausing after each forward thrust of her legs   15
and when she takes her first bite,
I grab the belt and beat her across the back
until her tears, beads of salt-filled glass, falling,
shatter on the floor.

I move off. I let her eat,   20
while I get my dog's chain leash from the closet.

I whirl it around my head.
O daughter, so far, you've only had a taste of icing,
are you ready now for some cake?

—1973

JIM HALL ■ (b. 1947)

*Jim Hall is one of the most brilliantly inventive comic poets in recent years.
He has also written a successful series of crime novels set in his native south
Florida, beginning with* Under Cover of Daylight *in 1987.*

Maybe Dats Your Pwoblem Too

All my pwoblems,
who knows, maybe evwybody's pwoblems
is due to da fact, due to da awful twuth
dat I am SPIDERMAN.
I know, I know. All da dumb jokes: 5
No flies on you, ha ha,
and da ones about what do I do wit all
doze extwa legs in bed. Well, dat's funny yeah.
But you twy being
SPIDERMAN for a month or two. Go ahead.   10

You get doze cwazy calls fwom da
Gubbener askin you to twap some booglar who's
only twying to wip off color T.V. sets.
Now, what do I cawre about T.V. sets?
But I pull on da suit, da stinkin suit,   15
wit da sucker cups on da fingers,
and get my wopes and wittle bundle of
equipment and den I go flying like cwazy
acwoss da town fwom woof top to woof top.

Till der he is. Some poor dumb color T.V. slob   20
and I fall on him and we westle a widdle
until I get him all woped. So big deal.

You tink when you SPIDERMAN
der's sometin big going to happen to you.
Well, I tell you what. It don't happen dat way.   25
Nuttin happens. Gubbener calls, I go.
Bwing him to powice, Gubbener calls again,
like dat over and over.
I tink I twy sometin diffunt. I tink I twy
sometin excitin like wacing cawrs. Sometin to make   30
my heart beat at a difwent wate.
But den you just can't quit being sometin like
SPIDERMAN.
You SPIDERMAN for life. Fowever. I can't even
buin my suit. It won't buin. It's fwame wesistent.   35
So maybe dat's youwr pwoblem too, who knows.
Maybe dat's da whole pwoblem wif evwytin.
Nobody can buin der suits, dey all fwame wesistent.
Who knows?

—1980

YUSEF KOMUNYAKAA ■ (b. 1947)

*Yusef Komunyakaa is a native of Bogulusa, Louisiana. Komunyakaa has
written memorably on a wide range of subjects, including jazz and his service during the Vietnam War.* Neon Vernacular: New and Selected Poems
(1993) won the Pulitzer Prize in 1994, and Pleasure Dome: New and Collected Poems *appeared in 2001.*

Facing It

My black face fades,
hiding inside the black granite.
I said I wouldn't,
dammit: No tears.
I'm stone. I'm flesh.   5
My clouded reflection eyes me
like a bird of prey, the profile of night
slanted against morning. I turn
this way—the stone lets me go.
I turn this way—I'm inside   10

the Vietnam Veterans Memorial
again, depending on the light
to make a difference.
I go down the 58,022 names,
half-expecting to find   15
my own in letters like smoke.
I touch the name Andrew Johnson;
I see the booby trap's white flash.
Names shimmer on a woman's blouse
but when she walks away   20
the names stay on the wall.
Brushstrokes flash, a red bird's
wings cutting across my stare.
The sky. A plane in the sky.
A white vet's image floats   25
closer to me, then his pale eyes
look through mine. I'm a window.
He's lost his right arm
inside the stone. In the black mirror
a woman's trying to erase names: 30
No, she's brushing a boy's hair.

—1988

R. S. GWYNN ■ (b. 1948)

R. S. Gwynn is the editor of this volume and (with April Lindner) of
Contemporary American Poetry. *He teaches at Lamar University.* No
Word of Farewell: Selected Poems 1970–2000 *appeared in 2001.*

Approaching a Significant Birthday, He Peruses an Anthology of Poetry

All human things are subject to decay.
Beauty is momentary in the mind.
The curfew tolls the knell of parting day.
If Winter comes, can Spring be far behind?

Forlorn! the very word is like a bell   5
And somewhat of a sad perplexity.
Here, take my picture, though I bid farewell;
In a dark time the eye begins to see

The woods decay, the woods decay and fall—
Bare ruined choirs where late the sweet birds sing.   10
What but design of darkness to appall?
An aged man is but a paltry thing.

If I should die, think only this of me:
Crass casualty obstructs the sun and rain
When I have fears that I may cease to be,   15
To cease upon the midnight with no pain

And hear the spectral singing of the moon
And strictly meditate the thankless muse.
The world is too much with us, late and soon.
It gathers to a greatness, like the ooze.   20

Do not go gentle into the good night.
Fame is no plant that grows on mortal soil.
Again he raised the jug up to the light:
Old age hath yet his honor and his toil.

Downward to darkness on extended wings,   25
Break, break, break, on thy cold gray stones, O Sea,
and tell sad stories of the death of kings.
I do not think that they will sing to me.

—1990

TIMOTHY STEELE ■ (b. 1948)

Timothy Steele has written a successful scholarly study of the rise of free verse, Missing Measures, *and is perhaps the most skillful craftsman of the contemporary New Formalist poets. Born in Vermont, he has lived for a number of years in Los Angeles, where he teaches at California State University, Los Angeles.*

Sapphics° Against Anger

Angered, may I be near a glass of water;
May my first impulse be to think of Silence,
Its deities (who are they? do, in fact, they
    Exist? etc.).

May I recall what Aristotle says of   5
The subject: to give vent to rage is not to
Release it but to be increasingly prone
    To its incursions.

May I imagine being in the Inferno,
Hearing it asked: "Virgilio mio,° who's   10
That sulking with Achilles there?" and hearing
    Virgil say: "Dante,

That fellow, at the slightest provocation,
Slammed phone receivers down, and waved his arms like
A madman. What Attila did to Europe,   15
    What Genghis Khan did

To Asia, that poor dope did to his marriage."
May I, that is, put learning to good purpose,
Mindful that melancholy is a sin, though
    Stylish at present.   20

Better than rage is the post-dinner quiet,
The sink's warm turbulence, the streaming platters,
The suds rehearsing down the drain in spirals
    In the last rinsing.

For what is, after all, the good life save that   25
Conducted thoughtfully, and what is passion
If not the holiest of powers, sustaining
    Only if mastered.

—*1986*

Sapphics stanza form named after Sappho (c. 650 BC)   **10 Virgilio mio** Dante is addressing Virgil, his guide through hell.

James Fenton was born in Lincoln, England, and educated at Oxford. Fenton has worked extensively as a book and drama critic. A brilliant satirical poet, he has also written lyrics for Les Misérables, *the musical version of Victor Hugo's novel, and has served as a journalist in Asia.*

God, a Poem

A nasty surprise in a sandwich,
A drawing-pin caught in your sock,
The limpest of shakes from a hand which
You'd thought would be firm as a rock,

A serious mistake in a nightie,   5
A grave disappointment all around
Is all that you'll get from th'Almighty.
Is all that you'll get underground.

Oh, he *said:* 'If you lay off the crumpet°
I'll see you alright in the end.   10
Just hang on until the last trumpet.
Have faith in me, chum—I'm your friend.'

But if you remind him, he'll tell you:
'I'm sorry, I must have been pissed°—
Though your name rings a sort of a bell. You   15
Should have guessed that I do not exist.

'I didn't exist at Creation,
I didn't exist at the Flood.
And I won't be around for Salvation
To sort out the sheep from the cud—   20

'Or whatever the phrase is. The fact is
In soteriological° terms
I'm a crude existential malpractice
And you are a diet of worms.

---

9 crumpet vulgar British slang for women   **14 pissed** drunk   **22 soteriological** relation to salvation

'You're a nasty surprise in a sandwich.   25
You're a drawing-pin caught in my sock.
You're the limpest of shakes from a hand which
I'd have thought would be firm as a rock,

'You're a serious mistake in a nightie,
You're a grave disappointment all round—   30
That's all that you are,' says th'Almighty,
'And that's all that you'll be underground.'

—1983

SARAH CORTEZ ■ (b. 1950)

Sarah Cortez grew up in Houston, Texas, and holds degrees in psychology and religion, classical studies, and accounting. She also serves as Visiting Scholar at the University of Houston's Center for Mexican-American Studies. She is a deputy constable in Harris County, Texas.

Tu Negrito

She's got to bail me out,
he says into the phone outside the holding cell.
She's going there tomorrow anyway for Mikey.
Tell her she's got to do this for me.

He says into the phone outside the holding cell,   5
Make sure she listens. Make her feel guilty, man.
Tell her she's got to do this for me.
She can have all my money, man.

Make sure she listens. Make her feel guilty, man.
Tell her she didn't bail me out the other times.   10
She can have all my money, man.
She always bails out Mikey.

Tell her she didn't bail me out the other times.
I don't got no one else to call, cousin.
She always bails out Mikey.   15
Make sure you write all this down, cousin.

I don't got no one else to call, cousin.
I really need her now.
Make sure you write this all down, cousin.
Page her. Put in code 333. That's me.   20

I really need her now.
Write down "Mommie." Change it from "Mom."
Page her. Put in code 333. That's me.
Write down "*Tu Negrito*." Tell her I love her.

Write down "Mommie." Change it from "Mom."   25
I'm her littlest. Remind her.
Write down "*Tu Negrito*."
Tell her I love her. She's got to bail me out.

—2000

CAROLYN FORCHÉ ▪ (b. 1950)

Carolyn Forché won the Yale Younger Poets Award for her first collection,
Gathering the Tribes (1975). The Country Between Us, Forché's second
collection, contains poems based on the poet's experiences in the war-torn
country of El Salvador in the early 1980s.

The Colonel

What you have heard is true. I was in his house.° His wife carried
a tray of coffee and sugar. His daughter filed her nails, his son
went out for the night. There were daily papers, pet dogs, a pistol
on the cushion beside him. The moon swung bare on its black
cord over the house. On the television was a cop show. It was in
English. Broken bottles were embedded in the walls around the
house to scoop the kneecaps from a man's legs or cut his hands to
lace. On the windows there were gratings like those in liquor
stores. We had dinner, rack of lamb, good wine, a gold bell was on
the table for calling the maid. The maid brought green mangoes,
salt, a type of bread. I was asked how I enjoyed the country. There
was a brief commercial in Spanish. His wife took everything away.

1 **his house** in El Salvador

There was some talk then of how difficult it had become to govern. The parrot said hello on the terrace. The colonel told it to shut up, and pushed himself from the table. My friend said to me with his eyes: say nothing. The colonel returned with a sack used to bring groceries home. He spilled many human ears on the table. They were like dried peach halves. There is no other way to say this. He took one of them in his hands, shook it in our faces, dropped it into a water glass. It came alive there. I am tired of fooling around he said. As for the rights of anyone, tell your people they can go fuck themselves. He swept the ears to the floor with his arm and held the last of his wine in the air. Something for your poetry, no? he said. Some of the ears on the floor caught this scrap of his voice. Some of the ears on the floor were pressed to the ground.

—1978

DANA GIOIA ■ (b. 1950)

Dana Gioia grew up in the suburbs of Los Angeles. He took a graduate degree in English from Harvard but made a successful career in business before devoting his full time to writing. The editor of several textbooks and anthologies, he is also an influential critic whose essay "Can Poetry Matter?" stimulated much discussion when it appeared in The Atlantic. *Interrogations at Noon,* his third collection of poetry, appeared in 2001. Gioia became chairman of the National Endowment for the Arts in 2002.*

Planting a Sequoia

All afternoon my brothers and I have worked in the orchard,
Digging this hole, laying you into it, carefully packing the soil.
Rain blackened the horizon, but cold winds kept it over the
    Pacific,
And the sky above us stayed the dull gray
Of an old year coming to an end.   5

In Sicily a father plants a tree to celebrate his first son's birth—
An olive or a fig tree—a sign that the earth has one more life
    to bear.

[handwritten margin note: prose structure paragraph]

[handwritten margin note: parallel structure of Hebrew psalms]

I would have done the same, proudly laying new stock into my
    father's orchard,
A green sapling rising among the twisted apple boughs,
A promise of new fruit in other autumns.   10

But today we kneel in the cold planting you, our native giant,
Defying the practical custom of our fathers,
Wrapping in your roots a lock of hair, a piece of an infant's
    birth cord,
All that remains above earth of a first-born son,
A few stray atoms brought back to the elements.   15

We will give you what we can—our labor and our soil,
Water drawn from the earth when the skies fail,
Nights scented with the ocean fog, days softened by the circuit
    of bees.
We plant you in the corner of the grove, bathed in western light,
A slender shoot against the sunset.   20

And when our family is no more, all of his unborn brothers dead,
Every niece and nephew scattered, the house torn down,
His mother's beauty ashes in the air,
I want you to stand among strangers, all young and ephemeral
    to you,
Silently keeping the secret of your birth.   25

                                                              —1991

[handwritten margin note: but beautiful]

RODNEY JONES ▪ (b. 1950)

*Rodney Jones was born in Alabama and received important national atten-
tion when* Transparent Gestures *won the Poets' Prize in 1990. Like many
younger southern poets, he often deals with the difficult legacy of racism and
the adjustments that a new era have forced on both whites and blacks.*

Winter Retreat: Homage
to Martin Luther King, Jr.

There is a hotel in Baltimore where we came together,
we black and white educated and educators,
for a week of conferences, for important counsel

sanctioned by the DOE° and the Carter administration,
to make certain difficult inquiries, to collate notes   5
on the instruction of the disabled, the deprived,
the poor, who do not score well on entrance tests,
who, failing school, must go with mop and pail
skittering across the slick floors of cafeterias,
or climb dewy girders to balance high above cities,   10
or, jobless, line up in the bone cold. We felt
substantive burdens lighter if we stated it right.
Very delicately, we spoke in turn. We walked
together beside the still waters of behaviorism.
Armed with graphs and charts, with new strategies   15
to devise objectives and determine accountability,
we empathetic black and white shone in seminar rooms.
We enunciated every word clearly and without accent.
We moved very carefully in the valley of the shadow
of the darkest agreement error. We did not digress.   20
We ascended the trunk of that loftiest cypress
of Latin grammar the priests could never
successfully graft onto the rough green chestnut
of the English language. We extended ourselves
with that sinuous motion of the tongue that is half   25
pain and almost eloquence. We black and white
politely reprioritized the parameters of our agenda
to impact equitably on the Seminole and the Eskimo.
We praised diversity and involvement, the sacrifices
of fathers and mothers. We praised the next white   30
Gwendolyn Brooks° and the next black Robert Burns.°
We deep made friends. In that hotel we glistened
over the *pommes au gratin*° and the *poitrine de veau.*°
The morsels of lamb flamed near where we talked.
The waiters bowed and disappeared among the ferns.   35
And there is a bar there, there is a large pool.
Beyond the tables of the drinkers and raconteurs,

---

4 DOE Department of Education   **31 Gwendolyn Brooks** African-American poet (1917–2000)
Robert Burns Scottish poet (1759–1796)   **33** *pommes au gratin* potatoes baked with cheese   *poitrine de veau* brisket of veal

beyond the hot tub brimming with Lebanese tourists
and the women in expensive bathing suits doing laps,
if you dive down four feet, swim out far enough, 40
and emerge on the other side, it is sixteen degrees.
It is sudden and very beautiful and colder
than thought, though the air frightens you at first,
not because it is cold, but because it is visible,
almost palpable, in the fog that rises from difference. 45
While I stood there in the cheek-numbing snow,
all Baltimore was turning blue. And what I remember
of that week of talks is nothing the record shows,
but the revelation outside, which was the city
many came to out of the fields, then the thought 50
that we had wanted to make the world kinder,
but, in speaking proudly, we had failed a vision.

—1989

TIMOTHY MURPHY ■ (b. 1951)

Timothy Murphy, a former student of Robert Penn Warren at Yale, returned to his native North Dakota to make a career as a venture capitalist in the agricultural field. Unpublished until his mid-forties, Murphy has brought four collections to print during the last decade.

Case Notes

for Dr. Richard Kolotkin
March 7, 2002

Raped at an early age
by older altar boy.
"Damned by the Church to Hell,
never to sire a son,
perhaps man's greatest joy," 5
said father in a rage.
Patient was twenty-one.
Handled it pretty well.

March 14, 2002

Curiously, have learned
patient was Eagle Scout.
Outraged that Scouts have spurned
each camper who is "out."
Questioned if taunts endured
are buried? "No, immured."

March 21, 2002

Immersed in verse and drink
when he was just sixteen,
turned to drugs at Yale.
Patient began to sink,
to fear he was a "queen,"
a "queer" condemned to fail
or detox in a jail.

April 1, 2002

Into a straight town
he brought a sober lover.
"Worked smarter, drank harder
to stock an empty larder,"
wrote poetry, the cover
for grief he cannot drown.

April 9, 2002

Uneasy with late father,
feared for by his mother,
lover, and younger brother.
Various neuroses,
but no severe psychosis.
Precarious prognosis.

—2004

Joy Harjo, a member of the Creek tribe, is one of the leading voices of contemporary Native American poetry. She is a powerful performer and was one of the poets featured on Bill Moyers's television series, The Power of the Word.

She Had Some Horses

She had some horses.
She had horses who were bodies of sand.
She had horses who were maps drawn of blood.
She had horses who were skins of ocean water.
She had horses who were the blue air of sky.   5
She had horses who were fur and teeth.
She had horses who were clay and would break.
She had horses who were splintered red cliff.

She had some horses.

She had horses with eyes of trains.   10
She had horses with full brown thighs.
She had horses who laughed too much.
She had horses who threw rocks at glass houses.
She had horses who licked razor blades.

She had some horses.   15

She had horses who danced in their mother's arms.
She had horses who thought they were the sun and
their bodies shone and burned like stars.
She had horses who waltzed nightly on the moon.
She had horses who were much too shy, and kept quiet   20
in stalls of their own making.

She had some horses.

She had horses who liked Creek Stomp Dance songs.
She had horses who cried in their beer.
She had horses who spit at male queens who made   25
them afraid of themselves.
She had horses who said they weren't afraid.
She had horses who lied.

She had horses who told the truth, who were stripped
bare of their tongues.   30

She had some horses.

She had horses who called themselves "horse."
She had horses who called themselves "spirit,"
and kept their voices secret and to themselves.
She had horses who had no names.   35
She had horses who had books of names.

She had some horses.

She had horses who whispered in the dark, who were afraid
    to speak.
She had horses who screamed out of fear of the silence,
who carried knives to protect themselves from ghosts.   40
She had horses who waited for destruction.
She had horses who waited for resurrection.

She had some horses.

She had horses who got down on their knees for any savior.
She had horses who thought their high price had saved
    them.   45
She had horses who tried to save her,
who climbed in her bed at night and prayed as they raped her.

She had some horses.

She had some horses she loved.
She had some horses she hated.   50

They were the same horses.

—1983

ANDREW HUDGINS ■ (b. 1951)

Andrew Hudgins, reared in Montgomery, Alabama, has demonstrated his poetic skills in a wide variety of poems, including a book-length sequence of dramatic monologues, After the Lost War, in the voice of Sidney Lanier, the greatest Southern poet of the late nineteenth century.

Air View of an Industrial Scene

There is a train at the ramp, unloading people
who stumble from the cars and toward the gate.
The building's shadows tilt across the ground
and from each shadow juts a longer one
and from that shadow crawls a shadow of smoke   5
black as just-plowed earth. Inside the gate
is a small garden and someone on his knees.
Perhaps he's fingering the yellow blooms
to see which ones have set and will soon wither,
clinging to a green tomato as it swells.   10
The people hold back, but are forced to the open gate,
and when they enter they will see the garden
and some, gardeners themselves, will yearn
to fall to their knees there, untangling vines,
plucking at weeds, cooling their hands in damp earth. 15
They're going to die soon, a matter of minutes.
Even from our height, we see in the photograph
the shadow of the plane stamped dark and large
on Birkenau,° one black wing shading the garden.
We can't tell which are guards, which prisoners.   20
We're watchers. But if we had bombs we'd drop them.

—1985

ROBERT WRIGLEY ■ (b. 1951)

*Robert Wrigley grew up in an Illinois coal mining town and studied with poets
Madeline DeFrees, John Haines, and Richard Hugo at the University of Mon-
tana. A past recipient of the Kingsley Tufts Award and the Poets' Prize, he lives
on the Clearwater River in Idaho.* Lives of the Animals *appeared in 2003.*

Thatcher Bitchboy

She had brought home just a single white wing was all,
only that one through all the hellish August weeks
the fat man's chickens kept disappearing into,

19 **Birkenau** German concentration camp in World War II

and that one wing I buried myself in the manure pile
behind the barn, so that by the time he finally arrived,   5
Fat Man oozing from his high-backed truck
like a gristly hock onto the hot black skillet of the county road,
mostly all I felt was the least yawny pang of nerves.
I sat with my dog by the front porch.
"Thatcher bitchboy?" he asked,   10
and I allowed as how she was.
"Daddyhome?" he croaked,
and soon we all were there,
Daddy and me, that good bitch hound of mine sleeping
in a mottle of the day's last sun and shade, and the fat man   15
brandishing his blurred implicational snapshots.
There rose then a cloud of Daddy's might-could-bees
and a cloud also of Fat Man showly-izzes,
the sudden stormification of
which could have been why the sky itself   20
came on so holy and dark just then, a dreadnought cloak
I hoped the Goddumb damn dog would run off under,
but it was only when the light from Momma's
lamp in the living room window showed them there,
that it ended, and the fat man tied a rope   25
to the collar that convicted her,
and she licked his blunt and bulbous fingers with love
and servility ("tastez lack chickin doe-nit daug," he chortled to
     the dirt).
Good cur hound, your eyes on me leaving were a blue
I believed the starved-blood likes of God's own ledger,   30
all the betrayals in all the lands of earth and more
recorded therein, a blue like the lost unredeemable sky
I would myself be forever falling into,
some heaven of hellfires and ice
I have since that mouthhot night learned to breathe in   35
as though it were the exhalations of the finest funereal orchids,
an air I believed would teach me at last
how to pray, and most certainly
God help me
what for.   40

Judith Ortiz Cofer was born in Puerto Rico, the daughter of a member of the United States Navy, and came to the United States at the age of four, when her father was posted to the Brooklyn Naval Yard. After college, she studied at Oxford and began her teaching career in the United States. A skilled writer of fiction and autobiography, she published The Year of Our Revolution: New and Selected Stories and Poems *in 1998.*

The Latin Deli: An Ars Poetica

Presiding over a formica counter,
plastic Mother and Child magnetized
to the top of an ancient register,
the heady mix of smells from the open bins
of dried codfish, the green plantains   5
hanging in stalks like votive offerings,
she is the Patroness of Exiles,
a woman of no-age who was never pretty,
who spends her days selling canned memories
while listening to the Puerto Ricans complain   10
that it would be cheaper to fly to San Juan
than to buy a pound of Bustelo coffee here,
and to Cubans perfecting their speech
of a "glorious return" to Havana—where no one
has been allowed to die and nothing to change until then,   15
to Mexicans who pass through, talking lyrically
of *dólares* to be made in El Norte—
                                            all wanting the comfort
of spoken Spanish, to gaze upon the family portrait
of her plain wide face, her ample bosom   20
resting on her plump arms, her look of maternal interest
as they speak to her and each other
of their dreams and their disillusions—
how she smiles understanding,
when they walk down the narrow aisles of her store   25
reading the labels of packages aloud, as if
they were the names of lost lovers: *Suspiros*,
Merengues, the stale candy of everyone's childhood.
                                            She spends her days

slicing *jamón y queso* and wrapping it in wax paper   30
tied with string: plain ham and cheese
that would cost less at the A&P, but it would not satisfy
the hunger of the fragile old man lost in the folds
of his winter coat, who brings her lists of items
that he reads to her like poetry, or the others,   35
whose needs she must divine, conjuring up products
from places that now exist only in their hearts—
closed ports she must trade with.

—*1995*

RITA DOVE ■ (b. 1952)

Rita Dove won the Pulitzer Prize in 1987 for Thomas and Beulah, *a sequence of poems about her grandparents' lives in Ohio. She is one of the most important voices of contemporary African-American poetry and served as poet laureate of the United States from 1993 to 1995. She is also a competitive ballroom dancer.*

American Smooth

We were dancing—it must have
been a foxtrot or a waltz,
something romantic but
requiring restraint,
rise and fall, precise   5
execution as we moved
into the next song without
stopping, two chests heaving
above a seven-league
stride—such perfect agony   10
one learns to smile through,
ecstatic mimicry
being the sine qua non°
of American Smooth.
And because I was distracted   15
by the effort of
keeping my frame

13 **sine qua non** an essential part (Latin)

(the leftward lean, head turned
just enough to gaze out
past your ear and always   20
smiling, smiling),
I didn't notice
how still you'd become until
we had done it
(for two measures?   25
four?)—achieved flight,
that swift and serene
magnificence, before the earth
remembered who we were
and brought us down.   30

—2004

MARK JARMAN ▪ (b. 1952)

Mark Jarman was born in Kentucky and has lived in California and Tennessee, where he currently teaches at Vanderbilt University. With Robert McDowell, he edited The Reaper, *a magazine specializing in narrative poetry. His most recent collection is* To the Green Man *(2004).*

After Disappointment

To lie in your child's bed when she is gone
Is calming as anything I know. To fall
Asleep, her books arranged above your head,
Is to admit that you have never been
So tired, so enchanted by the spell   5
Of your grown body. To feel small instead
Of blocking out the light, to feel alone,
Not knowing what you should or shouldn't feel,
Is to find out, no matter what you've said
About the cramped escapes and obstacles   10
You plan and face and have to call the world,
That there remain these places, occupied
By children, yours if lucky, like the girl
Who finds you here and lies down by your side.

—1997

MARK JARMAN

Julie Kane was born and raised in New Jersey and studied creative writing with Anne Sexton. For many years a resident of Louisiana, she has a Ph.D. from Louisiana State University and currently teaches at Northwestern State University in Natchitoches, Louisiana. Rhythm & Booze (2003) was selected for the National Poetry Series by Maxine Kumin. Skilled in such difficult forms as the villanelle (the subject of her dissertation), Kane recently co-edited (with Grace Bauer) Umpteen Ways of Looking at a Possum, *a collection of miscellaneous writings about Everette Maddox, a legendary New Orleans street poet.*

Alan Doll Rap

When I was ten
I wanted a Ken
to marry Barbie
I was into patriarchy
for plastic dolls   5
eleven inches tall
cuz the sixties hadn't yet
happened at all
Those demonstrations
assassinations   10
conflagrations across the nation
still nothin but a speck in the imagination
Yeah, Ken was the man
but my mama had the cash
and the boy doll she bought me   15
was ersatz
"Alan" was his name
from the discount store
He cost a dollar ninety-nine
Ken was two dollars more   20
Alan's hair was felt
stuck on with cheap glue
like the top of a pool table
scuffed up by cues

and it fell out in patches   25
when he was brand new
Ken's hair was plastic
molded in waves
coated with paint
no Ken bad-hair days   30
Well they wore the same size
and they wore the same clothes
but Ken was a player
and Alan was a boze
Barbie looked around   35
at all the other Barbies
drivin up in Dream Cars
at the Ken-and-Barbie party
and knew life had dealt her
a jack, not a king   40
knew if Alan bought her
an engagement ring
it wouldn't scratch glass
bet your ass
no class   45
made of cubic zirconia
or cubic Plexiglas
Kens would move Barbies
out of their townhouses
into their dreamhouses   50
Pepto-Bismol pink
from the rugs to the sink
wrap her in mink
but Alan was a bum
Our doll was not dumb   55
She knew a fronter from a chum
Take off that tuxedo
Alan would torpedo
for the Barcalounger
Bye-bye libido   60
Hello VCR
No job, no car
Drinkin up her home bar

Stinkin up her boudoir with his cigar
Shrinkin up the line of cash

65
on her MasterCard
Till she'd be pleading:
"Where's that giant *hand*
used to make him *stand,*
used to make him *walk?*" 70

—2004

NAOMI SHIHAB NYE ▪ (b. 1952)

Naomi Shihab Nye, a dedicated world traveler and humanitarian, has read her poetry in Bangladesh and the Middle East. Many of her poems are informed by her Palestinian ancestry, and she has translated contemporary Arabic poetry.

The Traveling Onion

It is believed that the onion originally came from India. In Egypt it was an object of worship—why I haven't been able to find out. From Egypt the onion entered Greece and on to Italy, thence into all of Europe.

—*Better Living Cookbook*

When I think how far the onion has traveled
just to enter my stew today, I could kneel and praise
all small forgotten miracles,
crackly paper peeling on the drainboard,
pearly layers in smooth agreement, 5
the way knife enters onion, straight
and onion falls apart on the chopping block,
a history revealed.

And I would never scold the onion
for causing tears. 10
It is right that tears fall
for something small and forgotten.

How at meal, we sit to eat,
commenting on texture of meat or herbal aroma
but never on the translucence of onion,   15
now limp, now divided,
or its traditionally honorable career:
For the sake of others,
disappear.

—1986

ALBERTO RÍOS ■ (b. 1952)

*Alberto Ríos was born in Nogales, Arizona, the son of a Mexican-American
father and an English-born mother. He won the Walt Whitman Award of
the Academy of American Poets for his first book,* Whispering to Fool the
Wind *(1982). He has also written a collection of short stories,* The Iguana
Killer: Twelve Stories of the Heart, *which won the Western States
Book Award.*

The Purpose of Altar Boys

Tonio told me at catechism
the big part of the eye
admits good, and the little
black part is for seeing
evil—his mother told him   5
who was a widow and so
an authority on such things.
That's why at night
the black part gets bigger.
That's why kids can't go out   10
at night, and at night
girls take off their clothes
and walk around their
bedrooms or jump on their
beds or wear only sandals   15
and stand in their windows.
I was the altar boy

who knew about these things,
whose mission on some Sundays
was to remind people of   20
the night before as they
knelt for Holy Communion.
To keep Christ from falling
I held the metal plate under chins,
while on the thick   25
red carpet of the altar
I dragged my feet
and waited for the precise
moment: plate to chin
I delivered without expression   30
the Holy Electric Shock,
the kind that produces
a really large swallowing
and makes people think.
I thought of it as justice.   35
But on other Sundays the fire
in my eyes was different,
my mission somehow changed.
I would hold the metal plate
a little too hard   40
against those certain same
nervous chins, and I
I would look
with authority down
the tops of white dresses.   45

—1982

JULIA ALVAREZ ■ (b. 1953)

Julia Alvarez published her first collection, Homecoming, *in 1984. It contained both free verse and "33," a sequence of 33 sonnets on the occasion of the poet's thirty-third birthday. She has gained acclaim for* In the Time of the Butterflies, *a work of fiction, and* The Other Side/El Otro Lado, *a collection of poems.*

Bilingual Sestina

Some things I have to say aren't getting said
in this snowy, blond, blue-eyed, gum-chewing English:
dawn's early light sifting through *persianas*° closed
the night before by dark-skinned girls whose words
evoke *cama,*° *aposento,*° *sueños*° in *nombres*°   5
from that first world I can't translate from Spanish.

Gladys, Rosario, Altagracia—the sounds of Spanish
wash over me like warm island waters as I say
your soothing names: a child again learning the *nombres*
of things you point to in the world before English   10
turned *sol,*°*sierra,*° *cielo,*° *luna*° to vocabulary words—
sun, earth, sky, moon. Language closed

like the touch-sensitive *morivivi*° whose leaves closed
when we kids poked them, astonished. Even Spanish
failed us back then when we saw how frail a word is   15
when faced with the thing it names. How saying
its name won't always summon up in Spanish or English
the full blown genie from the bottled *nombre*.

Gladys, I summon you back by saying your *nombre*.
Open up again the house of slatted windows closed   20
since childhood, where *palabras*° left behind for English
stand dusty and awkward in neglected Spanish.
Rosario, muse of *el patio,*° sing in me and through me say
that world again, begin first with those first words

you put in my mouth as you pointed to the world—   25
not Adam, not God, but a country girl numbering
the stars, the blades of grass, warming the sun by saying,
¡Qué calor!° as you opened up the morning closed
inside the night until you sang in Spanish,
Estas son las mañanitas,° and listening in bed, no English   30

---

3 **persianas** venetian blinds   5 **cama** bed   **aposento** apartment   **sueños** dreams   **nombres**
names   11 **sol** sun   **sierra** mountain   **cielo** sky   **luna** moon   13 **morivivi** a type of Caribbean
bush   21 **palabras** words   23 **el patio** outdoor terrace   28 **Qué calor** What heat!   30 **Estas son las
mañanitas** These are birthday songs

yet in my head to confuse me with translations, no English
doubling the world with synonyms, no dizzying array of words
—the world was simple and intact in Spanish—
luna, sol, casa,°luz, flor,° as if the nombres
were the outer skin of things, as if words were so close   35
one left a mist of breath on things by saying
their names, an intimacy I now yearn for in English—
words so close to what I mean that I almost hear my Spanish
heart beating, beating inside what I say en inglés.°

—1995

HARRYETTE MULLEN ■ (b. 1953)

*Harryette Mullen says, "I intend the poem to be meaningful: to allow, or
suggest, to open up, or insinuate possible meanings, even in those places
where the poem drifts between intentional utterance and improvisational
wordplay." Born in Florence, Alabama, Mullen grew up in Fort Worth, Texas,
and holds degrees from the University of Texas and the University of California, Santa Cruz. She currently teaches African-American literature and creative writing at the University of California, Los Angeles.*

Dim Lady°

My honeybunch's peepers are nothing like neon. Today's special at
Red Lobster is redder than her kisser. If Liquid Paper is white, her
racks are institutional beige. If her mop were Slinkys, dishwater
Slinkys would grow on her noggin. I have seen tablecloths in
Shakey's Pizza Parlors, red and white, but no such picnic colors do
I see in her mug. And in some minty-fresh mouthwashes there is
more sweetness than in the garlic breeze my main squeeze
wheezes. I love to hear her rap, yet I'm aware that Muzak has a
hipper beat. I don't know any Marilyn Monroes. My ball and chain
is plain from head to toe. And yet, by gosh, my scrumptious
Twinkie has as much sex appeal for me as any lanky model or
platinum movie idol who's hyped beyond belief.

—2003

---

34 casa house   **flor** flower   **39 en inglés** in English
Dim Lady See Shakespeare's *Sonnet 130*

KIM ADDONIZIO ■ (b. 1954)

Kim Addonizio is the author of four books of poetry and a book of short stories. Born in Washington, D.C., Addonizio earned a B.A. and an M.A. from San Francisco State University and has worked as a waitress, tennis instructor, Kelly Girl, attendant for the disabled, and auto parts store bookkeeper. She currently teaches private writing workshops in the San Francisco Bay area. Addonizio's poems achieve a delicate balance between the confessional and the universal, and manage to be simultaneously lyrical and gritty.

Sonnenizio° on a Line from Drayton°

Since there's no help, come let us kiss and part;
or kiss anyway, let's start with that, with the kissing part,
because it's better than the parting part, isn't it—
we're good at kissing, we like how that part goes:
we part our lips, our mouths get near and nearer,   5
then we're close, my breasts, your chest, our bodies partway
to making love, so we might as well, part of me thinks—
the wrong part, I know, the bad part, but still
let's pretend we're at that party where we met
and scandalized everyone, remember that part? Hold me   10
like that again, unbutton my shirt, part of you
wants to I can tell, I'm touching that part and it says
yes, the ardent partisan, let it win you over,
it's hopeless, come, we'll kiss and part forever.

—2004

Sonnenizio The sonnenizio was originated in Florence in the thirteenth century by Vanni Fucci as an irreverent form whose subject was usually the impossibility of everlasting love. Dante retaliated by putting Fucci into the seventh chasm of the *Inferno* as a thief. Originally composed in hendeca-syllabics, the sonnenizio gradually moved away from metrical constraints and began to tackle a wider variety of subject matter. The sonnenizio is 14 lines long. It opens with a line from someone else's sonnet, repeats a word from that line in each succeeding line of the poem, and closes with a rhymed couplet. [Addonizio's note]   **Drayton** Michael Drayton (1563–1631) see *Idea: Sonnet 61*

David Mason is best known for the title poem of The Country I Remember, *a long narrative about the life of a Civil War veteran and his daughter. The poem has been performed in a theatrical version. Mason edited, with Mark Jarman,* Rebel Angels, *an anthology of recent poetry written in traditional forms. A recent verse-novel,* Ludlow (2007), *concerns a 1914 coal-miners' strike in Colorado.*

Fog Horns

The loneliest days,
damp and indistinct,
sea and land a haze.

And purple fog horns
blossomed over tides —   5
bruises being born

in silence, so slow,
so out there, around,
above and below.

In such hurts of sound   10
the known world became
neither flat nor round.

The steaming tea pot
was all we fathomed
of *is* and *is not.*   15

The hours were hallways
with doors at the ends
opened into days

fading into night
and the scattering   20
particles of light.

Nothing was done then.
Nothing was ever
done. Then it was done.

—2004

*Mary Jo Salter has traveled widely with her husband, poet and novelist Brad
Leithauser, and has lived in Japan, Italy, and Iceland. A student of Elizabeth
Bishop at Harvard, Salter brings to her art a devotion to the poet's craft that
mirrors that of her mentor. She has published five collections of poetry and
The Moon Comes Home, a children's book.*

Welcome to Hiroshima

is what you first see, stepping off the train:
a billboard brought to you in living English
by Toshiba Electric. While a channel
silent in the TV of the brain

projects those flickering re-runs of a cloud   5
that brims its risen columnful like beer
and, spilling over, hangs its foamy head,
you feel a thirst for history: what year

it started to be safe to breathe the air,
and when to drink the blood and scum afloat   10
on the Ohta River. But no, the water's clear,
they pour it for your morning cup of tea

in one of the countless sunny coffee shops
whose plastic dioramas advertise
mutations of cuisine behind the glass: 15
a pancake sandwich; a pizza someone tops

with a maraschino cherry. Passing by
the Peace Park's floral hypocenter (where
how bravely, or with what mistaken cheer,
humanity erased its own erasure),   20

you enter the memorial museum
and through more glass are served, as on a dish
of blistered grass, three mannequins. Like gloves
a mother clips to coatsleeves, strings of flesh

hang from their fingertips; or as if tied   25
to recall a duty for us, *Reverence*
the dead whose mourners too shall soon be dead,
but all commemoration's swallowed up

in questions of bad taste, how re-created
horror mocks the grim original,   30
and thinking at last *They should have left it all*
you stop. This is the wristwatch of a child.

Jammed on the moment's impact, resolute
to communicate some message, although mute,
it gestures with its hands at eight-fifteen   35
and eight-fifteen and eight-fifteen again

while tables of statistics on the wall
update the news by calling on a roll
of tape, death gummed on death, and in the case
adjacent, an exhibit under glass   40

is glass itself: a shard the bomb slammed in
a woman's arm at eight-fifteen, but some
three decades on—as if to make it plain
hope's only as renewable as pain,

and as if all the unsung *could be an anapest, trimeter*   45
debasements of the past may one day come
rising to the surface once again—
worked its filthy way out like a tongue.

—1985

CATHY SONG ■ (b. 1955)

Cathy Song was born in Honolulu, Hawaii, and holds degrees from Welles-ley College and Boston University. Her first book, Picture Bride, *won the Yale Series of Younger Poets Award in 1983.* The Land of Bliss, *her fourth collection, appeared in 2001.*

Stamp Collecting

The poorest countries
have the prettiest stamps
as if impracticality were a major export
shipped with the bananas, t-shirts, and coconuts.
Take Tonga, where the tourists,   5
expecting a dramatic waterfall replete with birdcalls
are taken to see the island's peculiar mystery:
hanging bats with collapsible wings
like black umbrellas swing upside down from fruit trees.
The Tongan stamp is a fruit.   10
The banana stamp is scalloped like a butter-varnished seashell.
The pineapple resembles a volcano, a spout of green on top,
and the papaya, a tarnished goat skull.

They look impressive,
these stamps of countries without a thing to sell   15
except for what is scraped, uprooted and hulled
from their mule-scratched hills.
They believe in postcards,
in portraits of progress: the new dam;
a team of young native doctors   20
wearing stethoscopes like exotic ornaments;
the recently constructed "Facultad de Medicina,"°
a building as lack-lustre as an American motel.

The stamps of others are predictable.
Lucky is the country that possesses indigenous beauty.   25
Say a tiger or a queen.
The Japanese can display to the world
their blossoms: a spray of pink on green.
Like pollen, they drift, airborne.
But pity the country that is bleak and stark.   30

CATHY SONG

22 **Facultad de Medicina** Medical Faculty (building)

Beauty and whimsey are discouraged as indiscreet.
Unbreakable as their climate, a monument of ice,
they issue serious statements, commemorating
factories, tramways and aeroplanes;
athletes marbled into statues.   35
They turn their noses upon the world, these countries,
and offer this: an unrelenting procession
of a grim, historic profile.

—1988

GINGER ANDREWS ■ (b. 1956)

Ginger Andrews won the 1999 Nicholas Roerich Poetry Prize for her first book, An Honest Answer, *which explores the difficulties of working-class life in a Northwestern lumber town. Born in North Bend, Oregon, she cleans houses for a living, and is a janitor and Sunday school teacher. Her poems have been featured many times on National Public Radio's "The Writer's Almanac."*

Primping in the Rearview Mirror

after a solid ten-minute bout of tears,
hoping that the Safeway man who stocks the shelves
and talked to you once for thirty minutes about specialty jams,
won't ask if you're all right, or tell you you look like shit
and then have to apologize as he remembers that you don't   5
like cuss words and you don't date ex-prison guards
because you're married. The truth is you're afraid
this blue-eyed charismatic sexist hunk of a reject just might
trigger another round of tears, that you'll lean into him
right in front of the eggs and milk, crying like a baby,   10
your face buried in his chest just below the two opened
buttons of his tight white knit shirt, his big cold hands
pressed to the small of your back, pulling you closer
to whisper that everything will be all right.

—2002

Annie Finch is the daughter of a professor of philosophy and a doll artist who also wrote poetry. Having published her first poem at the age of nine, Finch continued her studies at Yale, the University of Houston, and Stanford. The author of an acclaimed critical work, The Ghost of Meter *(1993), on the effects of meter on free-verse poets (most of them women), she has published three full-length collections of poems and has edited anthologies of criticism and poetry. She teaches at Miami University.*

Coy Mistress

Sir, I am not a bird of prey:
a Lady does not seize the day.
I trust that brief Time will unfold
our youth, before he makes us old.
How could we two write lines of rhyme   5
were we not fond of numbered Time
and grateful to the vast and sweet
trials his days will make us meet?
The Grave's not just the body's curse;
no skeleton can pen a verse!   10
So while this numbered World we see,
let's sweeten Time with poetry,
and Time, in turn, may sweeten Love
and give us time our love to prove.
You've praised my eyes, forehead, breast: 15
you've all our lives to praise the rest.

—1997

A resident of Los Angeles, Gerstler has published six collections of poetry since 1986. Her seventh, Animal Planet, *appeared in 2010. A prolific writer of art criticism and book reviews, Gerstler has also collaborated with visual artists. She has taught writing at a number of universities, including Bennington, her graduate alma mater.*

Advice from a Caterpillar

Chew your way into a new world.
Munch leaves. Molt. Rest. Molt
again. Self-reinvention is *everything*.
Spin many nests. Cultivate stinging
bristles. Don't get sentimental
about your discarded skins. Grow
quickly. Develop a yen for nettles.
Alternate crumpling and climbing. Rely
on your antennae. Sequester poisons
in your body for use at a later date.
When threatened, emit foul odors
in self-defense. Behave cryptically
to confuse predators: change colors, spit,
or feign death. If all else fails, taste terrible.

—2008

REBECCA FOUST ■ (b. 1957)

*Born in Altoona, Pennsylvania, and educated at Smith College, Foust worked
for some years as an attorney, leaving law for motherhood and full-time writing.
Her chapbook of poems about raising her autistic son,* Dark Card, *appeared
in 2008, the winner of a competition sponsored by Texas Review Press; the
next year a second chapbook,* Mom's Canoe, *won the same prize. Her first
full-length collection,* All That Gorgeous Pitiless Song, *was published in
2010. She lives in Marin County, California.*

Family Story

Mom talked about how when the x-ray
they used in those day before the ultrasound
confirmed she was pregnant the second time
with twins, she buttoned up her best
going-out dress, wondering what are those dark spots,
adjusted her hat and left. Weeks later it occurred to her
they were tears, wept for the long year behind
the long years ahead of diapers, glass bottles,

nights without sleep, no help with wailing kids
but from wailing kids. She wept
like she lived; when tears dripped and bloomed
on the gray wool of her dress, she looked up
at the changing room ceiling, expecting to find rain.

—2009

APRIL LINDNER ■ (b. 1962)

April Lindner teaches at St. Joseph's University. Her first collection of poetry,
Skin, appeared in 2002, and she has also written studies of the work of
Dana Gioia and other contemporary poets of the American West. She is the
co-editor of Contemporary American Poetry: A Pocket Anthology *(2004).*

First Kiss

This collision of teeth, of tongues and lips,
is like feeling for the door
in a strange room, blindfolded.
He imagines he knows her
after four dates, both of them taking pains   5
to laugh correctly, to make eye contact.
She thinks at least this long first kiss
postpones the moment she'll have to face
four white walls, the kitchen table,
its bowl of dried petals and nutmeg husks,   10
the jaunty yellow vase with one jaunty bloom,
the answering machine's one bloodshot eye.

—2002

CATHERINE TUFARIELLO ■ (b. 1963)

Catherine Tufariello grew up in upstate New York and holds a Ph.D. from
Cornell University. Her first full-length collection, Keeping My Name,
appeared in 2004. A translator of the sonnets of Petrarch, she has taught at
Valparaiso University.

Useful Advice

You're 37? Don't you think that maybe
It's time you settled down and had a baby?

No wine? You're pregnant, aren't you? I knew it!

Hey, are you sure you two know how to do it?

All Dennis has to do is look at me   5
And I'm knocked up.
      Some things aren't meant to be.
It's sad, but try to see this as God's will.

I've heard that sometimes when you take the Pill—

A friend of mine got pregnant when she stopped   10
Working so hard.
      Why don't you two adopt?
You'll have one of your own then, like my niece.

At work I heard about this herb from Greece—

My sister swears by dong quai. Want to try it?   15

Forget the high-tech stuff. Just change your diet.

It's true! Too much caffeine can make you sterile.

Yoga is good for that. My cousin Carol—

They have these ceremonies in Peru—

You mind my asking, is it him or you?   20

Have you tried acupuncture? Meditation?

It's in your head. Relax! Take a vacation
And have some fun. You think too much. Stop trying.

Did I say something wrong? Why are you crying?

—2004

SHERMAN ALEXIE ■ (b. 1966)

Sherman Alexie is a Spokane/Coeur d'Alene Indian and grew up on a reservation in Wellpinit, Washington. While attending Washington State University as a pre-med major, Alexie attended a poetry workshop and soon began to publish his work. A prolific author of novels, poems, and short stories, Alexie has also performed professionally as a stand-up comedian.

The Exaggeration of Despair

SHERMAN ALEXIE

I open the door

(this Indian girl writes that her brother tried to hang himself
with a belt just two weeks after her other brother did hang himself

and this Indian man tells us that back in boarding school,
five priests took him into a back room and raped him repeatedly   5

and this homeless Indian woman begs for quarters, and when I ask
her about her tribe, she says she's horny and bends over in front
    of me

and this homeless Indian man is the uncle of an Indian man
who writes for a large metropolitan newspaper, and so now
    I know them both

and this Indian child cries when he sits to eat at our table   10
because he had never known his own family to sit at the
    same table

and this Indian woman was born to an Indian woman
who sold her for a six-pack and a carton of cigarettes

and this Indian poet shivers beneath the freeway
and begs for enough quarters to buy pencil and paper   15

and this fancydancer passes out at the powwow
and wakes up naked, with no memory of the evening, all of
    his regalia gone

and this is my sister, who waits years for an eagle, receives it
and stores it with our cousins, who then tell her it has disappeared

and this is my father, whose own father died on Okinawa, shot   20
by a Japanese soldier who must have looked so much like him

and this is my father, whose mother died of tuberculosis
not long after he was born, and so my father must hear
    coughing ghosts

and this is my grandmother who saw, before the white men came,
three ravens with white necks, and knew our God was going
    to change)   25

and invite the wind inside.

—1996

Pulitzer Prize winner Natasha Trethewey grew up on the Gulf Coast, the child of an interracial marriage (her father is poet Eric Trethewey). Her first collection, Domestic Work, *appeared in 2000, and her second,* Bellocq's Ophelia *(2002), focused on the life of a mixed-race prostitute in Storyville, New Orleans's notorious red-light district. A third collection,* Native Guard, *appeared in 2006. Trethewey teaches at Emory University in Atlanta.*

Domestic Work, 1937

All week she's cleaned
someone else's house,
stared down her own face
in the shine of copper-
bottomed pots, polished   5
wood, toilets she'd pull
the lid to—that look saying

Let's make a change, girl.

But Sunday mornings are hers—
church clothes starched   10
and hanging, a record spinning
on the console, the whole house
dancing. She raises the shades,
washes the rooms in light,
buckets of water, Octagon soap.   15

Cleanliness is next to godliness . . .

Windows and doors flung wide,
curtains two-stepping
forward and back, neck bones
bumping in the pot, a choir   20
of clothes clapping on the line.

Nearer my God to Thee . . .

She beats time on the rugs,
blows dust from the broom
like dandelion spores, each one   25
a wish for something better.

—2000

Craig Arnold's first book of poetry, Shells, *was selected by W.S. Merwin for the Yale Series of Younger Poets, and his second,* Made Flesh, *was published in 2008. Arnold won numerous awards and fellowships during his brief career, including a National Endowment for the Arts grant. He was in Japan on a U.S.–Japan Friendship Commission Creative Artists' Exchange grant, researching on the island of Kuchinoerabushima for his most recent project, a book of lyric essays focused on the trope of the volcano, when he disappeared, presumably the victim of a hiking accident. Despite extensive searches and world-wide concern, his body was never found.*

The Singers

They are threatening to leave us the nimble-throated singers
    the little murderers with the quick pulses
They perch at the ends of bare branches their tails
    are ragged and pitiful the long green
feathers are fallen out They go on eating and eating
    last autumn's yellow melia berries
They do not care that you approach cold corpses
    rot in the grass in the reeds
The gray-shouldered crows hobble about the wren
    barely a mouthful cocks her pert tail
and threatens to slaughter the white-footed cat in the bushes
    They do not understand that they are dying

They are threatening to leave us how quickly we forget
    the way they taught us how to play our voices
opening soul to weightlessness like the Spartan poet
    singing under the burden of his old bones
to the chorus girls with their honey songs and their holy voices
    how he wished he could scoot like a kingfisher
lightly over the flower of the waves who boasted
    I know the tunes of every bird but I Alcman
found my words and song in the tongue of the strident partridge
    Where will we find songs when the sleek-headed
mallards are gone who chase each other around the pond
    the reluctant duck and the lovesick drake

The way she turns her head to the side to scold him
    whack whack whack whack whack the way her boyfriend
chases off his rival and then swims back reeb reeb
    with feeble reassurances the way
he sits on top of her the way she flaps her wings
    to keep above water the way they look
pleased with themselves wagging their tails smoothing
    each feather back in its right place

They are threatening to leave but you may still catch them
    saying goodbye stealthed in the cedar and cypress
at dawn in the dark clarity between sleep and waking
    A run of five notes on a black flute
another and another buried deep in the mix
    how many melodies can the air hold
And what they sing so lovely and so meaningless
    may urge itself upon you with the ache
of something just beyond the point of being remembered
    the trace of a brave thought in the face of sadness

—2008

ALLISON JOSEPH ■ (b. 1967)

Allison Joseph was born in London, the child of immigrants from Jamaica and Grenada. When she was a child, her parents relocated to New York, where she attended the Bronx High School of Science. Following graduation from Kenyon College and the University of Indiana, she began college teaching and is now a member of the creative writing faculty at Southern Illinois University. She has recently published a sequence of sonnets about her father, who died in 1997.

The Athlete

    would like to be my friend,
    but between volleyball tryouts
    and broad-jump practice,
    there's just no time to chat,
    no time to hang out at lunch,   5
    blushing and gossiping over boys.
    Hell, there isn't anything boys

can do that she can't—she'll
throw a ball just as hard,
run gutsy miles on the track   10
to match their distances,
ski cross-country or downhill,
topping their speed and endurance.
I admire her toughness, her
out-of-my-way attitude, her   15
assignments in on time, grades
better than mine even though I'm
only on one committee. She even
works after school, selling shoes
at Lady Footlocker to weekend jocks,   20
slinky aerobics babes. And they have
no idea how fast that girl can move,
long legs trained to respond
to whatever command her brain
issues, whatever demand   25
she puts on her muscles.
Once she asked if I'd like
to run track, hoping to pull me
into her world, make me as swift
as she. And I had to laugh at that,   30
at her ability to see an athlete
when all I could see was a scrawny girl
with fallen arches. I told her no,
but thanks, glad that she saw something
to work with when she looked   35
at me, something to mold, shape.

—1998

BRIAN TURNER ■ (b. 1967)

After completing a degree in creative writing at the University of Oregon, Brian Turner served seven years in the U.S. Army, including service in Bosnia-Herzegovina and a year in Iraq. His book about his military experiences, Here, Bullet, *was named an "Editor's Choice" by the* New York Times *and was the 2007 recipient of the Poets' Prize.*

Here, Bullet

If a body is what you want,
then here is bone and gristle and flesh.
Here is the clavicle-snapped wish,
the aorta's opened valves, the leap
thought makes at the synaptic gap.   5
Here is the adrenaline rush you crave,
that inexorable flight, that insane puncture
into heat and blood. And I dare you to finish
what you've started. Because here, Bullet,
here is where I complete the word you bring   10
hissing through the air, here is where I moan
the barrel's cold esophagus, triggering
my tongue's explosives for the rifling I have
inside of me, each twist of the round
spun deeper, because here, Bullet,   15
here is where the world ends, every time.

—2005

403

SUJI KWOCK KIM ■ (b. 1968)

Kim received the 2002 Walt Whitman Award for Notes from the Divided
Country, *an exploration of the Japanese occupation of Korea, and of the
Korean War and its aftermath. Kim's family emigrated to Poughkeepsie,
New York, in the 1970s. She studied at Yale; the Iowa Writers' Workshop;
Seoul National University, where she was a Fulbright Scholar; and Stan-
ford University, where she was a Stegner Fellow. She lives in San Francisco
and New York.*

Occupation

The soldiers
are hard at work
building a house.
They hammer
bodies into the earth   5
like nails,

they paint the walls
with blood.
Inside the doors
stay shut, locked   10
as eyes of stone.
Inside the stairs
feel slippery,
all flights go down.
There is no floor: 15
only a roof,
where ash is falling—
dark snow,
human snow,
thickly, mutely   20
falling.
Come, they say.
This house will
last forever.
You must occupy it.   25
And you, and you—
And you, and you—
Come, they say.
There is room
for everyone.   30

—2003

A. E. STALLINGS ■ (b. 1968)

Alicia Stallings is the author of Archaic Smile, *chosen for the 1999 Richard Wilbur Award. Written exclusively in received forms, the book is noteworthy for the vigor and humor with which Stallings rewrites classical myths. Raised in Decatur, Georgia, Stallings studied at the University of Georgia and Oxford University. She composed the Latin lyrics for the opening music of the Paramount film,* The Sum of All Fears, *and has done a verse translation of Lucretius'* De Rerum Natura. *A second collection of poems,* Hapax, *appeared in 2006. She lives in Athens, Greece, with her husband, John Psaropoulos, editor of the* Athens News.

First Love: A Quiz

He came up to me:
    a. in his souped-up Camaro
    b. to talk to my skinny best friend
    c. and bumped my glass of wine so I wore the ferrous stain
       on my sleeve
    d. from the ground, in a lead chariot drawn by a team of
       stallions black as crude oil and breathing sulfur; at his
       heart, he sported a tiny golden arrow   5

He offered me:
    a. a ride
    b. dinner and a movie, with a wink at the cliché
    c. an excuse not to go back alone to the apartment with its
       sink of dirty knives
    d. a narcissus with a hundred dazzling petals that breathed a
       sweetness as cloying as decay

I went with him because: 10
    a. even his friends told me to beware
    b. I had nothing to lose except my virginity
    c. he placed his hand in the small of my back and I felt the
       tread of honeybees
    d. he was my uncle, the one who lived in the half-finished
       basement, and he took me by the hair

The place he took me to: 15
    a. was dark as my shut eyes
    b. and where I ate bitter seed and became ripe
    c. and from which my mother would never take me wholly
       back, though she wept and walked the earth and made the
       bearded ears of barley wither on their stalks and the blasted
       flowers drop from their sepals
    d. is called by some men hell and others love
    e. all of the above   20

—2006

Joshua Mehigan lives in Brooklyn, New York, where he works for a prep school communications department. His first book, The Optimist: Poems, *was a finalist for the Los Angeles Times Book Prize. His poems and transla-tions have appeared in many periodicals, including* Poetry, The New York Times, *and* The Formalist.

Riddle

I'm not a convict,   but sentries stand by,
reluctant to let me   leave my post.
Alone at length,   I leewardly wander,
but few times farther   than a few inches
as the wind whiffs   through my wide-open mouth.   5
Neither sinning myself   nor slack at my duties
(of which there is one   and one only),
it's capital   that I kill without mercy.
My motive's not mine,   my method impartial,
and, tough as I am,   one tug's my undoing.   10
Spare yourself   suspense and grief:
Don't do as I do,   but do as I say,
whether sure what I am   or sure what not.

—2004

Hilbert was born in Philadelphia and educated at Rutgers University and Oxford. With founding editor Garrick Davis, he helped to establish Contem-porary Poetry Review *as one of the most comprehensive online journals of literary criticism. He has been credited as one of several contemporary poets who had led a revitalization of the sonnet. He works as an antiquarian book dealer in his hometown.*

Domestic Situation

Maybe you've heard about this. Maybe not.
A man came home and chucked his girlfriend's cat
In the wood chipper. This really happened.

Dinner wasn't ready on time. A lot
Of other little things went wrong. He spat   5
On her father, who came out when he learned
About it. He also broke her pinky,
Stole her checks, and got her sister pregnant.
But she stood by him, stood strong, through it all,
Because she loved him. She loved him, you see.   10
She actually said that, and then she went
And married him. She felt some unique call.
Don't try to understand what another
Person means by love. Don't even bother.

SOPHIE HANNAH ■ (b. 1971)

The daughter of writers Norman and Adèle Geras, Hannah was born and educated in Manchester, England. Though she is primarily known as a writer of light verse, she has also published novels, short stories, and children's books. A collection of poetry, Pessimism for Beginners, *was published in 2007.*

The Guest Speaker

I have to keep myself awake
While the guest speaker speaks.
For his and for procedure's sake
I have to keep myself awake.
However long his talk might take   5
(And, Christ, it feels like weeks)
I have to keep myself awake
While the guest speaker speaks.

—2003

EMILY MOORE ■ (b. 1977)

Emily Moore teaches English at Stuyvesant High School in New York. Her poetry has been published in Ploughshares, The Paris Review, *and* The New Yorker, *where "Auld Lang Syne" originally appeared. She also performs with a three-woman band,* Ménage à Twang.

Auld Lang Syne

Here's to the rock star with the crooked teeth,
the cellist, banker, mezzo bearing gifts,
the teacher with the flask inside her jeans—
those girls who made us sweat and lick our lips.

To the *jeune fille* who broke my heart in France,   5
the tramp who warmed your lap and licked your ear,
the one who bought me shots at 2 A.M.
that night I tied your pink tie at the bar.

Who smoked. Who locked you out. Who kissed my eyes
then pulled my hair and left me for a boy.   10
The girl who bit my upper, inner thigh.
My raspy laugh when I first heard your voice

toasting through broken kisses sloppy drunk:
To women! To abundance! To enough!

—2008

ERICA DAWSON ■ (b. 1979)

Erica Dawson was born in Columbia, Maryland, and studied at Johns Hopkins, Ohio State, and the University of Cincinnati. Her first book, Big-Eyed Afraid, won the Anthony Hecht Poetry Prize. In a "self-interview," she says, "People, including me, feel comfortable with categories, labels. Some people feel comfortable saying, 'Erica keeps it real.' Sometimes they want to put me, and others, in a box based on our gender or race." Working largely in traditional poetic forms, Dawson writes "outside the box."

Somewhere Between Columbus and Cincinnati

If you die today, where will you spend eternity?

Jesus, it's stretch of few

And far between the repetitions: fenced-
In fields and Christ's billboard-dispensed
        Commandments. There **HELL IS REAL**
        Worn in the corners, peel-

ing like dead skins (**McRIB** beneath).
Fence posts decay like rotting teeth.
      Sun spreads dusk's morning *deux*.
      Pale pink eclipses blue

And it's all memorial, two brown
Bottles, the worms a wren will down.
      The shattered ambers burn.
      And if the salmon cloudlets turn

Pitch-black, I will believe in You.

—2007

STANZA, FIXED, AND NONCE FORMS

Acrostic Verse

Stuart, "Discovering My Daughter"

Accentual Meter

Bishop, "The Fish"
Brooks, "We Real Cool"
Cardiff, "Combing"
Hughes, "Harlem Sweeties"
Kane, "Alan Doll Rap"
Mehigan, "Riddle"
Wilbur, "Junk"
Wilbur, "The Writer"

Ballad Stanza (and Variants)

Anonymous, "Bonny Barbara Allan"
Anonymous, "Sir Patrick Spens"
Auden, "As I Walked Out One Evening"
Bogan, "Women"
Brooks, "The Ballad of Chocolate Mabbie"
Burns, "John Barleycorn"
Byron, "When We Two Parted"
Fenton, "God, a Poem"
Keats, "La Belle Dame sans Merci"
Kennedy, "In a Prominent Bar in Secaucus One Day"
Nelson, "The Ballad of Aunt Geneva"
Plath, "Daddy"
Poe, "The Haunted Palace"
Roethke, "My Papa's Waltz"
Rossetti, "Up-Hill"
Smith, "Our Bog Is Dood"
Tennyson, "The Lady of Shalott"
Whitman, "O Captain! My Captain!"
Wylie, "Ophelia"

Ballade

Disch, "Ballade of the New God"

Blank Verse

Coleridge, "Frost at Midnight"
Frost, "Home Burial"

Hecht, "The Dover Bitch"
Hudgins, "Air View of an Industrial Scene"
Stafford, "Traveling Through the Dark"
Stevens, "Sunday Morning"
Stevens, "The Worms at Heaven's Gate"
Tennyson, "Ulysses"
Yeats, "The Second Coming"

Cento

Gwynn, "Approaching a Significant Birthday, He Peruses an Anthology of Poetry"

Cinquain

Crapsey, "Amaze"
Crapsey, "Languor After Pain"
Crapsey, "Trapped"

Clerihew

Taylor, *from* "Brief Candles"

Common Meter

Anonymous, "Western Wind"
Burns, "A Red, Red Rose"
Cullen, "Incident"
Dickinson, "After Great Pain"
Dickinson, "Because I Could Not Stop for Death"
Dickinson, "The Brain Is Wider than the Sky"

Dickinson, "I Felt a Funeral, in My Brain"
Dickinson, "Much Madness Is Divinest Sense"
Dickinson, "Narrow Fellow in the Grass, A"
Dickinson, "Some Keep the Sabbath Going to Church"
Dickinson, "Tell All the Truth, But Tell It Slant"
Dickinson, "There's a Certain Slant of Light"
Herrick, "To the Virgins, to Make Much of Time"
Lovelace, "To Lucasta, Going to the Wars"

Concrete Poetry

cummings, "r-p-o-p-h-e-s-s-a-g-r"
Herbert, "Easter Wings"
Swenson, "How Everything Happens"

Couplets, Mixed

Dawson, "Somewhere Between Columbus and Cincinnati"

Couplets, Short

Blake, "A Poison Tree"
Blake, "The Tyger"
Finch, "Coy Mistress"
Housman, "Loveliest of Trees, the Cherry Now"
Housman, "'Terence, This Is Stupid Stuff . . .'"

Kennedy, "Little Elegy"
Marvell, "To His Coy Mistress"

Couplets, Heroic

Bradstreet, "The Author to Her
  Book"
Browning, "My Last Duchess"
Gunn, "Terminal"
Jonson, "On My First Son"
Pope, *from* "An Essay on
  Criticism"
Rich, "Aunt Jennifer's Tigers"
Swift, "A Description of a City
  Shower"
Tufariello, "Useful Advice"

Dipodic Verse

Whitworth, "The Examiners"

Double-Dactyl

Stokesbury, "Room with
  a View"

Fourteeners

Southwell, "The Burning
  Babe"

Long Meter

Donne, "A Valediction:
  Forbidding Mourning"
Frost, "The Need of Being
  Versed in Country Things"
Larkin, "This Be the Verse"

Ode, Irregular

Arnold, "Dover Beach"
Bishop, "The Shampoo"
Coleridge, "Kubla Khan"
Frost, "After Apple-Picking"
Owen, "Dulce et Decorum Est"
Wordsworth, "Ode (Intimations
  of Immortality . . .)"

Ode, Regular

Keats, "Ode to a Nightingale"

Ottava Rima

Yeats, "Sailing to Byzantium"

Pantoum

Cortez, "Tu Negrito"

Paradelle

Collins, "Paradelle for Susan"

Prose Poem

Edson, "Ape"
Forché, "The Colonel"
Mullen, "Dim Lady"

Quatrain, English

Blake, "The Little Black Boy"
cummings, "somewhere i
  have never travelled, gladly
  beyond"

Gray, "Elegy Written in a Country Churchyard"

Gwynn, "Approaching a Significant Birthday, He Peruses an Anthology of Poetry"

Hecht, "Third Avenue in Sunlight"

Longfellow, "The Arsenal at Springfield"

Robinson, "Richard Cory"

Quatrain, Italian

Merrill, "Casual Wear"

Toomer, "Georgia Dusk"

Rap

Hughes, "Harlem Sweeties"

Kane, "Alan Doll Rap"

Riddle

Mehigan, "Riddle"

Plath, "Metaphors"

Rime Royal

Wyatt, "They Flee from Me"

Rondeau

Dunbar, "We Wear the Mask"

Rondeau Redoublé

Cope, "Rondeau Redoublé"

Rubaiyat Stanza

Frost, "Stopping by Woods on a Snowy Evening"

Sapphic Stanzas

Steele, "Sapphics Against Anger"

Sestet

Byron, "She Walks in Beauty"

Frost, "The Road Not Taken"

Wilbur, "For C"

Sestina

Alvarez, "Bilingual Sestina"

Ashbery, "Farm Implements and Rutabagas in a Landscape"

Mayers, "All-American Sestina"

Sonnenizio

Addonizio, "Sonnenizio on a Line from Drayton"

Sonnet, Curtal

Hopkins, "Pied Beauty"

Sonnet, English

Drayton, "Idea: Sonnet 61"

Keats, "Bright Star, Would I Were Stedfast as Thou Art"

Millay, "If I Should Learn, in Some Quite Casual Way"

Millay, "Oh, Oh, You Will Be Sorry for That Word"
Morris, "Auld Lang Syne"
Nemerov, "A Primer of the Daily Round"
Shakespeare, "Sonnet 18"
Shakespeare, "Sonnet 20"
Shakespeare, "Sonnet 29"
Shakespeare, "Sonnet 73"
Shakespeare, "Sonnet 116"
Shakespeare, "Sonnet 129"
Shakespeare, "Sonnet 130"

Sonnet, Italian

Browning, "Sonnets from the Portuguese, 18"
Browning, "Sonnets from the Portuguese, 43"
Donne, "Holy Sonnet 10"
Donne, "Holy Sonnet 14"
Frost, "Design"
Hopkins, "God's Grandeur"
Keats, "On First Looking into Chapman's Homer"
Lazarus, "The New Colossus"
Longfellow, "The Cross of Snow"
Millay, "What Lips My Lips Have Kissed, and Where, and Why"
Milton, "How Soon Hath Time"
Milton, "On the Late Massacre in Piedmont"
Milton, "When I Consider How My Light Is Spent"
Robinson, "Firelight"
Wordsworth, "It Is a Beauteous Evening"

Wordsworth, "Nuns Fret Not at Their Convent's Narrow Room"
Wyatt, "Whoso List to Hunt"

Sonnet, Nonce

Barrax, "Strangers Like Us: Pittsburgh, Raleigh, 1945–1985"
Coleridge, "Work Without Hope"
Cullen, "Yet Do I Marvel"
cummings, "pity this busy monster, manunkind"
Herbert, "Redemption"
Gerstler, "Advice from a Caterpillar"
Kees, "For My Daughter"
Hilbert, "Domestic Situation"
Shelley, "Ozymandias"
Shomer, "Women Bathing at Bergen-Belsen"
Sidney, "Astrophel and Stella: Sonnet 1"
Wright, "Saint Judas"
Wroth, "In This Strange Labyrinth How Shall I Turn"
Yeats, "Leda and the Swan"

Sonnet, Spenserian

Spenser "Amoretti: Sonnet 75"

Syllabics

Mason, "Fog Horns"
Moore, "The Fish"
Plath, "Metaphors"
Thomas, "Poem in October"

Terzanelle

Turco, "The Premonition"

Terza Rima

Frost, "Acquainted with the Night"
Ruark, "The Visitor"
Shelley, "Ode to the West Wind"

Triolet

Hannah, "The Guest Speaker"

Triplets

Tennyson, "The Eagle"

Villanelle

Bishop, "One Art"
Thomas, "Do Not Go Gentle into
  That Good Night"

acknowledgments

Betty Adcock, "Voyages" from *The Difficult Wheel: Poems* by Betty Adcock. Copyright © 1995 by Betty Adcock. Reprinted by permission of Louisiana State University Press.

Kim Addonizio, "Sonnenizio on a Line from Drayton," from *What Is This Thing Called Love: Poems* by Kim Addonizio. Copyright © 2004 by Kim Addonizio. Used by permission of W.W. Norton & Company, Inc.

Craig Arnold. "The Singers" by Craig Arnold, originally published in Poetry in 2007. Reprinted by permission of the Estate of Craig Arnold.

Ai, "Child Beater" from *Cruelty* published by Houghton Mifflin Company. Reprinted by permission of the author.

Sherman Alexie, "The Exaggeration of Despair" Reprinted from *The Summer of Black Widows* © 1996 by Sherman Alexie, by permission of Hanging Loose Press.

Julia Alvarez, "Bilingual Sestina" from *The Other Side/El Otro Lado*. Copyright © 1995 by Julia Alvarez. Published by Plume/Penguin, a division of Penguin Group (USA). Reprinted by permission of Susan Bergholz Literary Services, New York, NY, and Larry, NM. All rights reserved.

Ginger Andrews, "Primping in the Rearview Mirror." Reprinted by permission from *The Hudson Review*, Vol. LV, No. 2 (Summer 2002). Copyright © 2002 by Ginger Andrews.

John Ashbery, "Farm Implements and Rutabagas in a Landscape" from *The Double Dream of Spring* by John Ashbery. Copyright © 1966, 1970 by John Ashbery. Reprinted by permission of Georges Borchardt, Inc., on behalf of the author. "Paradoxes and Oxymorons" from *Shadow Train* by John Ashbery. Copyright © 1980, 1981 by John Ashbery. Reprinted by permission of Georges Borchardt, Inc. on behalf of the author.

Margaret Atwood, "Siren Song" from *Selected Poems 1965–1975* by Margaret Atwood. Copyright © 1976 by Margaret Atwood. Reprinted by permission of Houghton Mifflin Harcourt Publishing Company. All rights reserved.

W. H. Auden, "The Unknown Citizen," copyright 1940 and copyright renewed 1968 by W. H. Auden, "Musee des Beaux Arts," copyright 1940 and renewed 1968 by W. H. Auden, "As I Walked Out One Evening," copyright 1940 and renewed 1968 by W. H. Auden, from *Collected Poems* by W. H. Auden. Used by permission of Random House, Inc.

Gerald Barrax, "Strangers Like Us: Pittsburgh, Raleigh, 1945–1985" from *From a Person Sitting in Darkness: New and Selected Poems* by Gerald Barrax. Copyright © 1998 by Gerald Barrax. Reprinted by permission of Louisiana State University Press.

Elizabeth Bishop, "The Fish", "One Art," and "The Shampoo" from *The Complete Poems 1927–1979* by Elizabeth Bishop. Copyright © 1979, 1983 by Alice Helen Methfessel. Reprinted by permission of Farrar, Straus, and Giroux, LLC.

Louise Bogan, "Women" from *The Blue Estuaries* by Louise Bogan. Copyright © 1968 by Louise Bogan. Copyright renewed 1996 by Ruth Limmer. Reprinted by permission of Farrar, Straus, and Giroux, LLC.

Gwendolyn Brooks, "The Ballad of Chocolate Mabbie" from *Selected Poems* by Gwendolyn Brooks. "The Mother" and "We Real Cool" from *Blacks* by Gwendolyn Brooks. Reprinted by consent of Brooks Permissions.

Gladys Cardiff, "Combing" Copyright © 1971 by Gladys Cardiff. Reprinted from *To Frighten a Storm* (Copper Canyon Press, 1976) by permission of the author.

Fred Chappell, "Narcissus and Echo" from *Source* by Fred Chappell. Copyright © 1985 by Fred Chappell. Reprinted by permission of Louisiana State University Press.

by permission of New Directions Publishing Corp.

Annie Finch, "Coy Mistress" from *Eve*, 1997 Reprinted with permission of the author and Story Line Press .

Carolyn Forché, All lines from "The Colonel" from *The Country Between Us* by Carolyn Forché. Copyright © 1981 by Carolyn Forché. Originally appeared in *Women's International Resource Exchange*. Reprinted by permission of Harper-Collins Publishers.

Rebecca Foust. "Family Story" from *Mom's Canoe* by Rebecca Foust (Texas Review Press, 2008). Reprinted by permission of the publisher.

Robert Frost, "Acquainted with the Night," "Design," and "Stopping by Woods on a Snowy Evening" from *The Poetry of Robert Frost* edited by Edward Connery Lathem. Copyright 1916, 1923, 1928, 1969 by Henry Holt and Company. Copyright 1936, 1944, 1951, 1956 by Robert Frost, copyright 1964 by Lesley Frost Ballantine. "After Apple-Picking," "Home Burial," and "The Road Not Taken" from *The Poetry of Robert Frost*, edited by Edward Connery Lathem. Copyright 1916, 1930, 1939, 1969 by Henry Holt and Company. Copyright 1994, 1958 by Robert Frost, Copyright 1967 by Lesley Frost Ballantine.

Amy Gerstler. "Advice from a Caterpillar" from *Dearest Creature* by Amy Gerstler, copyright © 2009 by Amy Gerstler. Used by permission of Penguin, a division of Penguin Group (USA) Inc.

Allen Ginsberg, All lines from "A Supermarket in California" *Collected Poems 1947–1980* by Allen Ginsberg. Copyright © 1955 by Allen Ginsberg. Reprinted by permission of HarperCollins Publishers.

Dana Gioia, "Planting a Sequoia" copyright 1991 by Dana Gioia. Reprinted from *The Gods of Winter* with the permission of Graywolf Press, Saint Paul, Minnesota, www.graywolfpress.org.

Thom Gunn, "From the Wave" and "Terminal" from *Collected Poems* by Thom Gunn. Copyright © 1944 by Thom Gunn. Reprinted by permission of Farrar, Straus and Giroux, LLC.

R. S. Gwynn, "Approaching a Significant Birthday, He Peruses an Anthology of Poetry" from *No Word of Farewell: Selected Poems 1970–2000*. Reprinted by permission of the author.

Jim Hall, "Maybe Dats Your Pwoblem Too" from *The Mating Reflex*. By permission of Carnegie Mellon University Press, © 1980 by Jim Hall.

Sophie Hannah, "The Guest Speaker" from *First of the Last Chances* by Sophie Hannah. Published by Carcanet Press, Limited, 2003. Reprinted by permission of the publisher.

Joy Harjo, "She Had Some Horses," copyright © 1983 by Joy Harjo, from *She Had Some Horses* by Joy Harjo. Used by permission of W.W. Norton & Company, Inc.

Robert Hass, "Meditations at Lagunitas" from *Praise* by Robert Hass. Copyright © 1979 by Robert Hass. Reprinted by permission of HarperCollins Publishers.

Robert Hayden, "Those Winter Sundays," copyright © 1966 by Robert Hayden, from *Collected Poems of Robert Hayden* by Robert Hayden, edited by Frederick Glaysher. Used by permission of Liveright Publishing Corporation.

Seamus Heaney, "Digging" and "Punishment" from *Opened Ground: Selected Poems 1966–1996* by Seamus Heaney. Copyright © 1998 by Seamus Heaney. Reprinted by permission of Farrar, Straus and Giroux, LLC.

Anthony Hecht, "The Dover Bitch" and "Third Avenue in Sunlight" from *Collected Earlier Poems* by Anthony Hecht, copyright © 1990 by Anthony E. Hecht. Used by permission of Alfred A. Knopf, a division of Random House, Inc.

Ernest Hilbert is an American poet, critic, and editor born in Philadelphia. Educated at Rutgers and Oxford, he served as the editor of the *Contemporary Poetry Review* from 2005 to 2010. Hilbert also edits a popular blog/podcast/web TV show, *E-Verse Radio*, and is a rare-book dealer. His collection *Sixty Sonnets* was published by *Red Hen Press* <http://www.redhen.org/> in February 2009.

Daniel Hoffman, "As I Was Going to Saint-Ives" from *Hang Gliding from Helicon* by Daniel Hoffman. Copyright © 1988 by Daniel Hoffman. Reprinted by permission of Louisiana State University Press.

A. E. Housman, "Stars, I Have Seen Them Fall," by A.E. Housman from *The Collected Poems of A. E. Housman*. Copyright © 1936 by Barclays Bank Ltd. Copyright © 1964 by Robert E. Symons. Reprinted by arrangement with Henry Holt and Company, LLC.

Andrew Hudgins, "Air View of an Industrial Scene" from *Saints and Strangers* by Andrew

of Ohio University Press/Swallow Press, Athens, Ohio.

James Merrill, "Casual Wear" from *Selected Poems 1946–1985* by James Merrill, copyright © 1992 by James Merrill. Used by permission of Alfred A. Knopf, a division of Random House, Inc.

W. S. Merwin, "For the Anniversary of My Death" and "The Last One" from *Migrations* by W.S. Merwin. Copyright © 1967, 2005 by W.S. Merwin, reprinted with permission of The Wylie Agency, LLC.

Edna St. Vincent Millay, "Oh, Oh, You Will Be Sorry for That Word!," and "What Lips My Lips Have Kissed, and Where, and Why" by Edna St. Vincent Millay. From *Collected Poems*. Copyright © 1923, 1951 by Edna St. Vincent Millay and Norma Millay Ellis. Reprinted by permission of Elizabeth Barnett, The Millay Society.

Vassar Miller, the text of "Subterfuge" (copyright © 1981 by Vassar Miller) from *If I Had Wheels or Love: Collected Poems of Vassar Miller* is reprinted with the permission of Southern Methodist University Press.

Emily Moore, "Auld Lang Syne" by Emily Moore, originally published in *The New Yorker*, April 14, 2008. Reprinted by permission of the author.

Marianne Moore, "Silence" reprinted with the permission of Scribner, a Division of Simon & Schuster Inc., from *The Collected Poems of Marianne Moore* by Marianne Moore. Copyright © 1935 by Marianne Moore, renewed 1963 by Marianne Moore and T. S. Eliot. All right reserved.

Robert Morgan, "Mountain Bride" from *Groundwork*, Gnomon Press. Copyright © 1979. Reprinted by permission of the author.

Harryette Mullen, "Dim Lady" from *Sleeping With the Dictionary*, by Harryette Mullen. Copyright © 2002 The Regents of the University of California. Reprinted by permission.

Timothy Murphy, "Case Notes," by Timothy Murphy. Reprinted by permission from *The Hudson Review*, Vol. LVI, No. 4 (Winter 2004). Copyright © 2004 Timothy Murphy.

Marilyn Nelson, "The Ballad of Aunt Geneva" from *The Homeplace* by Marilyn Nelson Waniek. Copyright © 1990 by Marilyn Nelson Waniek. Reprinted by permission of Louisiana State University Press.

Howard Nemerov, "A Primer of the Daily Round" from *New and Selected Poems* by Howard Nemerov, copyright © 1960 by Howard Nemerov (Univeristy of Chicago Press). Reprinted by permission of Margaret Nemerov.

Naomi Shihab Nye, "The Traveling Onion," reprinted by permission of Naomi Shihab Nye from *Yellow Glove*, Breitenbush Books, Portland, OR. Copyright © 1986 by Naomi Shihab Nye.

Frank O'Hara, "The Day Lady Died" from *Lunch Poems* © 1964 by Frank O'Hara. Reprinted by permission of City Lights Books.

Sharon Olds, "The One Girl at the Boys Party," from *The Dead and the Living* by Sharon Olds, copyright © 1987 by Sharon Olds. Used by permission of Alfred A. Knopf, a division of Random House, Inc.

Mary Oliver, "The Black Walnut Tree" from *Twelve Moons* by Mary Oliver. Copyright © 1972, 1973, 1974, 1976, 1977, 1978, 1979 by Mary Oliver. By permission of Little, Brown and Company. "Honey at the Table" from *American Primitive* by Mary Oliver. Copyright © 1978, 1979, 1980, 1981, 1982, 1983 by Mary Oliver. By permission of Little, Brown and Company.

Simon J. Ortiz, "The Serenity in Stones." Permission to reprint given by author Simon J. Ortiz, Copyright 1975.

Linda Pastan, "Ethics" copyright © 1981 by Linda Pastan, from *Carnival Evening: New and Selected Poems 1968–1998* by Linda Pastan. Used by permission of W. W. Norton & Company, Inc.

Robert Phillips, "The Stone Crab: A Love Poem" from *Breakdown Lane*, p. 32, by Robert Phillips. Copyright © 1994 Robert Phillips. Reprinted with permission of The Johns Hopkins University Press.

Marge Piercy, "What's That Smell in the Kitchen?" from *Circles on the Water* by Marge Piercy, copyright © 1982 by Marge Piercy. Used by permission of Alfred A. Knopf, a division of Random House, Inc.

Sylvia Plath, "Daddy" and Edge" from *Ariel Poems* by Sylvia Plath. Copyright © 1961, 1962, 1963, 1964, 1965, 1966 by Ted Hughes. Reprinted by permission of HarperCollins Publishers. All lines from "Metaphors" from *Crossing the Water* by Sylvia Plath. Copyright © 1960 by Ted Hughes. Reprinted by permission of HarperCollins Publishers.

Uncertainties: Poems 1970–1986. Reprinted by permission of the University of Arkansas Press.

Wallace Stevens, "Sunday Morning," from *The Collected Poems of Wallace Stevens,* copyright 1954 by Wallace Stevens and renewed 1982 by Holly Stevens. Used by permission of Alfred A. Knopf, a division of Random House, Inc.

Leon Stokesbury, "The Day Kennedy Died" by Leon Stokesbury. First published in *Crazyhorse.* Reprinted by permission of the publisher.

Mark Strand, "The Tunnel," from *Selected Poems* by Mark Strand, copyright © 1979, 1980 by Mark Strand. Used by permission of Alfred A. Knopf, a division of Random House, Inc.

Dabney Stuart, "Discovering My Daughter" from *Light Years: New and Selected Poems* by Dabney Stuart. Copyright © 1994 by Dabney Stuart. Reprinted by permission of Louisiana State University Press.

May Swenson, "How Everything Happens (Based on a Study of the Wave)" from *The Complete Poems to Solve.* Used with permission of The Literary Estate of May Swenson.

Henry Taylor, Excerpts from *Brief Candles: 101 Clarihews* by Henry Taylor. Copyright © 2000 by Henry Taylor. Reprinted by permission from Louisiana State University Press.

Dylan Thomas, "Do Not Go Gentle Into That Good Night" by Dylan Thomas, from *The Poems of Dylan Thomas,* copyright © 1952 by Dylan Thomas. Reprinted by permission of New Directions Publishing Corp. "Poem in October" by Dylan Thomas, from *The Poems of Dylan Thomas,* copyright © 1945 by The Trustees for the Copyrights of Dylan Thomas, first published in *Poetry.* Reprinted by permission of New Directions Publishing Corp.

Jean Toomer, "Georgia Dusk," from *Cane* by Jean Toomer. Copyright 1923 by Boni & Liveright, renewed 1951 by Jean Toomer. Used by permission of Liveright Publishing Corporation.

Natasha Trethewey, "Domestic Work, 1937" from *Domestic Work* by Natasha Trethewey. Copyright © 2000 by Natasha Trethewey. Reprinted with the permission of Graywolf Press, Minneapolis, Minnesota, www.graywolfpress.org.

Catherine Tufariello, "Useful Advice" from *Keeping My Name* by Catherine Tufariello, originally published in Tar River Poetry. Reprinted by permission.

Lewis Turco, "The Premonition" by Lewis Turco, © 2006 by Lewis Turco. Reprinted by permission of the author.

Brian Turner, "Here, Bullet" from *Here, Bullet* by Brian Turner. Copyright © 2005 by Brian Turner. Reprinted with the permission of Alice James Books, http://www.alicejamesbooks.org.

Ellen Bryant Voigt, "Daughter," from *The Forces of Plenty* by Ellen Bryant Voigt. Copyright © 1983 by Ellen Bryant Voigt. Used by permission of W. W. Norton & Company, Inc.

Margaret Walker, "For Malcolm X" from *This Is My Century: New and Collected Poems* by Margaret Walker. Copyright © 1989 by Margaret Walker Alexander. Reprinted by permission of the University of Georgia Press.

John Whitworth, "The Examiners" from *Being the Bad Guy* by John Whitworth (Peterloo, 2007). Reprinted by permission of the author.

Richard Wilbur, "For C." from *Mayflies: New Poems and Translations* by Richard Wilbur, copyright © 2000 by Richard Wilbur, reprinted by permission of Houghton Mifflin Harcourt Publishing Company. "The Writer" from *The Mind-Reader,* copyright © 1971 by Richard Wilbur, reprinted by permission of Houghton Mifflin Harcourt Publishing Company. "Years-End" from *Ceremony and Other Poems,* copyright 1949 and renewed 1977 by Richard Wilbur, reprinted by permission Houghton Mifflin Harcourt Publishing Company.

Miller Williams, "The Book" from *Living on the Surface: New and Selected Poems* by Miller Williams. Copyright © 1989 by Miller Williams. Reprinted by permission of Louisiana State University Press.

Williams, William Carlos: "The Last Words of My English Grandmother [First Version]," "Spring and All, Section I" and "The Red Wheelbarrow" by William Carlos Williams, from *The Collected Poems: Volume I, 1909–1939,* copyright © 1938 by New Directions Publishing Corp. Reprinted by permission of New Directions Publishing Corp.

James Wright, "Autumn Begins in Martin's Ferry, Ohio" and "Saint Judas" from *Collected*

index of critical terms

425

INDEX OF CRITICAL TERMS

426

index of authors, titles, and first lines of poems

Note: Authors' names appear in boldface type. Titles of poems appear in double quotation marks.

Note to Instructors: Any of these Penguin-Putnam, Inc. titles can be packaged with this book at a special discount. Contact your local Allyn & Bacon/Longman sales representative for details on how to create a Penguin-Putnam, Inc. Value Package.

Aeschylus, *The Oresteia*
Allison, *Bastard Out of Carolina*
Alvarez, *How the García Girls Lost Their Accents*
Anonymous, *Beowulf*
Anonymous, *The Epic of Gilgamesh*
Anonymous, *The Song of Roland*
Attar, *The Conference of Birds*
Austen, *Emma*
Austen, *Pride and Prejudice*
Basho, *On Love and Barley*
Boyle, *The Tortilla Curtain*
Cather, *My Antonia*
Cather, *O Pioneers!*
Chaucer, *The Canterbury Tales*
Conrad, *Nostromo*
Dante, *The Divine Comedy: Inferno*
de la Cruz, *Poems, Protest, and a Dream*
Homer, *The Iliad*
Homer, *The Odyssey*
Hwang, *M. Butterfly*
Hulme, *The Bone People*
Jen, *Typical American*

Karr, *The Liars' Club*
Kerouac, *On the Road*
King, *Misery*
Larsen, *Passing*
Lavin, *In a Cafe*
Marquez, *Love in the Time of Cholera*
Miller, *The Crucible*
Molière, *Tartuffe and Other Plays*
Morrison, *Beloved*
Morrison, *The Bluest Eye*
Morrison, *Sula*
Naylor, *The Women of Brewster Place*
Orwell, *1984*
Rushdie, *Midnight's Children*
Shakespeare, *Cymbeline*
Shakespeare, *Four Great Comedies*
Shakespeare, *The Comedy of Errors*
Shakespeare, *Four Great Tragedies*
Shakespeare, *Four Histories*
Shakespeare, *Hamlet*
Shakespeare, *King Lear*

Shakespeare, *Macbeth*
Shakespeare, *The Merchant of Venice*
Shakespeare, *Othello*
Shakespeare, *Twelfth Night*
Shelley, *Frankenstein*
Silko, *Ceremony*
Spence, *The Death of Woman Wang*
Steinbeck, *The Grapes of Wrath*
Steinbeck, *The Pearl*
Swift, *Gulliver's Travels*
Tagore, *The Home and the World*
Twain, *The Adventures of Huckleberry Finn*
Tzu, *Tao Te Ching*
Various, *Beat Down to Your Soul*
Various, *The Portable Beat Reader*
Various, *The Portable Greek Reader*
Von Goethe, *Faust, Part I*
Von Goethe, *Faust, Part II*
Wallace, *Big Fish*
Wharton, *Ethan Frome*
Woolf, *Jacob's Room*